Divine Enjoyment

Divine Enjoyment

A Theology of Passion and Exuberance

Elaine Padilla

FORDHAM UNIVERSITY PRESS

NEW YORK 2015

Fordham University Press has no responsibility for the persistence or accuracy of URLs for external or third-party Internet websites referred to in this publication and does not guarantee that any content on such websites is, or will remain, accurate or appropriate.

Fordham University Press also publishes its books in a variety of electronic formats. Some content that appears in print may not be available in electronic books.

Visit us online at www.fordhampress.com.

Library of Congress Cataloging-in-Publication Data

Padilla, Elaine.
   Divine enjoyment : a theology of passion and exuberance / Elaine Padilla. — First edition.
        pages cm
   Includes bibliographical references and index.
   ISBN 978-0-8232-6356-1 (cloth : alk. paper) — ISBN 978-0-8232-6357-8 (pbk. : alk. paper)
   1. God (Christianity) 2. Pleasure—Religious aspects—Christianity. I. Title.
   BT103.P33 2015
   231'.4—dc23
                                                2014024608

Printed in the United States of America

17 16 15   5 4 3 2 1

First edition

To Tirio,
the intemperate one

This book would not have been possible without the mystical walks on the beach of Ocean Grove, New Jersey, alongside my partner for life, Dale T. Irvin; the playfulness and leisurely nature of my cat, "Tiny"; the unconditional love of my mother, Gladys, and sister, Sigrid; the friendship of my stepsons, Douglas and Andrew; and the devoted prayers of my grandmother Rosario and my mother-in-law, Doreen. Each has been in her or his own way a source of vitality and encouragement to me. My late brother José, whom I lovingly nicknamed Tirio, continues to leave a trace of his festive and carnivalesque way of being in the world on the pages of this work, long after he passed away in the last semester of my doctoral coursework. Mentors such as Catherine Keller, Robert Corrington, Orlando Espín, Robert Ratcliff, "the collective," Miguel Díaz, the late Otto Maduro and Ada María Isasi-Díaz, and friends such as Krista Hughes, Dhawn Martin, Peter Phan, Michelle González, Gerard Manion, Laurel Schneider, and the late Helen Tartar, my wonderful Fordham editor, also journeyed with me in various stages of its writing, providing me with a surplus of nudging, good advice, and affirmation, alongside robust criticisms, great wine and conversations, food and dancing, encouragement, last-minute rides to the airport, yoga, and playtime. My deepest gratitude goes to the Hispanic Theological Initiative and its dedicated staff, especially its director, Joanne Rodríguez, for monetary and personal support; to the New York Theological Seminary, its former academic dean, Eleanor Moody-Shepherd, and the faculty and staff, who have truly embraced me; and to Drew University and its theological program for opening a space for this kind of theopoetic imagination to be nurtured. To all of you, my thanks.

Introduction

> You show me the path of life. In your presence there is fullness of joy;
> in your right hand are pleasures forevermore.
>
> *—Psalm 16:11*

> Pero la vida que buscamos y apreciamos es aquélla que sentimos como
> vida abundante: vida que es possible gozar junto con los demás sin poner
> en peligro el que los otros también la gocen: vida a disfrutar sin destruir
> la posibilidad de continuar disfrutándola hasta la vejez; vida digna
> de celebrar en comunidad y de recordar luego con añoranza . . . ¡la
> buena vida! Esa vida—la vida que vale la pena vivir y que nos incita
> a degustarla—no es pura lucha contra la muerte: es búsqueda del
> placer comun, la alegría duradera, el deleite profundo, el gozo gratuito,
> la dicha contagiosa. La buena vida—la vida que merece ser conservada,
> nutrida, comunicada, reproducida y festejada—es disfrute compartido
> del afecto, la compañía, el trabajo, la comida, el descanso, el arte,
> el juego, la oración, el baile . . . ¡y la fiesta!
>
> —OTTO MADURO[1]

Happiness. Enjoyment. Our time equates these terms with selfishness,
self-indulgence, luxury, bliss, and decadence. Owning and possessing as
much as one can, or securing one's place in the world, has come to define
the meaning of happiness. One can sympathize with the apostle Paul,
whose warning to the Galatians to abstain from "frenzied and joyless
grabs for happiness" is set amid his other warnings against "cutthroat
competition," "all-consuming-yet-never-satisfied wants," "small-minded
and lopsided pursuits," "the vicious habit of depersonalizing everyone into
a rival," and "ugly parodies of community" (Gal. 5:19–21, *The Message*).[2]
To think of God as having enjoyment can therefore be problematic. A
happy God, if happiness were to have the contours of overconsumption

and self-centeredness, would be an opulent God, a God who sought only God's own happiness in terms of fortune, honor, worship, power, and well-being. All that has existed, exists, and is yet to exist would be so only to fulfill or satisfy Godself. God's happiness would come at the expense of all that is creaturely.

Yet if this were so, why pursue the subject matter of divine enjoyment at all? Perhaps one could consider another dimension of happiness, one along the lines of what Otto Maduro calls *la buena vida*, "the good life." As seen in the epigraph above, enjoyment can also mean acquiring the fuller sense of life often associated with what takes place in *las fiestas*. One sketches the future or creates roadmaps whose paths lead one toward life's events worth celebrating in community with others—a source of much enjoyment. Even though the difficult conditions of life seem to stand in the way of achieving this ideal, we strive for it nonetheless, knowing that life is more than mere survival. When this impulse in us ceases, life stalls; we find ourselves being devoured by our circumstances, and perhaps turning others into scapegoats for the sake of our own so-called preservation. Consequently, in the midst of much struggle, as Maduro explains, the fuller sense of life evident in *las fiestas* is now more than ever necessary and urgent.[3] The good life in community, that which does not cause harm to others, deserves to be "preserved, nourished, communicated, reproduced and celebrated."[4]

In its concern for recapturing a zest for life exemplified in the regenerative performance of celebration, this book seeks to provide another angle on the cartography of enjoyment. It elaborates a theological model that allows for reciprocal forms of enjoyment between God and all living beings. Indeed, I believe that every generation must recapture and reignite a zest for life abundant if it is to overcome systems of belief that seek to impose a reality contrary to deeply relational, interdependent, egalitarian, and communitarian forms of living. In the same vein, a modus vivendi guided by a fuller understanding of enjoyment can serve as the basis for promoting mutually beneficial realities. Theologically speaking, the trope of divine love is a key element and impetus in this kind of relationship. It awakens us to the distinctiveness, interweavings, symbioses, and even parasitical and virulent elements that exist in the cosmos, even as it quickens in us a passion for enjoying the *whole* of life. The seductive love of God infuses our zest for life with an impulse to seek expressions of enjoyment that do not imperil the well-being of others.

Of course, theology is no stranger to the idea of the good life. In the thirteenth century, St. Thomas Aquinas, in agreement with Aristotle, argued that loving one's neighbor was the result of the "perfect love of God," which for him meant that loving one's friend as a neighbor was "concomitant with perfect Happiness."[5] And to love with benevolence was "to wish good" to another.[6] Once again, one might rhetorically retort, why not then a study of enjoyment? Particularly why not now, in light of how today our "pursuit of happiness" is being driven by self-centeredness and the pretense that one's enjoyments correspond solely to one's hard-earned successes? A main objective of what follows, therefore, is to abstain from constructing a model of enjoyment that, like a thief in the night, seeks to rob someone else of dreams. And by the same token, the goal entails accentuating the meaning of "fullness of joy" and "pleasures forevermore" that Psalm 16 prompts us to recapture anew in this day and age, a sense of joy and an experience of pleasure that this book situates within a paradigm of mutuality.

Consequently, this book aims to provide a fresh definition of enjoyment by constructing a theological model that challenges the notion of absolute self-sufficiency that in our time has come to define the successful contemporary human being, as Catherine LaCugna poignantly remarks.[7] Happy people who lack nothing, for "all good things belong to them already,"[8] as Aristotle explains, can no longer exemplify *eudaimonia* (or happiness), even as this expression of contentment is to be understood from within a concept of the life of virtue in relationship with others.[9] The modern person is considered to be superior on the basis of self-independence and autonomy, which basically means freedom from emotional and relational entanglements with others.[10] Furthermore, when we consider a theological argument that has God at its center—divine love as the impulse of the good life—we need to disturb *eudaimonia* even further. The manner in which we speak of God informs our ways of existing in relation to others. God could be viewed as condoning or, more strongly put, promoting a sense of divine enjoyment that grants us permission to disregard the needs of others, even to minimize their right to pleasure, and to seek to absorb their distinct expressions into a dominant view that is not theirs. Consequently, one way to challenge self-centered modes of being might be to imagine God and God's relationship with the cosmos as beyond the boundaries of the divine self, that is, as *passionate.*

That is why this book does not follow the usual route toward a moral theology of happiness. Indeed, the study is of a God of passionate enjoyment as such enjoyment pertains to creaturely living, seeking fuller expressions of communal enjoyment in mutually beneficial ways. The end or common good is rooted in God as an originary source of pleasure, just as is found in some forms of classical theism, but with a caveat. Because it is multiple and amorphous, the common good implicitly appears to be more adventurously welcoming of otherness, a point of transformation as well for the concept of beginnings, that is, of the divine will coming forth as an appetite. And since God's happiness has been defined over against creaturely need and temporality, another paradigm has yet to be put forth—a God who delights in the creaturely order through being shaped by the movements and processes of which God partakes.

Another Metaphysics of Love

To arrive at such a model, one that places a God of enjoyment beyond the divine self, I needed to embrace another form of metaphysics, one that would allow me to envisage more permeable forms of divine love—an erotic dimension of passion. This quest took me beyond Aristotelian metaphysics, a model that has prevailed in theological discourse since the apex of Scholastic thought.[11] Consequently, I have aligned myself with the critique that postmodern thinkers in particular pose to the metaphysics of self-sufficient love that protects God and the cosmos from intermingling. As Kevin Vanhoozer explains, postmodern thinkers raise some insightful questions concerning the simplistic manner in which scholastic metaphysics establishes "either/or contrasts,"[12] which for me is exemplified in classical paradigms. Seizing the capacities afforded by the language of panentheism (the belief that God and world are interrelated, with God and world being within each other), I give preference to teasing out the flux and fluidity of seeming oppositional relationships over analyzing categories of love that have become too insular and static. God and cosmos enjoy a loving relationship characterized by more permeable borders. The iconoclastic urge exemplified in my embrace of a divine-cosmic eroticism works against totalitarian forms of belief that can lead to idolatry either of God or of the cosmos.[13]

In my search for an erotic language with which to express this relationship of enjoyment that moves beyond either/or contrasts, I also pursue another definition of metaphysics, one ridden with erotic imagery. Although the dictum that all things are imbued with the divine presence is nothing new, the concept that God is capable of becoming in relationship with the cosmos has been little explored with regard to its sequela of divine enjoyment. Introducing a tint of Latin American feminism, I bring a balance to life's pain and pleasure, and place the cosmos more intimately within the inner existence of God as the source of fertility and vitality. Remarkably, this bodily approach to metaphysics helps me paint a beautiful analogy of mutually shared enjoyments akin to passion that also challenges patriarchal views. From a feminist standpoint, metaphysical models in which God is seen as purely and only active in creation, in the sense of exerting an independent and external control, while receiving nothing in return, are a projection of the archetypal male figure: dominant, inflexible, and independent.[14] Like theologies in which God is said to be mystically in all things as all things are in God, this model is "congenial to a naturally interpersonal approach to the God-world relationship," as Joseph Bracken keenly describes process thought.[15] Finally, hoping to further challenge seemingly oppositional categories related to erotic love (particularly within the scope of enjoyment), I found myself navigating the muddy waters of impropriety. Tropes such as *la fiesta* and views reminiscent of the ancient and modern-day carnivals, which playfully speak of eros with a touch of profanity, exuberantly guided my iconoclastic approach to metaphysics. They help suspend belief and disbelief, and show a level of ludic and profane activity that leads to deeper levels of communal vulnerability and greater understanding of the sacredness of passionate enjoyments.[16]

Such an iconoclastic model of love metaphysics is informed by my own sense of erotic mysticism and theopoetics. Mystics and poets grant us the freedom to playfully make use of erotic language. What I have found in these writers is the location from which to speak of the God-cosmos relationship through the metaphor of lovemaking, even when attempting to explain it away in metaphysical terms.[17] As we are reminded by Alfred North Whitehead, "philosophy is mystical" and "akin to poetry."[18] Through the former we gain "direct insight into depths as yet unspoken," while the latter helps us to understand "form beyond the direct meaning of words."[19] This poetic imagination that draws from a mystically embedded philosophy emancipates our theology from concepts such as a divine lover who while near, and possibly in the cosmos, as the cosmos is in God, remains unscathed by the fleshly enjoyments of the cosmos.

Hence, rather than the purely intellectual enjoyment of the unmoved mover and *actus purus* of Aristotle, in these pages I seek to unfold a theology of the passionate love of God such as is found in the works of mystics and poets. Of theology, Catherine Keller asks, "might it sound as much like poetry as proposition?"[20] Alongside the theoretical elements of theology, then, I reclaim its poetic dimension,[21] and urge a poetic imagery or a contemporary theopoetics akin to mystical dreams and imaginings.[22] I embrace theopoetics as a means of speaking of the divine mystical union with all living things, for it gives space to the imagination, which exhibits other forms of rationality. Poetry helps debunk what Ivone Gebara calls "a linear causality that ends with a first cause that appears to be Special, enlightening, and regenerative."[23] With a more ample imagination one goes beyond the bounds of strict forms of reasoning, and so makes room instead for embodied metaphors of the beloved lover God.

A mystically poetic metaphysics of love, furthermore, undergirds a model, akin to a lovers' embrace, that speaks of enjoyment in ethical terms, even as it also goes beyond the form of "morality" that keeps God from intermingling and becoming one with the cosmos. A morality established by patriarchy can reign supreme in models that emphasize linearity or categories that keep God enclosed within the divine self, such as the one that characterizes God as being self per se and absolutely subsistent. Accordingly, God showing us the path of life, and sharing the divine fullness of joy and pleasures forevermore with us (Ps. 16:11), would not necessarily render God a lover of the cosmos who partly embodies its multiple expressions of pleasure. As Gebara argues, "Linear thinking evokes a path of rectitude, a path that clearly manifests positive moral connotations. It is far removed from circuitous thought patterns, which imply twisting, morally devious ways."[24] Yet mystical and poetic language allows the lover to experience a painful pleasure generated by a longing for another who also loves, by receiving something from the beloved, and by being penetrated and becoming in part like the one who loves the lover. To speak of a *passionate* God in a relationship with the cosmos, and indeed somewhat "mixed" with it, is to dismantle the linearity and causality that try to keep divine enjoyment at a safe distance from all other living things.

Style and Structure of the Book

My baroque style of writing, typical of Spanish poetry, may seem disruptive: the book's arguments on divine enjoyment unfold through a series of choral motions. Evolutions, revolutions, and twists and turns give shape to the structure in which this basic idea moves from beginnings, to endings, to another set of beginnings. With a hint of a chiastic structure, Chapters 1 and 2 present incipient ideas that are more fully articulated in the later chapters, with the difference that the later chapters act as the feminist postmodern reconstructions of the first two. Chapters 1 and 5 and Chapters 2 and 4 may be seen as couplets, each member of which plays off the other's main aspects of enjoyment, with the third chapter providing the hinge that centers the ideas developed in those couplets concerning the metaphor of lovemaking. The last chapter moves the previous chapters' arguments beyond themselves, leaving them on the verge of opening up to another possible set of circular motions. Hence, the structure of the book seeks to imitate the open-ended and mutually indwelling "dance about" or choral movement of perichoresis (circumincession) through which the fellowship in the Godhead becomes characterized by intimacy, a "cleaving together" of God and cosmos embracing each other, as they enter into each other, permeate and dwell in each other in the Godhead, in this way transforming one another. Increasingly, they "become with" one another, metaphorically speaking, as lovers do when making love.

The series of choral motions evolves from a much modified version of St. Thomas Aquinas's model of the activity of the divine love that presumes God to be a lover, an activity that entails God going outside Godself into the world and returning all things to God (*exitus-reditus*).[25] After the first chapter, several circular motions subserve the work's analogical structure: the vulnerability of God that results from the inner life within God to the divine impulse of love in the cosmos; the return of all things to God; and finally the point at which God, as the eros of the cosmos, becomes one with the cosmos. The book culminates in a choral motion akin to the carnival or the *fiesta*, which deconstructs notions of the self as being its own sole beginning and endpoint, an enclosed self. In the end, the perichoretic dance of divine enjoyment is progressively open before the cosmos and vulnerable to it, as the multiple sites of embodiment of pleasure increasingly play significant roles in the subtle divine orgasmic crescendos. Five interrelated aspects of divine enjoyment specifically play major roles in this constructive move: pain (Chapter 1), yearning (Chapter 2), permeability (Chapter 3), intensity (Chapter 4), and impropriety (Chapter 5).

Chapter 1 serves as an introduction to an existing theological discourse on the passion of God. Spurred by the world wars and civil wars of the twentieth century, theology had to take another look at the notion of divine love in the form of pathos. At a time when such turmoil led many to conclude there is no God, authors of the cross argued that while there may be no God of impassive omnipotence, the God who experiences pain is alive and well. They symbolically joined efforts as they raised their voices in a theological protest that has reshaped God-talk today. Others followed suit and have presented a radically contextual approach to theology from the underside of history, from the perspective of the "crucified peoples" of the world.[26] Sadly, *pathos* has come to signify mostly suffering, rather than the fuller sense of passion. Understandably, one ought to underscore the capacity of God to suffer and the ethical path of love as a means to argue against impassibility, which in its most general terms means that God is incapable of experiencing the whole spectrum of creaturely emotions. Again, one may ask what a divine fullness that includes passion might look like when enjoyment is placed alongside pain. A starting point may be found in the works of Latin American feminist theologians. While as feminists they clearly wish to address suffering theologically (through a lens of liberation), they also assume that life's desires and pleasures endow life with a mobilizing principle of love.

Vestiges of an erotic divine enjoyment are to be found in classical theism, though eroticism per se is most prevalent in more relational theistic views. Both promise and challenges can be seen, for example, in the reflections of St. Thomas Aquinas on Denys the Areopagite, even as Aquinas remains faithful to some of the most influential views of Aristotle on the concept of enjoyment. As discussed in Chapter 2, the divine relationship with the cosmos propounded in the work of Aquinas resembles the loving union between lovers. For Aquinas, *yearning* or *appetite* initiates a circular motion in God by which God goes outside the divine self and into the cosmos to stir all things toward enjoyment, the end of which is union with God. Aquinas posits a God who seeks enjoyment with creation in amorous ways, for the good will of all things. This serves as an initial step in conceiving of a relationship between God and the cosmos that is reciprocal, and of a divine enjoyment that is mutually beneficial. But only to a point, for Aquinas (in accord with Aristotelian thought) also assumes that the divine lover ought to remain absolutely self-subsistent, that is, content within the divine self and impassible. Notwithstanding, the thoughts of Aquinas and other classical theologians prove essential in discussing in depth the notion of divine enjoyment.

Another element of enjoyment now emerges, for reciprocity and mutuality require a *permeability* that allows an intermingling in ways akin to erotic love. The works of Latin American feminists and of Aquinas begin to point in this direction, but they do not develop it fully. Hence in Chapter 3 the divine lover emerges as one who loves according to the flesh, erotically, in an explicitly reciprocal manner, a perspective developed in the works of postmodern thinkers who engage with the texts of the Christian mystics. Rather than a perfect and enclosed circle, a lonely affair with the self, or a perpetual virginity, what comes into view is an outline of "so good a Lover" that St. Teresa of Avila describes.[27] In imagery that shows the back-and-forth movement between lovers, their interpenetrative oscillations, another dimension of the divine loving nature begins to surface, the erotic dimension. Eros characterizing the divine love challenges the view that God receives nothing from the one who loves in return, from someone who, as St. Teresa describes, longs for an encounter with the divine lover that is akin to lovemaking. I therefore seek, along with these thinkers, to eroticize the language of passion, as the divine silhouette of the beloved lover slowly begins to take on flesh, a porous flesh that allows for the intermingling of selves as lovers intermingle.

Permeability drives the conversation to yet another element of enjoyment: *intensity*. Therefore, the need arises for a more explicitly panentheistic perspective as an aid to conceive of a God who becomes increasingly passionate with the cosmos. This God would endure passage from one form to another in a manner that adds fulfillment to the divine enjoyment (the cosmos intensifying God), and would change according to a partial transmuting incarnation (God becoming in the likeness of the multiplicity of the cosmos). Hence, loving intensely further challenges the notion of self-enclosure. As the cosmos flows into the divine life, thus partly intensifying the divine love, God stirs the cosmos toward fuller expressions of life. Their intimate relationship ensues in an intense passion in their distinct expressions. In Chapter 4, therefore, the divine love for the cosmos evolves into the principle of *intensity* that seduces all beings in the cosmos, a principle in se coconstituted by the many expressions of enjoyment brought together. As a result of the cosmos adding intensity to the divine enjoyment, God appears to continuously transmute into the lover who passionately loves others.

But what would it mean for God to welcome the many expressions of enjoyment in such a way as to be affected and coconstituted by them? What would it mean in relation to the imagery of lovemaking? And, even more, what would it mean for an understanding of the divine union with the cosmos as a festive dance akin to the Trinitarian perichoresis? How could a model of a God whose enjoyment also stems from the distinct pleasures of the many loves possibly provide an answer to the ethical concerns put forth concerning an enjoyment that if conceived as primary would be mutually beneficial? To answer these questions, in Chapter 5 I turn to the *impropriety* of divine enjoyment. The circular movement of selves within and beyond themselves speaks of a mystical intermingling analogous to a carnivalesque dance of passion. The trope of the carnival places divine pleasure beyond the language of propriety to which classical theism preassigns a set of postulates that preserve the logic of hierarchy (God above the cosmos) and exclusion (God unmixed with it). Something like a liberative perichoresis birthing an *ordo amoris* of radical communal vulnerability emerges from the figure of a God generously open to the multiple ways of loving manifested in the cosmos. In this concluding chapter the divine dance with a multitude of lovers—the Trinity, humans, animals, plants— transmutes God into hospitable generosity as God takes on the monstrous and yet-to be-finished shape of the *jouissance* of the many. Why not account for a kind of enjoyment that truly welcomes the other, that is, something truly other than the self, one's kin, religious affiliation or non-affiliation, gender, sexual orientations, tribe, or tongue?

The circular motion ends with a motif reminiscent of the Eucharist, which speaks of both remembrance of things past and an expectation of things to come. This eucharistic banquet imagery, like others such as the *exitus-reditus* and mystical union, is deconstructed and deromanticized so that the text does not appear to be arguing for a particular telos or ethnos (i.e., one bound to the Church or a particular gender or racial group) other than the dislocating union between the many and God. The book addresses the need to paint the figure of a God who opens up spaces of enjoyment in Godself, with the intent to offer a model of reciprocal forms of pleasure that resemble Maduro's *la fiesta*. Like a God who goes out into the streets welcoming the many to join the banquet, the book portrays an intimate and vulnerable God who incites us to daily enact communal life as a remembrance of events that speak of life fully, and places in us a longing for things yet to be manifested according to a new order of love. This picture of a God whom we can enjoy and who can enjoy us in community with others points in the end to a radical God-cosmos and intercosmic interdependence in the pursuit of happiness. At the incipit of the ethical call for mutual forms of enjoyment, I construct a model of divine enjoyment that, by deviating from the classical principle of self-subsistence (by oneself, and in an absolute manner), ascertains God to be already a community of affect. This thought inspires us, I suggest, to recognize the need for a deeper sense of vulnerability, for a radical generosity, and for equal access to sources of pleasure.

Pain: Groans and Birth Pangs of the Divine Enjoyment

> Neither metaphysically nor epistemologically was Greek thought
> prepared to ponder or believe in a crucified God.
>
> —JON SOBRINO[1]

What foolishness is the foundation of Christian thought—a God who endured the cross! The centuries-old debate about divine *apatheia*—the absence of passion—yields an alternative model of divine love to the classical theistic view of impassibility. For how could a God of love, whose outstretched arms on the cross offer eloquent testimony to the divine yearning, be incapable of receiving passion from the cosmos? To posit divine love for that which is other than God is consequently to raise a question about the passion of God. Being mindful of those on the underside of history, Christian authors such as Jürgen Moltmann and the liberation theologian Jon Sobrino have mounted compelling challenges to this idea. Their basic premise is that of a relational God, who willingly seeks to be "stirred by" the happenings of the cosmos. Their starting point is divine passibility linked with the experience of human suffering caused by the atrocities committed over the course of the past centuries.

I agree with some of the main conclusions these theologians have reached regarding the inadequacy of the argument for divine impassibility when set against the suffering of the world. At the same time, I seek to address the question from a different starting point: that of enjoyment. Hence the opening and closing arguments of this chapter, as if enveloping the trope of suffering, will steer the conversation toward the question at hand, whether a divine enjoyment can also stem from a *give-and-take* with the created order. This chapter furtively glances at the God who passionately loves the cosmos and introduces the concept of a God capable of experiencing a pleasurable suffering, a concept that arises in the context of Latin American liberationist feminism. Accordingly, the notion of a God who is vulnerable like us is explored, but with a theological twist: God's pathos is not reduced to suffering. The basic proposition is that a classical Aristotelian notion of an unmovable God cannot offer a full enough view of divine love, that God instead intimately relates to the cosmos, is in history confronting us, while also *painfully* becoming with and birthing in us a dream of and a passion for better things to come.

Therefore, through a constructive study of the trope of the *beloved divine lover* who suffers as well as enjoys the cosmos, I hope to challenge static views of divine love and definitions of passion that omit enjoyment or relativize its importance. In briefly laying out the history of the evolving thought about the passionate love of God, this first chapter does not attempt to provide an exhaustive account. Rather, offering a bird's-eye view, it quickly leaps from antiquity to early Christian thought, then on to medieval, modern, and explicitly feminist views. It introduces the reader to part of the corpus on divine passion, and to some of the arguments of those interlocutors who may help guide this exposition. The challenges raised in this chapter assist in examining the various historical answers offered to the problematic of the Aristotelian model as a way to carry forward, beyond its principle of impassibility, the nuanced God of enjoyment to whom this book introduces us.

God's Apathetic Happiness?

The Deity is thought of as a Being who abides in absolute calm.

Abraham J. Heschel[2]

Christian theology has long held views of God that are deeply rooted not only in Jewish or Hebraic thought but also in classical Greek thought. One of the foremost influences in this regard has been Aristotle, and specifically with respect to this project, his view of the enjoyment or happiness of God. Insofar as Aristotle is the primary proponent of the idea of apathy, of a dispassionate being, that this work challenges as it constructs the figure of a beloved divine lover, it may seem surprising to discover what a high value he places on *eudaimonia*, or enjoyment, which is, after all, a passion, in his discussions of God.

PHILEIC ENJOYMENT

In classical Greek thought, *eudaimonia*—happiness or enjoyment—is a good in and of itself. In particular, for Aristotle, it is the source from which all well-being stems and the end or goal toward which all things move.[3] In the circular movement between goal and end, goal as end, happiness denotes completion and thus self-sufficiency. Also, according to this definition, the good of happiness is to be found in it being both the beginning (source) and the end (goal) of happiness, thereby denoting perfection. Therefore, self-subsistence in relation to happiness comes to mean mostly to be in need of nothing, to lack nothing. Granted, self-sufficiency in Aristotle's paradigm has nothing to do with living in excess, such as in luxury, but rather with meeting one's basic needs, and finding much enjoyment in living well, as when heads of households are able to provide for the needs of the household, or a city is able to sustain itself with very minimal use of trade for its self-subsistence.[4] Also, happiness is a virtue in itself: seeking happiness for its own sake, which would mean for the sake of the good life just described, denotes completion. A happy life is a complete life of virtue in which even political and civic duties or pursuits find their end. By itself, happiness makes one's living worthwhile.

If defined to be solely about itself, happiness might seem to culminate in loneliness, at least according to our contemporary views of the individual self. But that is not the case, for happiness entails friendship when expressed in the context of human-to-human relations, a friendship, moreover, that is always linked to the well-being of the community. Although happy people lack nothing, for "all good things belong to them already," Aristotle also states that "it seems absurd, when people assign all good things to the happy person, not to grant him friends, which seems to be the greatest of external goods."[5] Friendship being a good and in addition to the good things already possessed means that happiness can come both before friendship and as a result of it. And here an apparent contradiction may be resolved. A happy person, who by definition is one who possesses all things yearned for, may also seem to be one who has the most friends. According to Aristotle, it would be absurd to construe the self-sufficient (happy) person as solitary, underscoring that happiness and friendship are intricately related in this perspective.

The significance of happiness being paired with friendship entails a reciprocated sense of active goodness that at first glance can seem attractive when one considers arguments for a God of passion. For one thing, its meaning could convey the image of a God who, while being happiest, is able to receive something in return from the cosmos, as friends commonly do. This relation would be most appropriate, since doing good and returning good for the sake of one's friends abolishes any notion of happiness being concomitant on greed, or on any compulsory return of love or goodness.[6] Well-being and friendship go hand in hand, for friends wish to do good for one another and act in ways that bring about happiness for one other. Happiness based on mutual well-being has to do with having the satisfaction of "loving more than . . . being loved."[7] So if this friendship model allows for it, God in a sense could love without concupiscence even when receiving something from the cosmos, for friends do not seek to obtain anything from each other and do not demand anything from one another in return. This concern could mean that God's love is found in the act of loving the divine self and others in ways that do not increase God's own pleasure at the expense of others'.

When it comes to kings and gods, however, in the Aristotelian model the possibility of God being a friend appears less plausible. For Aristotle, kings and gods (he places them in the same category) cannot be friends with those who are under them. Kings are considered to be greater in virtue, affluence, and self-sufficiency. This is not to say that kings in their self-sufficiency are necessarily without concern for others. A king, though in no need of the friendship of others, "looks to the things beneficial not to himself but to those who are ruled."[8] By contrast, the tyrant only "pursues what is good for himself."[9] So even when kings lack friends who are counted to be lesser than they, they can still behave in a manner conducive to benevolence, meaning not merely self-beneficial. A king might do well for an underling for the sake of the underling and not for the king's own sake. Yet could not this model of Aristotle pose a hindrance, particularly if we wish to postulate that God enjoys the cosmos, as I seek to do in this work, and when for him it is true that gods are self-sufficient to an *absolute* degree? Aristotle firmly states the division between gods or kings and their inferiors with these words:

> And this is clear if the divergence becomes great in virtue or in vice or in affluence or in anything else; for no longer are they friends, nor do they think to deserve to be. This is most manifest in the case of the gods, since they have the greatest superiority in all good things, but it is evident also in the case of kings, since those who are inferior do not even think they deserve to be friends with those who are best or wisest. In such cases there is no precise boundary up to which they are friends, for when many things have been taken away the friendship still remains, but when they are separated greatly, as from a god, it no longer does.[10]

To wish the good for the sake of a friend can only be done for another who is human, argues Aristotle. Humans cannot necessarily wish good for a god, since gods have no need of more good or good will; and this is all the more the case insofar as the gods cannot be one's friends. A hermetic barrier is raised. God would have no friends in that God would not mutually receive the love being reciprocated and respond accordingly. Summarizing Aristotle's view, Abraham Heschel writes, "if we love God, we cannot desire Him to return our love, for then he would lose His perfection by becoming passively affected by our joys and sorrows."[11] For the world to be a friend of God would mean for God to also passively receive something from the world, to be in the position of a recipient to whom something could be added or from whom something could be taken way.

Interestingly, Aquinas reads Aristotle otherwise, by interpreting him in accordance with some principles enunciated in the scriptures. According to Aquinas, when Aristotle says "If, as we commonly supposed, the gods have any care of men, we may well believe them to take delight in that which is best and most akin to themselves . . . the intellectual worker then will be the best loved of heaven," he is implying that God can also have friends.[12] Aquinas interprets this passage the following way: "This Holy Writ teaches, saying: *God guards all that love him* (Ps. cxliv, 20); and the Philosopher also teaches that God has especial care of those who love understanding, and considers them His friends."[13] In the passage quoted by Aquinas, Aristotle is speaking from the context of the gods being the most blessed and happy, and thus being somewhat also at work, not being asleep, like Endymion.[14] So an element of benign work or action on behalf of others is implied, which for Aquinas denotes divine-to-human friendship.

It is undeniable that Aquinas's reading of Aristotle differs from that of Heschel, who asserts that the God described in the work of Aristotle is incapable of having friends. I agree with Don Adams that Aquinas took certain liberties in his approach to the texts of Aristotle on enjoyment.[15] He creatively sought to bridge Greek thought with the scriptures and Christian classical views in order to demonstrate that wisdom may be also found in the wider world. As evinced by the established doctrine that God is love, he would not have been the only one who sought to add nuance to Aristotelian thinking, since Christianity has reinterpreted this paradigm by placing *agape* at its core. Perhaps this is the reason why for authors like Anders Nygren, the Greek concept of kingly *eudemonia* is comfortably replaced by that of a divine love that is benevolent: "an outflow," a love "that descends, freely and generously giving of its superabundance."[16]

Nevertheless, the views of the gods, or God, articulated by Aristotle still recognizably establish a chiasm between God and everything else that demands our attention. And while Christianity is clearly willing to narrow the distance between the two by granting friendship to God in the form of agape, with respect to Aristotelian influence on classical thought, a question remains. With an understanding of God as loving friend, can there be receptivity?

EMOTIONAL ENTANGLEMENTS

A lack of affect is where the Aristotelian principle of absolute self-sufficiency comes into fuller view, and the quandary deepens. Closely related to Aristotle's notion of divine happiness is the principle of the unmoved mover.[17] Happiness equals immutability. Immutability posits lack of affect. Though one cannot argue that divine happiness is nonbenevolent if viewed in this manner (for the principles of happiness still hold), it cannot be ignored that this nonaffective tone establishes a strict boundary that lacks vulnerability— true friendship—between the divine and the cosmos. God is immutably impassible, always actual, thus never in the state of potentiality. For Aristotle, there must be something unlike sensible things, "whose essence is actuality," something whose substance is eternal and unmovable while still "capable of moving all things or acting on them" actually.[18] This something is God, whose "self-dependent actuality is life most good and eternal."[19] In this already familiar view, God, who is a self-subsisting unmoved mover, is impassive and unalterable.[20] In Christianity, this principle has been held as truth. For Gregory of Nyssa, for example, the Godhead is free of all passion, and a good God "remains what it is . . . ever unchangeable," transcending "all addition or diminution."[21]

This view of a God who is the most self-sufficient, unalterable, actual being when maintained from the standpoint of impassibility also places an undue emphasis on entity (the good who is God is unmovable) and neglects the movement that occurs within God—the divine yearning, for instance. As Joseph Bracken explains, in placing the importance on things rather than on processes, Aristotle "sought to explain motion or processes in terms of a series of movers rather than a series of movers in terms of an underlying motion or processes common to all."[22] Motion becomes constricted by its antecedent cause, which ultimately is an unmoved mover. By placing the emphasis on entity or being, Aristotle is forced to claim that there is something that must remain unmoved, which in classical theism comes to be defined as God.

The problematic of God being "unmoved" is compounded when we consider happiness as stemming from a state of radical serenity intricately tied to a lack of passion. The deity can be in a perpetual state of contemplation, of "thinking on thinking," without affect.[23] Described in a positive manner, Aristotelian contemplation involves maintaining a state of calmness in the midst of misfortune, which for many ancient philosophers meant persisting in excellence while facing adversity. With a temperate character a person is able to maintain a steady pace in doing things beautifully and is able to accomplish things in accordance with virtue. From the point of view urged in this book, however, his argument warrants further interrogation, for contemplation also means allowing solely the intellect, the part in us that conceives of things beautiful or divine, to guide life. For Aristotle, to act for the sake of that which is virtuous means to perform actions according to the intellect, "the most powerful of the things in us."[24] Serenity denotes a *purely* rationalized passion that tames the flesh, and even such affections as sorrow.[25] And while attributing some form of intellectual activity to God is not necessarily negative, in what way would God respond to puzzling circumstances, even tragedy, if God's passion were purely rational? Would one attend to actions that are serious and beautiful only while in a state of apparent numbness to the intensity of the world's affairs?

Heschel's fitting response to immovability may prove fruitful. He quips, "It was such preference that enabled Greek philosophy to exclude all emotion from the nature of the Deity, while at the same time ascribing thought and contemplation to it."[26] Impassivity means calmness, an undisturbed state. Because affect is a disturbance of the mind, and thus a weakness, it cannot be attributed to God. This leads to what Heschel describes as the anesthetization of God: a God incapable of receiving anything is a God incapable of being affected.[27] *Apathes to theion*, divine impassibility, he explains, "becomes a fundamental principle in the doctrine of God for both Jewish and Christian theologians."[28] If God receives nothing from the cosmos, then God exists in a better state of contemplation (happiness) than we do.[29] Yet this renders God uninvolved in the whole of life's events. The notion of circular revolutions of divine thought enclosed in itself, even as it implies a concern for the created order, remains an issue to be wrestled with when placed in the context of the sufferings of history. Along these lines, Jon Sobrino asks the following:

> For Aristotle, God is the thinking process which thinks about itself, but which is apathetic with respect to history. For Saint John, God is love. Is that statement real? Is it supposed to be comprehensible in historical terms, not just in essential terms? If our answer to those questions is yes, then we must ask ourselves how God can express that love, his ultimate word to human being, in a world of misery without himself being affected by that misery.[30]

Admittedly, something close to the claim of a changeless love, in the sense of unfailing, eternal, and persistent, is surely appropriate for any

Christian theology. With Bracken, one could maintain that the divine love is an ongoing activity that is the ground of all existence, including God's, of which all things partake.[31] In some classical models this "motion" entails God going outside the divine self in demonstrations of love for creatures, to draw them into the divine self, for union with God. As in the case of Endymion, this activity can refer to a certain *being-at-work* that is contrary to being asleep in the sense of numbness, for it entails engaging in the beautiful and the good. Hence God being alert and aware of the affairs of the cosmos can translate into a divine ongoing motion that is love, and, as in the case of kings, even as benevolence or care. This claim of an unchanging love, in the sense of a persisting love, as it is found in Christian thought is therefore compelling.

In addition, as Mark-Robin Hoogland argues, affirmations such as that of Aquinas that "*God's love is the divine ousia*" can mean that "God is totally singular, perfect, infinite, eternal and unchangeable love."[32] This means that the divine essence is love, and by God being these perfections, the divine love is an incomparable love, an unchanging love like no other. Undeniably, a conception of a God whose love cannot be "comprehended," or shaped by manipulation or force, safeguards our understanding of the God of love.[33] Such an idea guards against the divine capriciousness attributed to the gods of the Greek pantheon. Rather than capriciousness, we therefore encounter a persistent divine love and a God who is unswervingly intimately close to us. Yet as Heschel indicates, a problem arises when conceiving of God as one who moves out of the divine self with an impulse not initiated by pathos—pathos in the Latin sense of *passio* or *pati*, "suffering"—for passion would then refer solely to something that happens to the creature as its soul is awakened by things external to it. How could God as Supreme Cause be affected internally or suffer in the sense of passion and from that passion or receptivity be moved towards an action of care?

The issue at hand consequently requires us to redirect our attention to *emotion* (in the sense of being acted upon) in this inquiry into divine pathos. It also entails challenging Aristotle's notion of an absolutely self-subsistent and unalterable state of happiness. Otherwise, divine immutability and absolute divine self-subsistence could translate into an aloof God whose loving motion resides in all there is without anything in any way affecting God. Aristotle rhetorically asks, "How could it be a mover unless it were itself unmoved? And if it were not aloof from the mixture of things, how could it dominate?"[34] Evidently an unquestionable presumption is at work. He is making an explicit theological statement about God who is happiest by being, above all, invulnerable, unmixed with the cosmos, and dominant. This development of Parmenidian (Socratic, Platonic) thought in Aristotle allows us to picture an unmovable God who, while being in absolute calmness within Godself, moves all things without pathos (affect). Similar to the concept of the soul with two floors—reason upstairs, emotions downstairs—Aristotle develops a figure of God who, while capable of self-contemplation, is invulnerable to the world. That is the classical view of the impassible God, unmixed in affairs of the cosmos.

Heschel and Sobrino therefore rightly put on trial this classical view even when speaking of the God of love. Divine pathos, viewed as deficiency, gives rise to an oxymoron. If God were aloof and unmixed with the world, that is, apathetic (without affect), God's concerns would be only for Godself. This aloof deity, "unmoved mover, pure form, eternal, wholly actual, immutable, immovable, self-sufficient, and wholly separated from all else," has one sole activity that rests purely in itself, and that is "thought, and thought alone."[35] Divine enjoyment consequently would equal imperturbability. Change in the divine could denote disturbance by those things considered to be unequal to or lesser than the divine. Nothing would affect the stillness of the serenity of God since God is "unmixed" with the affairs of the world. So divine impassibility as rest and immobility defines a Being who abides in absolute calmness. A God whose happiness stems from a self-enclosed calmness can be said to be "anesthetized" to or unaffected by the things of the cosmos. Again, how could this serene activity translate into the divine love?

The Aristotelian notion of divine impassibility therefore leaves no room for a passionate God of love, even in theology. Such a God, even while being "the ground of the love of all things," is a "loveless Beloved,'" as Jürgen Moltmann puts it.[36] Aristotle's God would also be "the beloved who is in love with himself; a Narcissus in a metaphysical degree: *Deus incurvatus in se.*" The only manner in which God would not suffer would be through being impassible. Moltmann asks rhetorically, "But in that case is he God? Is he not rather a stone?" How can this God be in relationship with the world?

How can one theologically disturb the unchanging divine imperturbability? I agree with Heschel: a God with whom one seeks relationship must be personally involved in the world in the sense of "being stirred by" the conduct and fate of human and nonhuman beings.[37] The alternative, therefore, to the God who "is conscious of Himself, but oblivious to the world" is the God who passionately loves the cosmos. This would not be to argue for a weak God, nor a divine martyr, not yet a capricious divine moodiness, but a God who in being concerned for the affairs of the cosmos is always vulnerable.[38] Perhaps this would imply another kind of friend, one that in agreement with Aristotle would be a source of comfort to the friend in misfortune in sharing her pain, but also beyond Aristotle in that a God of love would be extremely sensitive to and capable of enduring others' pain.[39]

With Divine Passion as Compassion

The question of divine impassibility has become especially prominent owing to the world wars, civil wars, the Holocaust, and the genocides that have taken place from the mid-twentieth century on. Jewish thinkers like Heschel and Christian theologians like Moltmann and Sobrino have symbolically joined their voices in a theological protest against the figure of the impassible God that undeniably has reshaped our views on the God of love today. These thinkers and theologians inherited the mantle of others who sought to delve into the trope of divine suffering, while more have followed suit and offered a view that presents theology from the underside of history, from the perspective of the "crucified peoples" of the world.[40] The witness of and stories told by some of these millions of people attest to the need to reflect on the issue of divine vulnerability. For why not consider the divine mystery of divine emotion—a God whose divine essence is unconditional love being also affected by the created order?

ON PATHOS AS SUFFERING

Incapability of suffering in this sense would contradict the fundamental
Christian assertion that God is love, which in principle broke the spell of
the Aristotelian doctrine of God.

Jürgen Moltmann[41]

Although there are glimpses of a God who is involved in the affairs of the world since early Christianity, the debate over divine impassibility has unfortunately dominated Christian theology, particularly with regard to suffering.[42] Even early theologians like Tertullian insisted that, to safeguard the Trinitarian distinctions, it could not be said that the Father experienced the suffering of the Son.[43] Hence the heresy of the Father suffering on the cross or *patripassianism* was declared.[44]

Certainly, many early thinkers embraced the Christian teaching that the Son of God became flesh and was born of a virgin. Quite the mystery for the Logos of God to become flesh by means of a womb and a birth canal![45] This Son also of the flesh of Mary enjoyed and endured and enjoyed from birth to death the full spectrum of human experiences. Jesus, says Athanasius, even while being the divine Logos, took upon himself "the other passions of the body too, in order that we may grasp eternal life."[46] Apollinaris of Laodicea went so far as to declare that "the singleness of an incarnate divine nature which is comingled [with flesh], with the result that worshippers bend their attention to God inseparably from the flesh and not to one worshipped and one who is not."[47] He is even mingled with us as humans.[48]

Hippolytus describes it beautifully in his treatise *Against Noetus:*

> Thus then, too, though demonstrated as God, He does not refuse the conditions proper to Him as man, since He hungers and toils and thirsts in weariness, and flees in fear, and prays in trouble. And He who as God has a sleepless nature, slumbers on a pillow. And He who for this end came into the world, begs off from the cup of suffering. And in an agony He sweats blood, and is strengthened by an angel, who Himself strengthens those who believe on Him, and taught men to despise death by His work. And He who knew what manner of man Judas was, is betrayed by Judas. And He, who formerly was honoured by him as God, is contemned by Caiaphas. And He is set at nought by Herod, who is Himself to judge the whole earth. And He is scourged by Pilate, who took upon Himself our infirmities.[49]

Yet an overemphasis on the divinity of Jesus, which then turns to the distinctions of the persons of the Trinity, has added to the obscurity of the notion of divine passion in what became the orthodox view. While the Logos became flesh, the passions had to remain proper to the flesh. Any suffering Jesus experienced he could only truly experience as a human, and not according to his divine nature. At the root of this argument has been the interrogation of the divinity of Jesus (Logos or Word). Against the Arian views, for example, the manner in which many argued for an "unbegotten Son" was by contrasting the human and divine natures. To argue for his peculiar sonship, they sided with immutability (as distinct from the Arian view of Jesus becoming divine at a later point in time).[50] For instance, Alexander of Alexandria argued that the inexpressible hypostasis that "possesses an immutable nature, being perfect and in want of nothing," is "as immutable and unchangeable, as the Father, and self-sufficient and perfect . . . an exact identical image of the Father."[51] Likewise for Athanasius: "For the Father is unalterable and unchangeable and always is in the same state and the same . . . the Son, being from the Father, and proper to his essence, is unchangeable and unalterable as the Father Himself."[52]

What has endured in classical views, as illustrated in the work of St. Thomas Aquinas, despite his innovative understanding of a friend who suffers, is that the divine nature of Jesus gained nothing from his human nature.[53] Even Jesus was impassible to the point that he suffered a perfect passion—kept under control by reason—while dying on the cross.[54] And to take it one step further in the direction of God, any compassion attributed to God is merely in appearance; it is at best an anthropomorphism. Interestingly, Aquinas was willing to ascribe an appetite to God, which could have meant that as lover, God would have been "inclined through love to act according to the demands and needs of the beloved," suffer for the beloved, and even experience "greater delight in the beloved in all he does or suffers for his sake."[55] Nevertheless, for him, to attribute passion to God is to contradict the idea of "the unchangeable God," and all the more so with respect to some passions, such as "Sadness and Grief."[56] Understandably, Aquinas sought to protect certain aspects of God, as he also conceived of a model that drew God intimately near the cosmos. Yet the sense one gets again is that at all costs, God must maintain an unsurpassable boundary between that which is affected and that which is protected from enduring affect.

Another model concerning the God who as a friend dies on the cross was therefore necessary, one in which God as friend could grieve and rejoice with the created order. In modern times, the Crucifixion as the cornerstone of Christianity had to acquire another meaning. One way of responding was by reflecting on how the suffering Jesus shared the joys and sufferings of the world with the divine essence. This idea acquired great significance in the work of Eberhard Jüngel. For him, in "responsible Christian usage of the word 'God,' the Crucified One is virtually the real definition of what is meant by the word 'God.' Christian theology is fundamentally the theology of the Crucified One."[57] The Christian faith that speaks of divine love concerns itself, therefore, with the crucifixion implied in the union of death and life for the sake of life that defines the very essence of God, which is love. And so in any argument regarding the existence of God, being the same as God's essence, the contention that God is love would be intricately connected to the divine humanity that suffered death.

Similarly, for some authors like Moltmann, the Crucifixion connotes *kenosis*, or a divine self-limitation.[58] On the cross God (and not simply the human Jesus) limits Godself. Self-limitation means that God, while being in no need of another, voluntarily and freely chose to suffer along with others. According to Moltmann, rather than being free from creation, from its needs, from the fetters of the flesh, and from others in the created order, God freely chose to suffer in order to liberate others.[59] "Out of freedom and not necessity" means that rather than positing suffering owing to self-limitation as a deficiency or imperfection in God, divine suffering is divine fullness and an aspect of divine perfect love. Rather than pathos being placed in a discourse of lack, it begins to fall within one of fullness, and in parallel manner as it falls within the discourse on happiness. God suffers out of the superabundance of God's love. God willingly suffered the humiliation and the death on the cross that Jesus suffered, pouring or emptying Godself out of God.

In a sense, the cross becomes the utmost symbol of the foolish wisdom of the God of love, who likewise eclipses the divine self through negation. For Moltmann, these two emphases point in the direction of a divine nature that suffers humanly and the God who suffered on the cross the abandonment of the Son by the parental figure.[60] And in agreement with Kazoh Kitamori, the emphasis is on the continuity rather than the discontinuity of the divine suffering among the members of the Trinity.[61] While the two kinds of suffering remain distinct in a way that prevents us from falling into docetism, the early Christian doctrine that Jesus was in reality incorporeal and so did not die on the cross,[62] the suffering of Jesus on the cross affected not only Jesus's divine nature but also God. In this manner divine love is rooted in God's pain, in the cross and what it represents, therefore being "in no sense an external act of God, but an act within" the divine self, as Kitamori writes.[63]

This notion of continuity, which challenges the either/or contrasts of Western thinking and is also explored in the work of Jung Young Lee, serves to dismantle the overemphasis on the distinctions of the Trinitarian persons, an emphasis designed to preserve the transcendence and uniqueness of God at the expense of mutuality or more relational forms with the cosmos.[64] Lee in particular draws from the popular Confucian classic *I Ching* or *Book of Changes* to propose a "both/and" understanding of the divine natures in order to ascribe the possibility of suffering to the nature of God. With this concept of both/and, rather than being an unmoved mover God could be the "moving mover" or "changing changer" in being highly continuous with the cosmos. With regard to the persons of the Trinity, the suffering of Jesus not only reveals that the other members suffer but also that the divine suffering extends into the world in the suffering of the Son. Both Kitamori and Lee, like Moltmann, seek to highlight the distinct sufferings of the Son, God and creation, while acknowledging that there is also continuity.

So there must be more to a God of love. Hewing to the view that such intradivine intimacy exists, one can maintain there is a bond of *friendly* love between God (trinitarianly) and the world that is more radically open to the cosmos. Thus one can press further on the quandary of the Aristotelian model of divine impassibility. A divine permeability that denotes suffering with the cosmos noticeably works against any concept of divine *apatheia*. God, by limiting the divine self, by becoming a friend, would not remain undisturbed, autarkic, or apathetic to the affairs of the cosmos as the intrarelations extended beyond the point of the cross and into the created order. The metaphor moreover grants permeability to the divine-human friendship. The Trinitarian God, by choosing to love through suffering, also becomes vulnerable to the world, which allows the suffering of the created order to become a part of who God is. More daring still, there is suffering in the cosmos because the cosmos, in continuity with God, also experiences the divine suffering.

HISTORY IN THE SUFFERING GOD

> On the cross God does not show up as one who wields power over the
> negative from *outside*; rather, on the cross we see God submerged *within*
> the negative.
>
> Jon Sobrino[65]

A history marked by tragedies like the immemorial bombing of Nagasaki,
by real human pain, is what gives rise to a theology of a God who suffers, as
Kitamori reminds us.[66] God suffers the suffering of the cosmos caused by
horrors such as these. They constitute dimensions of history that come to
be a part of the divine existence, Heschel argues.[67] When speaking of the
sufferings of those in Latin America through a discourse of liberation, God
is said to be present in a unique manner among "the suffering, oppressed,
and outcast countenance of our poorest brothers and sisters," among those
who suffer brutal oppression at the hands of military regimes that devolve
into civil wars, as argued feelingly by the Nicaraguan author Luz Beatriz
Arellano.[68] As theology remains closer to the cross, the suffering of the
crucified (victims and martyrs) in history becomes a linchpin for theological reflection on God, theologians like Sobrino insist.[69] In the figure of
God dying on the cross is "the death of the peasant, the native Indian, and
so forth."[70] Therefore, the victimized may become vehicles of revelation of
who God is.

The event at Golgotha thus takes some of the theological discourse on
divine love in the direction of a God who suffers in history. It declares that
suffering is a mode of being of God: love. A compassionate God who is free
to suffer "the otherness of the other"—to which, for Sobrino, the event of
the cross offers witness—"will give concrete reality to the most profound
intuition of the New Testament concerning God: i.e., that God is love."[71] A
God who loves as friends do (namely, they will lay down their lives for the
sake of a friend) can be typical of divine vulnerability. That is, a historical
love is revealed in the act of the Crucifixion. It tells a story of how God
loves by way of solidarity.

As exposed in history, God is prepared to become a victim. This narrative turns the Aristotelian view of kings and gods on its head in that it
posits another model based on love. In raising questions about "the authentic reality of the deity,"[72] we find that rather than a God viewed solely in

comparison to a king, a theology of the servant emerges, a more negative or scandalous view of God. No longer a king but a servant, God lets the divine self be affected by all that is negative. Such knowledge comes from following the path of negation. God is what God is seemingly not. Sobrino argues, "If there is some knowledge of God to be found on the cross, then some other principle of knowledge must be operative because the deity appears totally unlike anything we know."[73] An expression of the wounded God receptively hanging on the cross as a sign of love is quite a non-Greek demonstration of friendship. It is a *noetic* scandal.

God on the cross as a sign of love also challenges the eternal circle of divine contemplation, the notion of "thinking on thinking" of the Aristotelian deity, which posits a God who contemplates the divine self alone.[74] Sobrino rhetorically asks, "Does his solidarity with us mean that God himself must go by way of the cross in the midst of countless of historical crosses, or in the last analysis does God himself remain untouched by the historical cross because he is essentially untouchable?"[75] Suffering serves to reveal a concrete reality that, as Sobrino argues, is not merely human. God hanging on the cross narrates a story of such a divine reality that love is shown, in that "God is the partisan of human beings."[76] And this divine love of which Jesus speaks is unimaginable, for it is directed at the unloved and lowly, the crucified, rather than solely at the one who can equally correspond with pleasure. One who receives something from the cosmos thus is quite a scandal, to which the cross points!

Hence, while the Aristotelian notion of benevolence ascribed to kings and gods buffers the divine *apatheia* from tyranny, the motif of a God capable of suffering as a friend suffers further dislodges the idea of a totalitarian God and the totalitarian regimes that justify torture, mass murders, and disappearances. Likewise, the suffering of God calls into question the God of democratic capitalism, when the followers of that God fail to care for the needy or to engage in forms of trade that might benefit developing countries. The notion of suffering in God, therefore, becomes an element in the political arena. Accordingly, Sobrino argues, "It is in this point that we face the alternatives posed by Moltmann: Either the cross of Jesus is the end of all Christian theo-logy or else it is the beginning of a truly Christian theology, one that is a critical theory and a liberative praxis."[77] A God hanging on the cross offers the necessary critique of those who with insatiable thirst for power spare no lives.

This statement is consistent with that of Moltmann, for whom God is no "cold heavenly power"; neither does God "tread God's way over corpses" but is known as the human God in the crucified Son.[78] The picture of a crucified God with his arms outstretched contradicts the God outside history, offering a critique of the idolatry of power. Rather than all-powerful king, God is a fellow sufferer. For Moltmann, this is most evident in the statement of Cyril of Jerusalem: "O blessed tree on which God was outstretched." This "'outstretched' God of the Trinity"[79] suffers death internally. As Dorothee Soelle sees in Elie Wiesel's account of the boy who was hanged on the gallows, there lies the notion that God is neither an executioner nor a spectator (which would be the same), and not a mighty tyrant. But more than the figure of a benevolent king, God in choosing to be at the side of the victim is hanged.[80]

Thus, before we continue on this path to exploring who this passionate God can be when suffering and evil enter the equation, with much respect for those who have gone before us, we pause in silence. After considering earlier reflections on the God who suffers and on the manifestations of suffering in the cosmos, we quietly groan. Suffering—creaturely and divine—contains elements that are beyond our understanding. Just as the cross points to the inexplicability of some forms of suffering, so does the image of the God of pathos that the cross upholds. All suffering is a mystery. Particularly, when witnessing "extreme and gratuitous suffering" in the form of torture (the cross), as Kenneth Surin wisely contends, saying nothing is an appropriate response.[81] We pause in silence as we wonder what lies beyond suffering, and attempt to develop a discourse that holds a messianic view of the world order. In acknowledging the difficulty that surrounds speaking about this subject after confronting such a difficult set of vivid scenarios, we ask ourselves, "What else can be said after one takes suffering seriously?"

Yearning Pain

God is love, says scripture (1 Jn 4:8). If this is so, God must be first and foremost an object of desire—not of necessity, not of rationality. Theology—which is reflection and discourse about God's word—must therefore be driven and warmed by the flame of desire.

María Clara Bingemer[82]

Una palabra sobre el Dios de la fiesta y la belleza; una sabiduría profética de la experiencia viva del Dios vivo entre y desde los pobres, habitándolos de formas y colores, de clamores, es necesaria para hacer "poesía de la paz" (cf. Mt. 5:9), porque el que hace la paz es "poeta" de la paz.

María Teresa Porcile[83]

In locating the figure of the God who suffers within the main premise of this book, that is, a passionate God who enjoys the divine self with the cosmos, we encounter another question. What would it mean for us to affirm enjoyment when thinking of all things being in God in historical terms? How could a model of the God who shares history internally provide any resolution to our quandary about enjoyment? How should the theological implications of this God of love be pursued to their furthest limits, as we seek to move further toward that which undergirds even our protests and actions against life ruled by crucifixions?

HARMONY OF THE LEAST

In seeking answers to the quandary of divine enjoyment, when considering suffering in human history, one cannot overlook Aristotle's view of harmony. For him, happiness and friendship are essential components in maintaining the well-being of the city. Societal well-being founded on friendships contains an element of justice: a city filled with friends has no need for justice, for friends wish good things for one another, Aristotle says.[84] One might also dare to argue that prior views on divine passion aim at this kind of living that is *philadelphus*, that of loving friends who can truly enjoy one another. Generally speaking, the goodness that friendship might produce and whose end is happiness is bound up with yearning for beautiful outcomes of ordinary and possibly toilsome existence and delighting as one limits the self for the sake of others so they too can attain well-being (as one does also for the sake of oneself).

Notwithstanding how promisingly the Aristotelian model serves to address issues of injustice, its reach can go only so far. The Aristotelian model notably aims at living a life worth enjoying, but it disregards passionate modes of loving in favor of more pleasurable forms of it, which, being bound to the class systems of the time (including gender and ethnic classifications), places the weight of self-limitation on the shoulders of some more than others. Another goal would need to be in sight: a life lived abundantly can be so in ways that bring enjoyment to the whole, including the stranger and those in the lower classes, and without avoiding the element of suffering.

Particularly, for a life to be worth enjoying, suffering must remain an intricate component of harmony. Hence one ought to ask the tough questions that pathos demands. For harmony to be attained with an eye towards the contentment of the whole, how would all suffering be at least healed, if not eradicated, so that from the least to the greatest life can be lived abundantly? Sobrino rightly admonishes Christians to continue to grasp afresh the meaning of the cross, its scandal, so that the death of Jesus never becomes stated solely in "passive terms."[85] It is understandable that, in light of the injustices Latin Americans have faced as a result of civil wars and unfair international trade laws, for Sobrino there can be no placebo in the cause of liberation.

Yet, integrating suffering into harmonious living cannot be by means of establishing a dualism between suffering and enjoyment characteristic of some theologies of the cross. Sobrino, for example, also deemphasizes the joie de vivre activated by our sense of the resurrection.[86] Love, triumphant living, and the joy of living are secondary to or ensue only from suffering. As such, Sobrino even criticizes any theological reflection on festivities, especially those based on the liturgical calendar, such as Good Friday observances.

Furthermore leaving a wider range of paschal life unexplored would fail to challenge adequately the notion of divine absolute self-sufficiency, and to envision a God of pathos, of love. As Charles Hartshorne has wittily remarked, "He who refuses to rejoice with the joy of others is as selfish as he who refuses to grieve with their sorrows."[87] The challenge to the concept of divine *apatheia* cannot therefore remain confined to the argument of suffering in order to fully target what is most problematic about it, divine self-enclosure. Otherwise, a disconcerting view remains in place, the irrelevance of the cosmos to the inner enjoyment of God.

By affirming definitions of harmony that preserve the existing tension between suffering and enjoyment, it is possible to more fully demonstrate how joy is not absent from things unpleasant and physically painful, and conversely, that enjoyment can shine through moments of sorrow. "Joy is paschal," writes Luz Beatriz Arellano.[88] This is quite different from a simple view of pain mixed with pleasure. In the very act of loving another, as Aquinas states, "a certain transformation of affection" occurs, and "whatsoever the lover does or suffers for the beloved, the whole of it is delightful to him, and he is ever more stirred up, insofar as he experiences greater delight in the beloved in all he does or suffers for his sake."[89] In uniting with another, and in willing the good will of another, one wills it as for one's own sake. On the way to bringing this kind of enjoyment, there is pain.[90] That is, whenever there is a yearning for fuller expressions of life linked to mutual love, there is also the possibility of pain.

Accordingly, in considering the well-being of the whole, one would not only define enjoyment as lacking in worry. Enjoyment cannot be equated with serene calmness, with *apatheia*, or with numbness to the happenings of the world. Such is the sense of a lifeless and motionless kind of harmony that, like anesthesia, as Alfred N. Whitehead would say, serves as a "bastard substitute" for peace.[91] Even when perfected ideals are repeated indefinitely in history, staleness and anesthesia can settle in, causing any social group to sink toward nothingness, he affirms. Moreover, peaceful enjoyment cannot simply mirror everyone's idea of "getting along." As Porcile argues, with courage we denounce a false peace, and surrounded by inequalities, we raise our voices.[92] One looks beyond the sculpted body of Apollo and sees the multitude of children with inflated bellies. A sense of true harmony is necessary when one considers a love akin to passion. We gain a sense of equilibrium[93] in the use of resources that considers racial, gender, class, and other differences, as well as uniqueness.

A *harmony of the least*, therefore, comes into fuller view, for no one in this world can be described as fully self-sufficient. On the one hand, in the work of Aristotle we find that happy and thus self-sufficient people are friends of others, since they are virtuous in themselves and do good for the sake of the good. On the other, while this reflection on good living is noteworthy, we must also agree that it tends to be stated from the perspective of those whose sense of being in the world is considered to be the norm and whose resources are quite copious. Thus it becomes necessary to undertake a discourse from the perspective of those who seek a better life. While being vigilant of those who believe themselves to be "self-sufficient" and needing nothing, we must carefully note that there are those who actually are in need of much, and who lack the means to meet their basic needs.

PILGRIMAGE TOWARD THE PATHS OF SALVATION

Another essential element that stirs our hearts toward greater expressions of enjoyment therefore comes to the fore—the yearning for a harmonious living mindful of the least, a yearning that carries an element of pain (but can be also expressed in celebrations). Pain, with its disrupting effect, and in unison with enjoyment, points to things to come, to a reality not yet fully present. Pain ensues from the friction that past histories have with their future, of what comes from the contrast of the actual and the desirable, a loss intensified by the memory and hope of loving presence.

What would divine *yearning* mean in the context of this hermeneutical principle of liberation? Along with the mid-nineteenth-century Spanish philosopher Miguel de Unamuno, one might ponder the figure of the crucified Christ rendered in the painting of Velázquez as a depiction of divine yearning.[94] Rather than the *ens summun* or *primum movens* principle prevalent in classical theism, God is love, and loves with a love that is "full of suffering." And since God "loves and thirsts for love," that is, since God *yearns* to be in relationship with the world, God suffers, Unanumo holds, because "the flesh of reality" of which God and the cosmos partake is imbued with suffering.[95] This claim to a divine appetite is also part of the scandal of the cross, namely, that God becomes vulnerable to the cosmos because of love, and thus that God suffers because of the divine yearning for love. This notion of pain intrinsic to divine yearning requires further unfolding.

Pictorial images and narratives of the civil wars, the Holocaust, and the world wars inspire us to reflect on how the experiences of passion lead to the mystery of the divine self in which God confronts us.[96] From the perspective of those on the underside of history, one can say that God yearns as a friend, and God's mutual yearning toward greater forms of enjoyment (for the well-being of the whole) resembles a wound that wounds both God and the cosmos because of the element of yearning for something not yet fully actualized that resides also in the inner being of God. When suffering the tragedies in history, God groans in yearning with the cosmos for things that are still to come.

In that sense, it can be stated that the suffering of God and of the cosmos meet to incite the "all" to fuller expressions of life as the "all" finds itself in God's wound. The divine impulse stemming from suffering as much as from enjoyment might mean that this all comes to experience first-hand the suffering of God, as well as the divine enjoyment. This groaning impulse of God that drives us toward fuller forms of life is the mode of enjoyment toward which the discourse on suffering aims. Particularly for theologians of the cross, as humanity finds itself in God, it finds itself in the site and at the time of Golgotha, which confronts us with the abysses of history, as well as with the possibility of redefining those abysses according to a deep yearning for the impossible, a memory of the divine unchanging love time and again being reawakened as all things find themselves in God.

Humanity encounters the divine desire in its salvific pilgrimage, which for Sobrino would mean that we come into God's own historical process, that we participate in a process "with which we can actually experience history as salvation."[97] Our lives journey with God and toward God as we pass through the cross. We become icons of the impossible as we abide with God in God's "hour of grief."[98] In light of Sobrino's thought, the overtures of the divine pathos in the world are such that God drinks of the waters of history in order to turn their bitterness into a healing fountain of love. This can mean that God, by existing as love in history through the Crucifixion, suffers history in Godself, "the cry of Jesus on the cross and the cry of countless victims in history."[99] God takes on Godself the godless and the forsaken so that they can experience communion with God and have a foretaste of things yet to come, can imagine *u-topias*.[100]

This sort of imagining brings about much groaning, for it is not independent from "those groans and cries" caused by injustice, oppression, and death.[101] Thus the sharing refers to something internal, like a swap between God and us—a solidarity within God—for the purposes of gaining a new vision of the world. For Moltmann, for example, this inner solidarity means that God is "the event of Golgotha, the event of the love of the Son and the grief of the Father from which the Spirit who opens up the future and creates life in fact derives."[102] The event of Golgotha is God crucified, the "site" and "time" of future openings to new worlds, a representation of a crucified Trinitarian relation within God and with the cosmos.

An intimate solidarity, as I seek to define here in this project on passion, therefore raises the question of the present reality, but with a tone of divine desire for what might lie beyond it (in this life), ahead of it—another future. Along with Emmanuel Levinas, one might consider how yearning or desire stirs movement, propelling oneself to a "future never future enough, more remote than the possible."[103] Rather than nothingness, the not yet fully present rests on the horizon, a secret or a mystery without a visible appearance. Remaining desire at each instant, desire poses an unforeseen plane of enjoyment owing to the eros of its movement, which consists in going beyond the possible, perhaps the yonder of that which has constricted the familiar and choked the imagination. This form of desire would not necessarily locate oneself in the *after*life as much as in a possible future that inspires this side of reality, reimagines it.

Furthermore, the divine yearning would act as a weak impulse operating in the universe. In the words of Sobrino, God is either "wielding oppressive power or . . . offering and effecting liberation."[104] The critique embodied in the person of Jesus was against the power of the Roman Empire, God being neither emperor nor king. The power of God is love; God is love. And this love, for Sobrino, is universally political "in that it seeks to be real and effective in a given concrete situation."[105] God enters "the whole process of protest"[106] by drawing in and being with the crucified, so as to restore their dignity and humanity—the stance that placed Jesus on the cross at the hands of the powerful. God's unconditional love, revealed in its passivity, turns into active love in the historical process of transformation in which God joins us. Following in the footsteps of this divinity means to save by means mixed with suffering, a thought one might derive from Mahayana Buddhism, as Kitamori explores.[107] Suffering as an instrument of love is an ethic of love rooted in pain that transforms obligation into willingness[108] and, I would say, desire or yearning. Rather than seeking anesthesia, and contrary to being "spineless," this ethic is about taking a stance to deidolize any brute force trying to pass itself off as God.

This means that the God hanging on the cross, though a symbol of weakness, paradoxically does not connote mere passivity. As James Cone argues, if the main concern is with "what God in Christ has done about evil,"[109] then what needs to be done to eliminate evil remains very much our affair. This scandalous cross is the foundation of the Christian proclamation against those who crucify others and an indictment of ourselves, who in some way are a part of this system. God's suffering renders God accountable for a suffering cosmos; but it also renders us accountable, for we are complexly and intricately connected to evil. As others suffer, we not only acknowledge that we ourselves suffer, but also that we can be agents of true evil.[110] For Surin, facing this evil can be concomitant with regeneration, so that joy can occur. He states, "it is by following the pattern established by the life, death, and resurrection of Jesus Christ that one is enabled to transform evil and sin into that healing which lies at the heart of salvation."[111] And from this point of departure one can generate a discourse that leads to praxis, so that evil does not have the last word.

Experiencing the divine thirst for love within God's wound leads to having an authentic response of care for the crucified, that they might attain resurrection. This is an expression of divine love in us—agape. Sobrino posits,

> Moreover by its very nature and structure, sorrow, as the wellspring of knowledge, has its own distinctive and peculiar dynamism. Sorrow wells up in the presence of the evil embodied in oppression and injustice. When faced with this negative reality, however, sorrow cannot rest content with contemplation; it must issue into some sort of action. Sorrow must be active, and so knowledge tends to be transformed into *agape*.[112]

The hopes expressed through the recovery of a hermeneutics of liberation act like signs declaring that turns in history can be always possible. As Leonardo Boff eloquently notes, the proclamation that "God loves sufferers so much that he suffers and dies along with them" is not a mere "dolorism."[113] Its poignancy is such that it brings the person to "a commitment to make it gradually impossible for human beings to crucify human beings."[114] While the risk of a path of crucifixion remains a possibility, and in some ways it is a given as one follows Jesus, one pursues a cause that seeks to achieve victory over the torturers. God hanging on the cross shows the implications of evil and issues the call to eradicate it. We are called to take "suffering seriously," as Surin so passionately admonishes us.[115] By taking suffering seriously, we can imagine new worlds, and act in ways that liberate the all from evil. This "pathetic theology" sensitizes those hearing the call to gather the courage needed to be in solidarity.

ON BIRTHING PAINS OF JOY

Other entangling imageries gently woo us toward a path of divine vulnerability, perhaps a mystical one; toward metaphors that invoke a sense of intimacy. Perhaps an image of a friend whose *bowels* groan as in childbearing and birth by sharing another friend's misfortune can begin to emerge. The image of the friend would take on new contours. Like a woman with child, God groans with the flesh becoming flesh in this creative process. Such friendship is unlike an archetype that lacks *e*motion, being moved toward another, as in the Aristotelian model.[116] Yet also it is distinct from a God whose utmost representation is Jesus's death on the cross being employed as the primary metaphor with which to challenge the Aristotelian notion of divine enjoyment. Rather, in the imagery of the woman with child, God's passion can be viewed as being life-focused and painfully creative. In solidarity with the all, God mystically groans under the present circumstances, but also because things are being birthed anew in the flesh.

In drawing closer to this principle of groaning found in the element of *yearning*, we borrow from female body images that underscore intimate life in contexts of suffering and death, images that most male theologians have abstained from using. This imagery underwrites a wombic eros that provides the impetus to creativity. In the work of María Clara Bingemer, the term *rechem* serves to associate God with women's breasts and the womb, an association that closely maintains a female figure of God in relation to birth and nourishment. The term *chesed* similarly reinforces the image of a God loving compassionately in an infinitely tender manner. For Bingemer, "God's depths of mercy are likened to a womb (*rachamim*)" that draws in the Trinity along with the hurting in the world.

God construed in such female imagery becomes the site of conception, nourishment, protection, growth, and birth. God is an intimate, generative, and creative force that is revealed in its infinite mercy as "a womb that gives birth and stirs with compassion."[117] The womb is the site where God and the cosmos join, the site where suffering can see the rays of joy. Not only does God, as maternal father and paternal mother, remember and console the child of her womb; with receptivity she "accepts the seed of life and feeds it in her womb, so that it may become a full being in the light of day."[118] As with the birthing process, enjoyment is in sight—the joy of creation, of engendering something beyond the self, the joy of pregnancy, and celebration of it—as part of the ongoing creation based on *com*passion—a passion with—that is continuously being knitted in the divine womb.

This God-cosmos relationship of suffering and enjoyment serves to illustrate that God is not "solitary, invulnerable and impassible." Reflecting on the biblical witness, Bingemer argues that God is "the Mystery of life, who both begets and gives birth, participates and is involved in the sufferings of the people in Israel." This means that the womb-*rachamim*, "God's love for humankind, as it flows out of the trinitarian economy, is the image and form of God's deepest reality," according to Bingemer.[119] Permeability, while being particular to the inner life of the Trinity, expresses also the intimacy of the divine affect, a mutual sympathy (*syn pathein*) for the created order, and of the involvement on the part of God in its creative processes.

Life birthing is groaning breath, which links us to our neighbors.[120] We become like midwives by sharing in the birth of better living conditions, as we dream with others, and thus we come to express also the divine *rachamim* or divine *bowels* as we act on this common bond of love. This divine design of love among all living beings makes for a history that is womblike, "fruitful with new possibilities," says Ana María Tepedino.[121] With desire, one groans, announcing "the delivery of a New Creation," as Bingemer declares.[122] Life as breath means that the divine *ruach* (breath) that groans as women do when in labor connects one to the other, and in solidarity the all groans as a new future that is good for the whole is being born.

Some may argue further that the creative suffering joy of the cosmos necessitates a reversal, one in which God is also delivered to God for suffering the birthing processes, and through which the world attains salvation and restoration. Bingemer writes,

> In the passion of the Son the Father attains the maximum point of universal openness. In delivering the beloved Son, begotten and born from all eternity, into the hands of men to be crucified, the Abba is delivered over to suffer in the divine womb of the maternal Father, the infinite sorrow, the anguished omnipotence, the death of his maternal fatherhood. However, at the same time

and in the same unique movement of Trinitarian love, the passion of God who is maternal Father, who is Son, who is Spirit of love, opens wide the gates of salvation to all the abandoned of the world.[123]

God in a sense is be*ing* born, or is becoming because of yearning along with the sufferings of the cosmos. This process appears paradoxically open-ended; futures are salvific rebirths occurring in the midst of toilsome existence. Each person of the Trinity, as well as the cosmos as a whole, both limits each other and opens up each other to the future. The mystery of the love of God, *agape,* is shown in that "God's trinitarian being is not closed in on itself but is fulfilled by surrendering itself and giving itself freely out of the richness of its immanent being," argues Bingemer.[124] This imagery is in some ways similar to the concept of *zimzum* that Moltmann expounds in his engagement of Jewish theological concepts (mostly among mystics) in relation to the Holocaust. With a similar understanding of the divine continuity with the cosmos also found in *zimzum,* the cosmos becomes a part of an internal divine space that God opens within God. For Moltmann, *zimzum* is God contracting or withdrawing the divine self into the divine self so that the world can join in and share in the divine. God, by contracting Godself, "sets free a kind of 'mystical primordial space'" into which, out of which, and in which God enters in and makes manifest the divine self,[125] and, I would add, where God becomes intimately with another. In this divine and intimate space of self-limitation and negation that for some feminists is of the bowels or womblike, God both suffers with the world internally its limitations and enjoys its possibilities as they are actualized moment by moment.

MULTIPLE BEGINNINGS . . .

The idea of an interplay between joy and pain and of a creative impulse residing within a primordial space of God identified as the divine *bowels* and that is continuous with the longings of the cosmos leads us into other expressions of passion. God groans with desire and instills desire for better forms of living the very instant that the deepest cries as well as the highest hopes are inhabited within the divine inward parts or entrails, as God and cosmos share this womblike space. In this permeable imagery God's loving yearning can serve as the energizing vital impulses in close connection with the creative elements and enticement of beauty already existing in the cosmos. While distinct from the cosmos, this vital impulse, muddied with the flesh, can come to define the divine emotion, God being Greater Desire, as Bingemer argues, since desire is fundamental to life and is its primary vital impulse.[126] This view becomes most apparent when considering the statement, once again, that "God *is* love." For Alida Verhoeven, "the Presence of Creative-Recreative Spiritual Force, the source of Life and Love, is like an ongoing movement, an ebb and flow that moves in growing waves that wash over everything."[127] God's desires and the vital elements are erotically creative and re-creative in all their dimensions, in being and becoming, in the whole of the cosmos, and even in God. Nothing lies outside it.

Creation is a work of art in which the divine poet in collaboration with human artists participates through a desire for true harmony, their eros for beauty.[128] For why not consider the poor as subjects of beauty, creators of beauty? With this erotic force of life affecting the whole, the creative work of harmonious transformation can reach "all women, communities, the world, and the entire universe."[129] This emotive (in the sense of being affected or moved) eros of God that is internal to the cosmos erupts in a passion-like manner as liberating power. The divine passion stirs the erotic power that resides in all, activating a sense of being and becoming in common. All, even the poor and the victims of history, partake of this erotic impulse as they feel impelled to change their own situations as the divine love erupts among them. In the words of María Pilar Aquino, what many Latin American feminists seek to present is "God's ineffable absolute mystery, which erupts as love, liberating power, and hope among the oppressed of the earth, among the outsiders of society and the church."[130] At the peak moment, love "explodes with energy and vitality for carrying on the struggle," writes Tepedino.[131] In other words, the divine eros, in being tightly knitted to the vital elements of life internal to the cosmos, erupts as desire from within the cosmos, stirring the passion for life—its deepest cry.

Beauty becomes intrinsic to the ethical impulse rather than superfluous, supplementary, subsequent, or lesser to it. Harmony can be attained. Since beauty can be found through the terrible, there can also be cocreatorship of new realities. Porcile gives the biblical example of Jeremiah, who in being seduced by the beauty of God consoled those in exile (Jer. 20:7–9). Such erotic passion opens the future wide, and validates a sense of re-creative power that calls "into being what does not exist so that it may be," exclaims Aquino.[132] A new mysticism of life emerges in which death reigns.[133] New cosmic beginnings may take place, for spurts of life gush forth, birthing beautiful things anew, even after devastating cataclysmic events. We are enflamed so that we do not give up, and, as Aquino argues, so that "in the presence of immense suffering, we can change the environment into one of joy and liberation."[134] The divine desire is life's energizing capacity to engage in a messianic praxis mixed with beauty along with, not just on behalf of, those who suffer for the divine mystery permeates the whole.

Ethics and beauty must join hands, for, as Jay McDaniel observes, ethics without beauty is "morbid, lapsing into a rigid control of others in the name of being holy and pure," and beauty without ethics "is naïve, easily lapsing into a self absorbed narcissism."[135] This conversation can be risky. By placing ethics alongside beauty, so-called lustful impulses can be seen as accompanying transformative action. As Aquinas noted, even human passions may potentially become instruments of beauty,[136] might enact the impossible. For instance, Marcella Althaus-Reid narrates, "I have been a poor woman myself and I dreamed of warm clothes for my mother during winter, and nutritious meals for me and my family. But I also dreamt of having an education, a vocation in life to be a priest, and I dreamt of justice, love and lust in my life."[137]

Beauty present in forms of enjoyment is needed, to bring back the whole of life into our paradigm of harmony, even things seemingly trivial and leisurely, such as music, even laughter. As Porcile argues, "*fiesta* is the secret of the strength of the people who suffer, and from this one can add to the list of Human Rights 'the inalienable right of the poor to have a *fiesta*.'"[138] For her, and from a biblical perspective, the courage of Israel to depart from Egypt and to cross the desert began with a *fiesta* in view (Ex. 5:1). As if accompanied by desert songs and the worshipping leadership of Moses, Maria, and Aaron, one might be led to the liberation encountered in the *fiesta* of God. "The people create *fiesta*, seek unity, write poetry, produce their own ecstasy, in the dance of the enthusiasts (etymologically speaking, those 'filled with God')."[139] In dance and music, the poor may find the needed strength, hope, and "the gratuitous communion of beauty made in the anticipation of the celebration."[140] It can lead to a spontaneous epiphany of being beautiful and a vision of the kind of harmony that defies oppression. With a vision for the impossible yet to be actualized, probability disrupts the possible, uncertainty unsettles certainty, just as poetry and text can set free the narrative of a people. From within Latin America's dances, its poetry, songs, and even its silence, there can be born a theology that loves beauty, an understanding of God, and a knowledge that searches for beauty and loves it.

Play, music, and dance, alongside laughter, can interrupt proper orders that hinder access to the flourishing of the self, to the enjoyment of life. Festive elements of life such as these can vivify another imaginary, the good.[141] For beauty can bubble up into the very core of the self as a reminder of what means to be human, for the purpose of enacting the enjoyment of a better life that is being dreamed of. Playing, eating and drinking together, and dancing with one another celebrate that which remains to be fully expressed, Ivone Gebara intimates.[142] Through play and celebration, those who labor to provide for their basic needs, even those enduring the violence of war and political unrest, may enact and incarnate the not yet but possible. For in the struggle for life in the midst of "death, war, abduction, rape and abandonment" there's a remembrance that to be human is to dream.

With wings that reach out to the impossible, resurrections become possible—the substance of celebration. With love, hope, and faith one might dare to say, "Where, O death is your victory? Where, O death, is your sting?" (1 Cor. 15:55). One might stand against the unjust and dare to be human, a compassionate friend. And as Luz Beatriz Arellano argues, we can even be joyful and celebrate as life overcomes death, as we bear the sorrows of others so that together we can transform pain into happiness and hope.[143] For even as we endure horror, why cannot beauty, poetry, or peace be discovered through the terrible, as Porcile invites us to do in her text, quoted above, concerning the God of *fiesta*?[144]

In these pages I have argued that for God to truly enjoy Godself, there must be an element of mutuality, of God receiving into the divine self something other than God. The idea that happiness entails love for another, for example a friend, is a step in the right direction. God could not be happy being concupiscent, that is, by deriving pleasure at the expense of another being. Yet God must be conceptualized as being vulnerable to that with which God seeks relationship, as friends usually are, for without vulnerability there cannot be a full sense of reciprocity with God. Enjoyment therefore must be posited as an intrinsic element of divine love, but an argument for divine passion is also warranted.

This book seeks to adumbrate this fuller understanding of a God of love, which comes into view, therefore, as one first theologizes about the interplay between pain and joy—a kind of paschal joy. Rather than joy being privileged over pain, or vice versa, both elements recombine in various ways, disordering the logic of either/or. God joining us intimately in this quest for new beginnings pregnant with possibilities, and yearning for things refreshed gives way to a joyful body of pain that God becomes with us as if through a dance of passion. With a wombier eros in view,[145] experiencing all joys and pains increases a desire for the beautiful, a complex view of harmony. Desire, lust, passion, and life likewise enjoin the wombic eros with which God stirs us toward fuller expressions of enjoyment, even when such enjoyment entails suffering pain in common with other beings. Subsequently, the divine yearning mixed with the flesh of the cosmos erupts as a composite impulse of both enjoyment and suffering. The two concepts surfacing as equally belonging to the divine pathos contribute to an expanded understanding of a *liberative* praxis, which remains a main concern for those who seek to provide models of the God hanging on the cross with open arms before the cosmos.

In this model of a divine passionate God, we little recognize the impassible God of Aristotle. This God of passion suffers the suffering of all living beings and the cosmos; this God groans together with the whole of the created order as it longs for fuller forms of life. So, rather than downplaying the concepts of enjoyment or suffering at the expense of the other, or abandoning either one altogether, *why not expand the notion of divine yearning*, as primarily exemplified in the work of the feminist theologians discussed in the last section of this chapter? Why not discover a divine appetite that further dislodges Aristotelian models of divine absolute self-subsistence? Promisingly, therefore, in exploring the feminist paradigm, we begin to imagine a God who becomes with the enjoyments and sufferings of the cosmos, for the divine love is adventurous. In the birthing process too there is much enjoyment. Yet this exploration of pleasure in relation to desire will need to uncover other areas that, while assuming a commitment to a God who is in history confronting us, while also *painfully* becoming with and birthing in us a dream of and passion for better things to come, would lead further into the bottomless depths of the *bowels* of divine desire.

Yearning: Traces of the Divine Erotic Existence in the Cosmos

> I know how you love because I too have loved, and I know what
> passionate and obsessed love is and what it is to be madly in love
> with someone. And God is mad about me.
>
> —ERNESTO CARDENAL[1]

> The divine yearning brings ecstasy so that the lover belongs not to the
> self but to the beloved.
>
> —DENYS THE AREOPAGITE *(Pseudo-Dionysius)*[2]

> Dionysius says (*Div. Nom.* iv) that *the Divine love produces ecstasy*, and that
> *God Himself suffered ecstasy through love.*
>
> —ST. THOMAS AQUINAS[3]

The theological affirmations that God is love and that God loves the world, as noted in Chapter 1, are axiomatic for Christian theology. One can hardly turn anywhere in Christianity without encountering expressions to this effect. Sadly, the overwhelming witness to this tradition likewise emphasizes forms of love that are nonreciprocal or nonresponsive. Furthermore, God exercises a "pure" love in the form of agape or charity, not an erotic love, for an erotic love would mean that God desires something that God needs not (pure superfluousness). Anders Nygren, for example, in considering divine love as agape, juxtaposes God and eros, stating, "Eros is yearning desire; but with God there is no want or need, and therefore no desire nor striving. . . . 'God is Agape.' . . . Since Agape is a love that descends, freely and generously giving of its superabundance, the main emphasis falls with inescapable necessity on the side of God."[4] Particularly with regard to enjoyment, classical thought shies away from attributing a character of eros, yearning, and desire to the divine love, since much regarding reciprocity and desire remains tainted by an equating of the erotic with selfishness (increasingly so today, in light of the rampant consumerism). This is not the whole story, however, for mutual expressions of love cannot be reduced to these ideas.

A construal of the divine enjoyment that points in the direction of a divine yearning beyond selfishness would not be contrary to the long-standing traditions of Christian thought, either. I would even venture to say that it would be welcomed. As one investigates carefully some of the classical thinkers, the divine relationship with the cosmos appears in some models to resemble, in a pleasantly surprising way, an embracive love between lovers. As we explore these views, other models of the relational mystery of God begin to surface. Without ignoring the obstacles their work presents, some quite significant, we might unearth early roots of an expansive model of the love and enjoyment of God with the multiplicity that is the cosmos, a model that might reclaim a *movable* yet *restful* grounding of reciprocal or passionate love.

As a first step in exploring classical thought in an unconventional manner, this chapter takes up the work of St. Thomas Aquinas on the God who enjoys creation. The Aristotelian corpus on enjoyment with which Aquinas interacts cannot, of course, be omitted. As Jacques Lacan rightly argues, in the wake of Aristotle's "*jouissance* of being," Aquinas "had no difficulty in forging out of this the physical theory of love," whose awareness "of our own being, and everything which is for our own goodwill," is indeed by dint of the *jouissance* of God.[5] And while other early classical thinkers sporadically make their appearance, it is through Aquinas's specific understanding and exposition of *eudaimonia*—happiness—that a nuanced view begins to emerge, that of a happy God who seeks enjoyment with creation in amorous ways.

This chapter first sketches out an idea of the *beloved divine lover* whose enjoyment stems from stirring all things toward greater forms of enjoyment, but it does so cautiously, for in relation to this book's aim, an unreconstructed classical model would be deficient. Persistently, according to the classical model, God enjoys the cosmos only to a point, since the cosmos can add nothing to an absolutely per se subsistent God. Thus, this chapter undoubtedly stretches the concept of a divine relationship with the cosmos beyond the boundaries that classical thought would have observed.

The Divine Activity of Enjoyment in God and the Cosmos

O God,
   all-powerful and all-knowing
   without beginning and without end
You Who are
   the source,
   the sustainer,
   and the rewarder of all virtues.
                St. Thomas Aquinas[6]

In agreement with Aquinas, one of the affirmative statements that we can make about God is that "God is happy" and is *eudaimonia* (happiness).[7] In the *Summa contra gentiles* this concept undergirds the doctrine of the God of love. This affirmation is the product of combined philosophical and theological influences from which much of classical theism inherits the basic principle that God is happy because *eudaimonia* denotes perfection. The main argument is that God is God's own *eudaimonia*, that is, self-sufficiently happy in se. This concept of the happiest of all beings meets another key statement that seems to come from Aquinas's encounter with the writings of Denys the Areopagite, also known as Pseudo-Dionysius. While God is absolutely content with the divine self, and thus happy, argues Aquinas, God "not only desires happiness, as we do, but is in the enjoyment of happiness."[8] In other words, God desires happiness out of the divine contentment. Here we find the aspect of desire or yearning that offers one of most promising understandings of the doctrine of the God of love in relation to divine enjoyment found in Christian tradition—God, like a lover, desires or yearns with the created order.

This view of happiness as having a cosmological emphasis and being supplemented with a divine yearning unfolds from within a discourse that had gradually shifted from the simple detailing of mathematical proportions to the drawing of analogies between cosmic elements and the development of an epistemology of relations and harmonies between levels of reality.[9] Plato, for example, while sharply distinguishing between the world of appearances and the world of forms of ideas, proposed that love is a spirit that links the heavenly and earthly realms. Love stands in the middle between mortality and immortality. It seeks to beget the good or true goodness, which leads to happiness. The movement is upward, away from the bodily aspects of happiness. And through an upward movement that stems from the pursuit of wholeness, it seeks to catch sight of the divine beauty, and ultimately attain the eternal good. In its narrowest parsing, love is a restlessness in the soul seeking "possession of goodness for oneself."[10] This upward aim is achieved through *theoria* or contemplation (often differentiated from Christian or mystical contemplation), as the divine element in the soul (*nous*) receives revelation of the good and becomes assimilated with goodness.

The Greek idea of creator-creature resemblance, mostly described by a system of emanations or cause-and-effect relations, was likewise latent as a seed flowering within a concept of analogy bequeathed to thirteenth-century philosophy.[11] Prominent among those promoting this understanding of analogy was Plotinus, who sought to preserve divine transcendence by proposing that the created order is the result of emanations ex deus, and hence a consequence of divine existence. But Plotinus also moved beyond his predecessors, holding that "Lovable, very love, the Supreme is also self-love," a divine eroticism that lies beyond lack since "He is lovely no otherwise than from Himself and in Himself."[12] God is eros, and divine love links the heavenly and earthly realms just as it resides in the cosmos as the desire for the eternal, in the seeds of likeness that beget beauty.[13] Again, this divine erotic quality, while driving all toward loss of their particularity,[14] is solely self-directed,[15] a construal that omits concern for the cosmos as much as it denies any change in God, and one this chapter challenges.

To develop this principle of *eudaimonia* more fully (as characterized also by divine yearning), we might find it helpful to undertake the route of contemplation particularly as defined in Christian terms as aiming at union with God, by means of poetic or mystical language to explain it away.[16] With regard to the work of Aquinas (and other contemplatives), for example, we might approach his thought not simply as that of the renowned theologian, philosopher, and doctor of the church who taught in Paris during the thirteenth century but also as the production of a monk who regularly practiced contemplation.[17] This is also evident in how he engaged a liturgical theology centered on the celebration of the Eucharist and a mystical theology focused on tropes such as union with God and *visio beatifica* that he most likely found inspiring in the works of Christian thinkers such as Denys the Areopagite—ideas almost nonexistent in Greek thought.[18] As with much of the Christian contemplative life, his teachings fall within the ambit of the Christian community. Initially his work can appear burdensome to a contemporary reader, heavily laden as it is with philosophical postulates. Yet with continued reading, specifically through the lens of the discipline of contemplation he practiced, it is possible to recognize and embrace freely the novel touches that appear in his work. More vibrant understandings become possible. And joy and desire come to the foreground more explicitly.

His approach is sometimes poetically liturgical, crafting a contemplative enjoyment where others might not see it. For example, Don Adams indicates that Aquinas erred when he attributed to Aristotle "a view quite similar to his own contemplative view of happiness," yet goes on to say that Aquinas's views were "philosophically interesting, textually well motivated, and guilty of no interpretative crimes."[19] That it was Aquinas's custom not merely to reproduce or quote a thinker's work has been asserted as well by Mark Jordan, who notes the same interpretive phenomenon manifesting in the *Summa*'s dialogue with other authorities, such as Denys the Areopagite, Boethius, and Peter Lombard.[20]

There may also be traces of early Averroist influence in the Aquinan impulse toward the use of mystical language in the engagement of philosophical discourse. For Averroës, Aquinas's Muslim predecessor in interpreting Aristotle, the relevance of poetic—as in mystical—language can be found in that "one strives for an imaginary representation or exemplification of something in speech so as to move the soul to flee from the thing, or to long for it, or simply to wonder because of the delightfulness which issues from the imaginary representation."[21] While such an approach does not presume the representation to be the thing itself, there is no error in the substitution, for by substitution an attempt is made to move from the known to the unknown. Furthermore, poetry can stir "the souls of the multitude" toward "belief in a certain thing and towards doing or abandoning a certain thing,"[22] even in its role of serving as an imaginative representation, something that Averroës finds illuminating in the work of Aristotle. Rather than seeking to adjudicate the most faithful interpretations of these thinkers, then, and with a playful tentativeness and a sense of adventure, in the theological engagement pursued in this chapter a form of logic other than that of the "certitude of science" becomes evident, the logic of poetry.

More explicitly, Aquinas gleaned much from the *Divine Names* and the *Mystical Theology* of Denys the Areopagite, and followed the poetic path of the incomprehensible to search for the inscrutable mysteries of the divine infinite love to arrive at a path of excess. "We use whatever symbols we can for the things of God. With these analogies we are raised upward toward the truth of the mind's vision."[23] Thus, analogy leads theological discovery toward what Aquinas describes as "something virtuous by some excellent description" in seeking to introduce the reader to a wisdom built from similitudes, comparisons, "figures taken from corporeal things," or representations even of less noble things, with the goal of expressing, at least in part, the mysteries of divine reality.[24] Analogy reflects the intention to honor the eminence, excess, or infinity that becomes tightly knitted with an ultimate beatitude, a work inspired by a *visio beatifica* of love that awakens the imagination.

Early mystically poetic interpretations of the Song of Songs that Aquinas must have inherited are exemplary with regard to an erotic path of contemplation. Much of the early exegetical work done on the Songs' multilayered plot, extended poetic dialogue, and main protagonists reads anew God's loving relationship with "us."[25] To attain that fine level of symbolic interpretation, basic human representations in the Songs had to acquire meanings equivalent to things sublime. Recognizing the plain or literal understanding of its poetic imageries was simply the first step toward uncovering the deeper sense buried beneath the written text. For instance, in his commentary, Gregory the Great argued that figures in the Song of Songs are employed so that we may be introduced to things eternal by means of ordinary language. The soul drawn upward by means of allegory or earthly imagery and toward "the dense and overclouded mountain" where God speaks may discern that which is unknown.[26]

This path to the sublime, also present in the commentaries and homilies of Origen, assigned to God's love a certain erotic quality, particularly when illustrating the spiritual journey of the human soul toward God its lover. Not only does the power of love lead "the soul from the earth to the lofty heights of the heavens," or the desire of love serve as the only stimulus by which one attains the highest beatitude,[27] but a divine descending love precedes the contemplative ascent. The soul is moved by "a heavenly love and *longing*" (emphasis mine). On beholding the "beauty and fairness" of the Word of God, the soul (Bride) falls deeply in love with him who is in the image of the invisible God (Bridegroom). Divine love acts as a dart that wounds the soul with love and kindles the wound with the blessed fire. Origen describes this love as passionate love (eros or desire), implanted in the heart by and for the Creator, that seeks union with God, and says further that God is love, that is, *passionate love* (my emphasis), "from whom we have the very power of loving."[28] This union has the attribute of perfection in the sense of likeness (diligence in imitating God) fully reserved for the consummation, when that which is received at the beginning reaches its fulfillment at the end. It strives for becoming "the same, because undoubtedly in the consummation or end God is 'all and in all.'"[29] All things, particularly those who earnestly move toward or energetically pursue this end, find their "good house" in God.[30] This movement of love is also akin to the relationship between the Church and Christ.[31]

In the theological inquiries of Gregory of Nyssa, desire, having been divinely imbued, is the starting point of the creaturely movement toward the infinity of God. Gregory viewed the royal bed in the Songs as the site of arousal of the virginal bride for more intense desire, "for that spotless and divine marriage" with God.[32] Even as one reached such heights as those attained by Moses, one would remain "restless with desire," "more and more dissatisfied," thirsting for God, to be filled "to capacity."[33] The divine continuously invites us to further enjoyment.[34] Similarly, almost as if having not received anything, with desire one begs that God give more. Intensified by the hope of transcendence, this longing is inflamed at each stage in which it attains what is desired. Not being satisfied with receiving an image of the object of longing, the supplicant "wants to be filled with the very impression of the archetype."[35] Gregory adds, "The bold demand of the soul that climbs the hills of desire tends towards the direct enjoyment of Beauty, and not merely through the mirrors or reflections."[36] God, who is like "an infinite abyss of contemplation" that eludes pure presence, all symbols, is by his very nature infinite, unattainable, and incomprehensible. Not fully satisfying the seeker's longing, desire for the true vision of God has no end, for God's bounty is limitless. Like a hole in a rock, God is a place that is "so vast that he who runs in it will never be able to reach the end of his course."[37] Desire increases through eternity, with each limit attained becoming a new beginning[38] and every desire increasing in light of what lies ahead. Gregory describes the trajectory thus: "the true satisfaction of her [the soul's] desire consists in constantly going on with her quest and never ceasing in her ascent."[39] Desire itself is thus boundless.

Undoubtedly, the overall premise of divine enjoyment expressed in correspondence with the less than noble human experience present in Aquinas's work drew from the deep wells of poetic development of a biblical text already erotically charged. Discussions of God as love that imply a form of erotic desire abound in the scriptures, even though the figure of an erotic God must have posed some problems for early thinkers.[40] The Hebrew scriptures in particular describe God's desire for Israel using such analogies as the unfaithful wife whom God takes into the desert to allure her (Hos. 1:2–3:5) and whom God draws back so that she might become fruitful (Hosea 54:4–10); or of God calling forth the memory of the young wife who loved God, and whom God calls to return to that first love (Jer. 2:2, 3:1–13). In one instance the imagery of desired closeness begins as follows: "Later I passed by, and when I looked at you and saw that you were old enough for love, I spread the corner of my garment over and covered your nakedness . . . and you became mine" (Ezek. 16:8). Quite the erotic language, painting an image of a God who loves erotically! In the Second Testament marriage metaphors are more subtle yet still reflect a desire to consummate the loving relationship between Christ and the Church, both as a present marital reality (Eph. 5:23–32) and on a wedding day yet to come (Rev. 19:7–9).

By the thirteenth century, the time of Aquinas's life and ministry, fuller poetic expressions of a heavenly figure akin to a lover were being explored by many female Christian mystics as well. Some of Aquinas's contemporaries, for example, viewed God as yearning for the soul, much as the soul was viewed as yearning for the divine lover, the two ultimately achieving mystical union. In Mechtild of Magdeburg's *Flowing Light of the Godhead*, God calls out to the soul, saying, "Fair youth, I long for you. Where shall I find you?"[41] The soul is instructed to prepare itself, for the prince is about to visit her. The courtship is expressed as a dance, after which the soul enters the sacred chamber, which is the invisible Godhead. The soul, being so beautifully formed according to the divine nature, finds no separation between God and itself. They join as one. In one of her poems, Mechtild describes this yearning and consummation in overtly erotic language:

> Then a blessed stillness
> That both desire comes over them.
> He surrenders himself to her,
> And she surrenders herself to him.[42]

In the poetic assertions of the thirteenth-century mystic and poet Hadewijch of Antwerp (or Brabant), loving desire flows from God to the human lover, whence it returns to the divine lover who first instilled it. The courtly lover desires *com*penetration, that they both might dwell within each other. As the heavens open up, the hearts are filled with pleasure, sweetness, and joy.[43] It follows then that "the blissful soul is led into a spiritual inebriation, in which she must play and surrender herself according to the sweetness she feels from within." They penetrate each other: "mouth in mouth, heart in heart, body in body, and soul in soul, while one sweet *divine Nature* flows through them both (2 Pet. 1:4), and they are both one thing through each other, but at the same time remain two different selves—yes, and remain so forever."[44] The divine lover desires a reciprocal love, "to love him with that great love wherewith he loves himself, Three in One."[45] Love—God and the enactment of love—gives as much as it receives, for "Love counters this longing with her longing."[46] Inebriation enables the self to enjoy "the same bliss as God himself is, because it loves with love as much as it can see with wisdom, and sees with wisdom as much as it can love with love."[47] One of Hadewijch's poems depicts this reciprocity well:

> God, who created all things
> And who, above all, is particularly Love
> I supplicate to consent,
>   According to his pleasure,
> That Love now draw the loving soul to herself
>   In the closest union possible to Love.[48]

These images or visions of a divine yearning, already existent in the Christian philosophical and theological imaginary of the thirteenth century, can aid in understanding how Aquinas could view God as one who enjoys Godself also as lover. Aquinas's excessive use of analogical language, however, is not without its problems. The literal sense appears, in Denys Turner's words, to have become "barely more than a pretext for a typology."[49] And as the true erotic wordplays found in the scriptures are deemphasized, in the end sexuality is denied a true role in the economy of grace and salvation. Furthermore, any references to the divine passion as suffering, or to a change in God from potentiality to actualization, are formulated as no more than a mere divine condescending to the human condition and thus also a denial of the significance of a passionate God. As Aquinas purifies the analogies, Turner argues, "the role of human *eros* is reduced to the purely formal symmetries with which it maps onto the divine realities which it typifies."[50] Perhaps, to return to an earlier, mathematical view limning analogy as two parallel lines, these two realities "may never meet."

A clear example of the abstraction Turner warns about may be found in the words of Gregory of the Great in the preface to his commentary on the Songs. This can be illustrated by way of the "swallowing" imagery promulgated by William of Saint-Thierry, according to which the pleasures of the flesh normally shared in bodily manner are "taken captive by the Holy Spirit" and become a part of spiritual love.[51] Similarly, as for Gregory the Great, without the desensualizing of the flesh there is no progressive arousal of the soul.[52] To some contemporaries, Gregory's (and William of Saint-Thierry's) interpretation meant that the Songs pose the paradoxical request of asking us to purify ourselves of all passions. For it is through the language of carnal passion, uttered by lips "sullied by sinful words," that the soul looks toward chastity, as Gregory of Nyssa remarks.[53] Paradoxically, sensuous, carnal language serves to reveal the incorruptible. And while Gregory agrees that movements of the soul correspond to the motions of "the sense organs of the body," love awakens, arouses, intensifies the soul "by an ever greater desire," in much the same way as does the "angelic freedom from passion."[54]

Still, central to the Aquinan notion of divine *eudaimonia* or enjoyment that this chapter expounds is how analogical and metaphorical modes of defining the divine reality introduce us to the possibility of another logic, one that welcomes an erotic view. Logos, the language of reason, and eros, mystical or poetic language, can meet as complements in Christian theological discourse. Aquinas subtly presents distinct understandings of Aristotle's concept of happiness by supplementing it with the notion of yearning love that unfolds in the work of Denys the Areopagite. From the *Divine Names* Aquinas extracted a concept of the appetite that highly resembles the Areopagite's divine yearning for the created cosmos[55] centered on God (rather than on the Christ figure), the notion of grace perfecting nature rather than destroying it,[56] and thus a deeper penetration into a cosmological understanding of the love of God than some Christian mystics offered. What transpires in this theological dialogue is an aesthetic typical of medieval philosophical writing, as Umberto Eco so elegantly elaborates.[57] The metaphorical language allows the use of correspondences that describe passionate love alongside charity. It initiates an exploration of God's amorous enjoyment of creation. This activity of divine loving implies a lovers' dance initiated by divine desire or appetite.

A CONTEMPLATIVE GOD

That God loves as a lover yearns for the created order, and that God is eros, benefit from being set beside the logic of enjoyment in Greek thought. For any statement that God is love, particularly if enjoyment is among love's possibilities, must wrestle with Greek thought on the divine intellect and contemplation. In drawing from the views of Aristotle by way of Aquinas, Christian tradition might affirm that God is happy because *eudaimonia* (happiness) is "the proper good of every intellectual nature," which in the case of God means that *eudaimonia* is the proper good of God, since God's sole activity is of the intellect.[58] God is an intellectual being who eternally possesses *eudaimonia*, and since God by definition does not change from potentiality to act, God is continuously thinking. This principle is akin to what Aristotle said about contemplation being the activity that is "most pleasant and best."[59] According to Aristotle, "it must be of itself that the divine thought thinks (since it is the most excellent of things), and its thinking is a thinking on thinking."[60]

In this regard, Nygren's critique, namely, that happiness has "activity and the attainment of perfection" as its starting point and not love, is not entirely unfounded.[61] The logic of Greek *eudaimonia* downplays fellowship with God, the divine love, in favor of the "Good-in-itself."[62] As noted earlier, *eudaimonia* traditionally denotes perfection in that it entails a circular motion out from the origin and a return back to the origin. God grants it, and in turn it becomes the end that all things pursue, activating the pleasure of getting "exactly what one yearns for."[63] Christian thought might affirm that "happiness is a perfect activity" for it is bent upon itself, needing no habit to perfect it.[64] It is choiceworthy by itself, chosen on account of itself, preeminently good in itself. The view that God is happy and that happiness is sufficient in itself therefore literally translates into "God is happiness." That is, the divine essence is one of happiness, for God is the source of all happiness and the ultimate end of all pursuits.

The logic that God is God's own happiness consequently may be reframed as God needing nothing, lacking nothing, being wholly self-sufficient. A classical argument in keeping with Aquinas might postulate that God is happy because "God has no need of other things, seeing that His perfection depends on nothing external to Himself."[65] Hence Aquinas's view of the divine perfect activity of self-understanding combined with Aristotle's on divine "thinking on thinking," that is, thinking encircled about itself, comes to define God's happy essence and inclination toward contentment with the divine self.[66] God would take greater delight in God's own happiness, which is the divine self itself. In other words, God delighting in God's own happiness would mean that God is God's own happiness.[67] Since happiness is a virtue in itself, one that when sought for itself denotes completion, God would be happy solely within and with Godself.

It follows that certain aspects of Aquinas's thought on divine happiness are equally as troublesome as those discussed in Chapter 1, for they elide the divine love for the created order, since God appears to be the sole element necessary for divine enjoyment. At least, this is the common interpretation. The contemporary theologian Fran O'Rourke, for example, argues that Aquinas's view of self-sufficiency means "His activity is self rooted, abides in His own Being, and is directed through self-love towards himself as its final end."[68] Nothing can be added to God. *God is ipsum esse per se subsistens.* According to O'Rourke's reading, by the very divine essence, "God can receive no addition; in his purity and fullness he is distinct from all being."[69] So the divine *esse* is not merely (in this line of thinking) "the sum of all perfections and forms, but is their total simplicity and plenitude,"[70] their origin and end to which they return. Also, since God exists exclusively according to God's own existence, the divine plenitude is such that God "can become neither 'more' nor 'less'; in need of nothing, he seeks no alteration."[71]

The above construals of God as divine happiness, self-fulfilling, are reminiscent of Aristotle's figure of the benevolent king. On the one hand, the notion that God enjoys Godself and that out of this self-enjoyment may stem any other enjoyment God may experience in relation to the cosmos can be a positive point of departure when one takes up the doctrine of the God of love. God limned this way desires neither in compulsory ways nor out of capricious greed (such as to hoard external goods, power, honor, or fame).[72] In contemporary thought, this understanding situates desire or yearning beyond the notion of unsatisfied need, even beyond the basic dichotomy of satisfaction versus nonsatisfaction. Rather, reminiscent of Jacques Derrida's surplus of meaning, as desire arises from a surplus rather than a lack or need,[73] it recovers the relationship yearning has with an other beyond the self, turning generously away from fulfillment by means of pure self-gratification.[74] A model of divine happiness with such understanding of God's self-enjoyment as its point of departure would also challenge views that hold the sole duty of God is to provide material goods for a selected few, as well as the practice of amassing wealth and attaining elite status as a means of achieving happiness.

If left to itself, however, this view of happiness, centered on the idea of the divine thought and an understanding of God's own self, seems to lack a fuller appreciation of the divine relationship with the cosmos. Those searching for more reciprocal expressions of this relationship search in vain, for nothing has been added to the divine circle; God's absolute self-subsistent happiness lies in that it "already possesses its proper good."[75] And while the divine good benefits all creatures, there are some logical awkwardnesses. As the American philosopher of religion Charles Hartshorne has written, "The trouble is that our enjoyment of this good is no contribution to the divine good itself, which is defined as entirely self-sufficient."[76] God's act of happiness is circular within God, having God as both its starting and ending point and receiving nothing beyond the inner life of God, the cosmos thus adding nothing to the divine fulfillment.

To set free the Aquinan view of God enjoying the divine self with the created order from the self-enclosing grip of Aristotle's model, we may note first the aspect of circular "motion" that is part and parcel of the divine "proper good," which is God's nature. Again, for Aquinas as for Aristotle, happiness is a divine activity.[77] Here the analysis of the Catholic theologian Joseph Bracken is helpful in parsing the concept of divine activity more finely. In *The Divine Matrix*, Bracken sets forth several intriguing interpretations as he revises Aristotle's notion of divine activity in light of Aquinas's theology. His focus turns away from an entity that remains complete in itself and toward that aspect of motion as process that the term "activity" connotes. The activity of thinking, for example, would refer to a process more than to a complete "entity" or being.[78] Moreover, the entity would be derived from motion itself, which for present purposes I take as the impulse of divine contemplation, namely, yearning. The motion would likewise be progressively circular, starting and ending in divine happiness, the divine self as such, but in a more nuanced manner, one in which the circle took the form of lovers embracing.

The Greek form of contemplation takes as its focal point the activity of thinking, an activity productive of ideas—not the same concept that is expressed in the spiritual discipline of contemplation practiced by Aquinas. But Greek thinking and Aquinas's contemplation might draw nearer when the notion of divine yeaning is viewed through a more mystical lens. The move from the Greek version of "thinking on thinking"[79] to something akin to Christian mystical contemplation might unfold through a series of motions: the motion of the divine inner embrace, like an interpenetrative dance among the divine persons; the motion of God going ecstatically "outside" the divine self (yearning for the embrace of the cosmos); the motion of things enjoying themselves according to their nature in their embrace of God; and the motion of all things returning back to the divine self in ecstatic enjoyment (all things being embraced by God). The unfolding of the divine loving nature and the folding of the cosmos into God become evident in such motions, especially when the parallels that exist between the notion of divine enjoyment of Aquinas and that of the divine yearning of Denys the Areopagite are brought to light. God relates within and beyond the divine inner life in the same way that lovers relate to each other. The relationship within God is of love and fecund, and from it God goes outside the divine inner life and into the world. God goes out as an activity of love, sustaining all things, stirring them to enjoy themselves with a purpose, and wooing them into God, much as the Spirit does, in a tender and gentle manner.

YEARNING WITHIN

A second look at the concept of activity as circular motion contributes to further turning upside down the phrase "thinking on thinking," particularly if one considers the divine inner life as a loving process by means of which God stirs the world toward fuller forms of enjoyment. Coupled with the unique axiom of Aquinas that holds that the divine essence is the divine existence[80] but also beyond it, Joseph Bracken creatively asserts that God is "subsistent activity" whose *nature* is the activity of existing in unity with the persons of the Trinity and other beings. Specifically, if the Trinity is considered an analogy of a divine process akin to a circular motion, Bracken suggests, it can be construed as the mutual indwelling of three divine persons. They mutually indwell each other as "subsistent relations," namely, "interrelated subjects of one and the same activity,"[81] interrelated by love.

This activity (or movement), viewed through the lens of relations, draws on classical Christian thought in that the divine processes are those of knowledge and love, intellect and will, which correspond to the Son and the Spirit. That God is happy would mean that God enjoys the divine self through contemplation, but with the logic of the Trinity, three persons in one, now introduced, God's enjoyment is also with the Son and the Spirit. From Bracken, one might infer that when Aquinas equates the divine intellect and the divine will with the divine act of existence, he opens the door to deducing that the "proper object of the divine activities of knowing and loving is the divine nature" and that "the divine nature is co-terminus with the divine act of existence," which entails the enjoyment of the Son and the Spirit.[82] As Bracken suggests, it is therefore better to say that God is *subsistent relations* than that God is *absolute self-subsistence*, which is Aquinas's predominant view, for the acts of existence of the three subjects, God, the Son, and the Spirit, demonstrate a deeper dependence for their enjoyment on those of the other two relations, and possibly on the acts of the cosmos.

Moreover, since for Aquinas the divine essence is happiness and the divine essence is the divine existence, God's activity of joyous contemplation is also about amorous relationships (as with the mystics). That the divine enjoyment stems from subsistent amorous relations places value on the ground and the activity of love that are shared, rather than only on the activity of thinking per se. At least, it interlaces the two concepts. This theological view holds promise for those seeking to conceive of a passionate God of enjoyment. It is significant that for Aquinas, for example, on par with an essence that is of the intellect, *"God's love is the divine ousia"* or substance (being, existence).[83] Essence as existence would mean that the dynamic activity of God within God is love, and not purely a Greek thinking on thinking. That God is love therefore means that God has love first and foremost within the divine self and for the divine self, but as relations. The statement "God is love" thus points to the love among the persons of the Trinity, a circular motion from God to God that mirrors the relations between lovers.

In Aquinas, as in much of the Christian tradition, this concept is first developed in terms of the procession of the Spirit from the Father to the Son. The Spirit is a procession of the will that refers to an "impulse and movement towards the object" of God's love, which is the Son.[84] This impulse is akin to that of lovers. The object loved comes to be in the lover by way of movement of the lover toward the beloved. Aquinas explains, "So what proceeds in God by way of love, does not proceed as begotten, or as son, but proceeds rather as spirit; which name expresses a certain vital movement and impulse, accordingly as anyone is described as moved or impelled by love to perform an action."[85] In Trinitarian terms, the Son is begotten by way of a "movement" or an "impulse" in God called love, a form of desire that is also the bond between Father and Son called the Spirit.

This yearning love is circular within itself because it is an activity of divine enjoyment within Godself that grounds all existence, including God's. The impulse is toward another within God, in the sense of a "mutual indwelling" of one person of the Trinity in another. The abiding is such that the beloved is in the lover, "striving to gain an intimate knowledge."[86] The impulse is of the Spirit, which is "God's Love," searching *"the deep things of God."* The divine love is thus intensely *"intimate,"* even *"of the bowels,"* and reciprocal, of beloved and lover interpenetrating one another, "being both container and contents in different ways." And since "in God alone is His intellect His essence,"[87] of the same essence is Word and Love, which are processes of the intellect and the will, respectively. This intradivine yearning is expressed by way of intelligible emanations—processions of the intellect and the will. They are uniquely equal, intimate, fecund, and perfect processions from God the Father that partake of the same nature of God, which is love.[88]

In this circular movement of love there appear vestiges of the theological concept of *perichoresis*.[89] The term means "to cleave," and refers to the mutual interpenetration or indwelling of the divine persons, a commingling without the loss of distinctive attributes. Among some contemporary theologians, such as Catherine LaCugna, John Zizioulas, and Patricia Wilson-Kastner, perichoresis has been described as a dance between the persons of the Trinity, with the definition based on the Greek term *choreo*, or "movement around."[90]

While there is no direct reference in Aquinas's writings, Aquinas might possibly have appropriated a similar concept from such authors as Denys the Areopagite. For example, in the work of Denys the Areopagite we read, "In a house the light from all the lamps is completely interpenetrating, yet each clearly distinct."[91] According to LaCugna, this "analogy of the light of lamps" alludes to perichoresis.[92] And while she may not agree that this is also the case for Aquinas, Aquinas comes close to describing what the term perichoresis connotes, what LaCugna describes as "the dynamic and vital character of each divine person, as well as the coinherence and immanence of each divine person in the other two."[93] Aquinas does not explicitly use the term "perichoresis," but neither does Denys the Areopagite. Arguably, Aquinas was partly pointing in this direction in his use of the Areopagite's "circle" of love, with which he shared common views, to speak of the intradivine relations. In Aquinas we partly now see it in the image of container and content described above. Later it is disclosed more fully as a "divine dance" between the divine persons irrupting ecstatically into one another, and possibly with the cosmos.

Unlike in LaCugna, however, here the emphasis is not so much on the distinct persons as on the uniting activity that is their nature or ground of existence—which is love—and thus on the shared source of enjoyment of the divine self. That is, the focus is on the divine dance itself. Otherwise, as Bracken notes, if the focus remains on God as person, that is, on "an individual entity even when it is conceived as relational by nature, always in dynamic interrelation with other persons,"[94] other aspects such as the divine permeability to the cosmos may be difficult to grasp. Also, the shift of emphasis to divine love turns our attention away from the claim that God is a supreme being, which upholds a hierarchical logic. As Ivone Gebara argues, "we can no longer go on insisting on the traditional notion of a God/person—that is, a separate being superior to all that exists, a kind of superperson with the power to 'control' the universe, human life, and the morality of our actions."[95] Such a notion of the "superperson" is where the definition of God as *ipsum esse per se subsistens* leads. The purpose is therefore to temporarily bracket the question on person or being in order to bring to the fore the aspect of the dynamic divine activity of love.[96] As in Bracken's case, the present project attempts a reconsideration of a more "*bona fide* social ontology," one that sees God as the dynamic ground of divine existence, as well as the moving ground of all finite beings.[97]

This solicitude that Bracken shows toward the concept of thought in Aquinas as a relational process, movement, or activity in Trinitarian terms promisingly gives way to a positive inflection regarding a nuanced enjoyment—mystically contemplative. The coupling of the motion of thinking with the notion that the essence of God is love offers the possibility of another paradigm of divine existence, in a rather more poetic tone, that may widen the divine circle. In contradistinction to what Nygren posits with regard to God, eros, and yearning, might one unearth other principles of Trinitarian subsistence of which God is drawn, beyond the divine self?

YEARNING OTHERWARD

Inclinations toward a perichoretic dance with the cosmos in the work of Aquinas are first found in relation to the loving activity that for him begins with divine *appetite*. With a poetic flare, the grounding activity of God within the Trinity, which is love, also means that the existence of God in the cosmos is akin to a desiring love. Its significance can be posited by means of the definition that Emmanuel Levinas gives to desire, namely, desire is an expression of delirium, enthusiasm, or irrationality that puts an end to the solitary or inward thought. It announces "the beginning of a true experience of the new and of the noumenon."[98] Desire initiates a movement toward the other, to the unknown that is otherness, an opening within the self that disturbs self-circularity. Accordingly, whereas the notion of divine enjoyment would somewhat resemble Aristotle's views in that the circle would be perfect,[99] it would be markedly different in that God would have the capacity to enjoy the divine self by means of an appetite or loving longing for someone and something other than God.

There is evidence of something like an "opening" of the circle in Aquinas, for the divine longing poetically assumes the shape of an intellective appetite that contains the trace of something other than God embedded in it. Described in quasi-erotic terms, the intellective appetite is an *otherward* movement. This divine appetite is the impulse within God that "moves" God beyond the divine self as love, as Aquinas posits.[100] In agreement with him, one might even argue that "since power denotes a principle of movement or action, Dionysius calls love a power, in so far as it is a principle of movement in the appetite."[101] And while the intellective appetite is one way to describe the divine love as efficient cause, it can also simply imply an impulse or movement. As Aquinas indicates, "love is the first movement of the will and every appetitive faculty,"[102] and "love stands first among the soul's affections."[103] A logic other than the Greek *eudaimonia* is at play—a certain "madness," vividly expressed in Ernesto Cardenal's epigraph to this chapter—when God desires to unite with all things. Living things stirred by the divine power or movement of love, one may argue, may bring enjoyment to God in return.

That the divine longing can take the form of ecstasy and desire reveals another aspect of the intellective appetite. From both Denys the Areopagite and Aquinas, we might draw the notion that God is eros (yearning) and agape (love), going outside the Godself, seeking unity with all things.[104] Adding to Denys's understanding of that aspect of divine enjoyment, we might also in agreement with Aquinas innovatively say that God "desires happiness, as we do,"[105] which entails God suffering ecstasy. Aquinas argues, "And this is the sense in which Dionysius says, in chapter 4 of *On the Divine Names*, that 'even God himself suffers ecstasy through love.'"[106] As described by Denys the Areopagite, ecstasy is *"excessus mentis,"* which Aquinas interprets as "a going out of oneself by being placed outside one's proper order."[107] The divine ecstatic love is like an effusion, an overflowing, a bubbling over, outflowing or gushing forth, as Fran O'Rourke explains.[108] This overflowing motion of God beyond the Godself, beyond the "proper order" of God, therefore, comes by way of the intellective appetite, love and joy being a power and a principle of movement in God toward the cosmos.

So another circular motion is evinced in the manner in which God, out of the "realness" and fecundity of the divine intrarelations, sends the divine relations into the world as missions: word and love. Speaking specifically of love, the word breathes it forth, who is the Spirit. In Spirit being love, God dwells in the creature, the creature thus becoming a divine temple and love its sanctifying grace. By the gift of grace the soul becomes like the Spirit who dwells in the creature.[109] Love perfects the creature, which enables the creature to enjoy the gifting of the divine amorous activity. This divine sending, moreover, is from the origin: "as a tree sends forth its flowers," God sends the Spirit.[110] God sends from within the Godself and not externally, as a master would send a servant or an adviser would counsel a king. Since it is of the same origin, it is of equality as well. God sends Godself, or exits Godself into the world. Particularly through the Spirit, Aquinas states, "God is present as . . . the beloved in the lover."[111] So God in this sense can be said to be in the world and closely in relation to it through the divine mission as lover, through the divine activity of love.

God goes outside the divine self as lovers do, seeking friendship, intimacy, and union with the one loved (1 John 4:16). Aquinas reasons that "it belongs to love to move towards union, as Dionysius says,"[112] as if taking joy "in one another's presence, in living together, and in conversation" is the union that God seeks with the cosmos. Accordingly, along with Aquinas, we may say that therefore, God loves Godself "and other things." This notion of union is therefore the very definition of love, which for Aquinas is not too far distant from what his predecessors argued. As he puts it, "Hence, too, Dionysius says that *love is a unitive force* (*Div. Nom.* iv), and the Philosopher says (*Polit.* ii. 1) that union is the work of love."[113]

The notion of divine ecstasy may result in a preliminary engagement of the divine mutual indwelling with the created order. As Aquinas describes it, the proper nature of love is such that "the affection of the one tends to the other as to someone who is somehow one with him."[114] That God suffers *"ecstasy through love"*[115] parallels the manner in which the Spirit searches *"the deep things of God"* (argued above in relation to the Trinitarian persons). So an *otherward* movement akin to searching all things, *"even the deep things of God,"* is not too unrelated to another key aspect of the divine love: everyone who *"abideth in charity abideth in God and God in him"* (referring to 1 John 4:16).[116] In addition, it is quite significant that the divine will (intellective appetite) is moved by love to be *innermost* in all things, knowing them in their own nature.[117] Hence what comes forth is an image of God yearning for or desiring an intimate union of the divine bowels with all things. Along with Aquinas, one might caution that God unites with all things as a sweet and gentle agent that acts immediately *upon* them. So the imagery can also imply mere externality. God is not joined to their essence, for according to most classical views (such as those represented in Aquinas's work), to argue for a God who is in a thing as part of its essence would be to fall into error. Again, as stated above, God's union with creatures comes through an infusion of divine love, which also alludes to something internal and intimate.[118]

The same note of caution as above is needed here. This union, since it is still being expounded within the sphere of the intellective appetite, means that first, it is simple, and second, it is without passion. Both these principles remain under the influence of Greek thought (though not exclusively), particularly Aristotle's. As Aquinas explains, "Hence the Philosopher says (*Ethics* vii): *God rejoices by an operation that is one and simple*, and for the same reason He loves without passion."[119] Aquinas also states, "Now, according to the intellective appetite there is no passion, but only according to the sensitive appetite, as is proved in *Physics VII*. But no such appetite can be in God, since He does not have sensitive knowledge, as is manifest from what has been said above. Therefore, there is no passion of the appetite in God."[120] These two aspects will continue to pose a challenge to a sympathetic appropriation of views such as those of Aquinas for the construction of a passionate God.

Nevertheless, what is beneficial about the model of God as beloved lover that this book espouses is the aspect of an *otherward* and indwelling dance-like motion with the cosmos, or perichoresis, that begins to point to an amorous relationship. In this regard, one could agree with O'Rourke that the divine essence, which is love, is "the quiet leaven," that which is "most intimately and powerfully present within creatures" and which perfects and harmonizes all things.[121] Any movement in God as a result of the intellective appetite appears to draw God toward a fecund intimacy also beyond the triune relations, God seeking to unite and mutually indwell the cosmos as lovers do. Since God is love, therefore, God's essence is one of stirring up love in the created order. God is the lover whose enticing love awakens a desire for the good and the beautiful, and likewise initiates the movement of all things toward the utmost goodness and beauty.

AWAKENING PLEASURE

Another loving motion follows. The divine love stirs or lures all things towards enjoyment and pleasure in the cosmos. In Trinitarian terms, the Spirit moves the will with the love of charity, not as if this love was an instrument (which would therefore lead to involuntary acts) but rather as a superadded inclination to act upon it. That is, the love of the Spirit is not compulsory.[122] For there is an innate will to love already present that is only superadded to by the Spirit, who only inclines it to the act of love. Otherwise there would not be pleasure in the performance of love.[123] In a sense, the divine pleasure would lie in that things also enjoy themselves—find pleasure in themselves and their world—superadded to by love, so their enjoyment is with a purpose.

That God through the Spirit acts as a lover wooing all things toward enjoyment subsequently means also that there are forms of enjoyment fitting to each creature and that in a sense are nearly perfected with the divine love. The love of the Spirit is in accordance with Aquinas's view of God, who "*ordereth all things sweetly* (*Wis.* viii. 1)" and moves all things "to their due ends."[124] Furthermore, all things enjoy a common end, which is God, as they take delight in their different proper ends according to their diversity. God being the sustainer of each life form neither overrides creaturely desire, the pursuit of things desired, what is attained, nor the particular purposefulness of each life form. Rather, various enjoyments (proper ends) aiming at participation in the ultimate end result in "diverse relations of things to the ultimate end," which for Aquinas is the very meaning of "charity or beatitude."[125] God is the source and end of manifold pleasures, desiring all things to enjoy themselves and God, to attain higher levels of enjoyment. Life, according to Aquinas, is meant to be meaning*ful*. Hence love stirred within God, as subsistent relations, instills a gentle movement toward much pleasure—what entices all things toward the good and the beautiful in ways that maintain difference and distinction, and in a sweet and gentle manner, as lovers do.

Even more significant, God goes outside Godself and into the cosmos, because there is something innately good and beautiful found in the cosmos that God seeks to quicken so that it might attain a fuller life of enjoyment. A quality of goodness, love, and beauty is constitutive of the cosmos, even humanity.[126] The courtier has positive qualities that attract the one in love.[127] For Aquinas, grace constitutes "the state of grace," which renders something or someone other than God "a lover of God." This state of grace compares to a gentle prodding, a guidance toward an end to be shared with God.[128] This principle is also found in Denys the Areopagite, described beautifully in the following way:

> He is, as it were, beguilded by goodness, by love and by yearning and is enticed away from his transcendent dwelling place and comes to abide within all things, and he does so by virtue of his supernatural and ecstatic capacity to remain, nevertheless, within himself.[129]

So God is moved by love, the love of God within God, but also by something in the multiplicity of the cosmos itself that is lovely and attractive to God. In yearning for the cosmos, and without ceasing to be God or God's own self, God goes outside the divine self to unite with all that is creaturely. And since this movement of desire upholds the creaturely loveliness, something lovely draws God outside the divine self, and vice versa. It is a desire for a loving union that removes all coercion on both parts, in the way of lovers. God adds to the inclination to love in a sweet and gentle manner, aided by the love of the Spirit. Each acts according to love for one another willingly.

The abiding of the divine love with the cosmos also calls forth from what is already present for the well-being of the whole. For Denys the Areopagite, it entails the benign yearning of God "for all" that carries God outside the divine self in the loving care God "has for everything."[130] For Aquinas similarly, God "through the overflow" of the divine "loving goodness, goes outside" the divine self "in providence for all beings."[131] Creatures are inclined via incitement to act in lovely ways for the common good by acting in a harmonious or beautiful manner.[132] The divine yearning leads to the preservation and perfection of the whole of the cosmos by God as lover, for perfection and betterment are chiefly stirred "by the love of God."[133] Through this incitement, all living things seek union with each other, and ultimately with God, which is the true meaning of happiness. This is so because love responds to the divine yearning, which likewise acts as the alluring object that brings movement and activity outside the divine self in the form of abiding.[134]

THE LOVER DRAWN INTIMATELY NIGH

The alluring love of God instilling passion for all things to fully enjoy themselves leads to a fourth circular motion, one already hinted at toward the end of the previous chapter, a mutual indwelling within God, by way of a return back to God. This model is constituted by the Pseudo-Dionysian principles of God as source, preserver, and end. God as the source of desire goes outside the divine self without ceasing to be God, to draw all things into the divine self; holds them together; and maintains and preserves them because of an intense desire. All things culminate in a sort of mystical union—in Christian mystical terms known as the *visio beatifica*.[135] For Aquinas similarly, "owning to the fact that the very one seen is received into the seer, he unites the very seer to himself, that there may take place a sort of mutual penetration through love. For thus it says in John 4:16: 'He who abides in charity, abides in God and God in him.' Upon this union of what is maximally fitting follows the highest delight; and in this our happiness is brought to completion."[136] According to the life of contemplation, what ensues is our beatitude by means of visions of the Godhead. To see the divine essence is to have perfection "through union with God as with that object."[137] In union with God one sees the essence of God, the glory and the face of God (Exod. 32).[138]

As suggested by the poetic structure of the *Summa theologica*, creation therefore enjoyably flows from God (*exitus*) and returns to God (*reditus*), its source and end of enjoyment. Such is the divine perichoretic dance of love with the cosmos, "a kind of eternal circle,"[139] but one that, according to the model proposed here, welcomes in the cosmos. As O'Rourke indicates, "This universal panorama and cyclic scheme is the organic and architectonic structure of Aquinas' vision of God and the world," which for him also connotes that God is not enclosed in the divine transcendence.[140]

In desiring higher levels of enjoyment for all things created, God exits Godself toward the beloved in order to communicate the divine goodness and allow the participation of all in God. God going beyond the divine self entails God also drawing all things into the divine self, as in refilling them with pleasure. Also, God holds all things together, maintains and preserves them, because God simply desires the enjoyment of other things, for Godself "as for an end," because it befits the divine goodness.[141] That is why God can be called, in the words of Denys the Areopagite, "the beloved and the yearned-for," God being "beautiful and good."[142] God's contemplative love and appetitive power might thus be identified with an embracive motion that draws in all things and enfolds them so as to draw them intimately nigh to the source of all pleasure.

In the thought of Denys the Areopagite this is explained by God being the source "that extends goodness into all things" by specifically holding them in "some almighty receptacle" where all things are unified and held together for their preservation.[143] The imagery is of God sending forth and then regathering all things into the divine self. The sending forth and regathering together constitute a mystical motion, one of reciprocal yearning and desire (particularly the desire to be with God) that begins and ends this life's journey. God is the Beloved who is also the object and goal of all enjoyment, and who houses everything in Godself. Out of the superabundance of the divine goodness, God "makes all things, brings all things to perfection, holds all things together, returns all things. The divine longing is Good seeking good for the sake of the Good."[144] Just as for Aquinas, for Denys the Areopagite the divine yearning brings near the lover by way of the divine ecstasy for it "brings ecstasy so that the lover belongs not to self but to the beloved."[145] Furthermore, as Aquinas describes it in apprehending Boethius, God is happiest also because God is in that state of happiness "made perfect by a gathering of all good things," which Aquinas interprets as God containing them "in one single view."[146]

As the beginning and end of all things, God therefore comprehends the whole of reality—stirring the whole of reality through love intimately. The imagery summons up a lovers' dance between God and the cosmos, through which all things are moved by way of the divine appetite or yearning, even God. This motion of drawing near the cosmos and bringing all things into the divine self as into a receptacle (a gathering stirred by the divine yearning) constitutes the divine enjoyment.

As described in the contemplative life, "all things in God" means that potentially all things can partake of God, and be filled with all that is good. In agreement with many Christian theologians and mystics who preceded and followed Aquinas and with the theological views of the Latin American feminists discussed in the previous chapter, this state of grace, which undergirds all life processes, including the pain of birthing better futures, and consummates what is desired, defines happiness, which derives from being in union with God. As for Peter Lombard, the highest good is God, a knowledge that can lead to love, possession of love, and enjoyment of love.[147] Aquinas also puts it as follows: "From what has been said it evidently appears that in that final state of happiness which comes of the vision of God every human desire is fulfilled, according to the text: *Who filleth thy desire with good things* (Ps. cii, 5)."[148] This is because the desire of God encapsulates all desire (all that one desires ultimately is God), which ends with a joyous contemplation, for it means communion with God, and that, at times, as being in a banquet. He argues,

> By this vision we are made like God, and become partakers of the divine happiness. For God Himself by His essence understands His substance, and that is His happiness. Hence it is said: *When he appeareth, we shall be like unto him as he is* (I John iii, 2). And the Lord said: *I dispose unto you as my Father hath disposed unto me, a kingdom, that ye eat and drink at my table in my kingdom.* This cannot be understood of corporeal meat or drink, but must be spoken of that food which is taken at the table of Wisdom, whereof Wisdom herself says: *Eat my bread, and drink my wine that I have mingled for you* (Prov. Ix, 5). They then eat and drink at the table, wherewith God is happy, seeing Him in the way in which He sees Himself.[149]

The imagery of a banquet, the beauty of *la fiesta*, while always shrouded by the advent, not only points to an eschatological event but also to regularly partaking of the Eucharist, to sharing and being with one another, enjoying one another, and perhaps within one another in the act of sharing. Arguably, this eucharistic and festive sharing also hints at an incarnational interpenetration when referring to the partaking of bread and wine. A mutual indwelling, akin to the Trinity, of the *bowels* of God, thus intimate, is also affirmed on a careful reading of one of his written prayers. On serving and partaking of communion, he would say the following:

> I also pray that you bring me,
>   a sinner,
>   to that ineffable banquet where You dwell
>   with Your Son
>   and Holy Spirit.
>
> You who are for Your saints
>   true light,
>   complete fulfillment,
>   eternal joy,
>   consummate desire
>   and perfect happiness.[150]

In the movement of drawing in and bringing near there is therefore a divine trace that expands the circle. By God going outside to draw all things near, the circle offers openings in what seemingly are hermetic enclosures, for the circular activity of love appears to have several motions, within God for the divine self, and in relation to the world, which also incites toward diverse expressions of enjoyment that lures all things intimately near, better yet, within the divine self. The movement appears perichoretic, or akin to a mutual indwelling. The activity to which Bracken refers, then, can be seen as divine erotic love, which for Denys the Areopagite is a "simple self-moving power directing all things to mingle as one," a movement that starts in God, reaches to all creation, and stirs all things back to God.[151]

DIVINE PASSION, A POSSIBILITY?

So, while being enjoyment itself, one must emphasize, God yearns for enjoyment with the cosmos as Beloved, which, in respect to the one yearned for, also refers to rest.[152] For Aquinas, the appetite in moving toward the realization of the appetible object ends where it begins, an end that in creaturely terms is known as complacency, enjoyment, or happiness.[153] Aquinas states, "Accordingly, the first change wrought in the appetite by the appetible object is called *love*, and is nothing else than complacency in that object; and from this complacency results a movement towards that same object, and this movement is desire; and lastly, there is rest which is *joy*."[154] In other words, the appetite is love, the movement is desire, and its rest is joy, which is the result of attaining happiness. Delight or enjoyment denotes rest of the will or desire, a rest in the beloved that comes about with the actualization of the thing one desires.[155] God alone can lull desire, all things ultimately desiring only God as a lover, in whom the loved one finds complacency.[156]

In the poetic return of all things back to God as a beloved lover, one might argue that the divine enjoyment and happiness are likewise concomitant on rest. In mystical terms, God would find contentment and rest in union with another lover. This thought is adumbrated in Gregory of Nyssa's trope of the nuptial bed where the soul unites with God. The bed, for him, "represents the rest and happiness of the elect,"[157] where the divine lover delights in partaking of the sweetness and ripeness of the lover's fruit.[158] The divine yearning culminates in a divine "Sabbath," which is enjoyment. Again in the imagery of Gregory of Nyssa, this rest compares to the divine rest from creation: "Thus by Thine eyes, O Lord, I obtain the grace of being winged again, of recovering through virtue the wings of the Dove, by which I may have the power of flight. Now I can fly and can rest, and indeed in that rest which the Lord enjoyed when He rested from creation."[159] Rest refers to "the thing itself" being desired,[160] repose equaling God as Beloved; all things move toward rest, including God.

In models delineating mutual forms of enjoyment, the image of God resting or partaking of the Sabbath as beloved lover (as the above analogy of the nuptial bed helps illustrate) may invoke a divine passion, or passivity and receptivity. Might not Aquinas have thought of end as rest for God the lover as well? With Catherine Keller, we may characterize the "metaphor of 'rest'" as connoting "a dimension of divine passivity, passion, receptivity, altogether at odds with classical triumph of the *actus purus*, the purely active, unmoved Mover."[161] So rest as passivity can connote a recurrent receptivity on the part of God, the home of the universe.

A possibly mutually enjoyable lovers' dance unfolds when the circular motion includes an element of ongoing reception into the inner life of God. In relation to the concept of the lover God, this infinitely dynamic activity, narrowly parsed, is the act of loving or yearning of God and is not devoid of a kind of "rest" inclusive of the whole cosmos. The point of departure would be the motion within God that already includes the participation of all created beings in the dynamic existence of God, which is also a motion toward a being other than God, as implied in terms such as "yearning," a motion whose end is contentment, or "joy in the manner of an end."[162] Perhaps something like Keller's rhetorical question can prove to be insightful: "Might we affirm an *oscillation between divine attraction and divine reception, invitation and sabbath*?"[163]

As Bracken argues, what is potentially positive in Aquinas's understanding is that "all other beings participate in the act of existence through the creative action of God."[164] As with the analogy of the lovers mutually enjoying the delights of the nuptial bed, the "unlimited act of existence proper to God" in which all things participate is the very same as that in which the being of God is also "grounded" (that being the nature of God).[165] For Bracken, therefore, because all other created beings participate in the act of existence of God, they also participate in the moving but also restful nature or ground of the being of God.[166] Hence for Bracken the divine activity would be immanent, self-contained, and eternally of God concerning God, as initially stated above, but only through sharing the divine nature trinitarianly with all living beings. The Sabbath (of the cosmos and God) as receptivity is found in the shared nature of love, the medium of mutual penetration of selves that becomes the true source and end of enjoyment. So the divine love would entail activity and passivity, appetite (desire) and prehension.[167] God's love would be infinitely dynamic in the sense of the activity of existence of God or the divine nature being "a processive reality, a never ending conversion of potentiality into actuality."[168]

What would need to be maintained, if Bracken's view is adopted, is that God as the activity that grounds all existence would not be moved by something purely extrinsic to God but rather by something that is partly intrinsic, which as the principle of the divine existence is the "ground of all creatures."[169] In this sense God could be "self-moved," as Aquinas's model has it,[170] but more along the lines that Bracken proposes, in that God is also "the subject of an ongoing activity" that includes the participation of all other beings in God.[171] In agreement with Marguerite Porete, we might affirm that we share in "some part of the divine nature" in such intimate manner that love, who is God, has nothing outside us, and we ourselves have nothing outside of love.[172] In a seemingly Origenic mode, the end can be seen as the beginning of things, for "if the Three Persons of the Trinity will love me without end, then they have loved me from the beginning."[173] All partaking of the divine loving nature means that we are so intimately connected to God's inner being that we become an intricate element of the divine impulse to love (its beginning, which is yearning). As Porete says of love, "I am God, because love is God and God is love; this soul is God through love, and I am God by divine nature."[174]

Hence our enjoyment may partly enrich the divine life, add something to the divine enjoyment, as God also rests in offering the divine grounding activity of love as the site of participation. As Hartshorne suggests, "the all-knowing and all-loving cannot give happiness to others without fully participating in and possessing this happiness just because it is realized by others. For such is love at its fullest, joy in the joy, and sorrow in the sorrow, of others."[175] Without a fuller understanding of God as source and end of all things, that which all creatures ultimately enjoy, and which divine self enjoys, our understanding of the divine love would remain insufficient.

To sum up, there are two seemingly opposing aspects that describe the divine-cosmos relationship: God is an absolutely self-subsistent being whose happiness is solely God, yet God also goes outside the divine self, desiring to draw all things into the divine self. So the term "God" describes both a divine being that is seemingly fully content with the divine self and in need of nothing, and a point of departure concerning the divine love that allows for a God who romances creation into greater forms of enjoyment, moving toward a possibly mutual enjoyment between God and the cosmos. The movement of the divine loving activity, God's longing, appears to be *pericho-retic* and of the *bowels*, a movement that, if pressed further, as shown here, offers some possibilities for enlarging the inner circle of divine love to include the cosmos among the incipient forms of divine yearning.

Taking a Look at the Divine Mirror

> As the creature proceeds from God in diversity of nature, God is outside the order of the whole creation, nor does any relation arise from His nature; for He does not produce the creature by necessity of His nature, but by His intellect and will.
>
> St. Thomas Aquinas[176]

Before going any further, we should note that while the divine dance with the cosmos is in the relational sense perichoretic, according to classical theism, nothing can be added to the divine enjoyment because God is impassible and bound to a circularity of absolute sameness. While promisingly innovative, the trope of yearning in this regard does not violate impassivity, for as Aristotle argues, whereas all things can go in a constant cycle, "something must always remain, acting in the same way."[177] In short, both movement and permanence exist in God. And herein lies the sharp paradox of much of classical theism. The element of relationality present in this God of love lacks affect, mostly because God is seen as the impulse that stirs all things toward fuller forms of enjoyment, and ultimately toward God, with none of their expressions causing a "stir" within God.[178] God in *all* respects remains "the same way." The correctives briefly referred to in the previous chapter and earlier in this one with regard to a more intimate, if not mystical, participation are therefore fitting. Otherwise God would remain a mirror of the divine enjoyment.

INTELLECTIVE YEARNING

An important element that must be addressed is lack. Unlike what Nygren appears to propose, God moving ecstatically cannot mean that a need or a lack in God awakens the divine desire, rather yearning love itself. In agreement with Denys the Areopagite's argument, we may state that God created the world out of love. According to Andrew Louth, for Denys, the statement "God loves" means that creation is a product of the divine ecstasy, of God going outside the divine self and centering the divine being on the object of divine love: creation. The creatures in turn love God with the divine love (on its return journey) not out of striving but with desire. Louth explains that the circular motion of God and creatures going outside themselves in love,[179] particularly as expounded in the writings of Denys the Areopagite, indicates that eros takes on a new form that is contrary to Greek thought, which placed eros on a par with need. Yearning love or eros is "an overflow of divine goodness—it needs nothing, it is the source of everything," Louth explains.[180] Implicitly, creaturely yearning is more akin to love than is need that craves the divine favor.

Agape and eros spun into a single thread, love, is also evident in Aquinas. In part, this is why God loves without having any needs. For Aquinas, that God desires without needing anything means that the divine love is unrelated to concupiscence.[181] Otherwise the movement toward the thing desired, stirred by concupiscence, would be initiated by a lack of satisfaction in the one who sought it.[182] Earlier this was explained with regard to hoarding external goods, power, honor, and fame.[183] Love, on the other hand, draws the self outside the self and toward another in its intention to do good and because of care, as for a friend. It can be said that God in being drawn goes outside the divine self in the latter sense. The union created by friendship is according to likeness and based on love. Lover and loved one share things in common (communion). Aquinas argues, "they seek a suitable and becoming union;—to love together, speak together, and be united together in other like things."[184] Like a lover-friend, God lovingly unites with the created order, but not in the sense of possessing the loved one, for possession would mean concupiscence, which would be an error. This notion of possession safeguards God as much as the cosmos from becoming one in a manner that would obliterate one or the other. It preserves what each is.

In what way would this theistic model, which so positively affirms a divine appetite, stray from its potential to similarly affirm a mutually beneficial erotic relationship? Where would it fall short? As already alluded to in the discussion of Bracken's corrective, by insisting on a divine yearning being subsumed under the Greek thought of *ipsum esse per subsistens* or absolute self-subsistence, yearning remains bound to a similar view as that of Boethius. The divine relation would be posed more in terms of an individual substance of a rational nature, a God who could be called a person *solely* by being "the most perfectly intelligent being."[185] This mode of relating according to the logic of the Greek *eudaimonia* means several things.

First, the divine intellective appetite or divine desire in this view receives nothing from creation, and so acts independently of the situation that surrounds the creature. This would be quite troublesome if no divine sorrow or enjoyment could ensue as a result of life's events. As Aquinas states,

> When love and joy and the like are ascribed to God or the angels, or to man in respect to his intellectual appetite, they signify simple acts of the will having like effects, but without passion. Hence Augustine says (*De Civ. Dei* ix. 5): *The holy angels feel no anger while they punish . . . , no fellow-feeling with misery while they relieve the unhappy.*[186]

Though the creature can shape its own circumstances, for example, by pushing back into its own form, there is nothing that can bring about a change in God. And here a quandary surfaces that was posited in the first chapter: would not this mean that because God is "unfeeling" of the hurt of the cosmos, God has a kind of happiness that does not fully take account of its sufferings? The premise for which I instead argued in the first chapter is the one enunciated by Heschel: "Pathos means: God is never neutral, never beyond good and evil."[187] In a view that treats the intellect preferentially as an organ of impassibility, would God not be safeguarding the divine self from being contaminated with the world's "bodily" enjoyments?[188] Subsequently, a divine yearning that ultimately can neither experience pain nor find enjoyment in things other than God (in other words, a God who is absolutely self-sufficient) may seem superfluous to the created order.[189] Hence *eudaimonia* would basically remain a vacuous concept, as in the Greek sense.

Second, this doctrinal view of *ipsum esse per subsistens* would have an impact on the manner in which all things return to God and the state that characterizes their union with God. Early in the Christian era, impassibility appeared to have characterized this path of the soul, a dulling of all sensuality that purified the self from its pleasures. In his commentary on the Songs, Gregory the Great speaks of the fierce love of the soul for the divine, a love that ultimately turns away from any sensuous passion and transitions into "the virtue of impassibility,"[190] offering up the mind as "a burnt offering for the contemplation of God."[191] This translates into a state of happiness dangerously close to the Greek form of contemplation, which leads to "thinking on thinking." For as Gregory of Nyssa also says, "when every bodily disposition has been quelled, our mind within us may boil with love, but only in the Spirit, because it is heated by that "fire" which the Lord came to "cast upon the earth" (Luke 12:49).[192] As William of Saint-Thierry puts it, "in the happy consciousness in which [love] is rooted, the joy of the Lord is not disrupted by any worldly sadness that breaks in, nor is it obscured by any empty delight."[193] It steadily and uninterruptedly holds together, serene at every point, not undergoing any change.

God viewed as impassible thus also means that impassibility is the archetype to which all human beings return, since the element of passion was introduced later on, particularly after the Fall.[194] So the soul fixes "itself steadily on the inaccessible beauty of the divine nature," which for him is impassible, and seeks to become like it. The absence of passion points to that lost paradise, a primitive state of happiness, to the time when humans were not guided by the senses, particularly when the woman had no labor pains.[195] More akin to a nostalgic loss of a paradisical state, the sufferings of the body, our misery, tied to the human condition, are in contrast to the "joys we once had."[196]

Third, if only like is drawn to like, as in the impassible soul ardently longing for an impassible ground, what would become of the body? A response in more recent theological debates among some feminists has rejected this view, mostly because it blatantly neglects the body and disregards women. For example, Michelle González argues that "Aquinas contends that women's imperfect creation, as expressed in her bodiliness, reveals her inferior status."[197] Absolute sensuous distinctions between God and the cosmos also might translate into the manner in which beings that in human terms appear to be highly intellectual differ in terms of likeness to God from those that are not. Concerning the *imago Dei*, for example, Aquinas indicates, "Now man excels all animals by his reason and intelligence; hence it is according to his intelligence and reason, which are incorporeal, that man is said to be according to the image of God."[198] As LaCugna puts it, "This view of the human person fails to acknowledge our intimate bond with the earth and with the entire cosmos."[199] It also disregards the bond that God has with the embodied whole of creaturely reality.

A TRINITARIAN LOVE AFFAIR?

The absolute self-subsistence of Greek *eudaimonia* hence implies a self-enclosed mode of relating, even if that mode is perichoretic. The term *person*, Aquinas argues, "signifies in God a relation as subsisting in the divine nature."[200] For him this means that God is most perfectly intimate and fecund inwardly. As Aquinas explains, "the more perfectly it proceeds, the more closely it is one with the source whence it proceeds,"[201] an intimacy that stems from the divine intellect, which is the essence of God as love. The intimate processions define the divine fecundity, "for there is in Him only one perfect Word, and one perfect Love; thereby being manifested His perfect fecundity." Sadly, this intimacy and fecundity of God are described in terms of internally immanent triune relations, and solely in those terms.

In God there are only two real relations, involving Son and Spirit, and thus several realities that subsist in the divine nature in the sense that each is distinct from the others as relative opposites.[202] Only the Father is the Father, only the Son is the Son, and only the Spirit is the Spirit. In relation to the world, God is *really* distinct according to that which is *absolute*.[203] Absolute distinction means that though the created order relates to God in a real manner, there is no real relationship on the part of God toward the creaturely. What LaCugna remarkably brings to light is that "God's relation to creation is logical, not real, because being related to creatures is not a part of God's nature. The creature's relation to God is real because creation is constituted to be what it is by virtue of its relation to God."[204] That God does not need the world for God to be relational also means that God is independently relational within Godself, apart from creation. The created order thus adds no relationship to God.

Therefore, this model not only safeguards the divine relationship with the cosmos from cupidity (greed or selfishness), it also favors the divine freedom at the cost of real relations. Aquinas is not only able to avoid claiming that creation is of necessity, but also posits that God is therefore free from creation in ways that the creature cannot be of God. As LaCugna explains, "To be a creature is to depend altogether on having existence from another, whereas God alone is [absolutely] self-subsistent."[205] God's freedom connotes that relationship with the world in no way constitutes God's being. The relationship is maintained within the tension that the difference between God and the creaturely logically poses, the relation of God with creation being one of logic. That the creature is dependent on God denotes difference, unlike the divine processions that are "in one and the same nature."[206] So real relations are based on actions that are internal and not external processions in God.

The notion of absolute self-subsistence, therefore, harms the potential that aspects such as the intellective appetite may have. The attempt to keep us from thinking of divine enjoyment as being equivalent to creaturely experience is noteworthy, for it seeks to preserve the peculiarity and otherness of both God and cosmos. Still, such safety nets can be used in ways that are more inclusive of things other than God, things unlike God and that affect God's enjoyment. Needing nothing from the cosmos should not necessarily translate into receiving nothing from the cosmos, even as all things partake of God. A God who in the end is in need of nothing in the sense of being utterly independent from the cosmos would also lack desire for enjoying the divine self "with" the cosmos. But such is not the case with God, for the divine ecstasy implies desire.

OF A MIRROR-LIKE DIVINE INFINITE APPETITE

To press this matter more explicitly into the realm of pleasure and enjoyment, without accounting for passion and a more radical openness to the cosmos in constructs of a God of enjoyment, this view of yearning, as promising as it might be, would portray a divine enjoyment that appears self-concupiscent. If God is happy without the aid of any creature,[207] and remains happy solely in Godself, even while stirring all things toward fuller expressions of life within the divine self, the *Qui est* of God (Exod. 3:14) is one of God yearning only for Godself, hence contemplating only Godself.

A way to unpack this point on concupiscence is by looking into the nature of happiness as an activity of the proper good of God.[208] For Aquinas as for Aristotle, happiness is good in itself. And since the proper good is not something that God searches for, because God already possesses its proper good, God "desires happiness" only insofar as God "is in the enjoyment of happiness," and God is happy, properly speaking, enjoying only Godself.[209] Logically, the divine happiness being the same as the divine enjoyment equals God having pleasure in the possession of all ends, which refers to, as Aquinas puts it, *"a movement of the soul towards the enjoyment of God for His own sake."*[210] This would mean that the divine motion, in the words of Denys the Areopagite, "turns from itself and through itself and upon itself and towards itself in an everlasting circle."[211]

Thus we can affirm the theological concerns stated above. Whereas all living things are in movement toward the enjoyment of God, and whereas God is the end of our pursuits,[212] and thus our true enjoyment, God would remain exempted from the "acquisition or participation of something else."[213] Hence the cosmos would be superfluous to God's inner enjoyment. The harsh critique of Heschel is apropos. A God who is free of the very world that is dependent on God falls into a *theotropism*, an inward turning of God toward God.[214]

Paradoxically, among some thinkers, such as O'Rourke,[215] this superfluousness does not diminish the openness of the divine transcendence in creation models like those of Denys the Areopagite and Aquinas, since in God are found all the perfections, and God's love for Godself denotes absolute perfection (without any need for things external). Anything that God wills being good and for God's own end—God's goodness—means that "Creation is an outpouring of God's excessive goodness. In its most proper and positive sense, the created universe is indeed superfluous to God's being." God alone, O'Rourke remarks, is *"maxime liberalis."* Creatures being enriched by God because of God's goodness trumps the universe being superfluous to God. It appears to be a great honor to "add nothing" to the divine perfection, to be of eternal value to God as created beings.[216] For O'Rourke, this implies that the whole of the divine relation with us is a gift to us. Nothing is to be done on our part to add to the divine enjoyment within the divine self.

True, along with Denys one might argue that God "transcends the unity which is in beings," for God is "indivisible multiplicity, the unfilled overfullness which produces, perfects, and preserves all unity and all multiplicity,"[217] in this way maintaining a distinctive quality of enjoyment between God and the cosmos. Yet how are we to account for the manner in which the unique and peculiar forms of enjoyment of each thing have an impact on the divine enjoyment? Furthermore, how are we to interpret the statement that "all things are in God" (in classical theistic models like Aquinas's) beyond the qualifications of preexisting perfections in God as "all things" return to God? How would *alterity*, or otherness, factor into the equation of all things desiring the good, present in the divine desire and God's existence, and perfected in their search for the plenitude of the good (the end or goal of their existence), which is God? For while God stirs all things toward their own forms of enjoyment, and even to higher levels of it, why would they not exist in God in their particularity, and not solely in their perfection and likeness to God? O'Rourke admits that this model accepts no diversity in God.[218] God, who is One, disperses the divine essence through the multiplicity found in creation, but all things return to God in the form of their perfected simplicity.

But why love anything at all if in creating and infusing goodness,[219] and in moving all things to union with God in the act of giving them being and perfections, a likeness to God,[220] God is loving God's own perfections, and loves humans only as a result of the divine likeness in us? Though not in the sense of impassibility, as posited by classical thinkers, one might agree that likeness can be a vehicle of participation. We participate in the good by being good, that is, by being like God, who is good essentially.[221] Yet without anyone to love intimately near who is truly other, this circularity of love consequently means that the motivation of God's love is the divine love for Godself. The participation to which we are drawn is the God who loves Godself, and loves us *only* through that self-love.[222] Only in this sense can we say that God loves other things, a love that is "not only a true love, but also a most perfect and most enduring love."[223] So even as things unfold into God, God remains most content with and loving Godself more than anything else.[224] Would this not result in God gazing eternally into a mirror? Voraciously craving solely for the divine "good" self? Might God in the end only love the divine self—a form of pure narcissism?

Here the critique that Jean-Luc Marion offers of the present analysis is fitting. And while he is explicitly mostly arguing against a Cartesian form of solipsism, his words shed new light on the issue at hand. For him, this kind of love is found in the one who thinks that he or she can love him- or herself only by him- or herself. In the case of God, self-sufficiency is even more so since God's substance is absolute perfection. God becomes "ultimate substance." Substance is "constituting substance," which means "subsisting in itself exactly as itself." With respect to God, this means that God is "substance subsistent per se in itself absolutely."[225] This tautology again means that God equals an ego whose self-identity is with itself alone. The divine ego becomes equal to the divine ego—thus the solitariness of the tautological circularity of the metaphysical "I" that it creates.

More poignant still, "subsisting exactly as oneself" results in the erasure of the different forms of enjoyments and their sublimation into one's own. For Marion, erasure ultimately occurs when the *I* objectifies the other in itself, converting it into an alter ego, "a simple other 'me.'"[226] A lonely affair with the self ensues, for in objectifying the other, the *I* (ego) reduces alterity to the self that "loves," loving in the end a figure or representation of itself. It is the result of love that starts with the *I* and brings the other to the *I*, furthermore placing the other within the *I*, a love that at the very best "belongs to the domain of self-idolatry."[227] The one loving ends up loving only what is found within, in itself. To bring back the other in the shape of the self (*I*, ego) erases the other. For Marion, this means that there is only a return of the love of the self for the self and by itself. Marion states,

> If I love *in* myself the other, it will therefore be necessary that I love *myself* in the other—that I love in the so-called other only the idol of myself. Love, loved for itself, inevitably ends up as self-love, in the phenomenological figure of self-idolatry. My love always amounts to the love of myself. In other words, because in this love I love myself, I thus love concretely only those who love me.[228]

The solution would be to admit to a certain level of vulnerability that resides in there being something other than the divine love affecting all things as it is likewise being affected by their singular enjoyments. Otherwise the illusion remains of someone or something "being able to love himself by himself," argues Marion. Any such being is a *happy idiot*, who is under the illusion of being loved by everyone and believes that this love stems only from his own charms. He is "handsome, stupid, rich, and lucky, someone for whom everything turns out well, without any merit, difficulty, or failure, either."[229] Isn't the God of classical theism the example par excellence of this happy God whose love is absolutely self-sufficient? Marion is correct in that we have described God as a happy idiot whose love leaves no room for another lover. The solitary love of the happy idiot provides a false version of divine enjoyment, "the glory of a god,"[230] for God is not one whose "thought of the self [is] by itself."[231] For to whom would God be attracted?

Hence, the view that God goes outside the divine goodness to care for the loved ones without being bound by need or concupiscence has been in need of rethinking. In the end, unless we consider a divine inner circular motion of love that is open to the cosmos in ways that allow a shattering of the divine mirror, Aquinas's model fails because God is happier than any other being, in the sense that God's happiness is what God is from beginning to end. And if this is all that defines divine enjoyment, then God's satisfaction of desire ends up being purely masturbatory, as God looks at

God's own reflection of self in the mirrors of God. For God to truly enjoy Godself with creation, God would need to welcome true otherness (even nonhuman things) into the divine self, would need to be a passionate and vulnerable God. Therefore, our understanding of God's relation to the cosmos should expand to include an explicit theological affirmation of passion, the flesh, a porous space within God, perhaps even with multiple openings and sites of receptivity that can add to the divine enjoyment.

The purpose of this second chapter has been to listen to the whispering voice of classical thinkers like St. Thomas Aquinas, and particularly to those quiet insights I find surprisingly indispensable in developing a view of divine enjoyment that point to the radicality of yearning and drawing in something truly other than the divine self. The contemplative element evident in these teachings begs the imagination to consider a kind of divine longing with the cosmos that initiates a movement that ends with a lover's embrace, a eucharistic moment of loving union that allows for a more mutual and interpenetrating indwelling. That which I read as being liturgical or mystical theology directs our listening ears to what remains appealing, given as the strident noise of absolute self-subsistence seeks to absorb it.

As regards yearning, it is noteworthy that the divine enjoyment does not adhere to utilitarian ways. God seeks nothing that is solely for the aggrandizement of God. God is not capricious, nor can God be manipulated. God loves the divine self in ways that are simultaneously beneficial to the cosmos. Moreover, that God's goodness leads to a certain goodness of our own speaks of a God who stirs the world toward greater forms of enjoyment in ways that better define the common good. God's desire is truly the kernel of love that compels the world to love and thus enjoy itself, the creatures to love one another and God with a purpose, for the well-being of all.

Yet without the intended correctives that a view that favors reciprocity seeks to pose, we remain bound to the same traditional concept in which the divine circular motion, even if dancelike, lacks something of the other within itself—hence the aspect of "sameness" that hampers Aquinas's promising view on divine enjoyment. Even the far-reaching theological concept of perichoresis will sound more like the traditional view of the God of love whose love is bound to the self. The divine enjoyment comes full circle. Therefore, without a modified vision of participation at the point of the divine rest or Sabbath—God receiving something from the cosmos—the divine enjoyment, even if based on the circular motion or perichoretic dance of the bond of love, implicitly espouses a form of self-concupiscence. Because it remains trapped within the notion of likeness to God, even when unwilling to do so, it champions the very thing Aquinas argued against. The fullness of God ends up not leaving enough room for another with whom to enjoy the divine self. Therefore, the circle of perfection is meant to be porously open, so that we can begin to understand the intellective appetite as passionate. In so doing we may further challenge the androcentric view that is upheld by Aquinas (not surprisingly, given his historical context), according to which the passive principles in the human relations, even intercourse, are represented by the female gender.[232]

Permeability: The Open Wounds of the Lovers' Flesh

Thou art so good a Lover!

—ST. TERESA OF AVILA[1]

God does not only reveal himself through love and as love; he also reveals himself through the means, the figures, the moments, the acts, and the stages of love, the one and only love, that which we also practice. He plays the lover, like us . . . God practices the logic of the erotic reduction as we do, with us, according to the same rite and following the same rhythm as us, to the point where we can even ask ourselves if we do not learn it from him, and no one else. God loves in the same way as we do.
Except for an infinite difference . . .
. . . God surpasses us as the best lover.

—JEAN-LUC MARION[2]

"Come, my lover," says the Song of Songs, the biblical book that since antiquity has permitted its readers to evoke God as a lover. The vivid imagery of the lover God that it offers continues to be an invitation to explore the meaning of divine love in contemporary contexts. Moreover, the invitation is for an intimate nearness, the arousal of the lovers "under the tree" (Songs 8:5), perhaps of an intimate communion between God and the created order. New dimensions of divine intimacy become more self-evident, for in the embrace, lovers interpenetrate one another. New theological insights into the meaning of the divine ecstasy that theologians such as Denys the Areopagite and St. Thomas Aquinas explored can likewise come to the fore. If the statement "God is love" (1 John 4:8) can speak of joy admixed with pain, and even with desire or yearning, then could one say that this God is *passionate*, one who loves according to the flesh, that is, permeably? A God who responds to the agonies of the lover could by the same logic of relation also be viewed as responding to the advances of the lover to come and be intimate at some "way-

86

side inn" (Songs 7:12, *The Message*). If the initial unfoldings of the divine enjoyment that this book offers are correct, one could say that God enjoys the cosmos in loving the cosmos, that is, in giving and receiving the pain and the enjoyments of the cosmos. The question, of course, is how?

When divine love takes the shape of eros, particularly in the Songs, it invites certain positive assumptions concerning how mutually sharable the divine-cosmic enjoyments can be. The flesh comes to be seen as more porous once it is placed beyond the confines of the hermetic boundary or untraversable distance that even promising models in postmodern discourse can substantiate. In this chapter, therefore, I bring together various postmodern perspectives—the primary voices being those of Jean-Luc Marion and Luce Irigaray—and turn them on, primarily, the commentary of St. Teresa of Avila on the Songs to highlight the importance of the erotic dimension in the model of the passionate God that I espouse. Constructions of love that have become de-eroticized[3] regain their sensuous passion. And the divine wound, which began to emerge at the end of the first chapter, becomes a generating source of multiple enjoyments in this one, implicitly maintaining close ties with the notion of pathos as suffering and enjoyment, without remaining confined to categories of love such as agape.

The figure of the beloved lover God, by assuming these erotic contours, can emerge as a God who loves according to the flesh (pathos): a God who simultaneously can be self- and hetero-affected by, capable of intermingling with, and porous to that which is distinct and different from God. This chapter ascertains that God, in freely giving the divine self to another, simultaneously welcomes something that is truly other than God into the divine self. A more distinct argument on divine passionate enjoyment arises when I challenge not only the apathetic God of classical theism but also the proximate lover who remains safely near the created order but never mixed with it. Through intimate love, God is *in* the cosmos, enfleshing the divine self as well as delighting in a mutual enjoyment with the cosmos, which also interpenetrates and transforms God.

The Words Made Flesh

Poetic language such as that used by some mystics is quite iconoclastic, particularly as it has been appropriated by postmodern thinkers, who explicitly or implicitly make use of the via negativa to gain new insights into God.[4] That is why St. Teresa of Avila's poetic interpretations of the Canticles or Song of Songs, and her in-depth reflections, the result of a similar iconoclastic impetus, can amplify postmodern perspectives on the lover God. Nevertheless, the model of the divine lover espoused in this book is interpreted not only through a via negativa but also through what we may call a *via erotica*, a path of love, which by implication affirms the divine *flesh*. As we saw, Thomas Aquinas himself made use of the via negativa (in exploring the thought of Denys the Areopagite), which gave way to a *via eminentiae*, or path according to *excessus*, as he sought to know and even unite with God.[5] The path of excess grants access to God in a manner that deepens "the unknowing" and upholds "incomprehension" and even *infinity* without ending up with a simple or pure apophasis, as Jean-Luc Marion explains.[6] It is a step that allows for what I consider to be an excessive form of embodiment or incarnating silhouette of God to show forth. For example, Marion's superlative analogical affirmation of God as "the best lover" would simultaneously abstain from falling into mastery on the part of the beholder of God's beauty, even as one ascribes to God the attributes of a lover.[7]

A via erotica as imagined here is thus akin to Aquinas's poetic language, but only partly. Its analogical impulse would equally need to free the love of God from the bounds of self-idolatry. Otherwise it would pose a contradiction, since the pleasures of the lover of God cannot be peripheral to God's enjoyments. One would also need to wrest eros away from connotations of possession and appropriation that thinkers such as Nygren have invoked.[8] Outside the Song of Songs and mystical theologies, for the most part eros has been pinned against an erotic view of God, for God, who needs nothing (because God already owns everything), loves only as a friend, or as one who gives. Though the model discussed thus far has avoided such trivial distinctions between eros and agape, unless another paradigm is provided, one that by embracing the flesh sufficiently illumines the divine erotic dimension, the loving nature of God will continue to appear lopsided.

Even if one were to ascribe an erotic side to God, when placed in the metaphysical category of absolute self-subsistence or sufficiency, as indicated with regard to the concept of the happy idiot (briefly alluded to in the last chapter), God would be the kind of lover who is the only active partner in the relationship. In Aristotle there is a *jouissance* of a Supreme Being that Aquinas partly grafts onto his understanding of the God of love. Lacan, who is highly critical of this marriage with Greek thought, quips: "We ended up in Christianity by inventing a God such that it is he who comes!"[9] He refers to this paradox as the law of the phallic pleasure in the *Nicomachean Ethics*. It conflates the divine love with the other's own self-enjoyment, thus denying God the enjoyment of the other.[10] The Supreme Being of Aristotle, the unmoved mover from which all originates, he avers, has usurped "the opaque place of the *jouissance* of the Other—that Other which, if she existed, the woman might be."[11] In this Aristotle is compared with Freud, for whom "the pleasure principle is brought on only by excitation, this excitation provoking movement in order to get away from it."[12] The divine enjoyment excites the lover, yet does not go beyond its own pleasure, and thus cannot truly motivate the *jouissance* of another. Lacan asks further, "And why not interpret one face of the Other, the God face, as supported by feminine *jouissance*?"[13]

The poetic language found in the works of some mystics can resurrect the divine enjoyment from this Aquinan crypt of *ipsum esse per se subsistens*, not only without erecting an idol but also without erasing God's jouissant body of flesh, as well as that of the lovers, the multiplicity of cosmic life. Once again, this erotic path becomes alive when brought within the fold of postmodern thought, which to some extent engages the words of mystics such as those of St. Teresa of Avila, herself an avid reader of the Songs.

VIA EROTICA

The poetic prose of St. Teresa, as if taking a via erotica, evinces another living being whose pleasure God desires to enjoy in a permeable manner. Like some of her predecessors, this sixteenth-century Spanish Carmelite saw in the verses of the Songs of the divine troubadour the lyrics of a lover's delight. Longings, enticements, woos, passionate musings, all more evident in the words of St. Teresa than in those of previous male interpreters, hint at a lovers' dialogue. Calculating the precise starting and ending points of this erotic dialogue, that is, ascertaining who commences and who concludes it, however, can prove challenging. As with Aquinas's contemplative impulses, a good opening into it is the author's passionate prayers. Teresa prayerfully begs:

> So, my Lord, I ask Thee for nothing else in this life but that Thou shouldst "kiss me with a kiss of Thy mouth"; and let this be in such a way, Lord of my life, that even if I should desire to withdraw from this friendship and union, my will may ever be so subject to Thine that I shall be unable to leave Thee. May nothing hinder me from being able to say, O my God and my glory, that "Thy breasts are better and more delectable than wine"![14]

Seductively, she adds,

> Let us learn from this blessed soul, which has drawn near to this Divine mouth and been nourished from these heavenly breasts, so that, if the Lord grants us some day to attain to so great a favor, we may know how to behave and what to say. Her words are: "I sat down under the shadow of Him Whom I had desired, and His fruit is sweet to my palate. The King brought me into the cellar of wine and set in order charity in me." She says: "I sat down under the shadow of Him Whom I had desired."[15]

Undeniably, Teresa, like Thomas Aquinas, had inherited a wealth of allegorical interpretations in which this poetic use of language, based on the Songs, figures God as the subject-object of delectable pleasures. Already in the commentary work of William of Saint-Thierry, the cellar of wine (which becomes the wound in St. Teresa's imagery) is described as the site where a "torrent of delight" brings love "to a boil," overflows it "with elation," as God "delights in its object."[16] There "love and desire are nourished."[17] Likewise, as St. Teresa renders them in relation to the divine lover, body metaphors of breasts, lips, and bodily senses had featured prominently in earlier works of other Christian thinkers. For instance, in Origen, the Bridegroom (Christ) has anointed his breasts with splendid ointments and, thus nicely perfumed, seductively approaches the Bride (the Church), to whom the Father has sent him. The odor of his breasts moves the Bride to prayer, to desire to know the teachings of her Bridegroom. As the Bridegroom touches her, he anoints her, so that she may become of good odor.[18] Her entire body—"*thy neck, thine eyes, thy cheeks, thy hands, thy body,* thy shoulders, thy feet!"—is scented with the ointments of the beloved.[19]

Even so, the embodied sensuality characteristic of the Songs that St. Teresa so readily embraces must have posed some difficulties to her predecessors, for in many of them the divine pleasure fits more conventional views of intellectual passion, as previously intimated. In Origen, whereas the king's chamber contains "an incalculable multitude of riches," in which she rightly rejoices, the chamber is the mind of God, where the divine hidden treasures of wisdom and knowledge are stored.[20] This royal chamber, for both Gregory of Nyssa and Gregory the Great, is also where the divine mysteries or hidden things of God are stored.[21] The cellar of wine is the house of God, which is the divine wisdom, says William of Saint-Thierry. The hidden wisdom of God draws the mind via its illuminating grace and narrows the distance from this heavenly realm, "the Holy of Holies, solely by an interposed veil, that of a mortal body."[22] The flesh and its passions become eclipsed by, if not elided with, the divine wisdom and intellect. Freed from all bodily passion, in the end the divine pleasures remain insular and unaffected by the delight of another who also loves.

In a positive sense, the body metaphors based on the Songs point to an excess of meaning embedded in the scriptural passages themselves, which is also a prominent aspect of poetic prose that invokes a via erotica. In them there is a residue that stores through concealment fuller expressions of divine love incarnate. It is as if having endured negation, the breasts, lips, and mouth become icons of what is also yet to take on flesh even in its embodiment, appearing as a silhouette. As Gregory the Great argues, "because the bridegroom has wanted to make his wisdom known by way of the flesh, the bridegroom causes it to be concealed as it were in breasts of flesh."[23] That which is promised, fuller expressions of the lovers' delight, remains as its excess. As in Honorius of Autun, in longing the spouse becomes incarnate even as it is absent.[24]

Ironically, this would mean that the figure of the Shulamite is more fitting to their image of divine embodied passion, but with a caveat.[25] As Richard Kearney points out, "the passion of burning love and of endless waiting"[26] is mostly presented in the figure of one who seeks whom her soul loves (Songs 1:7). He argues, "It is the Shulamite who takes most of the initiative and does most of the talking in the Song of Songs."[27] The lover-king responds to her by restating her words, and so singing her song "from first to last." Contrary to those, like Origen, for whom longing is solely reserved for that something or someone other than the divine figure, in his case, the Church's,[28] God is transfigured into she who seeks her beloved, who desires beyond all desire. Consequently, transfiguration in the flesh, rather than a negation, deficiency, or lack, refers to the abundance (no end in sight) of her affirmation, the divine "Yes!" already present in her yearning, the incarnational love of God that crosses over,[29] as will be shown, a representation more akin to St. Teresa's views.

So, despite the many limitations apparently present in the various interpretations above, what endured was an imagery that welcomed an element of impropriety with which to promisingly set free conventional models. A fleshlike desire can be viewed as a primary impulse. For instance, what goads Bernard of Clairvaux is not reason, wisdom, or knowledge but desire. For him, this love is too bold. He admits, "Modesty, to be sure, issues its protest, but love overpowers it."[30] This love is reckless, unable to wait for judgment to be given. Being utterly immoderate and incapable of being constrained by modesty "or subjugated by reason," he begs, entreats, pleads, as St. Teresa does: "Let him kiss me with the kisses of his mouth!"[31]

Nevertheless, the uniqueness of St. Teresa's imagery of divine love cannot be overlooked, for the impropriety of God's love also lies in that it is mutually excessive. Coming close to the transfiguration that Kearney describes, it pushes the poetic language beyond earlier allegorical allusions. Through her use of the erotic language of seduction to represent the embodiment of love of both partners, she also verbalizes how the divine lover may not only desire but also enjoy her pleasures. For why not assume a response on the part of both lovers? Should we not be aware that in the prayers and answers to prayers lie the very invitations that both lovers beckon each other to love with incandescent passion, and even to come, or *jouir*? In her prayers, a lovers' dialogue is more vividly present. She prayerfully requests:

> O soul beloved of God! Trouble not yourself; for, when His Majesty brings you here and speaks to you as delectably as He speaks to the Bride in the *Songs*,— using many such phrases (as I have said) as "Thou are all fair, O my love," to show the pleasure which He takes in her—it is supposed that at such a time He will not allow you to displease Him; rather He will give you what you cannot yourself provide so that He may take the greater pleasure in you.[32]

The significance of her prayer lies in that she not only woos God, so that God takes delight in her, she also expects a response from her divine lover in relation to her pleasures. She turns to the lover again, longing once more to hear the seducing words of her divine lover, which in return tend to draw her even deeper into an erotic dialogue like that of lovers. The dialogue also carries tones of a mutual surrender, a surrender that, like the notion of ecstasy, is not bound to limits of the self. She adds:

> He sees that the Bride is lost to herself and enraptured for love of Him, and that the very strength of love has taken from her the very power of understanding, so that she may love Him the more. Yet, it is impossible that he should allow this, and His Majesty is neither accustomed, nor able, to fail to give Himself to one who gives Herself to him wholly.[33]

As Denys Turner explains, particularly in the work of St. Teresa, erotic love appears to be a universal and acceptable manner to express one's relationship with God.[34] She immodestly says, "Let the Lord kiss me with the kiss of his mouth, for thy breasts are better than wine" (Songs 1:1).[35] His question thus is fitting. "Why is the Incarnation a 'kiss of his mouth'?" Because the lovers can be described as unashamedly delighting "in each other's bodies—face, hair, breasts, eyes, limbs—the root image of the mutual pleasure of God and the soul in each other's presence."[36] In St. Teresa's appropriation of the Songs, God is drawn or seduced by the beauty of the lover, seeking to delight in the flesh of this lover. Likewise, the divine lover transgresses, seduces her, drawing her close so that she can taste the divine pleasures. As Phyllis Trible affirms, the expression "I belong to my lover, and his desire is for me" (7:10, NRSV) reflects the role of mutuality that desire plays in the Songs.[37] Both parties utter mutually gentle, sweet, and delectable words to woo the other, to delight in the other. The lovers *give* of themselves, as they are enraptured by one another. These descriptions, while inclusive of a love among friends (*philadelphus*), also go beyond it. For Turner, "These are the tones distinctively of *eros*."[38]

WOUNDING GOD'S BEING

Imaging God as a beloved lover, one who is also wooed by the words of the lover in ways that immodestly taste of the other's passions, further offsets views of God bound to models of an enclosed circularity as particularized in the concept of absolute self-subsistence. It challenges a metaphysics of love that holds God captive to "the empire of being" (the subject as absolutely self-sufficient), as Jean-Luc Marion argues.[39] The divine lover no longer can be viewed as one who is "subsistent being, permanently present, accorded value (of use and/or exchange) and finality (useful, without end, etc.), produced or destroyed by efficiency and calculation, shut in by the stranglehold of its causes."[40] Eros challenges such an interpretation by showing how as the language of "appetite" and "yearning" invokes not only the image of another whom God loves but also the transgression itself of God's love in partaking of the pleasure of another.

The lover is willing to love in advance, to risk the self in longing for another to love in return. Quite poignantly, as Marion explains, the lover is one who "can love, and whom one can love, and believes that someone must love him [or her]."[41] Hartshorne, following a more process logic, explains it thus: "Merely being known or being-loved is nothing to a thing; but knowing that one is known and loved—that may be a great deal."[42] In other words, the lover loves but also expects to be loved, to be in the place of the beloved, to be one who is loved. Loving has thus embedded in it the anticipation of being loved in return by someone or something "other than myself."[43] This notion of anticipation means that as lover, God would be affected by an "elsewhere" that assures God of being a lover. So God, rather than being "a presence subsisting in itself," receives assurance from something other than God of being indeed a lover.[44] The lover becomes a lover through the act of loving, which assures the lover of "making love," writes Marion. This is because love can only be shared when there are at least two lovers loving one another. In anticipating someone other than the self, the divine lover breaks free from the "narcissistic mirror." To anticipate love is "to renounce the status of the autarkic *ego*."[45]

The dialogue suggests an inexhaustibility of pleasure, a roundabout conversation that *infinitizes* the lovers. Vestiges of previous descriptions of desire or yearning more fully unfold here, for this desire is also excessive in that it is mutually shared. Through being loved, one's desire is increased. The statement "I love you" for Marion initiates an unending or inexhaustible dialogue of *jouissance* or pleasure. Even when the statement of love is affirmed in the now (and many times after a first time) by the one hearing the statement, there is a dissatisfaction, a moment of apophasis or withdrawal that leads to a moment of excellence or excess. The repetition of *jouissance* cannot exhaust it. To say "I love you" is also to ask, "Do you love me?" It invites the lover to "Come!"[46] No matter how many times the lovers say to each other "Here I am!" (commonly known as "I love you"), they turn around and say "Again!"[47] The lovers say to each other "now," "come," and "again." Jesus's question, "Peter, do you love me?" (John 21:15–17), exemplifies this erotic dialogue between God and humans, an act of unquenchable communion.[48] As Marion states, "Love enjoys eternity from the instant that it enjoys itself."[49] Between the instant when there is an anticipated enjoyment and the moment when one says "Again!" there is eternity.

In taking further Marion's model of a lover who anticipates another lover, and that infinitizes each, this concept of eros partly cancels out cause and absolute self-subsistence because it means self-abandonment. St. Teresa of Avila speaks of how she would give of herself, and how it would be impossible for God to allow, or be used to, and even fail to give the divine self to those who give of themselves to God wholly.[50] Rather than a self-sufficient being, God is "the *being-abandoned* [*l'étant-abandonné*]" that receives the divine self in that abandonment, says Marion.[51] This mutual *ecstatic abandonment* that makes room for the pleasure of another also compares to the metaphor of "the wound" used by St. Teresa. For her, quite "delectable" is God's "loving" pain concomitant on yearning, for it stems from the wound of Godself—divine longing.[52] Resembling the language of sadomasochism, the wounding of self-abandonment can entail a denial, if temporary, of pleasure that according to Karmen MacKendrick increases desire.[53] Each incarnation of "I love *you*" accompanies a voluptuous self-denial, a borderline cruelty that compliantly wounds the self (*ascesis*).[54] Self-abandonment may cause pain alongside pleasure, "the subject's paradoxical move against its own limits,"[55] which for MacKendrick increases pleasure by wanting more than the self, hence denying the self any sense of absolute self-sufficiency. The self becomes open to an infinite outside, much like the divine *zimzum* in Jewish kabbalistic views.

The roundabout of mutual pleasure of self-abandonment is evident in how St. Teresa of Avila, in seeking to be ravished by God, who is her lover,[56] succeeds in her seduction time and again. "Let him kiss me with the kiss of His mouth" (*con el beso de su boca*) is the prayer of desire of the soul on fire for her lover, the soul dying of love for God.[57] God too expresses a yearning for such an intimate relationship. "I have loved my Beloved," the divine lover responds, something she interprets as God desiring to be intimate with her.[58] In ecstasy, the divine lover draws near to her. And she, being drawn to that sacred side of God, draws near her lover as well.[59] Within the divine wound the encounter of sharable pleasures between the lovers takes place. The place where she sits is like a cellar of wine, under the shadow of the one whom she desires.[60]

In lieu of this poetic prose the divine passionate overtures begin to look like being wounded by another lover. As this *via erotica* shows, God longs to respond to her seducing words, gain pleasure from her pleasure, in a self-abandoning and infinitizing way. How else could one say that God is a good lover if there were no other whose pleasure could be said to add to the divine enjoyment?

A UNIQUE SONG

Eros is the desire to make space for another to enjoy her own *jouissance* and for another to "speak" of her own pleasures in her own poetic language ("lets be," in the sense of letting other forms of enjoyment become actualized), with an excess that follows a *via erotica* in which meaning cannot be confined; it is excessive. Regarding this point, I agree with Marion: it challenges the metaphysical concepts that confine the divine enjoyment to a system that operates under universal categories bound to a singular form of reasoning. Such concepts make God and the cosmos intelligible, interpretable, and consequently replaceable by something else, and in the case of God, by the male phallus. In short, the lovers' ecstasy opens up a space that ascribes pleasure or *jouissance*, a place beyond the confines of phallocentrism in that the pleasure of another cannot be fully comprehended.

At this juncture, St. Teresa of Avila is once again a significant dialogue partner, since for her the divine-human passionate union points to an enjoyment that is almost incomprehensible (uncontainable). For her, the Godhead is like a cloud of fire that leaves her immobile and even incapable of thinking, almost stupefied. As St. Teresa puts it, the soul "seems to be beside itself and in a kind of Divine intoxication, knowing not what it is desiring or saying or asking for."[61] The erotic union is "beyond the grasp of understanding,"[62] one in which the will can be awake but only to love more, to be a lover.[63]

An inability to speak coherently alongside a quasi-nonrational contemplation indeed characterizes the encounter with transcendence. That which is without limit cannot be limited within speech. For Gregory of Nyssa, "human speech finds it impossible to express that reality which transcends all thought and every concept." Even the attempt to express this divine reality, "to circumscribe the infinite in speech," could be offensive of God. God is beyond all *proper* description. When one seeks the incomprehensible, when one gives up the finite mode of comprehension, then the Beloved can be found, and brought into one's chamber, where God indwells.[64] For William of Saint-Thierry, more specifically, who described it as being "content with anything save the enjoyment of God and in God,"[65] this desire is as if partaking of a feast and an overabundance of pleasure, a state in which there is no thinking on thinking.

With a similar postmodern iconoclastic impulse, by turning this concept in the direction of St. Teresa in her song for God, and by comparing it to female *jouissance*, incoherence resembles a Levinasian *voluptuosity* that takes divine *wonder* or the element of the unexpected into account.[66] At the point of each satisfaction, as if with an unending reserve of meaning, more and new expressions of desire are born. Accordingly, there would be an encounter with the pleasure of another not foreknown and experienced in its simplicity by God, a difficulty that one encounters in the Aquinan model already hinted at in the previous chapter. The divine lover, in being both lover and beloved, is capable of wonder, of being surprised by the other lover, who is an active partner in its distinct manner. Without the element of the unexpected, how bored would God be?

In contemplating the sculpture of St. Teresa of Avila by Giovanni Lorenzo, Lacan arrived at similar conclusions. Teresa's ecstasy is beyond comprehension. He argues, "you only have to go and look at Bernini's statue in Rome to understand immediately that she's coming, there is no doubt about it. And what is her *jouissance*, her coming, from?"[67] In Bernini's famously ambiguous sculpture *The Ecstasy of St. Teresa*, she is portrayed as fainting with love. With her face lightly tilted to the back, her lips partly open, and her left breast uncovered, she seductively appears to be moaning as a result of the penetrating burning arrow of the angel.

Nevertheless, for Lacan,[68] while her lips are partly open, she remains silent about her *jouissance*. She lacks the words to express her pleasure. This physical gesture means that she is *not all, not whole*; that is, her *jouissance* would not fall within the bounds of the enjoyment of the One, the *signifier,* or what we could regard as the divine mirror of absolute self-subsistence. She too *comes.* In a positive manner, she cannot describe it, since her enjoyment is not a function of the concepts of enjoyment of the One, "the good old God of all times." It is beyond it. Lacan argues, "There is a *jouissance* proper to her, to this 'her' which does not exist and which signifies nothing."[69] Sadly, while her *jouissance* is properly hers, she herself may know nothing of it, "except that she experiences it—that much she does know."[70]

In the end, consequently, the Lacanian model, even if containing an element of wonder, confuses excess for lack, and hence does not accommodate the enjoyment of another affecting God in that there is no hearing of her speaking of her *jouissance.*[71] Through silence, her pleasure, as much as the cosmic enjoyments, would be reduced to that of the phallus or the circularity of an enclosed divine love. Enjoyment if silent is "a pleasure without pleasure," Luce Irigaray avers.[72] She, the cosmos, the silent partner, remains in many ways frigid with a pleasure of "silent" ignorance. For her, "'Saying' nothing of this pleasure after all, thus not enjoying it," is how she can sustain "the dual role of the impossible and the forbidden."[73] Elizabeth Grosz notes that Irigaray is critical of Lacan's understanding of St. Teresa because it simply "repositions women within the strictures of men's forms of self-worship, guaranteed by a God built in their own image."[74] It reifies the view that the female lover, not unlike the classical models of the cosmos, is merely a recipient of love, and not an active partner in the intimate relationship. Her love is an effect of *his* love, something done to her that she quietly and hysterically or orgasmically accepts.

Beyond Bernini's sculpture lies another St. Teresa of Avila, another form of *jouissance* unlike the *not all* and *not whole* that Lacan sought to describe in order to challenge the symbolic realm of the phallus. St. Teresa does speak of an excess of pleasure, even if incoherently, and compares her *jouissance* to a wound. Enduring the path of negation, the words that could be imagined giving rise to Bernini's figure are: "What greater blessing can I wish for? I cannot say; I know that this distress seems to penetrate to its very bowels; and that, when He that was wounded draws out the arrow, the bowels seem to come with it, so deeply does it feel this love."[75] The arrow is of fire, deeply wounding the "soul's most intimate depths."[76] It is quite paradoxical that, in the words of Irigaray, "the dart which, while piercing through her body, will with the same stroke tear out her entrails."[77] Her ecstasy comes in the form of a "delectable pain" and a "loving pain,"[78] a great pain,[79] and as an interior burning.[80] Pain and pleasure joining as one imply vulnerability in that the arrow penetrates and makes room for the other to join in the delight. God as well becomes wounded by the lover. Teresa: "Love is an arrow shot by the will, and flying with all the force of which the will is capable, freed from all earthly things and directed toward God alone, so that it must actually strike His Majesty. Once it has pierced God Himself, Who is love, it rebounds, after having won immense benefits."[81] The immensity of their mutual wounding exceeds meaning rather than lacking meaning; hence its incoherence.

St. Teresa may have borrowed from Gregory of Nyssa the concept of a mortal wound caused by the arrow of love, which is of the divine self and the desire (eros) that intensifies her yearnings.[82] She may have also inherited the language from St. Thomas Aquinas himself, who had described the lovers as entering into or penetrating each other "so that nothing remains not united to the lover, just as a form reaches the innermost recesses of that which informs it and vice versa."[83] According to Aquinas, this is one of the reasons why love "wounds," why it "is called 'piercing.'" Conversely, since the lover seeks transformation, love itself entails separation from oneself, from the bounds that contain the self, its limits. Love is like an ecstatic moving toward another lover that simultaneously makes room and wounds the self through penetration and piercing. Because of the delectability of this pain, the lovers, while mutually upholding that which is unique to each, expand each other's limits.

Subsequently, St. Teresa's desires are inexplicable as expressed partly because they exceed the bounds of phallic logic, in several ways. First, the orders of logic, by mixing joy with pain, turn upside down categories, and thus produce a surplus of incoherence in the exchange between two seemingly oppositional concepts. This interplay between two principles resembles but is not the same as some of the most recent revisions of the metaphor of sadomasochism.[84] The interplay between pain and pleasure facilitates the emancipation of "rigid dyads," such as pain and joy, that authors such as Althaus-Reid regard as necessary in erotic discourse.[85] This alternative to the binary methodology that has been in motion since the first chapter transgressively dislodges the *"logos spermatikos* of theology" by breaking free from "the binary pair in conceptual opposition," in Althaus-Reid's words.[86] "Pain" and "joy," even "death" and "life," change locations to the point that coherent descriptions of pleasure do not suffice.

Second, in St. Teresa's own flesh resides a surplus, which, like God's pleasures and desires, spills over the strictures of propriety—pure ecstasy! A Levinasian *voluptuosity* would again partly capture the meaning of the latter.[87] Levinas is correct: at each point of nudity, profanation, or immodesty there is no loss of its mystery in the discovery,[88] for it "precedes the artist's form."[89] The impropriety of her desires and pleasures is *non*sense in that it overflows preset categories, however, not because of the silence he posits.[90] As Irigaray would say, St. Teresa's *cryptic* words point to "a logic that challenges mastery," but not to a crypt to which she must remain confined.[91] Pleasure beyond the phallus, that is, beyond the symbolic and representational, would accord female *jouissance* a place of women's own, in the site of the "excess of the one (organ) demanded from women's bodies to render them definable in men's terms."[92] But it does so without erasing the flesh of her enjoyments. Any singular flesh or incarnated body becomes apparent in a painful ecstasy.

"In her own words" means, therefore, that she is not excluded from the discourse on divine enjoyment, and thus is not a prisoner of the *not all* that has defined her own *jouissance*.[93] It grants her the possibility of having pleasure, of speaking for herself,[94] and thus of disrupting the "complete *ring around*" of the divine attributes that inseparably become "the constituents" of the divine subject as self-same,[95] a "circularity that knows no end except the return, over and over again, upon itself/himself."[96] So marvelously solitary would be the pleasure of God if she would remained closed off and "buried in its crypt."[97] For this reason, by challenging the phallocentric views that have prevailed regarding a divine enjoyment confined to "absolute autarchy,"[98] her desires, pleasures, and words disturb "the whole." She who also enjoys herself in her own unique manner disrupts its organizing power and hierarchical logic with her desires and pleasures while causing wonderment. Hence her *song* does say something about another ecstasy. She describes a delectable and loving pain, and a wound that grants her a location, a birth of self-pleasure being shared *"Outside of all self-as-same,"* in Irigary's words.[99]

Therefore, if she did not sing her own song, the narcissistic pleasure set by the "phallic circulation" would deny both their pleasures. God alone would be enough to love Godself, as Marion points out.[100] And in the end, God would be like the good old God, the only one who comes, which Lacan's critique sought to iconoclastically demolish.

THE JOUISSANT FLESH

The via erotica grants flesh to words; words become flesh. For Julia Kristeva there can be no erotic *ecstasy* without *incarnation*. In the amorous dialogue, the lover welcomes another into her "loving swoon," love thus incarnating itself, becoming a body, a space of love.[101] This incarnational potentiality, argues Kristeva, locates God as lover not only metaphorically but also bodily. Without this enfleshment of love, as Irigaray points out (in response to Gilles Deleuze's use of the trope), what is left is a "body without organs," lacking pleasure and its own *topos*, its own point of reference.[102] In the sense of poetic language, in the struggle between appropriation and disappropriation of her ("she" being a lover who, like Teresa of Avila, enjoys herself), the divine enjoyments gain their flesh (even if not at the expense of the other). This topography, fleshly and beyond the divine "mind," needs to be reasserted in a new light. Without an embodied flesh, eroticism collapses into solipsism. Moreover, it contradicts the very definition of *jouissance*, incarnation even if as a silhouette, which speaks of loving according to the body's flesh.

It has been indicated that loving according to the flesh means that the lovers, in making room for one another in the flesh (through the wound), suffer pain. In St. Thomas Aquinas and other mystics such as St. Teresa, pain grants a regenerating spatiality that expands the lovers beyond themselves without dislocating their flesh. Pain holds a dual memory of other and self, of death and life, of multiple rebirths of desire and pleasure the end of which is not in sight—all by means of enfleshment. Pain establishes an expansive limit, the flesh itself. The limits, while preventing fusion (more fitting among those whose size and quality do not far exceed one of the lovers, and do not absorb either to infinity),[103] both locate the lovers and extend their flesh beyond themselves. It's a death worth living for, to mutually wound each other, with a trace of touch of self on the lover's flesh.

Once again, this concept appears quite evident, metaphorically speaking, in the language of sadomasochism. The wounding limits provide the spacing for the becoming of lovers through a "delectable pain," for the divine enjoyment, as much as hers, suffers the painful process of decentering itself.[104] The divine enjoyment shatters its own mirror (perhaps resembling the vulnerable act of wounding one's ego) and lets her gain her own flesh, so that she willingly withdraws and lets herself be expanded once again, wounded again—an excess. This bond of pain between divinity and the human body serves to enflesh the intensity of the mystery of love, for more wounding remains in sight. For St. Teresa, "just as the soul is about to become enkindled, the spark dies, and leaves the soul yearning once again to suffer that loving pain of which it is the cause."[105] Therefore, aspects of pleasure such as *yearning*, alluded to earlier, inevitably cause pain as the lovers actively refuse *teleology*.

This painful death is like life! A playful reversal ensues when even the marks of death can make the body of flesh visible, can grant it life. It produces a surplus of the flesh through which resurrections can carry the marks of the wounded flesh, Virginia Burrus explains. These reversals become what Burrus considers "a communion of painful pleasure, and extravagance of love, an 'economy of joy.'"[106] In the words of St. Teresa, the divine love appears to be "so excessive that it consumes the soul till there appears not to be enough of it left to live."[107] And "Blessed is the death that brings with it such a life!"[108] Death and life define the wounding process, for the wound is the "glorious slit where she curls as if in her nest, where she rests as if she had found her home—and He is also in her," says Irigaray.[109] There, in that wholly embodied site of eros—also of legs, lips, breasts, and her belly—the mystic discovers a divine passion that "neither can nor will translate."[110] Her own deathly *jouissance*!

In her death, there is life in the returning to herself. The erotic wound is where the "cloud of the Godhead" engulfs her,[111] and the divine breasts nourish her. She is in the arms of the beloved, looking at the beloved as the beloved looks at her.[112] She is in ecstasy. It is like a feast![113] She exclaims, "Thy breasts are better than wine" (Songs 1:1).[114] In union with the divine lover, she experiences all the "joys," "swoons," "mortal agonies" or deaths, "afflictions," and "delights," as described in the Songs.[115] Enkindled with the divine fire, she says, "Thou art so good a Lover!"[116] "So good a lover" for St. Teresa would be the divine companion who "never tires of praising her and encouraging her (auto)eroticism that has so miraculously been rediscovered," Irigary writes.[117] In this to-and-fro movement is a return to the self, an autoeroticism not unrelated to hetero-eroticism, each lover temporarily withdrawing so that the other lover may gain her own flesh.

God's wound makes things divine, that is, enjoy themselves, their own flesh, by means of withdrawal and expansion of limits.[118] The Word was made flesh "in this way" so that she could become God in her *jouissance*, says Irigaray.[119] There is an affirmation of the lover as lover when in climactic enjoyment the self is able to return to her self as she is drawn outside herself. If there is no return to the self, there is a rejection of her own flesh, no self-love. She would always be in exile from her own completeness.[120] There can be no enjoyment of the flesh but only on the other side of its limits. Similarly, that God returns to the divine self means that God loves the divine self, and enjoys the divine self, but as lover, through a space that is a painful opening before another lover, for whom God yearns, or is in ecstasy.

In affirming her flesh, the flesh of God is therefore also affirmed. It is a delectable pain for God to move beyond the divine limits (without fully abandoning the self), to receive enjoyment also from the enjoyment of the other, or as the other lover enjoys God in her enjoyment. An element of embodied vulnerability in the divine ecstasy or self-abandonment emerges: God receives the divine flesh by way of the other's flesh. God too gains God's divine flesh, and in a sense God's own limits when in relationship with what is other than the divine self. The divine lover incarnates, suffers the limits of the flesh, and thus the possibility of being affected or feeling another than itself, of receiving its flesh.[121] Without flesh there cannot be love, for love means affect (being affected by another), and without flesh there is no capacity to be affected. For Marion, "flesh allows itself to be affected without end by the things of the world."[122] This mode of loving according to the flesh is divine. "God plays the lover like us—passing through," Marion argues, "the flesh and the enjoyment of communion."[123] Through God being a lover, that is, in the flesh, as Irigaray argues, God can truly "savor the happiness of others."[124] So God receives God's own flesh in mutual enjoyment along with the becoming of the flesh of another. Otherwise, God would be an empty and dark well of eternity, a void born in the eternal mirror that has no flesh to enjoy.[125]

Without reference to an embodied *jouissance*, God too would become "disinvested of worldly predicates, and of all predication."[126] Does not the event of incarnation demonstrate what we can say about God and the divine love in the sense of ecstasy? In her return to her own flesh, her pleasure is an opening to speak about God, to know God, in her own becoming divine.[127] To say something about the lover is an element of the erotic language. That is, in the agreement with her own enjoyment there is no identification with or conflation of female *jouissance* and God's. Both go beyond the constraints of the "phallic circularity" in their affirmation of wonder. According to Morny Joy, there in that wound a "mutual illumination occurs, in which both God and woman in their absence or presence reaffirm the other in their fullness/nothingness."[128] There in that space, writes Cristina Mazzoni, "the two 'mysteries' of woman's *jouissance* and the ineffability of God" are not conflated.[129]

May we then infer that in feminist theology, to say that God loves in erotic ways, that is, beyond the "phallic circularity," means that God loves according to the wounding limits of the flesh? St. Teresa's poetic prose expresses exactly this concept by placing in the discourse a "body" of flesh that is delectably wounded. The whole bodily being of both lover and beloved reverberates at the touch of their incomparable loving caress, their union, and blissful loving encounter.[130] That the encounter leads to excess, and thus to a realm beyond the mind,[131] does not imply that there is no body. The element of wonder is there, but, as Turner might argue, it is not according to lack (Lacan's *not all, not whole*).[132] The via negativa would be akin to a "denial in the sense of superabundance,"[133] in this case of the flesh. Such is also the third path of Aquinas toward knowing God, an excess that can imply a form of embodiment that cannot be contained or mastered— another expression of the poetic path that expands the limits of logic. The other, feeling itself feeling, comes in the shape of enjoyment becoming enfleshed to the point of becoming visible and even felt corporeally.

With the flesh as starting point, the shift is from the Aristotelian thinking being to a feeling being, from the primacy of the mind to bodies gifted with sense. The lovers are therefore set free to enjoy their selves in multiple ways other than solely through the intellect or reason and morality. And as this approach grants flesh to God, God can once again be viewed as having the capacity to be affected (pathos). As it grants flesh to both lovers, they incarnate their pleasures, gain feeling and the capacity to be affected by each other's incarnation, even their pain. As Marion posits, such interpellations imply a dialogical relationship.

Perceiving God as a lover therefore challenges a model of metaphysics that describes divine love as being from itself and by itself (self-enclosed). Like the erotic dialogue in the Songs, the divine act of hearing the "words" of pleasure of someone or something other than God can imply a dialogue of mutuality that does away with the active versus passive schema. Furthermore, God is a beloved lover whose dialogue lies outside the bounds of mastery. As Irigaray highlights, outside mastery means a sight outside categorization and a speech "without a why," "without reason."[134] Such a view articulates a dialogue in difference without establishing an ontological opposition.[135] It challenges both certain metaphysical worldviews and patriarchal views that have portrayed the female, hence cosmic, lover as a silent partner. There is another who says "I love you" and immodestly pleads, "Love me!" The pleasures shared are distinct to each of the lovers. They experience wonder at the sight of the lover gaining her flesh. The slight shift in emphasis is noteworthy since it implies an embodiment akin to wonder that is partly missing from Lacan's work (not to mention from classical Christianity). Lacan's theological musings on God and on the divine relationship to another's *jouissance* are innovatively fitting. It is a unique way to provide the grounds for an analogy between the female *jouissance* and that of the cosmos, the latter having for centuries been held to be superfluous to the divine enjoyment. But Lacan's notion of female *jouissance* has been in need of further deconstruction so that it yields a more mutually reciprocal view of the divine relationship with the cosmos. That St. Teresa lacks neither in *jouissance* nor in words to express it points to another form of wonder, one that shows forth a yet more permeable flesh.

Of Flesh Saying YES!

> . . . it seems to me, something which represents feminine *jouissance* quite well, including in a movement of the sea, of going and returning, of continuous flux which seems to me to be quite close to my *jouissance* as a woman, and

completely foreign to what an economy of erection and detumescence represents. My movement, let us say of feminine *jouissance* is more maritime than scaling or descending a mountain.

Luce Irigaray[136]

With the divine erotic impulse wooing us to unique expressions of pleasure that I see implied in the conversations between God and St. Teresa of Avila, what other paradigms of divine reciprocity with the cosmos can we envision? What other imaginaries can be rekindled by the embrace of the divine lover? An important aspect yet to affirm is a *jouissance* that, like the waves of the sea, in its back-and-forth movement of continuous flux self-returns in a manner that intermingles with the other—an Irigarayan metaphor. In the climactic moment of *jouissance*, selves trespass the protective cover of each other's flesh. And as they draw back in, they become more multiple and permeably defined in terms of infinity.

IMAGING THE SONGS

One could say that St. Teresa's description of God as "such a good Lover" seems not too far distant from the view of Jean-Luc Marion that holds that God loves us "according to the same rite and following the same rhythm as us," God, "the best lover."[137] The statements are analogically metaphorical, even inclusive of the *via eminentiae* or path of excess of Aquinas that prevents mastery by pointing to infinity.[138] The God of flesh loves according to the same means, stages, rhythms, and practices as we do. The use of the terms "like us" and "as we do" clearly places the divine love in an analogical paradigm that grants God the freedom to love, and perhaps to be loved, as other lovers do and are. Moreover, in the statement "God surpasses us as the best lover" it is apparent that the divine passion is a mystery, the "moreness" of God that cannot be measured. Clearly, according to this view, which attributes mystery to the acts of love as a whole, the flesh does not stand against the mystery of the divine passion but rather magnifies it.

Yet the *via eminentiae* needs its complement, the permeability that a via erotica or the path of the lovers grants to the divine self, particularly when one considers the divine love, as Aquinas does. In the exilic movement of God going outside Godself and abandoning Godself (Ab-solute), God receives God's self. But such a going outside cannot occur except through an initial movement of withdrawal that never allows for invasion. Eroticizing the flesh would entail magnifying as a wound what Marion considers to be the narrow space between two bodies loving each other intimately.[139] The distance would indeed be minimal in that the flesh offers simultaneously hetero- and auto-affection. To feel someone else is also to feel oneself feeling.[140] Still, even if to love is to feel, and regarding the flesh, to feel that which differs from it, the distance that is to be preserved between the lovers cannot be hermetic. Distance from flesh to flesh cannot mean that the flesh of the other, though felt, is never internally wounding, *permeable.*

Without a wound, while loving another may be an act of the flesh, and very much a form of embodying desire, there would be no communion of the flesh. Marion wrongly puts it as "We commune, but within the distance of our two fleshes. They cross, through the same erotic reduction, in a unique amorous phenomenon—each appearing in the other without ever intermingling."[141] One feels oneself feeling, and so in a passive manner one receives oneself, yet not the other's flesh (transfiguration). Subsequently the flesh would bring the self alone back to itself by remaining hermetically encapsulated within itself. Marion argues, "It is still necessary to show how it leaves me to myself, without loophole or possible evasion. As soon as the ego takes flesh, it finds itself stuck to itself as to its ground . . . the taking of flesh assigns the ego definitely to itself and itself alone."[142] In itself alone, it takes flesh via the other, and returns to itself alone. The *I* becomes closer to itself than ever. "I am finally (given to) myself,"[143] the lover would exclaim. This is true even in the copulative act between lovers. Marion states, "But what one sometimes still names the 'carnal union' is characterized precisely by the fact that it provides us with the most questionable proof that the flesh of the other remains absolutely inaccessible to me, like mine to him or her."[144]

With distance shrouding *coitus* to the point of lacking the permeable aspect of *inter*course, what is there to be united in terms of the flesh? Would not this distance, while producing self-enjoyment, also remain an unconquerable threshold that preserves the same solipsism that postmodernity seeks to challenge? If not a wounded *whole*, the space that ecstasy opens would be external to the lovers. This type of distance preserves a kind of radical difference that hampers the use of poetic elements of the flesh to further dislodge the phallic logic of circularity. Without a concept of a flesh that can be penetrated, argues Irigaray, "all forms and all things risk being frozen in the icy rigidity of juxtaposed pairs."[145]

Indeed, Marion possibly fears falling prey to the views of René Descartes, for whom the thoughts of the mind (*res cogitans*) were granted a reality unlike any other, even unlike that of the body (*res extensa*). Things outside the mind are extensions of the mind even when they can be individual substances that subsist in themselves. Yet they can be contained eminently in one's nature because they appear before us, thus becoming available to our minds.[146] Only that which resides in the mind has certainty, which derives from the mind that grants it, thus producing the solipsism that Marion seeks to avoid.[147] An openness to exteriority, to the appeal of and response to the other, seeks to address this notion of mental solipsism.[148] For Marion, therefore, *jouissance* must involve a dual abandonment or movement toward each other (this being the definition of love) that undergoes distance (withdrawal). Otherwise it could lend itself to the objectification of one lover by another, as intimated in relation to the concept of the happy idiot in chapter 2. One way in which the other is not possessed by the other is if each *joins* the other without erecting two objects.[149] As Bracken explains, this concept of *intersubjectivity* connotes an "exchange of love between God and the human being" that can implicitly be understood as "dynamically interrelated subjects of experience rather than as logically related objects of thought within an abstract causal scheme (as in classical metaphysics)."[150]

This particular way of rejecting a Cartesian logic follows in the footsteps of other postmodern thinkers who seek to challenge the Aristotelian concept of the "prime mover" as "pure act" equated with "pure presence," which manifests possession of the flesh of the other (commerce).[151] Postmodern thinkers such as Jacques Derrida show how the Aristotelian concept of *ousia* as *energeia* corresponds to the movement of erotic yearning as it is motivated by an end, the pure presence of the object desired,[152] the lover becoming something to be grasped, calculated, categorized. The absolutely desirable, being possessed, places eros on par with the pure presence of the thing desired. Hence, it is this telos that "puts movement in motion, and that orients becoming toward itself, the absolute movement in motion, and that orients becoming toward itself, the absolute concept or subject."[153] Similarly, for Marion, a return to the self would not draw anything of the other into the self. By keeping the distance, the lover escapes this circularity of pure egoism, and thus the communion would be one of *givenness*, where there is a letting be, an abandonment or release, without drawing in the other as a copy of oneself.[154] Only thus can union ensure the alterity of the lovers, as in the case of Aquinas, and prevent the preservation of otherness and diversity in the return to the divine self. To have someone else who possibly provokes and loves brings a commonality of the experience of pleasure based on a dual honor, a pleasure without possession, which is the meaning of love.[155]

Nevertheless, like the two cherubs of the Ark of the Covenant forever facing each other,[156] in agreement with Irigaray, the lovers would "wait and wait for each other,"[157] a perpetual wait that, while not lacking in lure or desire, does fail to marry the lovers. Both lovers remain in a virginal or bethrothal state. Here lie traces of early Christian thought in which the "marital" bed is compared with this earthly existence, while virginity is compared with that which is transcendent and wholly other.[158] For instance, in Gregory of Nyssa, one of the early proponents of monastic life, drawing near to the unsearchable *cloud of unknowing*, of the divine nature, demands that one "must avoid customary intercourse" with one's spouse, which he equates with the senses.[159] Virginity (of the soul) equals the longing for incorruptibility that grants the power to see God (Goodness, Beauty, and Purity),[160] continence, perfect beauty.[161] In its austerity, it "destroys the passions with which it struggles."[162] For how else could one know when the other receives its flesh, as in Marion's purview, if not when the lover's body becomes glorified, when it ceases to be a body as such, and each of their faces radiates from a distance?[163]

This concept may also be illustrated through the work of Levinas, partly hinted at above in relation to voluptuosity. Using what he views as the fragility and vulnerability of the feminine as a trope, he describes the erotic union as an ultramateriality that never offers itself as the possible to be grasped, perpetually standing at the threshold of the real.[164] It appears as an erotic equivocation. While there is caress, it transcends the sensible,[165] seizes on nothing, expressing love but suffering from the inability to tell it, to live it and to express it bodily.[166] The caress seeks what is not yet bodily, denudes itself of its carnality, always in search of that which is future, always anticipating its dimension of absence, the not yet and absolutely ungraspable.[167]

Similarly, Kristeva's notion of the conjugal caress (what she finds exemplified in the Songs) locates the carnal union within the realm of the unnamed and virginal, purity, a flight and distance devoid of sexual intercourse. Conjugality and its fulfillment, as with Levinas, remain set in the future, "unavoidably missing the other who was barely touched and immediately lost."[168] That the divine lover is "imagined, seen, sensed," that is, corporeal, therefore would not mean represented, a divine incarnation that "would be accomplished once and for all."[169] She admits that by setting up flight "at the center of amorous yearning," the divine eros becomes an abstraction, an ideal sensuality.[170] This translates into a dialogue bound only to words, to speech, and not the embodiment of the jouissant flesh that she seeks to image.

What is to be preserved from their views is how they hold on to a promise of fuller fulfillments, something already established and that can be recovered by way of the tension that it holds with the present. A sort of *paschal joy* ensues.[171] MacKendrick considers it significant that the envisioned end is not meant to be settled but rather to be fluidly expressed at each point of consummation—a bottomless satisfaction.[172] Pain engages the physical pursuit of pleasure, an increased desire whose ends are also starting points. Its trajectory of pleasure with intervals of pain points to an openness toward what is to come—a want for more in the shape of another. Anticipation instills desire that remains desire at each instant, as argued above.

This concept comes into view when one considers the Christian spirituality of many mystics and their meditations on the Songs. As Denys Turner explains, the interplay of erotic metaphors provides an example of a wedding song of arousal and desire, "midway between the promise of betrothal and its fulfillment in sexual union."[173] The Songs, he writes, are "charged with a sense of sexual fulfillment anticipated" even when they also understood the mystical union as also occurring in the here and now.[174] The "Yes" of the lovers—the "Yes" of their flesh seeking to intermingle—encounters the "I love you," "Come!," and "Again!"[175] In the lovers' memory there is hope for recurrence, an increased desire to risk their very selves as they imagine reopening themselves once again, one before the other. The lovers' presence to and absence from one another speak of *successive phases* of anticipation and fulfillment, arousal and consummation, of *momentary presents* during which the lovers possess and elude one another, become one and are yet also other to the other. With each longing comes suffering as a result of each interval of separation, longing being suffering and suffering being longing.[176]

There is a long-standing tradition that ascribes this kind of yearning to God. Even Gregory of Nyssa himself, in describing a figure of God as Love inspired by a vision of surplus, said that the sweet dart of love that wounds the soul is a sweet pain that penetrates it, "for by tearing of the arrow she opens as it were, a door, an entrance into herself. For no sooner she receive [*sic*] the dart of love than the imagery is transformed into a scene of nuptial joy."[177] In another passage he describes the bride as a dove, who, "though she has enjoyed her share of good things as far as was in her power," grows in desire, seeming "to be beginning anew," like an awakened bride to whom the divine lover bids, "'*Arise*; and, when she has come, *Come* (Cant. 2.13).'"[178] Her intimate union occurs in a bed.[179] And as she arrives "in her lofty ascent at the peak of her desires," as she climaxes, the lover invites her to long for more.[180] She has attained only the beginning of things that lie ahead.

Several other early Christian thinkers even accorded a structure to the Songs composed of segments of arousals and consummations. William of Saint-Thierry, for example, divided the book into four sections, "each of which comes to an end with their lying together, that is, with the Bridegroom's and Bride's union."[181] The Song or epithelium serves to lead the couple into the "marriage chamber . . . brought to a conclusion when on the initiative of the Bridegroom she lies in his embrace."[182] Hence, rather than love being accomplished once and for all, consummation occurs in its prolongation of arousal, defying telos and the objectification of desire at each moment of communion.

At this point, the reasons for turning to the erotic imagery of the Songs become clear. For rather than virginity, why not further infinitize the flesh by means of a permeable communion? That neither of the lovers is the same after the erotic encounter cannot *only* be a matter of the lovers assuring each other of being lovers, of words being exchanged—not that this is not a significant aspect. Nor can it be a matter only of myself feeling my own flesh feeling another, another significant quality of the erotic flesh. In "a harmonious passage from external to internal, from the interior to the exterior of bodies," may lie the infinite consummation.[183] Each consummation entails surrender and abandonment; a giving of one lover to another entails such permeable nearness that, in the poetic words of St. Teresa, there is "no division between Thee and me."[184] One incapable of straying too far away from the other, each finds the self *within* the beloved. Specifically with regard to the soul, St. Teresa concludes that God "desires to have such intimacy with it that nothing can separate them."[185] Sealed and impermeable, this "carnal union" or copula would be otherwise. There would be no porous surface to let anything in or out, according to "the threshold" that the flesh provides. If affect remains something on the outside of my flesh, there is no true *int*imacy. Flesh viewed accordingly, even Marion admits, is without relation.

ON A "MARRIAGE"—A POSSIBLE INTERLUDE

It remains to be emphasized that the moreness of flesh that copulation embodies, its infinitization in the sense of a "marriage," differs from circumscribing the intimate union to the limits of a system of rules and proper actions that dictates the conditions for loving another. Erotic love, as indicated by terms such as *adonné* and *givenness*, falls beyond the law, even though at times it may seek a formally agreed-upon way of mutual self-surrender, its dual wounding. If it is beyond the law, then the notion of a "marriage" overflows the rims of the phallic logic often used to tame the flesh and assign strict norms to it, norms that often confine it to propriety.

Acting like an interlude in the Songs, lovemaking interrupts and disrupts its exclusionary sacredness. So rather than an erotic union sealed by a law that safely keeps the lovers *solely* knitted to prescribed forms of conjugal union,[186] passionate love freely gifts itself in its *givenness*, hence bursting the limits established by indebtedness. "Love makes only love," says Turner.[187] And while lovers desperately long for each other's embrace, as Alicia Ostriker argues, "the Song inscribes an alternative story of voluntary love and pleasure,"[188] an erotic freedom of a lover God whose desire, while holy and sacred, lies outside the law.[189] Even by evading being named, to be put in their proper place the lovers pull back from strict definitions of a marriage, possibly becoming vulnerable to the point of being identified with all lovers.[190]

Contrary to what obtains among some classical thinkers on the Songs, there would be no preference for heterosexual love when speaking of erotic manifestations of the lovers of the Songs. Erotic love lends itself to gender bending, blurring gender lines in indeterminate ways. In the Songs, Cheryl Exum indicates, female and male imageries are applied to both lovers, regardless of who the protagonist is.[191] In particular the woman of the Songs, Daphna Arbel argues, takes on different roles in her encounters with her lover.[192] Certainly, in queering the body one may be subverting the allegorical sense that many mystics use to expand the limitations of the divine "sexed" body. In particular the breasts of the Bridegroom are said to be "scented,"[193] "good,"[194] supple with milk,[195] and "sweet."[196] St. Teresa herself exclaims, "May nothing hinder me from being able to say, O my God and my glory, that 'Thy breasts are better and more delectable than wine!'"[197] The point is to interrupt the emphasis on androgyny with the queering of the lovers' flesh, for their sexed bodies becoming multiple.

Moreness may be also expressed in the multiplicity that comes into further view when different protagonists can join the erotic fest—a theme that will continue to unfold as this book's narrative progresses. So, rather than the language of the Songs pointing to an exclusive meaning of loving, it opens up the possibility of diverse couplings of love. As Trible describes it, "Throughout the Song, Eros is inclusive: the love between two welcomes the love and companionship of the many."[198] Even if in a voyeuristic manner, as Exum argues, the Shulamite "invites other women to share her gaze at him in 5:10–16, where she describes him somewhat intimately, much as the gaze at her in 7:1 [ET 6.13] is a group affair: 'Turn, turn, Shulamit, turn, turn, that we may look upon you', which is followed by a detailed description of her."[199] Further still, cosmic, floral, and faunal imageries adorn the loving depictions, welcoming less anthropocentric models of love incarnate. With regard to the divine lover, as discussed further in the last chapter, the many admitted to lovers' encounters means that the law has no hold on who, what, and how God loves. For Ostriker, "The happiness of the Song of Songs helps us, or can help us, to feel, to know," that the divine love that is present time and again "is extended to the world of which we are a portion."[200]

Consequently, this interlude-like impulse may locate a term such as "marriage" beyond arguments for or against the dissolution of the institution of marriage. Eros, flourishing beyond the "demands to remain a servant, wife, child-bearer, mother, commercial exchange object," as Kearney muses on the free love of the Shulamite,[201] is not about to reify another absolute limit beyond all expressions of marriage. For there can be a "marriage" among lovers according to eros, yet capable of maintaining the mysterious tension between freedom and faithfulness to which the lovers' union bids them (however that might be expressed). As Turner explains, "*Eros* imposes obligations more binding—and so in a sense more 'necessary'—than any which the force of moral laws could impose; and yet, within eros, the language of 'imposition' and 'obligation' can only be construed in contrast with the freedom of lover and beloved."[202] Rather than speaking of a marriage as no marriage at all, the language of the Songs frees erotic love from the language of imposition and obligation, of exclusion and limitations, that confines the lovers to prescribed definitions.

THE MYSTERY OF *JOUISSANCE*

But why highlight the point of self-exchange that coitus brings? When there is not even a partial bringing of the other into the self, loving according to the flesh lacks an important aspect of mutuality, the possibility of an embodied infinity. And without an exchange of bodily fluids that transforms the flesh, without this permeability, how truly eroticized it would be! Without a return to the self that brings something of the other into itself, even the aspect of *adonné* cannot be a givenness that gives anything of the self away but only fixes or roots the flesh in itself, receives solely itself. In taking flesh, consequently, while the lover is "altered by the other," as Marion posits,[203] without each leaving a trace on the other, without there being love, becoming, life, copula, would not there remain only a self-encircling loop?[204] If intersubjectivity and givenness are denied interchangeability, ultimately *jouir* remains bound to Scholastic metaphysics. For if in the case of God, God receives Godself and no other than Godself, if the other is not brought back into God, there is no shattering of the mirror image of the divine self (self-idolatry). There must be a ubiquitous opening that allows for passage, interpenetration, and fecund mixture, and that, even if as a wound, voids solipsism, undoing the divine return to the propriety of the same.[205]

Hence, as this imagery of a "marriage" is taken further into the realm of divine love, the meaning being sought is one in which God becomes one whose *ousia* is that of a lover, one who is God and already more than God in *loving* another.[206] God would indeed be "the best lover," when in a climactic "Yes!" God and lovers go beyond themselves, being welcomed and welcoming each into the other, without fully abandoning themselves. With each "Yes" there would also be a making haste in crossing the threshold of the flesh (Songs 2:10, 8:14), an entering in without much delay,[207] a coming inside, within the flesh that infinitize*s* it. As they enjoy themselves, they also enjoy each other by bringing into their selves something that is of the other. This expansive mystery of love takes on flesh, a most welcoming divine flesh that refuses to hermetically shut itself away from the world about it. It seeks to be wounded by the otherness that the impropriety of the lovers' encounters brings. As with the Songs, the body, the wound, the *bowels*, even the sexual organs can be the erotic topos of self-exchange (Songs 7). Each embodied flesh becomes the potentiality of the other while within each other—kernels of something new. Here resides the other improper aspect of infinity. The lovers become flesh while being *in*timate with one another.

The wounded cloud of the Godhead becomes the site of sharable pleasures as found in interpretations of the Songs like those of St. Teresa. Two arrows, and two wounds imply interpenetration.[208] And with Irigaray's rereading of mystical experiences such as St. Teresa's, the wound is where the female mystic "curls as if in her nest, where she rests as if she had found her home," and where the divine lover also rests and intermingles with her.[209] In a more intimate dwelling place, where interior and exterior become fecund, where activity and passivity meet, observes Irigary, would not something gather itself in "from a more secret consummation? In and through a mucous shelter that extends from the depths to the heights?"[210] Implying a decentering or withdrawal, and perhaps a distance, but quite contrary to Marion's view, their wound is the site of a fluid viscosity by which the lovers' flesh infinitizes through self-exchange. The very act of lovemaking rules out the either/or contrast apparently present in the distance that such intimate union simultaneously creates.

From within her wound, she is able to embrace her own lewdness and much more. In her self-embrace and climatic moments of becoming, a part of the self, her viscosity, inundates the fluids and membranes that nest within her. In the words of St. Teresa, "it is impossible to divide or separate the water belonging to the river from that which fell from the heavens."[211] The edges of a woman's lips remain open with inexhaustible "springs" that come from her, "the touching together (of her lips) . . . the break between, the hardening of the edges, the forgotten river that now divides them," says Irigaray.[212] Even more, springs intermingling refer to how her *jouissance* spills over the limits of her own flesh. As Irigaray asks, "the unceasing movement of two springs feeding each other could be the pledge of eternal happiness, could it not?"[213] The nest and home of the lovers, the cellar of wine of *in*finitizing pleasures, are the lips where lovers come and become themselves and another.

A copulative proximity of fluid exchange, the to-and-fro transgresses, further dislocates the divine love beyond the bounds of the proper (of classical theism). The movement is like the flow of ocean waters into the mouth of the river and back, a source of self-enjoying impurity. In the imagery of St. Teresa of Avila, the heavens too are capable of receiving her imprint, of being transformed by the waters of the rivers, the oceans, hers. The shared ripples, pulsations, and multiplicities of becomings generated by numerous withdrawals and expansions fluidly disturb the organic compositions of God. For Irigaray, "I not only have to draw near to the other, we must succeed in drawing near to one another . . . we must cross little by little towards each other while letting be both the one and the other."[214] In this sense, even in the prayer "kiss me with the kiss of your mouth" there is something of the other—the breath—that is taken in by God, a crisscrossing of selves. Like shared air breathed in, the divine self would not remain in its "proper place."[215] Hence erotic love achieves what Turner calls "a fuller differentiation within that union than either can possess without it."[216] It gives way to that which is "both *me* and *more than* me," a memory of my own multiplicity, without the loss of identity.

Desire unfolds toward a blossoming[217] of selves multiplied. In their going out (exile), they return to themselves modified, "towards a dwelling that will need to transform its frame in order to secure the memory of becoming—of oneself, of the other, of the world."[218] There is a mysterious passage that allows for something to arrive "which did not exist," brought about as a result of what the "two worlds" produce,[219] of this intertwining "little by little." The memory that it produces is of a "mysterious legacy"[220] of the encounter remembered without appropriation that connotes a surplus of physicality, an enfleshed infinity of self-combinations. The curling of the self inside its wound, as it also shelters another's becoming, entails combining with the flesh "of the other in an interweaving of spaces and times where visible and invisible alternate."[221] In the back-and-forth movement between lovers, unfoldings and refoldings are shared without any being reduced to what is revealed, each being irreducible to the *jouissance* of the other. Already an opaque distance that voids confusion arises out of the movement toward communion, for lovers can switch places and not destroy "their elemental Being," as Irigaray indicates.[222]

The divine yearning could very well be for an erotic mutuality akin to transfiguration, something that need not be in conflict with differentiation, nor does need be differentiation at odds with union. This erotic mutuality does away with such contrasts. Interpenetration, union, can be without con-fusion, and yet *trans*figurative. For Kearney, the divine flesh, more specifically in reference to the Shulamite of the Songs, becomes time and again by crossing over into the hallowed form of the creaturely "without consuming or being consumed by" the one whom God loves.[223] In the erotic transfiguration, by crisscrossing God becomes the "possibility-to-be rather than pure being in the manner of ontotheology, or as pure nonbeing in the manner of negative theology."[224] Like physical surplus (being more than one) is the mystery of the flesh that welcomes the unexpected to join itself and so to transfigure it. Even in the kiss the lovers become beyond themselves, are transfigured. Indeed, the silhouette of an erotic God whose flesh is "neither impermeable nor homogeneous,"[225] the silhouette of a God who is more than God, is quite improper.

Such is the language of erotic infinity in the Songs. It breaks free from the phallic logic of classical theism to express a mutual eroticism, to the point of transfiguration of the divine love. I agree with Turner that it speaks of the mystery of the interpenetrative union that occurs when lovers are intimate. As he insightfully states, "in the union of lovers is penetration, dissolution and absorption of each into the other in ecstatic self-abandonment."[226] As the divine eros makes room within itself, others can internally and intimately affect it. God's and St. Teresa of Avila's responding to one another's advances involves a wounding process of mutual expansion of the flesh through withdrawal that, to me, infinitizes the divine flesh subsequently by means of a process of transfiguration, thus the impropriety of the divine love. Her words describe a passionate surrender and return to her flesh in the act of enjoyment, even as the arrows afflict her bowels, and even her beloved's,[227] which points to the memory of being more than one. Infinity in terms of the porosity and elasticity of the flesh is implicitly embedded in these mutual forms of enjoyment. For why would God not be this *in*timately transfigured by the one whom draws as lover if God were to be "the best lover," that is, the most improper lover?

Yes, there are other modes of intersubjectivity and givenness through which God, like other beings, gains the divine flesh through the activity of love outside the confines of possession. That the act of love partly gives rise to the self of God in the act of return automatically implies that other subjects become the objects in God that provide for the divine "objective expression or actuality," as Bracken argues.[228] It describes what I consider an act of the divine incarnation. In the very invitation that God extends to another to come (*jouir*) there is implied the desire for the divine lover to welcome in that which God is not. Copula—*inter*course—means self-exchange. It means that at least one other becomes the underlying potentiality of God: thus God being God and other than God. In posing such a divine enjoyment with the cosmos, one might come to recognize, along with Bracken, that "the mastery of nature and of the world is transformed into the elaboration of a shared universe."[229] What an intermingled loving self that God is! That is, the essence of God whose love resembles our means, stages, rhythms, and practices is one in which the other is already intrinsic to it but not possessed. The essence of the mystery of divine love is highly impure, for the divine self becomes *itself* in continuous combinations with others. These are the ways of the via erotica or the path of love implicitly found in the concept of God as the best lover.

Nevertheless, this mysterious infinitizing of the divine flesh is in need of further exploration. To gain an understanding of how God can become

God as both one and many in the act of welcoming a more explicitly cosmic multiplicity into Godself and allowing it to passionately affect the divine actualizing of being implies a more risky chanciness than Irigaray's views allow. For how God enjoys Godself in becoming multiple with the cosmos requires another metaphysically relational model of divine enjoyment, such as discussed in the next chapter. The one described in panentheism may provide further relational models with which to explore the divine passionate love.

St. Teresa's texts on the Songs show that the figure of the erotic lover can grant God an embodied love, hence shattering the mirrors of absolute self-subsistence that keep the divine ecstasy trapped in the divine self. The imagery of the lover in the flesh implies an erotic intimacy that Luce Irigaray and Jean-Luc Marion find conducive to describing the kind of intimacy that occurs between God and another lover. It suggests an erotic dialogue, which—particularly when speaking of copula—also implies a self-return on the part of each of the lovers in the mode of at least a partial mixture that Irigaray recognizes. By breaking free from a dialogue that renders the cosmos a mere echo of God's enjoyment—a return to the same—God receives the image of its creation, its flesh, for in self-sameness is no love but paralysis, as Irigaray says.

To arrive at this erotic dimension of God's love, therefore, a permeable flesh that speaks of limits, but as a passage to the unlimited, and vice versa, was imagined. Limits prevent both dissolution and absolute separation. Limitlessness opens up at the point of granting passage of the limited into it, the moment of the lovers' delight. But limited being is also affirmed, as Michel Foucault indicates, "in the limitlessness into which it leaps."[230] Thus the God we seek to define might emerge from a space of the unlimited that affirms limited being, and again, the limitless affirmations of lovers saying yes. Such mutual infinity is nothing like homogeneity. The lovers copulate or love each other in terms of partial mixture.

That is why, in the permeable enjoyment of the cosmos and its life forms, God becomes excessive, that is, intensified with enjoyment. God's excess is enjoyment that delights in the multiple *yeses* of the cosmos. And in this immense plurality of enjoyments resides the infinite love of God. Consequently, that God is in the world as *infinite lover* or the best lover means that out of the activity of love, God becomes a distinct and unique lover *in* and partly *of* the cosmos. With this statement in mind, the erotic dialogue initially set forth in this chapter can help us discover concepts related to intersubjectivity in addition to the nonhuman elements that add to the intensity of the divine enjoyment.

Intensity: Passionate Becomings of the Divine Complex

> Love is movement.
> In the cosmic immensities
> as in bed
> love is movement.
> That one who is Love is Movement.
>
> —ERNESTO CARDENAL[1]

A God of enjoyment, one must imagine, experiences movement as the passage of oneself into another, the kind of "cosmic copulation" that Ernesto Cardenal's poetry implies. We can think of the language of seduction, of ourselves being wooed into the deepest *bowels* of the divine lover, and enticed to conceive of God as the very love that is incarnated in this kind of movement. Lovers in bed copulate and enact some form of passage from one self to the other. As they unite in love, they enact an expression of the divine lovemaking.[2] But how can we speak of the cosmos being in God in ways that allow us to gain a keen grasp of the significance of this exchange of selves? One possible point of departure is to rediscover how the flesh of lovers becomes one, and, as they join in, how each also partly incarnates or becomes in the form of the other, as lovers do. As Cardenal has written:

> Each one of the two
> already both.

> One already both, and
> two each of them.
> It's not a vague black hole full of nothing.
> Cosmic copulation.[3]

Cardenal's poetic vision is beautifully put. God and the whole cosmos copulate! They become multiple as they join as one jouissant flesh and partake of the attributes of each other. In its most mystical sense, the divine-cosmic copulation means that God is the one *in* whom the universe unfolds and the one that unfolds *in* the universe; and that in so doing, God enjoys the divine self with the cosmos without either abrogating the other's identity or unique form of enjoyment. Like a divine coincidence of opposites that, for Catherine Keller, refers to how the "all" is relational in God and unfolds to become "God" in "all things,"[4] the divine *wound* would gain an intensified sense of passion ensuing from the many living beings expressing their unique forms of enjoyment in God. And out of this fleshly site that welcomes even ancestral memories, God could also in turn vivify the cosmos. How adventurous is God's love for the cosmos, as God offers hospitality to its manifold expressions of enjoyment that emerge in a zest for life! This kind of *passage* would lead to a union not only in the form of heterogeneity but also in the sense of *transmutation*, that is, God partly incarnating the contrasting elements of life.

In this chapter, therefore, I assume a "reality-in-process"; that is, I consider those whose model subscribes to God's being as movement, which for me is seemingly copulative, stemming from the divine activity of intimately sharing the divine nature with living things other than God.[5] The reality in process that it describes is therefore mainly panentheistic. Hence I draw on the works of Alfred North Whitehead and authors who are explicitly in dialogue with him, and on the writings of Ivone Gebara, who, while not a self-professed process thinker, both embraces panentheist principles and takes them further. The intention is to shed some new light on how this kind of quasi-mystical intermingling can be imagined. In entering onto panentheistic grounds, I will be able to more specifically press against Christian classical views that deny God fuller expressions of intense pleasure. An intensity of flesh and blood, ridden with ambiguous and complex living, is what God seeks to incarnate. Might such a God, "who may be" and whose ancestral existence ensues from the many, lure life ever more toward something novel, in the first instance by being imbued with the passions of the cosmos, its joys as well as its sufferings?

The Divine Interstitial Givenness

> It should be said that love pertains to the appetite.
>
> St. Thomas Aquinas[6]

> Appetition is immediate matter of fact including in itself a principle of unrest, involving realization of what is not and may be.
>
> Alfred North Whitehead[7]

There is a lovers' dance of passion akin to lovemaking between God and the variegated cosmos that leads to intense forms of enjoyment not only for the cosmos but also within God. This perichoretic dance entices all things toward union with God, and also constitutes the divine self in the divine "abandonment" so that other living forms may self-enjoy themselves in their own unique manner. In this, God is quite the poetic lover, who enjoys the cosmos in ever and new ways. Alfred North Whitehead describes this concept beautifully. For him, God is "the poet of the world, with tender patience leading it by his vision of truth."[8] But what would it mean for God to be this poet in the sense of the beloved lover, as has previously been figured? How would God be affected by the cosmos, as the many gain their flesh or incarnate themselves in their abandonment or *givenness*? And what would it mean that God is also always becoming—in a state of potentiality—in relation to the cosmos? To better consider this passionate dance of God with the cosmos through the lens of panentheism—all things in God—I draw on the two interrelated principles of *multiple passages* and a *transmuting incarnation* of the many in the one, which provide the basis for my argument.

MULTIPLE PASSAGES

As discussed in Chapter 2, for Aquinas, love is a unitive force or power that incites within God a desire or yearning to go outside the divine self ecstatically. Love in this construal is a simple enactment of "the will having like effects,"[9] for it seeks to move toward the desired object, to unite with it, so that there may be a perfection of the good in all living things.[10] The movement refers to an intellective appetite in God.[11] There is something in the created order that is already attractive to God, something good, if corporeal, that compels God to go outside the divine self and unite with the creaturely. The divine love, in desiring the perfection of the loved one, "moves all things to union, for, in so far as He gives them being and other perfections, He joins them to Himself in a manner in which this is possible."[12] Ultimately, union yields a perfected enjoyment in the cosmos. The divine love stirs desire for enjoyment of life (wholeness), even physical enjoyment, which ultimately leads to a final enjoyment, which is union with God.

Not quite the same but similar is the divine love that Whitehead describes; it is an erotic power *in* but also *of* the universe that creatively aids in the advancement of all things toward fuller expressions of life. Engaging Plato, as Aquinas perhaps did in reframing the views of Denys the Areopagite, Whitehead argues that the divine eros impartially conditions "the whole process of the Universe."[13] The primordial nature of God is erotic, lodged in the intellect as well (the mental pole); the divine eros values and is "the urge towards the realization of ideal perfection."[14] Similar also to Aquinas's notion of the intellective appetite, this erotic nature is immediately the source both of enjoyment and also of appetition that "melts into action."[15] The erotic power is the divine erotic appetite as "the principle of unrest, involving realization of what is not and may be."[16] Unique to Whitehead's thought, to be more precise, is the postulate that "God is the organ of novelty, aiming at intensification."[17] In the world, God's primordial nature is a thirst for something different, an appetition for something new within permanence—"towards something relevant, something largely identical, but something with a definite novelty."[18] An appetite for novelty is for Whitehead "the primary meaning of life," each creature *transforming* itself through an "insistent craving" for a zest for existence.[19] Contrary to some Aristotelian principles, in the end, I argue, this perfection can take on the contours of meaningful contrasts and even chaos, adding intensity to the divine enjoyment.

While Aquinas and Whitehead each develop the concept in unique ways, for both, enjoyment or zest is of importance to living. In both paradigms, this principle of life is quickened by the divine appetite or God's loving desire—life's impulse toward meaningfulness. As in Aquinas's model, "enjoyment" in Whitehead relates to "well-being" more so than to simply existing, being, or surviving.[20] This form of enjoyment is worth noting. As Otto Maduro argues in motivating the concept of *la buena vida*, this form of enjoyment points to the following: "That life—life that is worth living and that incites us to overuse it—it is not pure struggle against death: it is the search for common pleasure, enduring happiness, deep delight, free enjoyment, contagious joy."[21] For Aquinas and Whitehead explicitly, the whole of existence rests on this form of *la buena vida*, in that all living beings move toward it, seeking to attain it. Similarly, in the form of self-enjoyment a proposed good takes on meaning beyond the divine self as it becomes a value for others.

There may also be some similarities in how the two authors understand the concept of mutual immanence. For Aquinas, God *passes into* the object of the divine love to unite with it.[22] God "joins them to Himself in a manner in which" perfection is made possible.[23] Yet the notion that the divine self remains *"internally complete"* hinders classical views like those of Aquinas, as Whitehead's general critique of Greek thought indicates.[24] According to Whitehead, Christian classical doctrine ended up affirming a divine realm in which "there is *no passage*," in the sense of there being "no loss, no gain . . . complete in itself . . . self sustaining."[25] It promotes the dualism traditionally believed to exist between the static realm of God (perfection, completion) and the dynamic realm of creation. For Whitehead, the divine realm is without loss or gain, and is characterized by terms such as "'completely real,' 'perfection,' 'certainty.'"[26] In the classical model, this view translates into a creation that belongs to an inferior realm, because it is transitional. Transitional reality (creation) is derived from a changeless, ultimate, and perfect reality, which has erroneously defined the notion of divine enjoyment as something that is unchanging and *absolutely* self-subsistent. As indicated in Chapter 2, God puts on the garments of an unmoved mover who is eminently real, and is in relation to a transitional world that is real only derivatively. God is real by virtue of the divine self, and the world is derivatively real, for it exists solely by virtue of who God is.

As implied throughout this book, in a model that allows for a more radical form of mutuality, perfection is shaped differently. For one, the divine love, rather than urging all things from the outside in, actively entertains all potentiality from an internal sharing of selves akin to loss and gain (transmutation). God and cosmos mutually indwell one another through God being primordially in all things in the form of an eternal desire for things to continually "create" themselves anew.[27] Second, God becomes something other than God in relation to "every other creative act," that is, as the whole of the cosmos comes to be a part of God to which God reacts.[28] Just as lovers do, both the cosmos and God adventurously receive from one another, and incarnate one another, through the movement of love. The cosmos receives from God the divine persuasion or erotic appetite, a "lure" or an "urge" to actualize itself in ever new and creative ways, and God receives the creative past expressions of the life of the cosmos. The purpose is tender care: "the love in the world" passing into "the love of heaven," and then flooding back into the cosmos.[29] At each moment of passage, the cosmos gains the potential to transform itself, just as God is able to everlastingly transform the divine self "in the Being of God" in relation to the cosmos.[30] These *multiple passages* are due to a back-and-forth movement of love akin to desire or yearning—"the insistent craving that zest for insistence be refreshed by the ever-present, unfading importance of our immediate actions, which perish and yet live forever."[31]

For Roland Faber, the "love in the world" passing into "the love in heaven" means that God provides space for the world to grow and evolve according to hope.[32] God makes space and gives Godself to reconcile the world. Whitehead calls it "the union of the actual ground with the novel consequent,"[33] at which point God receives a reaction from the world, through which God becomes a "fellow sufferer."[34] In reacting to the world, God deposits in the cosmos the desire for it to take hold of the many possibilities. In this sense, the divine passion, in receiving something from the cosmos, also exercises the power of love that brings hope for life in the midst of tragedy. So, as the cosmos passes into God, God opens the cosmos to the wholly unexpected, the infinite potential, the unrealized possibilities of God. Consequently, the complexity of God's *givenness* lies in the fact that God would suffer and enjoy the divine self with a purpose.[35] As Faber puts it, "in 'suffering' God does not merely passively suffer or endure, but actively provides an opening toward (ambivalent) life itself."[36] And as the divine love passes back into the cosmos, God becomes the *advent*, or the yet to come of the now in the present. A form of this thought was shared by the theologians of the cross and feminist thinkers of Latin America introduced in Chapter 1.

Rather than the Aristotelian *actus purus* taking on the form of the divine love as cause, in the panentheism espoused here, therefore, what we find is a poetic eros that is the "reservoir of potentiality" and lures all things with love in fusing the divine self with them. Much as the divine love is depicted by Aquinas as sweetly stirring all things, but even more distinctively so from within a process paradigm, the divine love in this construction is not certainty but possibility. It is neither a "productive" nor a "destructive force" but an urge toward novelty—persuasive love, says Whitehead.[37] With the divine immanence of the infinite love in the finite, finitude is imbued with potentiality as "the finite possibilities of the universe travel towards their infinite realization."[38] The divine desire is both the "foundation of order" and "the goad towards novelty."[39] The lover God is adventurous, the advent of "the possible" in the world, something that the world cannot provide solely for itself and by itself.

Closer to Whitehead's view, God's proposed good for becoming (primordial valuation) leads to a self-value crafted by each creature, each self-actualizing itself according to its own purposes. There is no one ideal for all, and the possibility of altering God's plan is characteristic of the divine love.[40] According to Faber, this is the theopoetic aspect of God to which Whitehead alludes when stating that God is "the poet of the world."[41] God bequeaths God's potentialities, granting the cosmos *"a space for the eschatological adventure,"* he argues,[42] for each living thing self-creates as each arises from the infinite possibilities that God offers and assesses, forming multiple self-realizations determined by the living thing itself.[43] God becomes the cosmic lover who adventurously draws into the divine self all there is and transforms it into a heavenly existence that *passes* back into the cosmos, but still according to the world's creative self-becomings.

In a sense, therefore, the beloved divine lover is like an adventurous poet who nurtures within the divine self the creative incarnations of the possible, arising from the lived experiences that are intensely relevant to it. This means that each creature enjoys its experience in its particular form within the divine self out of its own complex unity with God. For Aquinas, this could mean that all things participating in God as the ultimate end are able to preserve their distinct proper ends of enjoyment,[44] thus affording the diversity that is housed within the Godhead. For Whitehead, more specifically, all living beings in God self-select their "intensive relevance," which accords value on the basis of what is preferred for the adaptation to a particular environment. All the while they also seek the best possible form of life that, as Whitehead argues, provides "that way of enjoyment."[45] As each creature self-selects from the many alluring forms of enjoyment available to it, it attains a determinate "satisfaction," "a unity of feeling of the one actual entity."[46]

In addition, similar to Aquinas's understanding of contentment, for Whitehead, enjoyment refers to the cusp or satisfaction of an actualized desire. Yet it is particularly significant for Whitehead that each moment of enjoyment is also the death of self, which again passes into life. As old meets the vivifying novelty of the divine eros, there is an immediate self-enjoyment that constitutes that living being, immediately in its perishing it readies itself for another similar but novel way of enjoyment.[47] Passion, death, even the death of another, the *passage* of the self, a passing on to something other than the self after each completion—all these are the marks of enjoyment. So self-enjoyment also refers to its potentiality, in that it motivates yet another purposeful self-creation for and beyond the self at each moment of death.[48] At each moment of satisfaction there is a complex unity characterized by both enjoyment (fulfillment) and appetition (yearning), by things concrete or actualized and things in their potentiality, ready for something new.[49] In the cosmos, the divine enjoyment is about a process *in* which completeness is granted yet another beginning, death its rebirth, *passage*, another becoming that brings freshness to wholeness, such that life becomes continually refreshed anew.

Hence self-enjoyment is the result of entities being-in-one another. The selves are as intimately connected as in the act of lovemaking. And because each is in the other, one self can become the potential for a new existence, evident in the life of another. As each self infuses its own particular potentiality into another entity, it becomes "an element of the *givenness* of the universe," while partly remaining as it is at that moment.[50] The selves *give* of themselves and pass from one self to another. In a non-Cartesian manner, substances internally affect one another in their *givenness*.[51] They *add* something to each other. Subjects emerge out of a process of *passage* in that they incorporate new possibilities from other subjects, "perishing" as they rise as events, and exerting influence on other subjects while they become their objects. Their "self-loss" births new possibilities beyond themselves, *infinitizes* them, which explains the loss and gain they endure (passage and transmutation). In the words of Faber, "nothing can be *in and for itself* that has not already become *from something else* and is not capable of becoming efficacious *for something else*."[52]

TRANSMUTING INCARNATIONS

The possibility of all living beings adding something to the divine enjoyment lies in this form of adventurous passage. The divine enjoyment is because of something other than Godself,[53] when others are a part of the satisfying becoming of God. Other actual entities come to formally constitute the divine subject when God, in being capable of feeling (*sentire*), *prehends* them.[54] This model of enjoyment is not according to an entity "*formaliter*" or to its "own absolute self-realization"; rather, it is in the sense of "other things" being "components in its own constitution."[55] The passage is one in which "contentment" or "satisfaction" with Godself (becoming actual) is also accompanied by enjoyment of the many forms inhabiting it, and then passing into others to become a possible ingredient for their enjoyment.

Passage therefore means that at the point selves welcome others, they are also transformed by them, becoming *other* themselves. Subsequently they also undertake somewhat of an immortal function through love, in the sense that in the act of loving they become part creators of other entities as they enter into one another. In this sense *passage* is analogous to what has been proposed in conversation with classical and postmodern thinkers. The lovers join one another, and become as a result of loving and being loved by another, to the point that Aquinas can poetically say, "love transforms the lover into the beloved, it makes the lover enter into the interior of the beloved and *vice versa*, so that nothing of the beloved remains not united to the lover, just as form reaches to the inmost recesses of that which it informs and *vice versa*."[56] Furthermore, in Aquinas a "certain transformation into the thing loved"[57] bears a resemblance to the concept of *transmuting incarnation* I espouse in this study. In his dialogue of love as an appetite and thus what I see as a possible passive-active power of transformation ("the moved mover"), he remarkably adds the following: "And since anything that is made in the form of something is made one with it, through love the lover becomes one with what is loved, which becomes the lover's form."[58] The lovers incarnate one another, as explored by Irigaray in regard to lovemaking and by Kearney in relation to the figure of the Shulamite in the Songs. Implicit in the lovers' copulation is an intimate distance that breaks free from pure nothingness (*ex nihilo*). As Cardenal points out, "It's not a vague black hole full of nothing / Cosmic copulation."[59]

The distinct enjoyments of the lovers are uniquely expressed even as they are intrinsically transformed by these expressions. Each subject enjoys itself through the flesh of another as much as it is transformed by it. The lovers, in other words, give of themselves and receive themselves through giving, as well as let go something of themselves that comes to be a part of the other lover, as much as the lover returns to herself modified—a clear example of passage and transmutation. In agreement with Joseph Bracken, we can articulate a view in which God and creatures are not inert thoughts that objectify each other but rather are "subjects of experience in dynamic interrelation."[60] *Givenness* would hence mean something else for Whitehead, for whom it simultaneously connotes both mutual immanence and the freedom to enjoy oneself in distinct forms.

This lovemaking and dynamic interrelation between God and cosmos is mutually transforming because, as Bracken explains (in drawing Aquinas's views closer to Whitehead's), a dimension of God lacks in actuality.[61] Aquinas would frown at this proposition. "In the divine will there is no potentiality," he firmly states.[62] For him, that which lacks in actuality is imperfect, for it implies lack or the need for something not possessed in se—God's "so great perfection, to which addition is impossible."[63] Aquinas would reject this theological premise since for him, although all things seek their own forms of enjoyment, for each tends to a good suitable to itself, as O'Rourke reads Aquinas,[64] God enjoys all things singly and continuously (seamlessly), that is, not as a result of regathering their unique diversity and unique self-actualizations. For Bracken, both would be implications of Aquinas's Aristotelian thought. But if one presses this mode of thinking further, as Bracken does, the opposite can also be true. God as subsistent activity or motion can make room for ongoing stages of actualization, or "an ongoing series of separate acts of existence with each individual act serving as potentiality for its successor."[65] This process of actualization would imply infinity, and thus another way to define perfection, since as potentiality God would be "purely indeterminate and thus unlimited in an absolute sense."[66]

The divine enjoyment, therefore, can also occur as a result of God incarnating the cosmos. To elaborate on a form of passage that ensues in transmutation or incarnation, God as primordial, in being "purely indeterminate," also needs a "complex integration with physical feelings"—indeed, the flesh of the cosmos—for there to be actualization of the infinite and the potential.[67] Whitehead: "Thus a process must be inherent in God's nature, whereby his infinity is acquiring realization."[68] This process is made possible by another dimension in God, the physical or consequent nature (the cosmos passing into the reality of heaven). That is, God becomes actual only in relation to the cosmos and not apart from it. One can say that God *transmutes* or undergoes passage from potentiality to actuality as the divine self gains flesh in relation to the cosmos. The divinity desires *passage* through a process of realization of the divine infinity through the consequent nature of God. God *passes on* to more incarnational forms without ceasing to be God (identity), since the *givenness* of God is the result of an *internal* determination (as it is also with other creatures).[69] That is, God selects and orders the divine self in ways appropriate to God, all the while God also becomes *physically* as God perceives all living beings.

As lovers do, God internally completes or perfects the divine self, but not alone, rather in relation to the cosmos—a position distinct from classical theism. Whitehead emphatically argues that "there is no entity, not even God, 'which requires nothing but itself in order to exist.'"[70] Internally, as consequent, God is composed of "the organic actualities of the world"[71] that bring into the divine self the "physical experience derived from the temporal world."[72] God welcomes the cosmos into the divine self so that something of it becomes an intrinsic element of God's nature. This is the reversed act of love, which complements well what Aquinas said, remarking on Denys the Areopagite: "thus Dionysius says (*Div. Nom.* iv) that *Paul being in ecstasy through the vehemence of Divine love* exclaimed: *I live, now not I, but Christ liveth in me.*"[73]

This union akin to lovemaking is an act of feeling deeply. Once the cosmos is in God, the primordial eros receives the physical feelings from the consequent nature that feels the world immediately as the world also feels God's consequent nature.[74] The principles are similar to the concept of the regathering of all things into a "receptacle" that Pseudo-Dionysius and Aquinas articulate, as discussed in Chapter 1, but with a twist. God is internally affected by the heterogeneity of the cosmos, and becomes in part this heterogeneity. Furthermore, it means that the starting point of divine enjoyment is also the complex unity, something better expressed as an *I/we* or something already heterogeneous—the memory of a "mysterious legacy"[75] briefly intimated in the previous chapter in conversation with Irigaray. Here lies the element of intense divine enjoyment that avoids a sense of a final perfection akin to *closure* or the *propriety* of the divine process. There contrasts meet and are directed by the erotic nature in a manner that brings in novelty to the cosmos and contributes to a realization in God that is fully harmonious, "free from inhibitions of intensity by reason of discordance."[76] And, one might argue, a "perfect multiplicity"[77]—of all enjoyments in God—which harmony contains meaningful contrasts akin to chaos can thus begin to shape the divine enjoyment itself.

Consequently, the divine eros as the starting point of the divine movement toward the cosmos starts with potentiality seeking physicality in relation to the cosmos—seeking to become divine, but only in relation to another. This is not a process enclosed in se, as already discussed. God is the open-ended future before the cosmos, which comes to define the divine enjoyment, an enjoyment that also ensues from this internal process of incarnation (unity, actualization) derived from the divine "lovemaking" relationship with the cosmos. This cosmic eros, also internal and thus elemental to the universe (while similar to the intellective appetite that Aquinas posits), is therefore unique in that it seeks passage rather than expressing an absolute completeness derived solely from the divine self. This form of passage, one that does not stem from self-completion, defines the divine enjoyment in ways that do away with numbness (apathy). God purposefully lures all things toward novelty while seeking to feel the physicality of the cosmos, namely, to embody it or transmute with it. The divine enjoyment is realized by means of all living beings of the cosmos coconstituting the divine self in such manner that the cosmos partly trans*forms* God.

The Multidimensionality of the Poetic Eros

This eschatology comingled with earth—the cycle of life, the year's seasons, the bodies of animals, plants, and flowers—this human and larger-than-human eschatology warms the heart a great deal.

Ivone Gebara[78]

A wombier divinity, by contrast, will always materialize, mix, mingle and multiply with her offspring.

Catherine Keller[79]

The erotic dance requires a space within God that possesses a permeable membrane through which cosmic and divine self-becomings mutually intensify one another. This space would take on the contours of mutual loving encounters in which for St. Thomas Aquinas the divine love is intensely "*intimate*," even "*of the bowels*," and reciprocal, of beloved and lover interpenetrating one another, "being both container and contents in different ways."[80] It would even be like the wound where God nestles the divine self, and the "cloud of the Godhead" that engulfs St. Teresa of Avila[81] and in which she finds it difficult to distinguish a "division between Thee and me."[82] This would be the site of erotic loves joining as one, to the point that there is "both *me* and *more than* me" without the loss of identity.[83]

With the element of permeability, the waters of the cosmos flow back into the divine oceans of love. But how do they also constitute the loving essence of God? What kind of passion do we encounter in this model when we consider that for Whitehead, "God is the organ of novelty, aiming at intensification"?[84] How could the enjoyments of the cosmos in being many and variegated add intensity to it? In other words, how can the cosmos add intensity to the divine enjoyment, as the erotic nature (*esse eros*) of God hears the words of the many lovers saying yes to life, even in their seemingly contrasting forms of loving? This could entail considering not only the manner in which the primordial *eros* is "*infinitely intensive*" by virtue of healing "all contradictions and discordances in the world," as Faber argues through Helmut Maasen, but also how it is infinitely intense as a result of the many intensities being components of the one complex unity of God.[85] God's intense love can be one that endures a *multipassage* that allows God to incarnate our own intense experiences.

INDETERMINATING INDETERMINACY

One way to interpret Whitehead's view of the divine intensity is by way of the relation it holds to the grounding activity of the divine erotic love. Two passages are key. First, for Whitehead, "The absolute standard of such intensity is that of the primordial nature of God, which is neither great nor small because it arises of no actual world."[86] And second, "Thus an event is a matter of fact which by reason of its limitation is a value for itself; but by reason of its very nature it also requires the whole universe in order to be itself."[87] So, as Charles Hartshorne remarks, God is "in one respect of his being maximally absolute, and in another aspect no less strictly or maximally relative."[88] These statements, held together, can translate into God's intensity being absolute only as a value for Godself but, by reason of God's erotic nature, also requiring "the whole universe." Self-valuation occurs through the processes of self-selection that all beings, including God, undertake. God self-creates the divine self or becomes according to the divine self-determinative process, so God is always God, and furthermore, God is always a beloved lover. Whitehead finds it significant that "there is no entity, not even God, 'which requires nothing but itself in order to exist.'"[89] This has to do with potentiality as *givenness*, with an other-directed love expressed as *passage* in terms of value, but also as an other-received love that can add to God's intensity in terms of God's nature (transmutation). Neither an "unmoved mover" nor an "unmoved love" seems to be what I seek to describe in scrutinizing Whitehead's stance.[90]

As initially intimated in Chapter 2 in a discussion of Bracken's thought, we can interpret Whitehead as presenting a model in which an intimate threshold of intensifying feelings is tightly knit to Aquinas's view on the divine loving *nature* or Godhead.[91] Something like the very *bowels* of God, and specifically pertinent to the discussion here, as Bracken indicates, the concept of *esse* found in Aquinas could be drawn nearer to the principles of creativity and the continuum of relatedness that Whitehead poses.[92] These two principles can relate to the axiom of Aquinas that the existence of God is the essence of God, that God's activity is the same as the divine nature.[93] Lastly, that God's initial impulse towards the cosmos is initiated by the divine intellective appetite with which God stirs all things towards fullness of life, might serve to show in agreement with Bracken that latent in the above axiom is the notion of a moving reality of erotic love that grounds all things, including God's existence. For Bracken, this grounding activity of all that exists is "the indeterminate subject of the divine act of existence."[94] We may say that the element of indeterminacy is the result of the primordial eros being the dimension of God that is in a continuous state of potentiality. It also reflects the complex unity of all beings as potentialities, having perished and passed as objective immortalities into the divine life. In this version of the process model, therefore, God's movement toward the divine self originates in God's unity of conceptual feelings found in the primordial eros that includes "among their data all eternal objects," which in a sense refers to the many residing in God.[95]

This view of the divine love could yield an understanding of Whitehead that shows another side of the initial divine movement of love or yearning when put in relation to the wounded God of Sobrino and the "cloud of the Godhead" expressed in the work of St. Teresa. The divine movement grounded by the multiplicity already existing in the Godhead denotes that the divine enjoyment as stemming from God's intimate union with others and not as solely from itself, in itself, and for itself (divine absolute self-subsistence). Here therefore, in this model, the principle of novelty and nontemporal accident of creativity, which is "the universe conjunctively," is grounded by the *nature of things,* for example, the many being a *complex unity.*[96] The starting point for the divine love or eros is the "universal of universals" continuously becoming a complex desire, not being a simple one. Divine simplicity in itself would lack a relational passage. So the other-directed love being espoused here differs from classical strands of thought, such as Aquinas's, concerning union with God that locate the divine simplicity as its starting point, the divine enjoyment having already taken place in the will of God, and all at once conceptually. Here lies a deep mystery of the divine loving nature—its intensifying love.

Consequently, the dynamism of the love of God as the process of one moved and moving simultaneously would be more akin to the Trinitarian perichoretic reality, in which the divine persons, though distinct, are of the same *indeterminate nature*, as Bracken purports. The "underlying nature of God" would be "the dynamic principle or ground of the divine being, and as such the ground of all finite beings," says Bracken.[97] This loving ground in movement also speaks of *one* ultimate erotic reality already conditioned by passage or sharing, because this reality refers to what Bracken, in citing Jorge Luis Nobo, argues is " 'the becoming, the being and the solidarity of all actual entities,' including God as the primordial entity."[98] So this grounding erotic activity is a vital ground of life that is already many (composed of all living beings), a complex of relatedness, not only as a Trinity but also as the many are in God as potentialities. This dynamic aspect within God is indeterminate in the sense of being always as becoming, according to loss and gain, as stated above. In view of this dynamic divine nature of love, then, we may say that even the poetic eros can also be a *conditioned* condition of all things even as it lures all things toward a wide-open future.

That the grounding activity of love provides the space for the intensifying enjoyments of all that exists, can mean that the trope of *khora* that Whitehead uses is such an erotic ground. Khora is that which Timaeus asked about, and answered, "What power, then, and what *nature* should one suppose it to have? This especially: that it is a *receptacle* for all becoming, a sort of wet-nurse."[99] Whitehead appropriates the concept of the Platonic khora to speak of the site of all becoming, which at least in the physical world is a becoming of the many actualities being "components *in each other's natures*," having an intercommunication of "*mutual immanence*."[100] Like a site of intimate encounters, the receptacle is also related to the concept of the soul, which is not separate from the whole of a living body viewed as society and in relationship with other societies. For him, "The everlasting nature of God, which in a sense is nontemporal and in another sense is temporal, may establish with the soul a *peculiarly intense relationship of mutual immanence*."[101] In the soul, life is set in motion by eros, all of which is also a life-motion activity within the "the matrix of all begetting," or khora.[102] From this peculiar intensity resulting from a mutual immanence that takes place in the khora, the primordial eros incites all things toward order by way of the world's immanent relation with an immanent God (consequent). At this juncture, Whitehead does not state how this intensity affects the primordial eros in its relation to the consequent nature and the cosmos, yet the term *mutual immanence* in relation to intensity remains vague enough to lead to various forms of interpretation, particularly the one being espoused here.

With this trope of the divine khora of love or erotic nature of creativity and relatedness, one can shift the argument at hand to a divine receptacle in which an exchange of intensifying subjects occurs. The work of Faber hints at it. Though for him, the khora is not a *formal* nature of God[103] (though I agree with Bracken that it is), he would affirm that it is the place in God that is all receptive, the divine matrix or mother of all being *by means of a mutual immanence*. There, events relate to one another, have a common medium, and God and world disappear into each other. The divine matrix is the space of relationship between God and world, and between world and God, where God is "world sensitive" and a "fellow-sufferer."[104] That is, in being capable of "feeling," and so enjoying the cosmos, God is also capable of suffering with it. This divine matrix that forms some sort of "pantheistic nimbus," consequently, cannot be one-sided and unidirectional. For example, even when speaking of the khora, one cannot solely emphasize that God insists in "being" or "becoming" as *eschatological ad-vent*" or an eschatological *advent*ure in which God originates in a distinct manner as "God."[105] This indeed is needed. But one must go further and examine the possibilities of God being likewise primordial in the sense of becoming a complex desire, of being adventurously receptivity; affected by the consequent nature as a true site of world thus the possibility of the cosmos truly affecting the divine primordial love with its multiple expressions of intense living.

In considering Bracken's understanding of the Godhead, which he draws from principles found in Aquinas's work, as I also seek to do, "the dynamic principle or ground of the divine being, and as such likewise the ground of all finite beings,"[106] implies that this life-giving process can intensify the divine lover, for it leads to passage in the mutual partaking of natures. This quasi-Aquinan concept is both latent and implied in Whitehead. According to Bracken, it speaks of "one reality" that exists primordially in God since it constitutes primarily the divine nature or ground, and secondarily the world.[107] This allows Bracken to conclude that the relatedness between God and world is naturally perichoretic in its mutual loving immanence.

And while "God is all that God can be at this moment in the divine existence," for God self-determines the divine self, "in the next moment God can acquire a new determination so that God is in some sense other than (though not better than) God is here and now."[108] This is so because the erotic activity of God and the ground of all existence, a premise he finds present in the work of Aquinas, "serves as the 'relational complex' for all actual occasions" (Whitehead's thought) in the same manner that interrelates the divine persons.[109] The underlying activity of all existence is "God-Love," or the self-emptying activity or loss in the sense of opening up space that creates "an all-encompassing 'energy field' or 'matrix,'"[110] which can be a mutually immanent intensifying process, as all things are found in God. Similar to St. Teresa of Avila's concept of the wound or "the cloud of the Godhead," in which the lovers find it hard to distinguish one from the other (hence their mutual pleasure), this concept of mutual immanence can help define the intensifying process of the divine love.[111]

The multiple in God could be the element of the divine intensity of enjoyment. As Faber and Keller observe, in the concept of this "perfect multiplicity"[112] are glimpses of a *theoplicity* and an expression of *polyphilia* of God in the form of intensification as a result of the *passages* that define the creative complex of relatedness.[113] The beloved lover God opening up space for the cosmos could also be interpreted as God insisting on a process of self-creativity from the many in their own many forms affecting God primordially with their self-creativity. That would be true indeterminacy! True adventure! One could argue that this power of divine love resists such definitions of self-determination. Otherwise, would not God's enjoyment be of satisfaction, once again, as in self-enclosure (something absolutely finished or accomplished once and for all), something like an "unmoved love" most akin to the Aristotelian model we have challenged thus far?

MEANINGFUL CONTRASTS OF ADDED INTENSITY

"For God the conceptual is prior to the physical," Whitehead writes.[114] This means that the movements of the love of God toward the cosmos are initiated by things not yet actual. But what does this mean if the starting point of the divine movement is potentiality in the sense of becoming a complex desire? This principle of novelty might mean that love as the grounding activity opens the medium of a divine passionately intense enjoyment, by which God acquires more permeable "physical" boundaries, without God and world collapsing into one another. Further, it might mean that all living beings in God can intensify the divine intensity according to the ways and by means of passion, in this way adding something to the poetic eros through the consequent nature.

In God, seeming contrasts, such as joy and sorrow, meet, possibly intensifying the divine passion for life.[115] In Chapter 1 this was posited in relation to the divine suffering with the world. If we understand God as the home of our insatiable longings and as becoming with the cosmos, God would *yearn* with a joy mixed with sorrow, as God endures within, moment by moment, the physical actualizations and the partly present and delayed fulfillments of greater forms of enjoyment of the cosmos (in our time and place). An excessive physicality characterizes this divine yearning, for climactic fulfillments engender greater desire for more delight not yet present, bottomless desire. In affirming this bottomlessness mixture within a more radical openness to the cosmos, one agrees to carefully consider a God who takes into the divine inner life "all the currents of feeling in existence," as Hartshorne insightfully argues.[116] God would suffer and have joy with the "all" simultaneously, hence the intensified desire that ensues (other than a plain sense of God as source and end of enjoyment).

With a more explicitly panentheist flare than in Chapter 1, I argue, therefore, in agreement with Hartshorne that the divine influence within a broken existence would take on the form of a being who is "most open to influence" and most "adequately moved by what moves" all creatures.[117] From the most intense pain to the most exhilarating joy, the whole spectrum of it, God would not only know what all creatures feel but also how they feel, and would find a divine joy mixed with pain in sharing their lives in all their contradictory elements, "lives, lived according to their own free decisions, not fully anticipated by any detail plan."[118] This all-encompassing sufferer suffers with the whole array of highs and lows of the cosmos that Gloria Schaab, in drawing from evolutionary scientific principles, describes as belonging to the creative processes of life. In a "dynamic process of ongoing creativity and growth" inherent in the created order lies an intrinsic measure of risk toward enjoyment that both God and all beings are willing to take, which introduces the possibility of God and us suffering in, with, and under the cosmos's own advancements (even if at times these may come by seemingly destructive means).[119] This would be like what Hartshorne views as the natural consequence of the "democratic self-ordering of a world whose members not even the supreme orderer reduces to mere subjects with the sole function of obedience." It would be another instance of the Aristotelian emperor-God of chapter 1 being turned upside down. God would not be a mere ruler but a supremely sensitive God who allots to all creatures the "privilege of participation in governing which goes infinitely beyond a mere ballot."[120]

Jay McDaniel describes it as God feeling the terror and suffering of a gray whale being killed by an orca as much as the satisfaction the orca feels as it kills the whale. Humans, animals, and plants seek to *survive with satisfaction*," which invites tragedy when incompatible yet legitimate aims come into play. "God is not One-over-many but, rather, One-embracing-many," says McDaniel.[121] In this sense the God of history would embrace "the biological, geological, and cosmic as well as human history," as the whole of the cosmos unfolds in God.[122] Although God is not bounded by the processes of the universe, the universe becomes an element of the intensity of the divine enjoyment. And although this view is not arguing for a divine will ruling over all things, and neither for all things being equally ethical, it seeks to affirm that all things, even if seemingly contradictory, come to be a part of the adventurous love of God. What an intense contentment might God's be!

Another way to explain it would be in terms of the individual elements or different expressions of a single work of art, as in the colors and strokes of a painting that appear to be contrasting but are not. For Whitehead, "every actual fact is a fact of an aesthetic experience," which is an "intense experience," of "feeling arising out of the realization of contrast under identity."[123] In art, many seeming contrasts compose a single identity or artistic expression. We know this is also the case for all living beings, for they are composed of many parts, for example, as embodied. But how can one speak in similar terms regarding God? Could one say that the primordial eros is "the absolute standard of intensity" in that God's complex desire acquires flesh in ways akin to a harmonious contrast through the consequent nature (i.e., "joyful body of pain," as evidenced in the discussion of sadomasochism in Chapter 3)?

Arguably, Faber would provide a partly negative answer. For him, nothing of the cosmos can intensify what is already *"infinitely intensive."* In an argument against Hartshorne's views regarding the difference between the temporal process of God and the cosmos, a different view from what I am seeking to describe here, he firmly says:

> God's primordial nature, rather than needing a world, is instead itself pure gift for the self-fulfillment of events. God's consequent nature, on the other hand, does not acquire extra intensity through its reception of world events—for God is already *infinitely intensive* by virtue of God's own primordial nature; instead God's consequent nature purposelessly heals all contradictions and discordances in the world. This is what enables God to perceive the world *undistorted* in its freedom from purpose and save it in a surprising, unanticipated integration in divine harmony (groundlessly and without 'functional' intension) (Maasen 1988). God's infinite intensity pours itself out, without any dark reserve, like the good (*bonum diffusvum sui*).[124]

In part, Faber seeks to speak of the consequent nature as the space that God opens within Godself so that things can remain multiple and differentiated, and can be reconciled in that differentiation. God, while being relationally transcendent (not external), would remain *"differently* immanent."[125] Also, in his view he seeks to describe an inner divine process that starts with satisfaction, may we say, self-enjoyment or contentment, which in God is defined by an eschatological sense of potentiality (the not yet actual). This is according to Whitehead's understanding of the "absolute standard of intensity,"[126] which, as Faber explains, implies that God as primordial is pure potentiality, not in the sense of deficiency and lack but as the site of novelty that withdraws to bequeath possibility and creative communication.[127] In this way, we may say once again that the divine love is unconditioned in that it is potentiality itself. So God gifts Godself out of God's own satisfaction and pleasure, and thus is the fount as potentiality of all cosmic intensities in their peculiar forms.

Yet as we follow this line of reasoning, a question arises. Could even the consequent nature receive any intensity from the cosmos, or would it instead do so solely from the primordial nature of God? Would that mean, then, that the divine harmony in healing all contradictions with a purpose is devoid of meaningful contrasts? How would God not love according to sameness, that is, as an autarkic ego? Would it not also place receiving intensity from the cosmos on a par with God needing nothing from the cosmos in the sense of the cosmos being superfluous to the divine enjoyment, as argued in Chapter 2? If so, how different would Whitehead's view be from that of Aquinas, which affirms that the divine love lacks passion in that it receives nothing from the cosmos, for it needs nothing from the cosmos? How could we then argue for a God of passion, that is, a divine beloved lover who feels *intensely* things other than God? As Hartshorne quips, "And how can a perfect being change (as it must if relations to the changing world are internal to it)?"[128]

The answers can be found in Whitehead, I suggest, for whom intensity points to the principle of multiplicity.[129] This is a key concept in the process model and to any understanding of the divine loving nature that Faber himself embraces. For Whitehead, "'givenness' and 'potentiality' are both meaningless apart from a multiplicity of potential entities."[130] With regard to the erotic nature, this means that "God is primordially one, namely, he is the primordial unity of relevance of the many potential forms; in the process he acquires a consequent multiplicity, which the primordial character absorbs into its own unity."[131] There the primordial eros could feel the cosmos intensely as it encounters the consequent nature of God. The primordial eros can achieve an intense satisfaction at each moment of unity as many contrasting elements become meaningfully defined within God and by Godself in relation to the cosmos.[132]

A principle of "aesthetic contrast" comes into play. What I see happening is the multiple creating a meaningful and harmonious contrast that the erotic grounding activity continuously puts into play—the manifoldness of the perfections. The many not only mutually "disturb" one another as they unite in one experience, they also disturb God. The exclusion of these feelings would be perfection, but one can say that in God, this perfection carries the sense of "a *positive* feeling of discordance," which is disruptive in nature and thus does away with anesthesia or staleness.[133] In this respect, the Whiteheadian model counteracts the Aristotelian understanding of enjoyment that, according to Heschel, results in a form of divine anesthesia.[134] In Whitehead what we find instead is a principle of unity of individual intensities joining together without "a tame elimination or a tame scaling down" of both unity and individuality.[135] This erotic unity is a harmonious discord or a harmony of contrasts. In this sense, intensity is the result not only of "the positive feeling of the whole as Harmonious" but also of the "whole as discordant."[136] Harmony and discordance are felt as such individually and each in relation to the other. As for Whitehead, "For the understanding of Harmony and Discord it is essential to remember that strength of experience, in massiveness and in intensity, depends upon the substratum of detail being composed of significant individuals."[137] Hartshorne explains contrasts as "contrary determinations in the same entity" that preserve polarity and are "necessary for co-presence and mutual dependence of opposite determinations."[138]

So how can something that is *infinitely intensive* or perfect in every way gain added intensity by means of added value? How can one say that the divine love gains an increased intensity without attributing necessity and lack to the divine enjoyment? Perhaps one can consider the manner in which for Hartshorne the term perfect means "worthy of admiration and respect."[139] Like Aquinas, he takes the path of excellence. The primary good is for every creature to "enjoy rich harmonies of living, and pour its richness into the one ultimate receptacle of all achievement, the life of God."[140] God is enriched by the knowledge of our love—as "we present God with a more beautiful creation than he enjoyed before."[141] Our enjoyment adds value to God, a concept that places "value" at another level of adventurous relatedness. Furthermore, with his view on added value, concepts such as "perfect," "absolute," and "infinite" acquire the sense of the enjoyment to all relations as they are in all their respects—being inclusive of all reality.[142] For Hartshorne, "Supreme dependence will thus reflect all influences—with *infinite* sensitivity registering relationship to the last and least item of events. Is this not genuinely something eminent and supreme?"[143] In this sense he is revising the way of excellence by saying that God is ideally good and great, not by being an absolute unincreasable value "but by being *unsurpassable by another* than himself . . . only God can surpass God, but this he perpetually does by ideally absorbing the riches of creation into himself."[144] God is supremely relative to all beings in their otherness, and our very existence enhances God, for we ultimately contribute to "the evergrowing divine treasury of values."[145] In that sense God contains the unique divine value (identity of God as God) and also additional value (meaningful contrasts or differences), both combining to define the term "better" in the sense of excellence or eminence,[146] perhaps another dimension of God as "the best lover" that one can envision along with Marion.[147]

The divine matrix activates a passion for acquiring an intense physicality via its openings that porously receive the whole of the cosmos within. As Keller describes it, the divine matrix is "a layered complexity, a multidimensionality of becoming, in which differences are neither kept separate (as in a clearly bounded dyad of Creator/creature) nor fused (as in a pantheistic substance) but held in contrast."[148] Seen through the lenses of the khora, God is "the *Not-Other*" or *non aliud* in the sense of God being the *Manyone* that Keller speaks of in conversation with Nicolas of Cusa and Faber.[149] It unfolds into what Cusa calls a "*coincidentia oppositorum*," which then comprises the multiplicity of the universe, and, in agreement with Faber, refers to the One not "withdrawn from the many" nor yet distinguished from them.[150] The grounding activity of divine love continuously provides the threshold into physicality by means of all things being welcomed into God. For Keller, God incarnates the many as God houses the universe in the sense of the many things that are not God being in God. In the divine act of differentiating, all things become out of everything and return to the everything, "the many-becoming-many ones."[151] God is the "*differential plenum*" that is not opposed to the many but contains it— God is a collective, even in terms of race, gender, and species in all their seemingly contrasting forms.

One might ask, therefore, if the khora is the site of intensification of the many forms of intensity coming together as one without scaling or taming down the divine intensity,[152] and if one considers this notion of harmonious contrasts as some form of perfection that is found in the khoric site of mutual immanence between God and the cosmos, could one say that the many perfected in God according to their own individuality can intensify the intensity of the divine Eros as it meets the consequent (physical)? Perhaps the perfected many as if contrasts can add to the intensity of God, for fullness of divine enjoyment, while each internally self-enjoy themselves in their individuality. The divine intense love therefore would be increasable by means of God's grounding activity, God's intensely manifold perfecting processes, and *polyphilic* in that it also "feels" by way of the multiple "feelings" encountering each other within the divine matrix. God opens space within God for a differentiating differentiated whole of intensifying intensities.

The multiple self-enjoyments, all in connection with one another, can be the reason for the infinitely intensive aspect of the primordial eros seeking physicality. Along with Keller, we may say that "differences are intensified by being brought into relation."[153] All things in God come also to contribute to the divine intensity as a result of being together in an open-ended manner (potentiality). The *in* of the *in*carnation of the divine as a *Manyone* acts as a trace of desire for each life form to designate "an active indeterminacy, a commingling of unpredictable, and yet recapitulatory, *self-organizing relations*."[154] Each in their own self-expression of organizing enjoyments intermingling as lovers within the divine lover might then intensify one another and God.

This speaks of a Trinitarian reality according to openness to the cosmos that can *add* something to the divine primordial intensifying organ of novelty, as the primordial meets the consequent already wounded by the cosmos. The khoric or zimzumic "within a within" activity that results in God contracting Godself can lead to an intensity of God, God's self-enjoyment in the opening of space within God for *différance* and multiplicity.[155] Allowing differences to reside in God intensifies God,[156] as God grounds all meaningful contrast within God. Each living being's enjoyment or cusp of contentment coincides within God, appearing *as if* opposites or contrasts. This means that God as lover feels intensely.[157] Along with Keller, we can even consider "the zoological fecundity, the bestial intensity," where nature appears as undomesticated within God.[158] Going beyond the anthropological, the divine intensity is also about "their lives, their patterns of eating, mating, birthing and moving."[159] What a divine intensity ensues from the multiple forms of enjoyment of the cosmos joining God! How else could we describe this celestial form of lovemaking with the cosmos?

INCARNATING ESSENCE

The wounded *bowels* of God open themselves before the cosmos to offer a space within not only for intensifying loves and pleasures but also for passage akin to transmutation. The divine khoric womb of love where lovers exchange selves has incarnating and transmuting capabilities by which God can begin to take on the form of the one whom God loves as in lovemaking.[160] This divine space provides God with the pleasure of incarnating the joys and pains of the *pluriverse*.[161] This *in*-between site of pleasurable becomings allows God to receive a flesh of intense loves from the cosmos, and, as a lover, for God to be present in the form of a silhouette, as foreshadowed in the previous chapter. With the marks of the cosmos on its flesh, this silhouette smells like the scented passions of the cosmos.

At this juncture one returns once again to the initial argument made with the discussion of Bracken concerning Aquinas's view of the divine loving nature or Godhead of which all the persons of the Trinity as well as the created order partake. For Keller the notion of the "divine matrix" that Bracken places analogous to the "Godhead" provides a panentheistic model that allows for some expression of apophatic commingling, that is, a preservation of otherness.[162] Furthermore, in the work of Keller, the notion of a divine matrix implies that God has a body, something "that suggests the radically incarnational *nature* of that God." Hence one might say that the divine intensity refers in part to the divine nature as something shared with the many, something that is intrinsic to God as the many that God enfleshes, at least in part.

Another way to express this thought of the divine nature is through the work of Ivone Gebara, which harmonizes somewhat with panentheism. In commenting on Sallie McFague, she writes, "The distinction McFague proposes requires deeper reflection. To say that in the panentheist perspective God does have a body and is incarnate, but not necessarily or totally, means that the last word on the mystery that enfolds us is not our own. It signifies openness to the possibility of all that is different, unpredictable, and unutterable."[163] Agreeing with McFague, Gebara argues that the divine embodiment or "divine milieu" is sacramental (incarnational mystery). Furthermore, *relatedness*, for Gebara, being inclusive of all in the one (as the one has been classically perceived as being in the all) is an expression of the "esse-diversity of God."[164] Particularly by considering her expression of divine *esse* or *ousia* of eros (apparent also in the work of Bracken) one can turn explicitly to the many as the mystery of embodied diversity (more explicitly so than Bracken has done thus far).

Of course, Gebara in her writings shows no evidence of seeking to directly engage Whiteheadian thought, much less the views of Bracken or

Keller. She briefly shares similar theological inclinations with McFague, whose work is an explicit response to Hartshorne,[165] but not exclusively so. Gebara admits to engaging with the ideas of various astrophysicists and of ecofeminists whose focus is a "reality-in-process."[166] Her thought is also grounded in her Latin American contexts, for example, her life among the poor of Brazil. So here I am not arguing that she is a process thinker, or explicitly a panentheist. Yet Gebara's concepts can shed some light on Bracken's views, particularly how for him relatedness can be seen as an expression of creativity and the extensive continuum, as well as on the concept of multiplicity that Keller espouses. In particular, her understanding of *relatedness* is useful when conceptualizing the incarnational aspect of the *Manyone* and its relationship to intensity, since Keller has remained interested in Gebara's ideas on embodiment herself.[167] With God's loving nature being relatedness, as Gebara argues, we can be in some way the creators of relatedness, for "we are of its substance and it is of our substance."[168]

That we are cocreators might mean that the site of becoming has incarnating attributes. For Gebara, otherness being incarnate as relatedness is—like the concept of "*esse*-diversity"—life as God. In this regard, Gebara is unique. She refers to God not as a person but as the ground of all life, thus the mystery of life itself. As discussed in Chapter 2, she seeks to avoid some assumptions of classical theism concerning God. For her, "we can no longer go on insisting on the traditional notion of a God/person—that is, a separate being superior to all that exists, a kind of superperson with the power to 'control' the universe, human life, and the morality of our actions."[169] A "superperson" resembles the definition of God as *ipsum esse per se subsistens* that I am challenging. Likewise, temporarily placing the question on person or being in the background aids in considering the aspect of the loving nature of God and a more "*bona fide* social ontology" that Bracken, and now Gebara, can help us visualize.[170]

Furthermore, the connection of the concept of "*esse*-diversity" with "life" itself points more specifically to the divine nature of dynamic love seeking embodiment. At this juncture, Gebara's views can become tightly knitted with the views of various feminist theologians, discussed in Chapter 1, who speak of life as a divine source of vivification. Gebara describes relatedness as "the *underlying fabric* that is continually brought forth within *the vital process* in which we are immersed," "a *constitutive reality* for the universe and for life" or "the ultimate ground of all that exists," and that which *"animates all* living beings."[171] In this sense, one can argue for an "*esse*-diversity" that finds its home in God (without the loss of its earthly attributes) and that enlivens the whole cosmos. One might say, therefore, that the divine matrix that Bracken and Keller describe intensely vivifies all things in receiving the happenings of the cosmos. So without diluting the differences, but rather preserving the all-encompassing mystery, as stated above, the ground of all life, relatedness, is unspeakably binding— "*utterance, word, attraction, flux, energy, and passion*."[172] It is the embodying ground that vivifies everything, as all beings vivify one another, even God.

Subsequently, with reference to Bracken's thoughts on the Godhead, discussed above, we may also consider a nuanced view of Gebara's understanding of *esse*-diversity. God's incarnational *esse* points to the verb "to be." God *is* love, the *ousia* of God being love,[173] but in the sense that God's embodying being "links everything with everything, and everything with all" in ways that make it difficult to dissociate the one flesh from the many.[174] So the incarnating capacities of God's very *bowels* can be seen in that God's being "constitutes the cosmos and all life forms," by maintaining both "multiplicity and unity" and interdependence.[175] Furthermore, it might mean that the ground of all becomings continuously longs to receive flesh from the cosmos, and so becomes flesh of its flesh, an erotic flesh, in all its magnificent difference, perhaps another key manner to draw from Marion's metaphor of God as "the best lover."[176]

The khora or *bowels* of God is therefore the site in which the divine erotic love can partly embody the cosmos. As exemplified in the model of St. Teresa of Avila, "the cloud of the Godhead" can also take the shape of a wound, an opening in God's flesh. God is wounded and penetrated as much as she herself is wounded by the arrows of divine love, at which moment distinctions, while not being annulled, become blurry. Hence one can affirm that just as the cosmos is an enfleshment of heaven here on earth, so the divine eros incarnates a myriad of cosmic intensities, even if accounting for seemingly contradictory expressions of all living things saying "Yes" to life, "Come," and "Again!"[177] The divine love is adventurous in that God allows all these expressions to affect God intimately, to the point that the love of God acquires an intense physicality in relation to the cosmos. In the divine wounded bowels, the interminglings of God and cosmos acquire flesh, as lovers do, by trading places in some measure (passage).

NEPHESH, FLESH OF MY FLESH

As already noted in our discussion of St. Thomas Aquinas, God has desires that lie within the intellective activities of God. Aquinas states that whereas in creatures, intellect and appetite are two distinct aspects, God's appetite is of the intellect, and a single activity.[178] Following this logic, one can say that God loves only in the sense of having an intellective appetite. Because of this, Aquinas argues, God does not love according to passion, something already posited in previous chapters. Passion corresponds to parts, primarily bodily, and to a succession of events, and thus to change. And since God, who is simple, does not change, for him love is according to the intellect. Aquinas sets this statement in the framework of his understanding of Aristotle, saying, "Hence the Philosopher says (*Ethic.* vii): *God rejoices by an operation that is one and simple*, and for the same reason He loves without passion."[179] In Aquinas, in the act of the intellective appetite there is no transmutation, even less a body of God to speak of.[180]

In Whitehead's model, as a supplement to Aquinas, there is room for transmutation of the divine eros as God acquires physicality, that is, embodiment, arising out of the divine relationship with the cosmos. Here Hartshorne's analogy of the body may be employed again. Apart from his arguments on the Platonic model of the soul-body,[181] his view of the body of God as society may help us gain insight into how the *Manyone* shares the divine nature with a myriad of creatures seeking to enjoy and enjoying themselves in their own unique intense forms. So God would be a body of enjoyment, of multiple pleasures and pains, or a "creaturely society" coming together at each point of the divine complex differentiated unity. The divine bodily society would contain "not merely a multitude of radically subpersonal entities, such as cells or molecules, but also multitudes of multicellular plants and animals, including persons and those nearly personal creatures the apes and whales, and who knows what other forms of life on the astronomically probable billions of planets?"[182]

Here Faber's caution, divulged earlier, is fitting to a point, for one cannot conceive of God purely as a sequence of events. According to Faber,

Whitehead's concept of the primordial eros safeguards God from being bound to world processes in ways Hartshorne purports, according to Faber. Instead, for Faber, the movement of the divine eros rightly does not stem from the world events. So God, who is the *"unconditional condition* of that world process,"[183] is also unconditioned by and independent of its process.[184] Here we must also consider the aspect of adventure that is characteristic of potentiality (primordial eros). For Faber specifically, God as unconditioned love is eternal and the inexhaustible source of possibilities (the primordial nature), recoiling into the divine self and turning toward the world in its activity of becoming. In the process of ordering itself there is always this element of unconditioned adventure.

Yet here again, in complementary fashion, rather than simply contradictory, the concept of the *Manyone* already belonging to the divine loving nature provides a quasi-Hartshornian alternative—God would partly transmute the divine self according to the diverse intensities of the cosmos in ways such that God did not cease to be God. In Whitehead's terminology, God would become God not "from the world itself,"[185] in terms of the divine self-creative capacity but (as Bracken argues) in reference to the divine erotic nature of love. As consequent, God would evolve as the world evolves "without derogation to the eternal completion of its primordial conceptual nature,"[186] yet God's primordial love would also take on the shape or transmute itself partly in accordance with the cosmos because of their shared nature.

As lovers do, and as implied above, categories become blurry when one considers a passage of earthly realities into the divine realities, and vice versa. For example, the memories of the past inform the future, as much as the future does the past. The craving for novelty would be affected by the "terror at the loss of the past, with its familiarities and its loved ones," as Whitehead would say.[187] But also the joy of the new years, accompanied by the terror of the loss of "friendship, and love, and old association," can lead to revolting from mere preservation. Furthermore, the body analogy comes closer to the manner in which God incarnates the cosmically multiple in ways that also account for the element of novelty alongside disharmony, the manner in which God brings freshness and hope out of the wreckage.[188] The point is to preserve the divine perfection, and by the same token to accord complexity to the dimensions of God. And unlike the flesh of Marion's lover God, this God appears to be quite heterogeneous, comprised of many ostensibly contrasting and thus internally intensifying elements of permanence and novelty, of intellect and body, of inner and outer. Similar to the experience of sadomasochism defined in Chapter 3, God feels all things and in all things their differences, without them being tamed down or anesthetized. It is quite significant that with the body imagery, the divine intensity can begin to gain tangibility—real bodies and their histories, earthly becomings—alongside an intellective appetite.

This is key as one considers how the happenings of history can thus intimately affect the beloved divine lover in terms of passion, as God partly incarnates them, so that healing may occur, a concern already shared in Chapter 1. The many in the one bring in something of the past living histories and traditions with them, their perpetual perishings (*passing* on, passage), perhaps even as something objectively immortal (transcendence).[189] Here Gebara's views are also helpful. More specific to her, just as all living beings, past and present, are linked in God, and like life itself, we become a "Sacred Body" or the "'divine milieu' in which we live and have our being," that is, we collectively take part in history in the making.[190]

Accordingly, the divine *manifoldness* has a body memory, for as one body, we are of one substance. Memory is a concept that automatically implies being influenced and not just influencing, as Hartshorne explains.[191] "It is objects as such that influence subjects," he writes. God remembers as God prehends us and our histories. So memory can be seen as God "utilizing previous events as materials for new syntheses, the syntheses themselves furnishing new such materials, and so on forever—this principle expresses not only how the world hangs together, but also how it depends upon and yet also influences God."[192] So one can say that God enlivens not only from an open-ended future but also with the traces of a lived past that God receives as God unites with us, and we find ourselves within God.[193]

Gebara, distinct from Hartshorne but somewhat relatedly, describes memory as a Trinitarian reality that integrates all things (even things past) accordingly:

> I am, but at the same time I am thousands of lives and circumstances that have gone before me to weave and prepare for my personal life. I am myself, but I am also the countless lives that went before me. I am my ancestors, with their

personal histories; their voices and traditions run through my veins. I am I, but my being goes beyond my individuality, beyond the personal story limited by the years of my own life. This does not mean I cannot call myself "I," as a person who is to a certain extent free and autonomous, who loves and hates and hopes. But it means that my personal reality, my autonomy, is always relational, "dependent on. . . ."[194]

With the metaphor of the body one can incorporate some form of body memory into our understanding of eschatological hope (derived from Faber). Those whom we have loved become a part of us and God, a memory not static in form but dynamic and interconnected.[195] In that sense, God would be the "universal brotherhood/sisterhood" that, like a "collective pregnancy," simultaneously is an "ancient newness"[196] and the sap of all life that vivifies all things. The divine love and appetite flowing back into the cosmos might connote a sort of ancestral vivification—*being* as in living intensely even in relation to ancient pains and endured horrors. As Gebara says, the "esse-diversity" of God is "life in its extraordinary richness . . . that unfolds in the complexity of a vital mystery."[197] So the divine intensity would be an eschatological adventure in that it is akin to this sense of "ancient newness" that acquires a flesh.

So why not affirm a divine passion akin to this kind of vivifying incarnation of an "eschatology" that is "comingled with earth" that one finds expressed in Gebara's work? Why not say that as an "ancient newness" most akin to a relational *"esse*-diversity", God loves intensely, and thus intensifies all living beings in the divine incarnation? Further, why not account for an explicit body imagery, and present a more fluid understanding of the intellective and physical dimensions of God? Why not account for a passionate love of God flowing back into the cosmos? How should we describe this complex form of intense embodiment when we consider these elements of harmonious contrasts? What would the divine silhouette begin to look like? This speaks to a Trinitarian reality in which there are passage and transmutation rather than self-enclosure and mirror-like enjoyment (Chapter 2); hence the element of disordering orders. The divine matrix or complex of relatedness would therefore be not only harmonious but also a chaotic nexus, not only a grounding but also groundless, hence disruptive of orders that ensue in a divine enjoyment akin to sameness.

DISRUPTIVE INCARNATIONS

In embodying the cosmos, the *multiple passages* between God and the cosmos occurring in the depths of God are akin to eruptions, disruptions, and interruptions, something "cosmically" destructive or seemingly deathlike out of which new life bursts forth. As Burrus explains, death can grant life to a body of flesh as it makes it visible, that is, as flesh becomes flesh.[198] This concept, too, is akin to Cusa's notion of the *complicatio* that Keller creatively identifies with "'the chaos which contains all.'"[199] The chaotic nexus holds a relation to "appetition" or desire in that each individuated potentiality is in an in-between phase of becoming actual in relation to its past and desired future.[200] In the divine process, God is (as actual) also a God who may be (possibility)[201] in ways that appear disorderly, as the potentialities with their immortalized past histories join a complex desire that cannot be defined according to a particular order in the future.[202]

An element of groundlessness would come into play in ways that affirm divine indeterminacy as potentiality. The quality of disruption within permanence of the chaotic nexus is not too unlike the principles on the *harmony of the least* espoused in Chapter 1. And, as Whitehead observes, a certain quality of disorder, in the arrangement of musical notes can be "harmony standing amid dissonance"[203] that has the potential to give rise to new forms of social orders and divine becomings. They are what they have always been as musical notes, yet when rearranged, they have the potential to become something new as well. Harmony is both the depths of unplumbed potentiality and permanence.[204] These seeming contrasting elements are not mere opposites; rather, as coincident they carry the intensity of transformed orders.

So, alongside the grounding process of the primordial eros there is also the welcoming of the "right amount of chaos" that disrupts stasis. In other words, not only does an ideal future reside in it, so also does this "intensity of space—that chaotic potentiality which (try as you might) cannot be kept outside and other," as Keller writes.[205] Being of God, and as God seeks physicality, in that intermediate state, the divine eros partly incarnates our intensities, and to an extent becomes us and so embodies us, appearing to be indeterminately disruptive of order as well. She writes, "As God becomes our bodies, as our bodies relax, breathe and bleed into the Sacred Body of all bodies, let the formal relation of 'God' to 'chaos' begin to take flesh as well."[206]

Why not consider this "Body of the universe" according to the concept of a meaningful disorder that disrupts categories with their neat associations? For God to be a harmony of contrasts means that the divine enjoyment would stem from a "milieu" that is not a socialized version of a perfect "being in itself" but rather as an open-ended or groundless realm that embodies even seemingly destructive forces with a purpose.[207] As throbbing energy flows through us, we are attracted to others, and can be disruptive toward one another, which is a part of the enigma of *life*, as Gebara indicates. For Whitehead specifically, "Perfections of diverse types are among themselves discordant. Thus the contribution to Beauty which can be supplied by Discord—in itself destructive and evil—is the positive feeling of a quick shift of aim from the tameness of outworn perfection to some other ideal with its freshness still upon it."[208] This means that a certain lack of perfection, one that is not purely evil, can lead to yet a greater form of perfection, which is the very definition of beauty and harmony.

While this view of a sacred embodied milieu would not mean that God causes evil in the cosmos (for God is not evil), or even needs it to feel intensely, as Faber warns us,[209] it would mean that God is capable of embodying this element of disruption that seems destructive. As Gebara indicates, if there is a "continuity of the universe's creative process"[210] among all living beings, including God, then both "creation and destruction" must be a part of the Trinitarian reality-in-process since both "are expressions of a single vital process."[211] Relatedness is the place where one discovers both the cross and its resurrections.[212] God embodying life or *being life* means that God, while not being evil, is capable of embodying death for the purposes of birthing new forms of order. It is an attraction that "pours forth from every direction: from persons, animals, and vegetables; from the sun, the moon, and the stars; from love poems and loneliness; from today and even from the garbage."[213] This seemingly chaotic divine body, therefore, can appear to be negative or opposite to God, but it is not. Particularly, for Gebara, it is the mystery of God being "man, woman, breeze, hurricane, tenderness, jealousy, compassion, mercy."[214]

The beloved lover God partly becomes us, as the divine dimensions are partly turned upside down, an intensifying ordering disorder, as the divine love feels intensely the many all at once in the khoric pantheistic nimbus.

The intensity is of *mutual immanence* and can be akin to a chaotic intensity of many loves, which to me only quickens a passion that is a life-giving novelty, that ruptures the same, thus does away with ataraxia. So beauty would be more in the sense of a harmonious unity akin to an ordering disorder that enhances potentiality for new things to emerge out of the wreckage.[215] Like "an aesthetic value of discords in art," God partly becomes turmoil and wreckage,[216] the divine "milieu of milieus" composed of many dimensions also in the sense of groundlessness and ordering disorders (memories of horror integrated so as to be healed) that God becomes, at least in part.[217]

Here Keller's captivation with the Deleuzian reading of the Leibnezian Baroque aspects is helpful, for she places it in direct relationship to Whitehead's philosophy of becoming, and in comparison to a chaotic multiplicity. So God's aesthetic dimension with its "curls, spirals, labyrinths, drapes, pleats" would be more Baroque than perfectly arranged with all intensities permanently pre-ordered.[218] Likewise for Gebara, "God's Baroque" eschatological face would show forth the harmonious contrast of the "esse-diversity," its groans and celebrations, "God as part of our own bodies."[219] Otherwise God cannot be a process, or a being who incarnates the cosmos (complexity rather than simplicity). The divine intensity too is manifold, unfolding and enfolding in multisited urgings and labyrinthic pulsations that grant depth to the God-cosmos relationship, as I reread Keller's views.

The beloved lover yearns for becoming with the cosmos, and so God chooses to be wounded and penetrated, as St. Teresa would say, and partly becomes us, enjoys us with a purpose. The divine bodily mystery of relatedness and interdependence of all with all is an *esse*-diversity, which passion enlivens all things as it links each one with another, as God also links the divine self to them is for life. Each becomes in touch and is touched by the wreckage. God, humans, and nonhumans are vivified by a passion capable of enduring the tragic. Life with its vibrant mortality invites us to love intensely or passionately so that with this passion we can see new things being born in conversation with the old. Gebara explains,

> In some ways, things that appear negative are an energy that is capable of developing within us the capacity for loving others: for bending to those who have fallen on the road, for taking in an abandoned child, for replanting a ravaged forest; for cleaning up a polluted river, for feeding animals during

a time of drought. Out of the garbage we accumulate, a flower can bloom.
Dry bones can return to life; the horror of war can become a cradle of
compassion.[220]

It means that the "horror or pain" and "freshness of hope"[221] that Whitehead speaks of are the very expression of who God is in continuity with us,
as we are with one another, so that there might be collective hope. Rather
than being above the "filth, ostracism, and destruction," God could in some
mysterious way be mixed up with it, "in the squalor of our lives," as Gebara
writes.[222] In that lack of divine absence from "the hell of warfare and from
the hell of betrayal and destruction . . . from the most serious situations of
social injustice and exclusion"—simply put, "from what we call 'evil,'"[223]—
the whole of what we are as a body becomes "the site of multiple resurrections."[224] And as Whitehead describes it, even tragic events are not a total
loss.[225] One can also agree with Keller, therefore: in the *complicatio* lies "the
materialization of the possible" not devoid of "a folding-together of our
species' gifted and crucifying history."[226] May we therefore agree with Gebara that all things, even if ridden with death, can become the potential for
an intense life, even in God (Trinitarian reality) since "the potentialities of
the universe, the potentialities of life, and the potentialities of human life"
can be viewed as being always open-ended?[227] God as life is open-ended.
The not yet of the open whole is an adventure not devoid of paradoxical
intensities of which all partake.

Creation out of turmoil means that along the borders of chaos, life moves
restlessly. At its borders are the "eruption of difference," the emergence of
"self-organizing systems," or states that are far from equilibrium and seemingly unable to maintain "any ordered complexity" says Keller.[228] Yet, as she
also indicates, "the channeling or self-organizing of this 'depth of original-
ity' allows organic life to stabilize, evolve, and socialize."[229] The chaotic disruptions of the depths of life can bring new reconfigurations according to
love. This is salvation through creativity, a creativity that is in many ways
poetic. For this reason we would agree to be guided by poetry along paths
that are deviant, nonlinear, that lack certainty and disrupt categories. God
would be the poetic lover who chooses to be wounded, to partly become in
the likeness of the cosmic poem, to trade places within a divine intimate
space, to become God and not God, and yet a God who again incarnates

a love not fearful of adventure. I concur with Gebara, who insists on the poetic, for "linear thinking evokes a path of rectitude, a path that clearly manifests positive moral connotations. It is far removed from circuitous thought patterns, which imply twisting, morally devious ways."[230] The divine poetic eros aids us in imagining even—or above all—God as being deviant from the norms that enforce harmony defined as *uni*formity!

Perhaps this will take us into other incarnational paths and help us conceive of the beloved lover as "the disorderly deity who brings on the carnival" that Keller invites us to explore in the work of Althaus-Reid.[231] The metaphors of the erotic nature press even further against the membrane of the Platonic khora, and turn the metaphor of perichoresis into a carnivalesque dance of many lovers. This will entail disrupting the view of any neatly organized chaos that fails to perceive concepts such as "the moist uncertain zones of our bodies, of every body,"[232] and, I would add, other improper forms of embodiment that take the notion of *in*carnation into unchartered territories. How adventurous is God when considering the divine openness to embodiment! One of these devious ways can be a less proper difference, one that is out of order, where the poetic bears an even greater ambiguity. Perhaps as Althaus-Reid would have envisioned, this *Manyone* is quite carnivalesque in that God provides passage for Godself to incarnate the many strangers in a carnivalesque manner.

A reality immersed in intense ways of loving and in Trinitarian or perichoretic life giving movements entails passion in the sense of passage and transmutation: all things joining the divine nature of love of God as God also incarnates their contrasting elements to the point of the cosmos becoming a divine body. For one thing, the divine enjoyment stems from placing in each living form a desire or an aim for enjoyment, for life being lived in ever new ways, that is, according to novelty. It points to an existence that is, as Whitehead puts it, "more than a succession of bare facts," and to an enjoyment that is "the quality of the quality" in life.[233]

Yet, since there is such a thing as *la buena vida*, zest for life inclusive of joy and grief, the self and others, even our ancestors, the failures and successes of life weariness and resurrections had to be included. I mused, since perhaps the divine intense enjoyment mixed with ours is a trace of love in all things that interconnects us, that which disrupts stasis with its yet to come attribute not devoid of memory. Thus in this chapter, the divine appetite of Aquinas had to become the divine goad toward a zest for life, already intensified by the many joining God in their unique forms of enjoyment, with their memories of life past sighing for a better future. God is life! As Whitehead wisely puts it, "Life refuses to be embalmed alive."[234] To me, this is how God can be open-ended or infinite in the divine passionate love, and in the life-giving and vivifying indeterminacy that grounds all things.

What would it mean for us to say that God is this poet of the cosmos, who loves the many in their unique forms of loving, perhaps cosmic copulation? What would the metaphor of lovemaking then entail when considering that, classically speaking, the mystical union with God has been compared to the Eucharistic moment of partaking in ways that point to that which "may be" (potentiality) in the sense of a grand banquet or celebration? The God of *la fiesta* briefly introduced in Chapter 1, whose yearning vivifies the created order in the second, and who embodies how each is in the other in ways briefly introduced by Irigaray and more developed in this chapter through the lens of panentheism needs to be further explored in dialogue particularly with festive and indecent theologies. This reality in process points to an activity of love that aims at the intensity of life of the other in God with amplified meanings that draw from metaphors of excessive love and hospitable flesh that give shape to a grotesque kind of incarnation, as we shall see in the next chapter.

Impropriety: Incarnations of Carnivalesque Passion and Open-Ended Boundaries

> The unfinished and open body (dying, bringing forth and being born) is not separated from the world by clearly defined boundaries; it is blended with the world, with animals, with objects. It is cosmic, it represents the entire material bodily world in all its elements. It is an incarnation of this world at the absolute lower stratum, as the swallowing up and generating principle, as the bodily grave and bosom, as a field which has been sown and in which new shoots are preparing to sprout.
>
> —MIKHAIL BAKHTIN[1]

> What is at stake here is not just God devolving itself in Christ but in the Trinity, and in the Trinity understood as an orgy, that is, a festival of the encounter of the intemperate.
>
> —MARCELLA ALTHAUS-REID[2]

The idea of a divine lover who suffers with the cosmos in yearning to be in an intimate relationship with it, and whose flesh is porous and welcomes the cosmos into the divine khoric *bowels* so that both God and world can live intensely, that is, passionately, seems to locate the divine relationship with the cosmos quite out of its proper order. This trope of impropriety has been unfolding all along in ever-increasing spirals that culminate in this chapter, only to spiral one more time into the future, with a heightened, if not hyperbolic, cosmic celebration of the immodest type. Without explicitly locating itself there, it draws from an imagery of which many mystics have spoken—the grand banquet (Luke 14:13), celebrated alongside the passion of the Christ through the Eucharist. Yet by means of poetry, play, and assorted literary devices, as well as by expanding the final imageries of the first chapter, God here appears as a God of *fiesta*, one who dances and laughs, who is drunk—for the cosmos, that is, outside of God's wits.[3] A playful portrait of this banqueting communion, of lovers' ecstatic intoxication with each other's passions, with its mystical intermingling of selves, further challenges Aristotelian expressions of enjoyment and classical images of God.

Analogous to a carnivalesque dance of passion, this idea points to that which is open, always becoming with the cosmos; it points to death and life, multiple incarnations, and even to the lower stratum, to the pelvis.[4] As if enduring the literary devices of simile, metaphor, onomatopoeia, and hyperbole, in addition to irony and sarcasm, the Trinitarian dance can be understood as poetically orgiastic. This poetic turn would not plunge us into the "orgiastic love germane to pagan worship" about which Julia Kristeva warns us.[5] Rather, like a dance of a multitude of lovers within each other, humans, animals, and plants can be seen as intermingling, becoming the other and not, within and with God, as God becomes with them, *polyamorous*.[6] The carnivalesque dance of passion is viewed as luring forth all living things toward a more hospitable coexistence than at present.

The path first followed is the one paved by the festive theologies and their impetus toward an aesthetic praxis. These theologies then are assumed in a turn toward the contributions of more explicit "indecent" theologies of the festive type. The inspiration of this part of the book mostly comes from a deep Spanish and Latin American sense of the sacredness of festive life, introduced earlier with my discussion of Otto Maduro's *Mapas para la fiesta* to explore "*la buena vida*." We are to live life in ways worthy of celebration, ways that benefit the self as well as others. In this chapter, what comes into play are things considered too common to be divine, as adumbrated by Luis Maldonado, Rubem Alves, Roberto Goizueta, and Marcella Althaus-Reid. Even when I interweave the philosophical work of Friedrich Nietzsche and Mikhail Bakhtin with these authors' work, the conversations remain closely connected through the language of these festive and indecent theologies and the modes of being they underwrite.

I have dared to create these categories and place the work of these authors within them; few of the authors I discuss explicitly refer to their work as festive or indecent. I am not joining a "seamless dialogue" already taking place; even though some of the authors share the same language, only a few engage in an explicit conversation with each other. Nonetheless, I hope that what ensues is a promising and challenging exploration of the God of enjoyment according to the festive elements of life. Also in this chapter the divine festive carnival becomes the culminating trope of several constructs and motifs discussed in all the previous chapters in relation to the lover God: yearning, ecstasy, *la fiesta*, passion, suffering, pain, permeability, the limit, the intermingling of selves, passage, transmutation, potentiality, the divine khora, plural unity, intensity, chaos, and a sacred body of love. In redefining these terms according to the beauty and harmony of *la fiesta* and carnivals, this chapter aims to make room for a God who can endure a metamorphosis from the ambiguous performance of the festivals to grotesque images characteristic of carnivals—the poet of the universe incarnating its ecstatic poem, so that the poem itself also incarnates this most hospitable divinity.

Dancing Earthly Rhythms

> As for being out of one's mind and wits, which follows drunkenness, in God's case it must be taken to mean that incomprehensible superabundance of God by virtue of which his capacity to understand transcends any understanding or any state of being understood. He is beyond being itself. Quite simply, as "drunk."
>
> Denys the Areopagite [Pseudo-Dionysius][7]

> Dionysius says (*Div. Nom.* iv) that *the Divine love produces ecstasy*, and that *God Himself suffered ecstasy through love*. Since therefore according to the same author (*ibid.*), every love is a participated likeness of the Divine Love, it seems that every love causes ecstasy. *I answer that*, To suffer ecstasy means to be placed outside oneself.
>
> St. Thomas Aquinas[8]

Throughout this study, I have implicitly brought the imagination to bear on our theological musings on the passionate God of enjoyment. An investment of the imagination moves the analysis from the categories of theology proper toward what has been called theopoetics. As the work of Amos Wilder attests, theopoetics broadens the language on God to include elements such as dance and music, characteristic of the festivals.[9] But placing the figure of the lover God in a festival context poses difficulties to a classical understanding of divinity. The masks, satire, and revelry found in some expressions of the festival take our understanding of the divine outside its customary boundaries. These disconcerting expressions of the festive show up in many places: in the ancient Roman Saturnalias or festivals; in the medieval festivals of Europe, such as the "feasts of fools," the "feasts of the ass," and the "feast of the "Boy Bishop"; and in more modern-day festivals and events such as Mardi Gras in New Orleans, the Korean mask dance, the Puerto Rican El Carnaval de Ponce, and many others.

Nevertheless, a festive theopoetics might be worth the trouble. Theopoetics opens wide the divine dimension to a "moreness" or a *sensus plenior* imbued with a hermeneutics of excess. The excess of this understanding of God spills over settled definitions and disrupts conventional meaning; it allows us to reimagine this world and perhaps welcome a long-received God of love differently. For example, St. Thomas Aquinas spoke of "moreness" when taking the path of *eminentia* or excess in his references to God. In his teachings on the love of God he embraced reason and logic, and infused them with imagination.[10] Hence, an entry point into theological reflection is the way in which this aspect of "moreness" connects with the theopoetic dance, linked in previous chapters to *perichoresis, multipassage,* and *transmutation*—all relevant to the notion of the divine passion.[11] Also, as previously discussed, perichoresis can refer to the manner in which God relates to the cosmos and to us in permeable and quasi-mystical ways, thus akin to lovemaking, cosmic copulation. But what would it mean for the concepts of perichoresis and God as the best lover to be analogous to the path of excess or *sensus plenior* evident in the festival? How might the figure of the God who dances inform our previous views on the divine dance of love with the cosmos? How can a festive sense of the path of excess help us gain new insights into the passionate enjoyment of God?

EARLY INDECENT IMAGININGS

An improper discourse on the passionate God progressively transforms the divine lover into the *disruptive* figure of the festive God of the carnival, a happy God enclosed in the divine self; into one who immodestly goes after many lovers, leaping and running free from the circumscribing solitude attributed to the sacred. This adventurous form of enjoyment is considered inappropriate in most classical models of divine happiness since a passion for the enjoyment of the created order disrupts the auto-dissemination ensuing from the divine "pen/is" and "God's testicles," a word written by God the Father as "the scribe of his lonely creational pleasures,"[12] as Marcella Althaus-Reid's critique serves to show. It means that rather than a narrative of a solitary God whose love is of and for the divine self alone, in yearning to be in relationship with the world, God suffers *"ecstasy through love."*[13] The cosmic lovers affect God, take part of the divine erotic essence. And as the divine lover transfigures Godself into a dancing lover, God delights in the sweet fruit of love of the ones whom God loves, at the banquet hall, until fainting with love (Songs 2:3–5; 6:13). The divine self loves ecstatically, which speaks of God loving, like the Shulamite who drinks and dances, beyond the divine composure. In seeking to be otherwise (perhaps excessively so), "God is trouble," John Caputo remarks, for driving the divine self to the extremity of the divine existence.[14]

Gaining this festive sense of passionate enjoyment between God and the cosmos would first entail accepting God's hospitable welcoming into the paths of excess, that is, into the superabundance of God and of the divine eros. That is why the journey begins with a festive lover who, according to Denys the Areopagite suffers an *"excessus mentis,"* or an aberration of the mind, which for Aquinas occurs when one is "placed outside one's proper order."[15] As a way to interpret this view, the initial impulse driving God beyond the divine self is impropriety itself, God yearning to be intimate with the created order to such a degree that God willingly seeks to become improper. Specifically when linked with the notion of *eudaimonia*, or enjoyment, God's improper love is what stirs the whole of life toward union with God through a path of excess. Here the notion of *excessus* as something overflowing the proper order implies a disruption of stale categories concerning the happiness of God. The disruption becomes evident as the path of unknowing (via negativa) is followed by one of excellence (*via eminentiae*).[16] God invites us to affirm, negate, and ultimately encounter a divine excess of ways of being a lover.

This welcoming journey is joyously perichoretic, dancelike, of playful lovemakings. Already enticed by the loveliness of the created order, God becomes "without mind and without perception."[17] God loves excessively, is enamored to the point of seeking union, for knowing is about union, and loving "far beyond the mind," in the words of Denys the Areopagite.[18] That is why for Aquinas, God is in excess of the mind more in the sense of being beyond the divine self because of love and of the self as being united to God as "to one unknown," such union coinciding with an excellence or superabundance of the divine attributes.[19]

And further: superabundance or a *via eminentiae* can be about an excess of metaphors, similes, perhaps even hyperboles, that counteract silence without doing away with mystery. Thus God would not be "beyond being" solely in the sense of being *purely* infinite and unknowable. Rather, God being beyond prescribed forms of defining beingness, as Jean-Luc Marion distills from Aquinas's texts, can mean God as "the best lover" because of the excess of God as love. Thus God would be a lover, an *ego amans*, in that the divine abundant love is what defines the divine nature of God. God is an excessive lover, and so the divine nature is excessively loving; God's love lies beyond proper descriptions of love. Outside the proper order of things concerning God or literal categories of God means that the indecent love of God exceeds ways of loving according to myself, my clan, tribe, and tongue, and categories of loving.

Subsequently, the path of theopetic excess we are drawn toward allows a dissimilar similarity that more playfully still disrupts understandings of God by utilizing improper analogies drawn from the ambit of festivals and carnivals, such as intoxication. For the Areopagite, that there is an "incomprehensible superabundance of God" and that God is "outside of all good things, being the *superfullness* of all these things," correspond with the state of God being "drunk."[20] This poetic view of drunkenness refers to a metamorphosis of names that are excessive and hence inappropriately passionate, such as God as the most extravagant lover, owing to the superfullness of all loves with which God loves, excess being the improper ecstasy of the drunk. A transfigurative impropriety of loving "according to the same rite and following the same rhythm as us,"[21] as Marion has it, can therefore be described in troublesome ways.

The hospitable enjoyment of God subsequently displaces others out of their proper order. It poetically lures them into a relationship characterized by a playful immodesty so that they too can love excessively. God being something in addition to the divine self, in the sense of being a poet who disrupts all proper meanings, also means that all things drawn beyond themselves *daimonically* partake of the intoxicating superfullness. Denys the Areopagite would call this immodest ecstasy "the good procession" of God's own *transcendent unity*,[22] for all beings thereby find themselves excessively desiring God, hence also immodestly in God, as a result of the divine impropriety. In seeking to be otherwise, that is, in yearning excessively, God is the source of "out of order," trouble, disruption and interruption; the source of irregularity, disordered, and displaced orders—lovers loving disruptively.[23]

Several statements from the lips of mystics illustrate this dual journey toward loving ecstatically, hence as if intoxicated. Bernard of Clairvaux in being besides himself declares: "I am not unaware that the 'king's honor loves righteousness' (Ps. 98:4 = 99:4); but reckless love does not hang about waiting for judgment to be given: it is not moderated by good advice, or constrained by modesty, or subjugated by reason. I beg, I entreat, I plead: Let him kiss me with the kisses of his mouth!"[24] Gregory of Nyssa too would immodestly put it as: "All intoxication causes the mind, overwhelmed with wine, to go into an ecstasy."[25] And speaking of Paul, Gregory says, "for this ecstasy was a movement toward the Godhead." Gregory also speaks of himself having "experienced that divine and sober inebriation."[26] Similarly, St. Teresa of Avila, in her mystical experiences, for example, in the cellar, the Godhead and site of the encounter of the lovers, is "deeply inebriated and absorbed" to the point that she is beside herself, "in a kind of Divine intoxication."[27] Intoxicating herself with the divine passion, St. Teresa exclaims, "Thy breasts are better than wine!"

An intoxicating yearning improperly becomes the primary and gentle impulse within and beyond God that guides the whole of life toward a festive dance akin to perichoresis. It also becomes the gateway, at least potentially, to fuller expressions of transformative interminglings and incarnations. *Distance* adventurously draws near another, differentiates while intermingling with it, enabling communion without confusion. The divine yearning would hold a relationship to an "indivisible multiplicity, the *unfilled overfullness* that produces, perfects, and preserves all unity and multiplicity," for which the Areopagite argued.[28] The lovers begin to resemble one another, so much so that Aquinas, paraphrasing Denys the Areopagite's statements on divine love in his response to Peter Lombard, is able to say, "love bears the lover into the beloved, so that he now lives the life of the beloved."[29] The principles discussed earlier in relation to lovemaking then would unfold another layer of the divine impropriety. To speak of the divine eros is to shift everything—even God—out of place. Nothing stays in its given "proper place" when "interpenetration and unbounded exchange" are in play, as Luce Irigaray rightly argues.[30] The divine impropriety prevents all things from returning to "the essence of the proper" in the form of their "return to the same,"[31] for in making love, all lovers return to themselves modified, God breaking free from a phallic circularity.[32]

By becoming the host and in being hosted, this festive God exposes the divine self to the risk of becoming flesh of the cosmos's flesh, improperly divine.[33] In this sense the happy God likewise enters what John Caputo describes as "constituting an open-ended whole, an internal complexity, a complex chaosmos, a nontotalizing chaosmic process of self transformation, of autopoiesis, of auto-deconstruction, the complex play of perhaps."[34] The divine flesh risks itself in no longer falling within a mold of certainty characteristic of classical views of perfection when binding itself to what Caputo says, "for better or for worse," is "the unavowable vow of our marriage to the flesh of the world, to the world of the flesh."[35] Placing itself beyond the prescribed purity, even in the place of indecency, is the playful chanciness of God when choosing to enter into the realm of the flesh, when porously destabilizing sameness, when actualizing an otherwise, when refusing to remain bound to the solitary exile of *pure* self-enjoyment.

Our way forward will take us into further immodest metaphors. Might one perhaps, in partaking of the divine superfullness, desire to love life excessively, to seek celebration? In its superabundance of poetic meaning the transmuting unity points to the festive and carnivalesque elements of life. It highlights the mystical union through the imagery of the many gathering together to celebrate life while enjoying wine and food. Aquinas's *eudaimonia* unfolds from within the scene of a banquet, "*that ye eat and drink at my table in my kingdom.*"[36] For St. Teresa as well, the surplus of wine is like a "delectable feast."[37] This metaphor of the festival paints more explicitly the image of the divine enjoyment that I seek to convey. The divine enjoyment, as multiple source and end, points to a lover God who is intoxicated with the many enjoying themselves within the Godself with a surpassing sense of sympathy, perhaps with a greater sense of disorderly praxis, quite abundantly festive.

This festive journey of impropriety that gleans from the divine superabundance would need to ground another expression of theopoetics that more playfully flirts with the trope of *fiesta*. How can one account for a divine life that embraces "the dancing, the music, food, drinking and play," as Irigaray argues?[38] After all, would not God as lover also enjoy good wine and music while in the company of the many whom God loves?[39] María Teresa Porcile rhetorically asks, "what can be better than to imagine together a God who wants the people to have a *fiesta*?"[40] The flute playing and dancing on the plaza would be according to new forms of order.[41] Several biblical accounts point to this kind of incarnational poetry when they refer to Jesus as "a glutton and a drunkard" (Matt. 11:17–19; Luke 7:32–34). A perichoretic loving passion could be intricately connected to the excitement found in the creative process, to the eruptions and disruptions of wine and laughter, of music, festivals, carnivals, and like celebrations. The disruptive superabundance and exuberance of the elements of life would further provide a framework from which to speak of the divine ecstasy in the improper sense.

ODES TO A DANCING GOD

They feast
>> on the abundance of your
>> house;
> you give them drink from
>> your river of delights.
>>>>>>> Psalms 36:8

The poetic imagery of the many dancing about in intoxication within God opens new possibilities for understanding the divine enjoyment. The concept of perichoresis unfolded earlier began to welcome the festive elements of life such as dancing, music, banqueting, food, drinking, and play.[42] With this theopoesis in view, aesthetics and a love for beauty can resurface when one ascribes passion to God. Theological reflection on the passionate God of enjoyment, the source and end of which are excessive love, can best explore in detail the idea of divine festivity.

The intuition of Luis Maldonado takes us in this direction. The God "who can dance," a construct partly evolving from the work of Friedrich Nietzsche on the Dionysian elements of art,[43] provides a significant point of entry. We may glean some ideas from the *teologías dionisiacas* or *festivas*, or the Dionysian festive theologies that emerge from the Spanish-speaking world.[44] Similarly, we may reflect on a certain "moreness" of the sacred as a sign of the divine mystery among the common.[45] In this respect also, this theological reflection holds a vinculum with the *via eminentiae* in that it affirms analogy through the interpretive path of "moreness." It ties analogy to the festive elements of life as a way to demonstrate the surplus of theological meaning that festivals encompass.

To return for a moment to the statements of the previous section, "moreness" does not necessarily always mean heaviness or weightiness, as in things holy, but may also be expressed in lightness, in things considered less sacred. In the festivals, other, more lightly held orders become more prominently linked with God, an association that arises when one considers something like the "chaotic nexus" to which I alluded in the fourth chapter. There is even an element of mockery of gravitas, of that which is considered settled and unquestionable. The divine figure of a "god who could dance" is a not too "serious, thorough, profound, solemn" god, as Nietzsche argues.[46] It is a laughing, dancing God, a God capable of lightness. Hence Maldonado's point: the festive element evident in Nietzsche's *Rauschhafte* or drunkenness is about the ecstatic, the frothy, seething, murmuring aspects of life that are "anarchic, counter to . . . Apollonian clarity."[47] This is not to argue for a lack of reason, for, as José Vasconcelos explains, the Dionysian elements of art are not devoid of reason.[48] Rather, it is to liberate divine enjoyment in the direction of new norms lightly held.

Analogizing the concept of *sensus plenior* with the intoxication that happens during popular festivals allows us to gather some key principles to playfully speak of the mystical union of God with the many.[49] In Nietzsche, for example, the many are revelers who join together in less proper ways than Denys the Areopagite and Aquinas envisioned. The analogy of *sensus plenior* with intoxication draws from less sacred aspects of life. This festive eros of reason admixed with the vital impulses of the cosmos becomes the "ecstatically luring call of the Dionysian bird"[50] for a primal joy found in the bosom of the "primordially One" through music, dancing, and wine.[51] All things are called to return to the "primordial unity."[52] But beyond Nietzsche and the Dionysian pagan rites, unity is composed of the many, as in a festival without fusion, totality, or fullness.

Similarly, intoxication is akin to an ecstatic or rapturous emotion being drawn forth. In Aquinas, "emotion" refers to a power "borne towards something else, so that it goes forth out from itself, as it were."[53] With Paul as his example, Aquinas elaborates on how a temporary passion can drive someone to experience the *visio beatifica*, which relates to the Eucharist and grand banquet.[54] Yet the rhapsodic state can be more explicitly tied to things viewed as common, for wine and music can lead to laughter and dancing. As Nietzsche pointed out, this would be a God capable of saying, "Raise up your hearts, my brothers, high, higher! And don't forget your legs! Raise up your legs, too, good dancers; and still better: stand on your heads!"[55] The divine dance and even God can appear to be upside down. Thus a Dionysian exuberance situates Aquinas's playfulness in his use of terms such as "ecstasy" and "intoxication" closer to a more explicit God-talk on the impropriety of the intoxicating dance of the lover God, whose cosmic eros lures the many toward rhapsody, inciting the enthusiasts toward unashamedly bizarre behavior.

Implicit in this *Rauschhafte* is also the biblical imagery of a grand *fiesta* of universal reconciliation of the many, in which everyone shares a common meal of peace and justice in earthly ways, as Maldonado indicates.[56] Aquinas's image of the grand banquet as the ground (for him, source and end) of all enjoyment, and the delectable feast of St. Teresa, come close to expressing this idea. Again, the concept is more festive and excessive than they would allow, for, as Porcile has it, it is disruptive in that many revelers dance about in ecstasy, like maenads.[57] For Nietzsche, the "singing and dancing crowds" *whirl* themselves "from place to place" under the "Dionysian impulse" in a reveling manner.[58] The anarchic crowds with their rhythmic movements expand the limits of their flesh as the Dionysian impulse lures them toward intoxication. Their rhythms and dynamics of joy penetrate all nature, awakening emotions, and growing in intensity.[59] Hence the banquet imagery expands even further to include an intoxicating dance that leads to the unique corporeal expressions of exhilaration, enthusiasm, pleasure to the fullest, great delight, and the passionate love of the many.

The festivals lead us to a form of passion that is abundantly and immodestly a collective passion. Unlike in the Apollonian and perhaps Aristotelian divine figures, intoxication widens the individual consciousness, "thinking of thinking," to include the many, as Maldonado indicates.[60] And hence the reason why Vasconcelos argues that the Dionysian elements of art speak of a "God of Passion," and why he avers that "the Dionysian passion is expressed in the *Bacchae*, assured that the whole of the universe could grant it anything better than a rapturous fire."[61] Hence the divine ecstasy prominent in the festivals of old forms a vinculum of creativity that leads to happiness, as the many "living beings" become "one living being, with whose creative joy we are united," says Nietzsche.[62] Intoxication unites the many and takes the divine enjoyment to an increased level of impropriety, an explicit, fiery, or intense divine passion of the many in the one for the purposes of collective enjoyment.

Seen through a festive lens, divine love is no longer immutable but rather involves erotically embodied movement, change, and transmutation of the many. Happiness also would not be about *pure* activity without receptivity, or about stirring all things toward an *absolute* stillness and calm repose, the classic view of God as unchanging and the end of all things toward which all things move. Rather, the divine festive eros stirs all things in the form of an adventurous dance of receptivity and activity that builds in intensity owing to the participation of the many in the Godhead. In Aristotle, calmness refers to a purely rationalized passion that tames the flesh and affections such as sorrow.[63] It would be the stillness of all storms in that it is an *absolute* calmness, devoid of movement and mixture.[64] One of its manifestations is an anesthesia to puzzling circumstances and even tragedy, as Abraham Heschel has pointed out.[65] But the festival points to a series of movements performing receptivity and mutual becomings, followed by another performance of movement and receptivity, and so on.

This God would feel everything sympathetically, embodying the highest intensity of emotions of the gods, from suffering to jubilation.[66] A certain cruelty or voluptuousness shaped as resistance is involved when desiring desire is not overcome by the calmed telos of a subject, a once-and-for-all satisfaction of God and other beings, a completion of being God properly speaking. With a flare of sadomasochism, as in the work of MacKendrick, the divine eros would act like a lust "that demands eternity . . . bursting time with subjectivity—repeating, accelerating, freezing, exploding."[67] In such a model, which confronts Nietzsche's view of the ascetic lifestyle, the expenditure of the divine self is loss; hence the demands for co-occurring satisfaction, joy becoming intricately linked to desire—a counterargument also to a teleological economy of productivity, as discussed later.[68]

This understanding of the way that God's being *emotionally* incarnates the cosmos takes into account permanence, but it also expresses an extravagant life outside the realm of stale order. The dancing about in a reveling manner could be like the tragic dithyrambic musicals or the tragic chorus of goatlike satyrs that Nietzsche describes, and God and cosmos could be "subject and object, at once poet, actor, and spectator."[69] Rather than a categorized order that separates audience and participants, the rhapsodist would see herself as being "one with a host of spirits," as entering into "another body" or "into another character."[70] Specifically, God could be seen as empathetically becoming with the cosmos, poetically being God and not God, and the cosmos could be seen as partaking of the divine nature, analogically becoming divine—thus playfully trading places. Indeterminacy would therefore characterize this "moreness" of love, in that the starting point is potentiality (excess of meaning). Potentiality, not actuality, is the point of reference, which tells us that the divine nature of love is not settled owing to its complex unity. So how indeterminate can the divine erotic nature be when the many as potentialities are mutually indwelling the divine erotic nature?

In light of God and the many living forms improperly dancing about and interchanging places and roles, one might say that this form of poetic enjoyment cannot be encompassed or mastered. But when positing a union that is beyond mastery, particularly in relation to intoxication (ecstasy), one must also take into account a theological discourse that preserves the notion of boundary while also disturbing it. Unlike in Nietzsche, the limits of the proper must expand without abrogating distinctions. As in Marion's work on Dionysius, the abandonment of self in the Dionysian *yes* and *Amen* cannot mean that the cosmos and God collapse into one primordial being, which would imply idolatry and possession.[71] For Marion, the *yes* must free the cosmos from collapsing into the divine, so that neither becomes an idol and none can possess the other. Without *différance* there is neither divinity nor *worldhood* to speak of. And yet, in a more radical sense of intersubjectivity than Marion proposes, and advancing further into the Dionysian-Nietzschean model, perhaps to involve a deeper sense of intoxicating passion, we might consider the multiplicity of loves as a plural unity rather than a simple one, as already discussed. The playful transmutations of one living form into another, happening within a type of divine khora or Godhead, entail empathy without abrogating the limits of the many in the one, and the one in the many. Otherwise, how could it be a manifestation of true passion?

BORDERING DRUNKENNESS

Music, laughter, wine, and dancing can awaken empathy and passion by means of elasticity. The concept of the expansion of limits is reminiscent of the festivals themselves, which are circumscribed both in space and in time. In expanding these limits, they serve as occasions for an ordering disorder. As Roberto Goizueta explains in reflecting on the work of Maria Goldwasser, in the festivals there is no sense of stasis or chaos exclusively but of "shared flowing" of one aspect into the other.[72] Festivals are like a "river bank" that provides elastic borders for the river to flow, for there to be some form of "sweet disorder" or an expression of antistructure within an opening space—or a space that opens wide.

In Maldonado's work, for example, the rituals and symbols prevalent in the festivals pose an excess of meaning, a *sensus plenior* that exceeds in respect to practice while other definitions of location and temporality are held constant.[73] *La fiesta* is about beauty that inspires one to view all things through the senses of enjoyment. Territories seem to expand their limits in *la fiesta;* the streets expand with "the dancing, the music, food, drinking and play."[74] *La fiesta* is also about beauty in mixed landscapes of nature and human invention. On the way, the path becomes that fountain of aesthetic experiences carefully sought by those "who know the possibilities of beauty in combined zones of human input."[75] Even the ways that lead to it, the ways through the rivers at sunset, roads of *sinpecado* (windy roads), illuminated by the refulgent sun, are an aesthetic manifestation of *la fiesta.* Moreover, people of all ages participate in the great festivities of the year. Childhood, youth, and even those who have *passed on* (died) are revived.[76] As if expanding time, even the dead may join in the dance, a custom observed in the Day of the Dead festivals.

Similarly, in the festive Godhead, the limits of the many bodies (even metaphorically speaking) joining as one remain, yet also expand, and can be crossed. Roberto Goizueta implicitly refers to a similar aspect of expansion and dislocation of the *fiestas* in his understanding of *liminality*, a concept appropriated from Victor Turner. For Goizueta, it provides the postmodern deconstruction of "the modern subject-object dichotomy that grounds the modern autonomous subject-as-agent."[77] In the interchange of subject-actor roles that takes place in the festivals (for all are participants in that space of liminality or displacement), orders with their prescribed boundaries become more "we" oriented, which can indicate that there is a particular passion akin to elastic vulnerability even as the limen remains.[78]

Like an antistructure overflowing a riverbank, the divine limitlessness also becomes vulnerable to the ordering disorder of the festivals of old. And as in the festivals, this would be akin to mockery, a turning upside down of what is usually considered to be divine. We may consider again the God of passion described in the words of Jon Sobrino: "If there is some knowledge of God to be found on the cross, then some other principle of knowledge must be operative because the deity appears totally unlike anything we know."[79] The God whom we create in the image of an emperor becomes a crucified servant capable of being wounded, and beyond that *persona*, a festive deity capable of being intoxicated with love near the limit that the flesh imposes. In the shape of Jesus, the deity turned upside down can mean that God is "a debunker, a jester," as Rubem Alves argues.[80] The limitless letting itself be wounded by the limit refers to knowledge gained through the path of negation, which sets free the boundaries of "I" and "we" in the infinitizing movement toward the all to the point of debasement (kenosis).

In this festive union is the divine *yes* to the many, but in ways unlike some concepts of the Dionysian elements of art of Nietzsche. Particularly in his critique of the Apollonian sense of art, Nietzsche errs, in that measurement and ethics are completely opposite to excess or impropriety. For him, the Apollonian imagines the individual as a boundary of freedom exacted in the forms of "self-knowledge and measure,"[81] being best described by the *principium individuationis* or principle of individuation. The "apotheosis of individuation" is a law that delimits boundaries and measure, restraint and proportion.[82] By exacting measure and requiring self-knowledge, the Apollonian sense of art would give rise to the ethical individual. For Nietzsche, "side by side with the aesthetic necessity for beauty, there occur the demands 'know thyself' and 'nothing in excess.'"[83] The Apollonian seeks to save us from "the Dionysian flood and excess,"[84] a world not alien to it in which there are no exact measures or boundaries. And so enjoyment, and even the whole of reality, as envisioned by Nietzsche in terms of excess, belongs to the realm of inexactitude, which escapes these aspects of the ethical being.

How does this "we"-oriented passion akin to intoxication relate to the limit of the "I" in the framework of the festivals? On the one hand, one may raise the criticism of the sort of exactitude that creates the illusion of uniformity and continuous permanence (stasis), and the type of individualism that seeks to do away with the concept of *multiple passages*, as described in Chapter 4. Some levels of measurement and exactitude do indeed lack the element of adventure in that they erect rigid boundaries that keep beings and their worlds apart. Yet on the other hand, as Nietzsche urges, unity cannot do away with the boundaries in ways in which ethics plays no part. So, whereas in this study one finds an affinity for some aspects of the notion of movement, mixture, dissonance, and chaos that Nietzsche espouses in valorizing Dionysian art, the manner in which he criticizes the self with limits, and hence what he considers to be the ethical person, are particularly problematic. If there is no boundary between one flesh and another, and if this limitlessness can even be expressed as violence against other living beings, then his concept of limitlessness lacks the ethic of love needed for a life in union with others. How can there be dissonance if within this unity there is no return to the self, no *différance*, as to one's limits and those of others? Hence, as stated above, even when there can be a sense of "sweet disorder" and antistructure as found in the festival, the limits and boundaries of the flesh, because they are elastic and dynamically fluid, remain in place, upholding an ethical equilibrium between change and permanence.

Once more, the point is to allow for a *jouissance* open to otherness, which would challenge the *principium individuationis* against which Nietzsche also argues, and also go beyond him, in that to become a maenad would not be to self-forget or self-annihilate in order to become one under a "universal will."[85] As lover, the dancing and laughing God gains flesh through the enjoyment of the other, who also returns to herself; and God, in returning to Godself something of the lover, is welcomed in. In the playful exchange of places, the many remain mindful of the selfhood and flesh of each one.

Otherwise, as Irigaray asks rhetorically, would not the Dionysian dance, music and drunkenness, be too much of an unnatural beat, too fast for the body? Would it not even "destroy the body?"[86] In this way the festive life within God also spurs an ethic of love that parallels the limits that the festivals impose, an ethic conversant with liminality.

In posing this critique of Nietzsche's contempt for ethics, we must remember its other face: the type of celebrations that take place in certain villages of Brazil during which young girls are sold into prostitution, as Gebara describes. At the cost of the girls' bodies and dreams, the people get to celebrate the arrival of "fresh meat." Gebara concludes, "Feast, festival, competition, exchange of money—all take place over the bodies of young women. They offer their bodies to follow the course of a celebration, to be used and then discarded."[87] Such concepts of celebration do not honor the limits of the flesh, and hence demonstrate the need for an ethic that expands boundaries without abrogating them.

Certainly, freedom of expenditure more than restraint according to measurement is characteristic of festivals, but with a proviso. As Goizueta remarks, in being at one with others, the world, the cosmos, with the "Giver of life" there is implied an *aesthetic praxis*, a praxis based on a love that is open to reciprocity—to give back life in enjoyment—without the enforcement of it. This celebration of life as gift is "a wellspring of motivation" for social justice, as Elizabeth Johnson remarks in respect to some Latin American authors on the trope of *fiesta*.[88] We do because we love, situating notions of labor as they should be, as undergirded by enjoyment.[89] And as Vasconcelos remarks, "In its highest form, ethics is aesthetics, that is, service out of love, not out of duty; service with joy and life, action as enjoyment, the final stage."[90] Enjoyment, therefore, does not necessarily lack purpose when connected to love. Things are enjoyed as such, not outside ethical confines, but as that which sustains them.

And, conversely, this ethic of love is not devoid of excess. The act of enjoyment disrupts order with its lack of measure and upsets the monopoly or commodity of pleasure that the imagination sets free, argues Alves.[91] For example, the anarchic element of pleasure comes into view from the "wide range of psychic, religious, mystical, aesthetic, and bodily experiences which are extremely rewarding and which are not commodities."[92] Alves finds a seditious danger implied in this type of freedom. As he puts it, "the free areas of pleasure beyond institutional control may eventually give rise to the notion that other forms of social organization are possible." Pleasure is dysfunctional and subversive in that it "conspires against the closed rationality of the system."[93] The many and not the few, the whole of the community and not a minority, as in Aristotelian musings on happiness,[94] can have access to enjoyment through the festivals. In a way, this form of aesthetic enjoyment is about freedom to abdicate the power that dictates what and how this pleasure ought to be expressed.

Festivals can affirm excess by extending the confines of enjoyment also beyond the market even as it also finds itself providing pleasure at a certain cost (to name a few, ring toss and roulette wheels on the boardwalk, and dunk the local celebrity, fried dough and cotton candy at a traditional U.S. county fair). Thus, celebrations like those of the festival type, while partaking of elements of economy, do not altogether lie under the control of the factuality "that controls economic life in society," as Elizabeth Johnson remarks.[95] And so in unison with her one can exclaim, "To be human is to celebrate." Embedded in creation is an element of enjoyment of life for the sake of enjoyment: pure expenditure. It seeks to fall outside a system of exchange value that controls enjoyment.[96] This is the element of excess through which one can become "ready and capable for loves that enlarge the understanding: the sea, the desert, the mountain range, the loneliness," as Vasconcelos writes.[97] Expenditure proclaims through enactment that life is not made of water-holding cisterns but of overflowing springs, as Alves says.[98] And so the limitlessness found in the limit of the *fiesta* can be seen as awakening a passion for life itself.

Like the festivals, the limit according to the divine flesh infinitizes, but without it there is no true excess. These tunes of enjoyment allow for what I believe is a fitting understanding of the God of *fiesta* that Goizueta ties to his view of the "triune Community whose love *is* life" and the "God who *is* Life."[99] This divine figure of the Godhead articulates an ecstatic dance that maintains its earthly roots by upholding the limits of the flesh and expanding them. It poses a carefully constructed reflection on an ethic of love, without obscuring another essential argument: the intoxicated God who can dance and laugh, the God characterized by love of the many joining in celebration. The limitlessness of the limits of enjoyment is what *teología dionisiaca o festiva* accomplishes. In it is the divine *yes* to creation's array of moods and emotions, as well as its many forms of love and enjoyment. Its views on divine drunkenness point to another kind of loving excess, one defined by the many in the one with their many expressions of enjoyment—*polyphilia*. As its tunes lead us to new incarnations of the God of *fiesta*, the one becomes a "we." This form of divine disruption enhances definitions of the divine adventurous love.

And yet, with this festive imagery of drunkenness of the many in the one in sight, what would be the purpose of a divine dance of passion that expands limits, in addition to the communally ethical? How can the divine dance awaken a passion for life amidst sorrow, and a vision of a more just world order that the first chapter introduced?

THE COLLECTIVE YES TO ANOTHER ORDER OF LOVE

The divine drunkenness akin to an adventurous lovemaking—God going outside Godself and drawing all things into Godself and intermingling with them—stirs all things toward a passion for life, for fuller expressions of it in that it says *yes* to the imagination. This dance of open boundaries enacts potentiality even when in the midst of circumscribing circumstances. This affirmation of life is for Alves another component of theopoetics: empty cages opening up to infinite horizons.[100] A God who can dance with intoxication leads us into the dance, for becoming is through enjoyment, by performing that which is yet to come: a just world order according to love. The perichoretic dance between God and the cosmos consists of yearnings and mystical unions, as well as music, dancing, and wine. Through the lens of the festival, this lovers' dance also draws more explicitly from the theatrical element of performance.

Here also the concept of the festive Godhead is ambivalent, in that God holds the suffering of a life of resurrection, the enjoyment of a death on a cross. The notion of the banquet at which the slain Lamb is present each time we celebrate the eucharistic liturgy points to this ambivalence. This God is one whose tunes of celebratory mockery are not easily definable.[101] In relation to the festive elements of life, the imagination affirms something of the Godhead in the form of disruptive excess, which is also a form of indecency that affirms a flesh capable of both suffering and joy. The limen reaches out to an abundance of affirmations of life itself, so that it can encounter joy in the abysms of pain.[102] Hence apparent contradictions can be seen as playing a part in the festive divine inner life as it moves toward a passionate enjoyment, for something "powerful and pleasurable" can be a part of pain, as Nietzsche points out.[103] This lover God would be as much about lament as about songs of praise, since pleasure and pain are not opposites but equal partners in the divine enjoyment.[104]

From Chapter 1, one welcomes a vision for celebration that accounts for the hearts of the hurting. It provides what Porcile describes as the eros or desire for beauty, a greater harmony capable of enduring the travails of the harshest of deserts.[105] The enthusiasts, those filled with divine excessive passion for life,[106] *por vivir una vida con gusto*, of pain mixed with joy, of the holy mixed with lust, become icons of the impossible, bodily interpreting that which is yet to be actualized in the present reality. As God provides space (*zimzum*) within the divine womb, the enthusiasts come to incarnate history within the God of *fiesta* and the anticipated celebration via ecstasy, song, dance, and poetry.

In the festive Godhead, the divine impulse is more akin to the movement toward opening of boundaries of potentiality. It purposefully stirs us toward saying *yes* to a fuller enjoyment of life with its highs and lows so that there can be an ordering disorder that leads to becoming. It disrupts forms of order that deny life by inviting what is yet to become to take part of the now through the enactment of potentiality. Alves explains that in saying *yes* to the whole of life in dance, celebration, laughter, and wonder, one affirms *pathos*, for it means that one would rather love life too much, dream and create out of frustration and suffering, than be like the living dead.[107] It is like being intoxicated with the divine love and passion for all things to experience the divine intensity. Hence, the festive *yes* enacts that which the status quo cannot control, "the possibility of a different social order," one akin to the utopian grand banquet, as Alves argues.[108]

The impulse of divine intoxication, like the liminal mode that Goizueta appropriates to describe *la fiesta*, opens boundaries so that one can affirm life in the form of "supposition, desire, hypothesis, possibility" similarly abounding in "the carnival, festival, theatre, film, and similar performative genres."[109] Life as a verb is something dynamic and transitive, something that cannot rid itself of the ambiguous and thus the proliferation of its possibilities. The enactment of possibility is what the divine intoxicating dance does when expanding its boundaries with this *yes* to life. As Johnson indicates, in reference to Goizueta, the subjunctive mood of possibility in the concept of *la fiesta*, unlike escapism, is about being "aware of pain and tragedy" as well as "fullness."[110] In the enactment of such openness to life (possibility) lies a refusal to lose hope in the midst of the struggle.[111] An affirmation stated in such terms can bring meaning to life in the form of "desire and future possibility."[112]

Here the performance of enjoyment parts ways with Nietzsche's comparison of intoxication to a purging process that ends up in disgust with reality. Nietzsche's view seals shut reality by seeing tragedy only as a means of purification or discharge of "the whole life of the people."[113] For him, the one who has partaken of the Dionysian reality comes to understand "the wisdom of the sylvan god, Silenus," and becomes nauseated at "the horror and absurdity of existence."[114] He cries over the complacency of the everyday (mostly under the Apollonian veil) and speaks of death in the ways of Hamlet—"not to be born, not to be, to be nothing . . . to die soon."[115] As Irigaray explains, in this respect the Dionysian element of art can act as a "drunken passion" that seeks to arise far away from one's earthly roots,[116] and so ultimately lacking in the abundance characteristic of ancient feasts. As Irigaray quips,

> An old noon your hour is, and the sun has to give his all for a single drop to be drunk from it. From so high and so far such force must he beat if the taste of a single moment again to be savored. Quite separate from the feast and plenty of old.[117]

On the contrary, in the festivals the element of divine intoxication parallels the performance of the not-yet from within the common, and expands boundaries to move beyond stale restrictions; hence the potentiality of which the present comes to partake. It breaks free from determinism in a manner that falls into neither nihilism nor superhumanism. Performance, like child's play, is not full presence; rather, it preserves open-endedness and ambivalence. It can be seen more in the sense of prolonged and expanded desire, already discussed with regard to lovemaking. With a vision of the future, one keeps an eye on that which cannot be fully possessed.[118] Accordingly, very much in keeping Gebara's views,[119] for Goizueta, *la fiesta* is the enactment of "the ultimate goodness of life." Even when it happens in the "midst of suffering" it accounts for "the 'subjunctive' denial of the ultimacy of death."[120]

Perhaps, as discussed in the previous chapter, a primeval chaos of unity exists within God defining the divine life shared with the whole of the cosmos in a manner that nurtures the potentialities with their immortalized past histories. As the many become a part of this complex unity and intensify one another and God, they stir and gain passion for their desired future.[121] The divine eros stirs us toward adventure, things newly conceived. In the festival, more specifically, intoxication is linked with performing a passion for an earthly existence in which the many are one, akin to solidarity. As Goizueta explains, *las fiestas* link the present to "the past (often in the form of the 'dangerous memory' of suffering) and the future (as the anticipated, full realization of *communitas*)."[122] So, in celebration is the *yes* to life of the many as a sign of the possibility of performing what is imagined in terms of life with others (while one's feet are here on earth).

The Godhead viewed through the trope of *la fiesta* brings back the liminal aspect of the adventurous performance of the not-yet, and its ambiguity found in the erotic excess of the many joining as one (ecstatic love). To use the words of Alves to explicate it, intoxication could be about saying *yes* to an "*ordo amoris*" that can be considered utopian (a commitment also of the theologians of the cross).[123] One can go beyond the purely factual by enacting another order of things more akin to an *advent*urous love. The rhythms of this *yes* "contain promises of freedom, love, and life," and remind us of a community according to the "'not-yet,' the aperitif of a banquet still to come," Alves writes.[124] To perform the gifts of the future, as we do when dancing, is to have a taste of a community according to creative love, the great experience still to become manifest more fully.[125]

Through a lightness of being and the natural instinct characteristic of festivals, life creatively weaves in adventure. With passion, all living things in God (as God is also in them) are stirred toward life together with one another. A cacophony of voices says *yes* to life resolutely in the midst of pain and in communion with one another. With their own unique desires and ways of enjoyment within God, they declare that even if life is dissonant, it is worth living, for in affirming life they become open to imagining new forms of love-order in this world. In this lies the adventure of eros.

Rather than being stopped at the sight of the classical theological impossibilities and contradictions, in adopting the principle of festivity, one wishes to see how new horizons pregnant with the imagination knitted to an ethic of love can emerge. For example, one can embrace both suffering and joie de vivre as expressions of divine passion. In the festivals, death and life are not enemies. And what is more, one can fluidly embrace new ways of describing the *light* becomings of God that subvert full presence by accounting also for the concept of the divine embodiment of the many. Opening spaces of boundaries can, as festivals do, nurture the imagination, even perhaps make way for other improper ways of speaking of the divine perichoresis and the adventurous love of God.

But, we might ask, if the festive God is one who comes out of order, what would this mean in relation to the way in which God becomes analogous to the many loves and lovers? According to other literary devices evinced in the festivals, the *grotesque*, the many joining as one in the form of celebration, each in their unique expressions of enjoyment, gain an element of impropriety not fully discussed in these previous festive theological views. It exposes us to an exploration of "keys," gay and light, minor and major. And so, to delve into current understandings of the orgiastic elements concerning the divine passion, one would need to look into the contributions of explicitly indecent theologies, some which open the divine self to unique mutations, that is, incarnations analogous to the monstrous.

Incarnations of Dangerous Liaisons

Songs, hymns, shouts, growling, grumbling, yelping . . . praise and blame . . . delirium and wisdom . . . exclamations, affirmations, interrogations . . . groans, laments, gaiety . . . and dancing, running, leaping . . . All those (male and female) things at once and together. Banished from the order of the city, buried far from the sun, sunk beneath the city, slumbering under the appearance of serenity, calm, peace.

Luce Irigaray[126]

If theology has its own cowardice and fears, the horror of uncontrollable bodies and especially of the orgy made up of unrestricted bodies may be the stronger. There are bodies whose fluids overflow the metaphorical discourse of theology, but they have lost materiality and sensuousness.

Marcella Althaus-Reid[127]

In the more grotesque elements of the impropriety of the festivals, such as the orgiastic, reside something like a *monstrum tremendum* that protects our imaginations from idolatry. The monstrosity of the grotesque disturbs our way of thinking about God as usual. As Kearny writes, "the monster is not only a portent of impurity (the root of *monstrum* in *monere*, to warn) but also an apparition of something utterly other and numinous (from the root *monstrare*, to show)."[128] The grotesque monstrosity challenges settled definitions, for the carnivals free up space for mutations of selves to occur hyperbolically. Other literary devices, forms of poetry, come into play. Better said, they engage in play in which seriousness is expressed as a hypercomic truth. What we encounter is the excess in the images themselves, like the accentuated facial features of a mask that point to and participate in a "moreness" of meaning and incite laughter. While not devoid of reality either (for the seriousness of the situation is included in the use of the symbolic), the excess of the grotesque challenges full presence through superabundance.[129] It is equally analogical and thus indeterminate to what has been encountered so far, but with greater intensity.

The limits of the grotesque elements of the carnival, like other festive elements, also penetrate the limitless by not remaining bound to definitions of the divine incarnation in the proper sense. Even further, the poetic license inclusive of ludic indecency pinpoints more explicitly the "obscurities, twisted categories and queer details which appear in disorder, and with or without apparent continuation," as Althaus-Reid affirms.[130] Queerer[131] disruptions occur when potentially transgressive constructions of the divinity explode in the scene of the carnival: the drag queen, the cross-dressers, the semi-nude dancers, the *vejigantes* or clownlike characters, the Saga men, and the many other personifications that put into play the elasticity of limits according to hyperbolic incarnations.[132]

The divinity exists as *passage*, beyond being, by deterritorializing itself through the carnivalesque monstrosities.[133] As if wearing a costume, it can undergo metamorphoses, changes, and travesties. For Bakhtin, this would mean that a gay God can represent an uncrowned God, an abused, exposed, debased, and humiliated God,[134] but also a God that in a divine debasement opens the eyes to a new truth—a *corpus Christi* whose blood is being changed into wine.[135] And rather than a virginal Mary, a drag queen Mary Magdalene, as Althaus-Reid depicts the carnivalesque, can kiss the wounds of the Christ.[136]

Contrary pairs, like Don Quixote and Sancho Panza, so ingeniously challenging realities from different vintage points and coming together in the same continuum, can serve to show that mysteries can appear in the festive spirits of eating and drinking. *All things lead to the sacred knowledge.* Incarnating bodily life in ways akin to the lightness found in the *via eminentiae* or *sensus plenior*, shows another way of truth, quite unofficial (never intending to be official). The "comic monster" exposes another truth not by pure certainty but by openness to the ironies, playfulness, and jestings of life.[137] Playfulness of words incarnates lightened truth according to a gay festive wisdom. Another type of symposium of profound wisdom lies here, where there is a leveling of lower and higher, a finding of truth according to the festive flesh.

But what would it mean for this "moreness" of meaning—playfully twisted, queer, deterritorialized, debased, monstrous divinity—to encounter the path of eros or via erotica described in the third chapter? What if the *via eminentiae* of the festivals were to take a turn toward the carnivalesque elements of the festivals discussed in this chapter? A theopoetics that embraces the grotesque offers another way of describing the mystical union with God. Without doing away with the ethical commitments of the Dionysian and festive theologies, and while doing so also assuming the principles of *différance* embraced thus far,[138] the carnivalesque theopoetics draws from a hermeneutics of excess that explicitly appropriates the language of the orgiastic, and thus disrupts understandings of love and sexuality needed to expound on the metaphor of the lover God.[139]

This kind of hermeneutics, equally light in kind, seeks to reconfigure "the individual and collective praxis of bodies dealing with bodies, and with the body of the sacred itself."[140] A carnivalesque theopoetics subverts the frontiers of God's amorous relations as "the excessiveness of God" or *libertinaje* is expressed in the very act of intermingling in immoderate, intemperate, and scandalous loving ways.[141] One can say therefore that the vulnerability or passion of the God of this festive eros so foolishly expressed serves as a scandal portrayed in the multiple expressions of improper embodiment of the divine polyamorousness. Without this stumbling step toward the embodiment of God's passionate enjoyment, would not the intoxicated God who dances miss something of the radical implications of "all" things being in God loving God and one another?

ANOTHER TOPOGRAPHY . . .

Instead of emphasizing an ascent and a higher status granted to immovability or calmness of "thinking on thinking," as Aristotle might posit,[142] the carnivalesque points to sensuous movements of *la carne*, the flesh. It's a "dance" of flesh that descends to the depths of the underworld, even the anal and pubic regions, not as the site furthest removed from the divine enjoyment but as the very being of a God whose nature is love. As Althaus-Reid argues, God loves also from the pubis.[143] There is a downward shift that poetically reconstructs the medieval and modern physical cosmos, its metaphysical and moral world orders. This shift challenges the Neoplatonic hierarchy of higher and lower worlds, with heavenly powers and intelligences driving the world of God and that of earthly creatures.[144] The highest in the hierarchy were outside time, while the carnivalesque were within the world order. In the carnivalesque divine dance, as in sadomasochism, bottom and top trade places and mix with each other.[145] This is also unlike what we read in St. Thomas Aquinas, who, while keeping the concept of *excessus mentis* in close relation to the divine enjoyment, also remains bound to a model that links God solely to the intellect.[146] And despite his profound resistance to Platonic disembodiment and his restoration of a richly material creation theology, not only would God have no body (even metaphorically), even less could the divine enjoyment take place in relation to that body's external or lower parts.[147]

God is outside the proper place of categories of God in that God is ironically also upside down, and continuously mixing and turning around like dancing! As argued above with regard to the festival, the carnivalesque inverts the divine topography in order to mock the preestablished language about God. We can imagine quite an anarchic khora when the carnivalesque takes poetic license in depicting God as being indecent, as exposing the external and lower parts of the body. As *vejigantes* seek to show, the *bowels* of God become exposed, the divine wound opens before the cosmos. And as God's metamorphosed exposure descends to the pubic regions, in an earthy manner, "She lifts her skirts and shows the parts through which everything passes (the underworld, the grave) and from which everything ensues."[148] The bodily hierarchy turned upside down points to a topography in which the lower stratum becomes the path to rebirth. In this is also a vulnerability expressed through the anarchic exposure of the genitals as conduits of life, so not so much as enfeeblement but rather as a peaceful identification with the rest of nature.[149]

In gaining earthly tones, God too becomes made up of "gay matter," a creative term used by Bakhtin to describe gaiety.[150] A God of "gay matter" is ambivalent. Transfiguring the divine self into the earthen flesh would mean that as much as womb, God is grave, more *carnally* the becoming of all things. As Bakhtin writes, the "lower stratum is productive," "gives birth," points to immortality, and is the sign of resurrection.[151] "The death of the old is linked with regeneration."[152] Even death appears as being pregnant, as giving birth, the grave becoming a symbol of "the earth's life-giving womb."[153] Perpetual perishing as well as rebirth, death and birth, and from there growth and multiplication in ever-increasing quantities, are all a part of this "gay matter." It can be linked with excrement and viewed as regenerating and renewing the earth from that standpoint. Thus "gay matter" adds a bodily character to the mystery of the incarnation, drawing all elements into a closer intimacy.[154] God giving birth and regenerating would point also to "gay time" in which there is a dancing about movement toward a better future, yet the first fruits are quite grotesquely of the lower stratum, more so than Alves and Goizueta envision.

Bodies with porous openings, and even the genitals with their convexities and orifices, become the focal site of interchange.[155] Similar to what occurs in the process model of the previous chapter, the movement is into and outside of God, things dying and being conceived and being born within God, but via the lower parts. As in bodies, air coming in and going out renews the old, ferments it to the point of freshness. The continuum is an unfinished wholeness of degradation and renewal interplaying poles and swinging motions of "top and bottom, heaven and earth."[156] Inward and outward interplays also mean that heart, bowels, and other internal organs are in relation to the outside parts of the body. The body inside out and turned upside down is playfully porous. "It represents either the fertile depths or the convexities of procreation and conception," swallowing and generating, giving and taking.[157] Consequently, rather than on the whole, the emphasis is on the (w)holes that allow passage. Here the metaphors of Aquinas and St. Teresa concerning the very bowels of God more explicitly relate to the external parts of the body that also serve to speak of the act of creativity.

This emphasis on God's lower parts, at times even playfully exaggerated, pose a mocking way of becoming divine according to the flesh. Althaus-Reid gives the example of a G(od) spot based on the playfulness of the fun fair photographs commonly found in carnivals in which one can place one's head in a hole and look like something or someone one is not. There is an excess to the board that allows self-identification in ways that stir up the imagination; any head will do. God as "an open, gigantic red vulva" or the G(od) spot draws on the grotesque to reverse and go beyond what is the norm.

This playfully gendered and erotically charged poetic imagery of the lower stratum therefore is also essential to encountering the lover God of the carnival. We can consider Dionysius as Marion does, as going through a passage. According to him, toward the end of Nietzsche's work, Dionysius passes from a male to a female deity, and appears in an eschatological manner (not fully present).[158] For Marion, "between the *Songs* and the *Dithyrambs*, masculine tomfoolery becomes feminine desire, a fantastic torture, a pain from elsewhere, the call to return, the appearance of the god in person."[159] But in doing so, this female deity should be seen in more grotesque ways than Marion envisions: her passionate yearning naked, hybrid, always becoming while fully embodied as a silhouette.

Even if we recognize that "God's position is a sexual option in itself," this position is out of its proper order in terms of set gender categories; hence the ambivalence of the analogy, as Althaus-Reid demonstrates.[160] God is an adventurous lover who can also embody something like what Althaus-Reid calls a "third sex" or an intersexual monstrosity.[161] Other symbols of the divine eros can be celebrated. This "analogy by excess" resembles St. Teresa of Avila's queer descriptions of the divine body: delectable breasts, wounds, openings, perhaps a slit? In appearing in ever more grotesque forms, the oddly gendered God that intoxicates welcomes other ignored topographies.

THE ADVENTUROUS DANCE OF BECOMING

When deterritorializing the divine flesh, particularly as the world is turned upside down, with southern poles factoring into the divine becomings with the many dancing about, what transpires is something mystically orgiastic, a wider opening, a more permeable porosity, or "loopholes" of the flesh. Otherwise, would not the festival also be in danger of falling into the normativity of patriarchy, which seeks to tame passion and pleasure, rid itself of bodies? Something of the Aristotelian God remains when one tames the excess of meaning with regard to the divine enjoyment. Phallic order prevails when all the possible outbursts of the archaic powers of the earth are averted, and more ludic kinds of passions are exorcised, as Irigaray argues.[162]

Not the hermetic enclosures but the porous openings to the world resembling passage are key to the orgiastic images of the divine mystical dance of cosmic copulation. Applying this principle of openings to the Trinitarian dance of God with creation, in combination with Althaus-Reid's hermeneutic of excess, one finds a divine relationship with the world embodying a type of carnivalesque perichoresis. There is a mutual indwelling and encircling about one another, closely resembling the orgiastic embodiments of the flesh that Bakhtin and Nietzsche describe. The choreography of mutual interpenetrations of the divine persons "with openings" serve to illustrate that "God-talk on loving and pleasurable relationships," like the carnival, produces a queer image of God that can appear offensive in that it borrows from a language of sexuality decoded by the underside, a notion of love proscribed by dominant society.[163]

In the poetic welcoming of the many strangers, the triune God transmutes its triune self into the monstrous lover dancing about with the many orgiastically. Quite carnivalesque is a Trinitarian theology that exceeds "the borders of the divine three," as one might say in agreement with Althaus-Reid,[164] for in the elasticity of the monstrous the limits of modes of loving can be like a bounded infinity. The scene that it paints goes beyond the proper "intimate reunion" of monoloving relationships or dyadic prescriptions of love (father-mother, male-female, God-creation). The divine eros becomes wounded by the excluded queers or others and becomes the hospitable ground to strangers, sharing their bodies and "complex sexualities."[165] Those "other sexualities expelled from the Eden of loving" are also what the festive divine lover becomes hospitable. Bodies interrelating and combining themselves within God share a common ground that transgresses the proper and traditional images of the divine three, which usually degenerates into a father-son relationship.

Indeed, the carnivalesque God who loves the multitude with their unsettled multiple loving relationships refuses not to incarnate "vulgarity, horror, and impurity," as Altaus-Reid tells us.[166] Keller would describe this erotic form of transmutation as the *Elohimic Manyone* having strange manners, being iconoclastic. The divine eros for the many, the carnivalesque perichoresis with the many lovers, when one considers play and humor, is more like the "the *cosmic eros*, with its mythic bisexual, hybrid and playful atmosphere."[167] The poetic language used to described its impropriety is Bakhtin's "sea of heteroglossolalia," indicative of the hyperbolic otherness inherent in the divine dance of love with the many cosmic lovers. The chaotic carnality, as in Althaus-Reid's imagery, is sexually charged, articulating a "queerly erotic universe" and a not too proper Lord, says Keller.[168] A Godhead whose Trinitarian dance is orgiastic is indeed quite indecent, decentered, anarchic. What are the implications of God loving in such improper manner and of embodying such adventurous forms of lovemaking?

DIVINE POLYFIDELITY

In the law of hospitality what is theologically posited for us is that the Trinity would give hospitality by becoming the stranger and trespassing beyond the border of current theological discourses.

Marcella Althaus-Reid[169]

Why the need for an erotic path of excess when interpreting the element of passion in the divine enjoyment? Why embrace this aspect of the *via eminentiae*, that is, en route to the indecent excess that the via erotica offers? The carnival gives way to a mystical vision of an open Trinitarian reality of intermingling bodies that nurtures a vision of a God of passion that incarnates the improper, in order to draw the improper into the divine self, in whom bodies touch other bodies, in whom sensuous interactions can occur in an adventurous way, hospitably. This Trinitarian reality akin to the orgiastic elements of the carnivalesque comprises sexuality while broadening its poetic implications. For Althaus-Reid, this can become a type of conciliatory element of the Trinity, an element of "hospitality by inclusion in itself."[170] By opening space within itself, does not the divine provide space for other possibilities and interpretative lenses, other ways to "contemplate redemption . . . consider the beatification processes in the holiness of our everyday living . . . reflect on celestial spaces . . . with their iconics of sacred carnival?"[171]

With more than three in the divine triad, including many loving friends and lovers, it is difficult to locate God in a single place and according to one mode of loving. Going beyond one's clan, tribe, tongue, nation, rites, rituals, and religious and political persuasions, an aesthetic praxis welcoming of the many expands its limits. God's love is shown to be multiply excessive. In carnival imagery, God is a polyamorous God "whose self is composed in relation to multiple embraces and sexual indefinitions beyond oneness, and beyond dual models of loving relationships."[172] The sacred carnivalesque encounter forms a "polyfaithful group of sacred friends," multitudes of lovers.[173] The Godhead becomes that kind of space of intimate reunions, a polyloving God who delights in having multiple partners and demonstrating many ways of loving them. Categories of the divine love burst open as the many dancers join together within God!

Who is the divine neighbor? God becomes polyfilial, loving in all body forms, all backgrounds and places, even in obscure alleys. The divine impulse is "an erotic overflowing of the divine" into different neighborhoods.[174] God repudiates the picture of God as lacking flesh, embodiment, and particularly skin color. Instead, God exists in excess of relationship, and creates a multicolored scene of actually too much color all at once, forming too *dark* a skin. These dark enthusiasts, people of passion, many of them from the Southern Hemisphere, with their bodies that have been considered too dark and dirty, too sensuous, and uncivilized to be of God, are also embodied by the God of the carnival.[175] This God stands outside the civility and propriety of the ones who determine through the symbolic certain "good" manners, ways of speech, and even bodily gestures preestablished by those seeking to colonize dark bodies. A system in which everything must fall within a universal norm is totalitarian in nature.[176] The carnival perturbs control and uniform propriety by metaphorically "mutating" God, that is, by presenting a "disrupting" silhouette of God.

That is why, one might argue, a God in community whose polyamorous love shares in the language of the orgiastic gives way to another "topography of eros"[177] in which there is no mastering. God incarnating the multiple ways of loving offers no false hospitality that follows the law of the Same of Aristotle, and sadly even of Lacan. God is hospitality itself by becoming in part the stranger, by welcoming and intermingling with the polyfaithful group of friends, even the animal neighbor. God is a semideterritorialized body in love that, though shared by everyone, *wholly* belongs to no one. It would be a more nuanced way of describing Aquinas's view of the perfection of the divine happiness, which "embraces happiness according to the most perfect mode of each," and can correspond to government, but not of "one man, or of one house, or of one city, or of one kingdom, but of the whole universe."[178] In becoming multiplicity, God's love is out of control! Never fully fixed, it is always becoming hospitable, always becoming a stranger. As with Althaus-Reid, in reference to the orgy, in becoming the stranger, God is a queer lover whose love is *advent*urous—going out—always in the here and now and simultaneously yet-to-come.

Not mastering God is due to the divine body in transit, shifting as it is constituted by the multiple compositions of the orgy and the multiple encounters with strangers. The divine adventurous eros is of the carnival, of the flesh, of the cosmos, of *carne*; it partly deterritorializes itself within the divine permanence, and hence welcomes in flux. God becomes the "Queer Other in transit" and finds the divine self in different and unfamiliar territories of nomadic bodies traveling about in spaces of grace.[179] How exuberant in beingness is a God beyond Being, who may also be a God of becoming, perhaps a monster? With this theopoetic imagery, the lover God goes beyond Marion's views, in that the notion of "being" takes on grotesque contours as it points to the ambivalence of being not yet complete in the sense of continuously acquiring multiple shapes as the many join together in the complex unity. As it occurs before our very eyes in cinematographic transmutations of human to monster, and then back to human, the embodiment of deformed flesh, but more multiply so, refers to a divinity also in a state of becoming. The grotesque images are "ugly, monstrous, hideous from the point of view of 'classic' aesthetics, that is, the aesthetics of the ready-made and the completed," as Bakhtin explains.[180] The incompletion is not in the sense of Lacan's *not all* and *not whole*, according to lack, but rather results from the many shapes and forms of love and lovers that the complex unity can endlessly take on; there is continuity in the discontinuity set by the limits of the flesh.

Excess! A theophany of the God who in being God continuously crosses God's own borders, a border-crosser is the playful God of the carnival who partly lets go of proper metaphors of God and lets the divine self exist as the transgressive company of the Bacchae without being conquered. God disaffiliates from the proper and prescribed ways of loving and refuses to be "normal," "en-bordered," and forgetful of a love that is different. A God of no fully secured borders,[181] perhaps an alien-like God, is a God whose affiliations hold a permanence (God being God) that likewise is constantly on the move (God being many others than God). How like the crowds moving and dancing about from place to place is the playful God of the carnival, who resists recycling no longer fitting theological borders of the divine self.

The picture of the monstrous silhouette evolving here points to this turbulent intimacy of queer strangers participating in God and being a part of the mutual dance: a stormy sea of love that stirs up the calm lake of no feelings, or divine anesthesia. It is an exuberant mystical union that abounds in the mysteries of the erotic flesh that sweats and bleeds.[182] What lack of mastery is shown in the metaphor of unrestricted and uncontrolled bodies whose fluids overflow the metaphorical discourse on God! Such enthusiastic mysticism contains too much materiality, too much sensuousness, too much wine. In introducing the carnival one draws on the scandalous ways in which God lets the divine self be loved, intoxicated with passion, and lets the "scandalous lovers" love one another. How adventurous is the God who loves in these scandalous ways!

COSMIC MONSTERS OF POLYMORPHIC PROPORTIONS

God's dance-like transmutation with others enfleshes a kind of orgiastic union not only between God and humans but also with other living beings in nature, as they also intermingle among themselves. It evinces in housebound and botanical, micro and macro, as Keller has it, in images of "zoological fecundity" or "bestial intensity," of animals, especially wild ones, procreating and even laughing. She poetically puts it the following way:

> Do we consider their lives, their patterns of eating, mating, birthing and moving, so far beneath the dignity of theology, so much less important than human suffering, so much less interesting than human discourse, that we politely skim the poetics of creation? Have we cared so little that we colluded in the rapid discreation of all of these crafted species? Might our indifference reflect the uncultivated distaste for the chaos of creation?[183]

Humanly speaking, this open-ended whole forms no simple geometric shape.[184] There is a collective unity that is mystical, materialized, embodied, yet also embracive of plant and animal shapes seldom included in theological reflection, and that orders itself in an open-ended manner that can be but lightly settled. It lies beyond human mastery. As Caputo puts it, "God and animals have a great deal in common. . . . Both God and animals are 'strangers' that an excessive and inhospitable humanism would like to master and assimilate."[185] Rather like a collective consciousness of all things, the ancestral memories would be of trees, oceans, and rivers, being renewed as they universally embrace.

The Godhead more explicitly could be "a mysterious primordial unity"[186] akin to the festivals that seek to unite the broken ties between humans and nature, between "the beasts of prey,"[187] and between the gods and all living things. Like a cosmic dance floor, it could restore "a mystic feeling of oneness" and an incarnate spirituality that refuses to see the human, particularly the person of civilization, as the center of the universe, as one might glean from Nietzsche's work.[188] Also, this exceedingly hospitable space transposed into the trope of the carnivalesque could enhance a vision of the many "mixed together in a primeval chaos" (though not completely devoid of orders as found in his view) as the intoxicated many join in the celebrations.[189] In this welcoming shape the gods are proximate, and the festive companions, including animals, can feel each other's pain, as Nietzsche describes them.[190]

Such oddly shaped incarnation of a divine enjoyment whose "gay matter" is also bestial may appear to be quite hideous.[191] This is so because the element of the grotesque, which derives from the Italian feminine noun *grotta*, speaks of God as an opening for the passage of all living forms into one another. It refers to the vases that contained a diversity of mixed figures of plant and animal-like humans and gods, for example. Accordingly, becoming divine in the form of the grotesque can appear in the playful terms of plant, animal, and human forms giving birth to each other, as "the *passing* of one form to the other, in the ever incompleted character of being," as one envisions from Bakhtin's description of the grotesque.[192] The grotesque divine body is cosmic, containing all the elements of the universe— earth, water, fire, air, sun, stars, the signs of the zodiac, mountains, rivers, seas, islands, and continents.[193]

God poetically becoming this cosmic poem has a grotesque body perhaps not too unlike the baroque unfoldings and multiple dimensions of the khora of which Keller speaks.[194] Not only the collective body of a renewed past, the divine monster is of cosmic, animal, vegetable, and human forms—dark-skinned and moor, even—dancing about, as in the Spanish carnivals.[195] The divine nature of love of God according to a cosmic-divine perichoresis is quite polymorphous.

Even the "strangest metamorphoses and debasements" that would accompany the festive and mystic depths of which Nietzsche spoke regarding the Dionysian elements of art can play a part in these sensuous mystical unions.[196] The uniting dance of the festival transmutes shapes in a mythical manner. The gods, the earth, its beasts and humans, and even kings, along with the folk, metaphorically intermingle with one another, trade places. As exemplified by the bearded goat-human-satyr of the Greek festivals of old, these images of festive enjoyment elicit a sense of embodied mysticism in which there is an excess of life's sensuous expressions, even bestial ones, becoming flesh of our flesh.[197]

The carnivalesque transfigurations described thus far, these metamorphoses of the monstrously grotesque, are not too unlike the "esse-diversity" of God that for Gebara sacredly incarnates this web of bodily interconnectivities. It is about the mysterious unfoldings of the complexities of life.[198] It is the vital mystery that we are, and also that which is beyond us, the cosmic embodiment of God. With the carnivalesque undertones of Bakhtin, the many are rather shapeless, when bestial living things are included. God's monstrous mixture incarnates, therefore, "an inexhaustible and many-colored life."[199] It shows that God's body would also be "at home" in the cosmos, for God would be of "the cosmos' own flesh and blood," even if the divine life is "its leading force," Bakhtin argues[200]—of the cosmos as an open-ended variegated being in the sense of being an unfinished whole of the many in the one, grotesquely embodying "the immortality of the becoming of being."[201]

Creativity in the form of fertility as well becomes the principle of open-ended reshapings that add intensity to life. In the festive union there is an "excess of countless forms of existence which force and push one another to life," says Nietzsche.[202] In an orgiastic manner, and concretely and sensually pressing against each other, they form a complex and differentiated space of physicalities touching each other en masse.[203] This intermingling of many within the (w)hole generates an intensity toward fuller expressions of life.

Such cosmic fecundity! And like lewdness and lust, play and laughter, the elemental passions that remind us of fertility and vigor are another expression of the divine passionate love awakening joy in existence, cocreating beautifully in relation to nature, feeling the whole intensely, and imagining interconnectedly. It is a celebration of the adventurous potentiality of new beginnings in which the collective body is eternally open and birthing, collectively and orgiastically becoming anew as plant, animal, humans, and nonhumans empathically touch.

ANOTHER AESTHETIC PRAXIS AT PLAY

With the monstrous in mind, an aesthetic praxis is also one in which the gay, liberating, and regenerating laughter is of the essence of becoming, with all its virtuous abundance and increase.[204] Not surprisingly, the emphasis is on preserving the limits while also expanding them, infinitizing the many forms it can take by means of elasticity. Implicitly there is something more like the type of passage in which there is an identification of one with the other—a form of ludic empathy. The carnivalesque pathos expands boundaries between spectator, actor, and god, between human and nature, and between heaven and earth in ways that can lead to monstrous reshapings deeply mindful of givenness. They are all participants in the act, and can trade roles and shapes as if wearing masks or in costume to feel deeply what the other feels. They partake of infinite possibilities nurtured by empathy as they become dissonant lovers within the divine *carnivalesque home of monstrous becomings.*

With this playful image of the divine adventurous love, the *vita activa* takes on new contours. The grotesque indecency points to another ethic that does not shun the orgiastic elements of the carnival, one in which physicalities, by gathering without stationary beginnings or ends,[205] disrupt exclusionary orders. One is reminded of John Caputo's definition of ethics. For Caputo, ethics is tightly knit to a concept of "difference" or "alterity" that assumes the form of an-*arche*, or a decentering to the farthest point of those things considered to be outside the inner circle of the divine love, or social good will. It is an eccentric kind of ethics, what Caputo calls a "hyperethics," that locates itself "where the trace of God is inscribed on 'the other one,' the neighbor, the stranger or the outsider."[206] It places itself outside the proper order of things themselves, perhaps another virtue that speaks of a radical hospitality "to the stranger, to those who are 'out' rather than 'in.'"

A gathering, or welcoming of the many, including the farthermost strangers, such anarchic hospitality that excites bizarre ways of communicating the flesh can announce a new thing still to come, alternative ways of living harmoniously, the virtue of humorous becoming. The imagination's birthing other perceptions of the presence of God in unfamiliar surroundings—a Trinitarian model of a divinized orgy, for example[207]—recedes the actual so other forms of ordering may arise. Through play, space becomes roomy, and when entering the scene the carnivalesque God shows that other multiple realities according to love are still possible. Such an ethic exposes the law to grace, its limits to the khoric chaotic edges, where otherness is not excluded. In being beyond normativity, this ethic is immodestly gracious, of no *statically* defined borders. Love's disordering of laws porously expands definitions of being by wooing the whole, the many dancing about, to become hospitably elastic.

There is an excess to justice in the carnivalesque ethic, perhaps such a hyperethics, arising from the possibility of a queer *amoris* that inspires Althaus-Reid's views on justice.[208] Within an orgiastic dance of unity, justice is not about having a correct, just, or exact measure in the sense of things being placed in their proper or prescribed order (by class, race, gender, sexual orientation, or religious or even nonreligious views). Nor is it about being restrictive or staying in a space that cannot be exceeded. Discontinuities, disruptions, and new beginnings characterize the limits of the orgiastic love. Things delayed and just about to start stand at the limit, the limit being not simply that which points to the end of something but also that which initiates something. It is an ethic of multiple openings and a becoming virtue according to potentiality that, as noted by Gebara, leads to a vision of a praxis of happiness that works toward the happiness of all living beings.[209] This anarchic ethic is an internal breathing *urge* inclusive of those at the margins yearning for fuller expressions of enjoyment that benefit the whole. To clamor for no form of enjoyment at the expense of the other places a demand for the whole to be watchful of the marketplace with its global and self-perpetuating systems that give rise to nationalisms that keep ethnic and religious groups apart, of political and economic systems that benefit from alienation and impoverishment, of racism, homophobias, and class inequalities—a false enjoyment that strips the flesh from delighting itself in the fruit of its communal fervor and the potential of mutually beneficial dreams and labors.

Because this ethic is outside the assemblage of things put together as they should be (*poiesis*), on the outskirts of the normal versions of behavior, possibly humorous, at the khora, its eros can be set free not only from the production of dominant images of being human but also from a utilitarian view in which expenditure consumes the nonhuman.[210] A groan "within our flesh" collectively has the capacity to improve the ability within us to construct a world that reflects our shared life, and that affirms the needed adaptations to life of each living organism. Their becomings, too, are of the many in their sorrowful endings and hopeful beginnings. This vital mystery favors the displacement of "hierarchical boundaries" that presume the superiority of "some over others," Gebara says.[211] Even as there are indeed natural orders, cycles of life by which some nourish others, in lieu of a grotesque God embodying nature, we may reorder and decenter exclusive claims to enjoyment, do away with the claims to the supremacy of rational forms over those called irrational or less rational. Such divine monstrosity debunks the Aristotelian model of happiness by factoring in the enjoyments of plant and bestial life.[212] May the whole self-organize itself in matchless ways! Within the fertile divine loving nature composed of the many forms of life enjoying themselves in their unique ways, the picture we paint is of a polymorphous divine love that stirs all things stemming also from bestial life toward adventurous forms of loving. Something of God and other living beings returns to us, in the back-and-forth movements, helping us welcome the possibilities for imagining monstrously shaped limits giving rise to another way of defining the neighbor, to envision sustainable cities and states, to live also according to the living breath of our plant and animal friends.

Visions of a hetero*normat*ive God and alternative body configurations of the polyamorous love of God can mobilize people en masse, welcome their fervor enacted in their performance of the imagination, even that of the poor, their passion being actualized toward just acts that promote love for the stranger, the queer, the alien, the excluded other, as well as our animal and plant neighbors. We can dance among friends who are not a mere mimicry of ourselves, and we can offer a truer hospitality, one that does not place otherness, including the nonhuman, under the scientific gaze or exclusionary laws of the Same. Fervor, this collective desire engendered in the mysticism of the festivals, can act as a social process and a living force that poses a material spirituality.[213] We consider the acts of divine compassion along with a laughing God who takes pleasure "while pursuing a divine destiny of the kind of transgressive justice which disorders the law."[214] Laws that were stringently erected to keep bodies impoverished in the first place, that ghettoize to maintain a certain class- or race-based order,[215] that caricaturize the religious other, that define certain sexualities in subhuman terms, that strip the migrant of her humanity, and that destroy entire ecosystems and deplete the environment of life can be disordered. Through fervent desire or intensity of collective passion, hegemonic powers can be brought down and exposed to a recurrent deconstruction.

The point to affirm is that bodies orgiastically touching other bodies, out of control in the anarchic sense, can be purposely disruptive. They have the potential to open the path for something new to emerge, as the khora does to stale order. "The Queer carnival dancers of vision and the travelling circus of anarchists can be seen as standing in the tradition of the marginalized Hebrew prophets of resistance," writes Althaus-Reid.[216] For Nietzsche, this is most evident in the festival because some form of "mythopoeic power" is at hand.[217] He writes, "we shall now recognize in the Dionysian orgies of the Greeks, as compared with the Babylonian Sacaea with their reversion of man to tiger and the ape, the significance of festivals of world redemption and days of transfiguration."[218] But beyond him, the Bacchae are adventurous nomads who come back from that which is yet to come. With a vision of potentiality, an *ordo amoris* of the carnivalesque type, the intemperate bodies gathering to form a multitude are "unequilibrated, excitable and incorrigible" with a purpose.[219] The mystical orgy becomes a site of transgressive excitement where the multitude becomes conscious of its solidarity within a greater collective and arises to seek a future not yet established, not yet conquered. Might in the collective passion be the impulse of the many mobilizing and being mobilized by the many, even if playfully, toward countless forms of abundant rejoicing and celebrating a "good life" collectively![220]

These incorrigible bodies point to an image of a God of enjoyment whose graceful laws are also on the move, in the sense of being unfixed and diverse, of ever becoming more just, according to a "collectivity" of no hermetic borders.[221] With boundaries of affiliations lightly settled, orders disorder the image of an ethics devoid of love for the stranger, whatever stranger might be in vogue.[222] The immodest image of "a festival of the encounter of the intemperate"[223] means that the divine righteousness has yet to be defined, for God is *grace*fully God even when in transit. As if joining the divine becoming, love would lack not in exuberance, for God goes out of the bounds of propriety, expands hospitably, and calls all things to love immodestly, that is, excessively. In this, anarchist affections (as in decentered) could play a role in disrupting political and exclusionary religious discourses. The divine affections refuse repression, admitting rather to the creative capabilities of disorder that favors possible "better orders" that come about in the mysterious form of "monsters of grace," as Keller says.[224]

Rather than remaining bound to repressive laws, we welcome laws according to love in new ways. For Althaus-Reid, the underlying principle is that to be just is not the same as being always compliant with order, to be decent. An orgiastic ethic gives way to another artistic behavior, a virtuosity that is at times anarchic. It has an excess of justice that, for example, can be described more in terms of the graffiti representing the disappeared in Argentina painted right next to the Holy Family frescos on a church wall, as Althaus-Reid describes.[225] There's a reminder to do justice, and not merely within the bounds of the proper. With these graffiti representations, we are mindful of how needed are the holy Frankensteins in our time so that one's love for the stranger becomes active.[226] With cosmic visions of those many others that are unlike us to the farthest borders of being human, in being hospitable one might also create a virtuous space for the springing forth of the natural elements of life such as the nonhuman that also *in*form the human flesh.

With the carnivalesque elements of festive life, like laughter and play, and including the mystically orgiastic, the many shape the plural unity in ways that appear humorously monstrous. Mystics and early thinkers partly led us onto this improper path as they wrote of their union with God and the divine yearning by following the ways of unknowing and excellence. Their anarchic poetry burst free from the logic of propriety, rending possible an impression of the beautiful silhouette of God, one also present in the carnivalesque elements of the festivals. They spoke of a God with an excess of *being* love, and made it possible for other imaginations shaped in sensuous ways to conceive of a divine yearning akin to intoxication. Drunk with love for many others, so one might imagine, God goes outside the divine self in improper ways and draws all things into the divine self, including the many, as in a banquet or delectable feast.

Différance affirms the flesh with limits, yes. Yet, in affirming *différance*, we also embrace an aesthetic praxis in which there is a ludic empathy. What we hope for is the emancipation of the imagination so that it can grasp a festive depth in which God becomes the lover of many in many different forms. This is a God capable of lightness of being. The wish is for a playful God to be lightly touched, smelled, tasted, seen, and heard in the many shapes of nature as God welcomes in the stranger via the divine dance with the cosmos. It is a playful God who incites enjoyment and receives its flesh back in the voluntary and willing response of the celebration of the many who dance and laugh. The dance is of passage of bodies with openings that can be penetrated, and so also can empathetically transmute from one shape to another without the loss of self. And unlike a uniform flow of melody, the lyrics of the divine poetic lover express a nonsyncopated and abrupt cacophony of sounds.

With all things coming from God and returning to God, what emerges is a picture of a divine enjoyment analogous to a plural unity characteristic of a common good diversely composed. God becomes an open-ended *whole* that enjoys the divine self in nurturing the flourishing of the many others and for mutual sake. What exuberance! It is a dithyrambic dance generated by life's seeming contrasts. It is an intense dance of passion through which the whole is delightfully stirred to live life to the fullest, *una vida a vivir con gusto*,[227] with much plenitude in mindfulness for the well-being of each, apart from selfish pursuits, even when there may be pain. How improper is the dance of a passionate God of enjoyment whose excessive love stems from pain, yearning, permeability, and an intensity of harmonious contrasts that the cosmos brings, and with which God stirs it!

Might this primordial mystical union of grotesque enfleshment act as a fertile creativity imbued with joy? Life in the excess of God's love shown as a smile may come to us like rain showers in times of drought, making us laugh. We love, dance, laugh, celebrate, perhaps even beyond reason, because life is worth living. Dancing, laughter disrupt orders of fate by allowing us to taste the first fruits of new ways of loving the many as we celebrate.

Our love becomes adventurous. Its ethic, being grotesque as well, and its ambiguity give way to a hospitably expansive view of love, according to multiple shapes of justice that overflow the discourse of stale exactitude, strict order, and sameness. Indeed, here God queers the divine self, takes on strange flesh, as a reminder for us to *make* love and act kindly toward the queer others, the strangers in our midst, even plant and animal life forms.

So why not conclude a study on the divine enjoyment with a celebration, for surely even the dead—our ancestors—are dancing with us! Let us inaugurate the age of the God who belly laughs out loud in disruptive ways! Let us welcome play! And let us join in a celebration that welcomes the elements of air, fire, water, and earth, the interconnectivity with all living beings! Our love of and for the many, a monstrous grace, will be demonstrated in this act of laughter.

INTRODUCTION

1. Otto Maduro, *Mapas para la fiesta: Reflexiones sobre la crisis y el conocimiento*, Temas de formación sociopolitical 40 (Atlanta: Asociación para la Educación Teológica Hispana, 1998), 31. My English translation of this quotation is as follows: "But the life that we long for and treasure is one to be lived abundantly: life that is possible to enjoy together with others without putting in peril that others might also enjoy it: a life to be savored without destroying the possibility of continuing its satisfaction until one's old age; life worth celebrating in community and of remembering later with yearning . . . the good life! That life—the life that is worth living and that incites us to taste it fully—is not a mere struggle against death: it is the quest for common pleasure, for lasting joy, for deep delight, for free enjoyment, that contagious happiness. The good life—the life that deserves to be preserved, nourished, communicated, reproduced and celebrated—is the shared enjoyment of affect, the company, the labor, the food, the art, the game, the prayer, the dance . . . the celebration!"

2. The passage is rendered into contemporary language by *The Message*, a contemporary version of the Bible translated from the original Hebrew and Greek by Eugene Peterson. As it appears on the title page, "The Message is *a contemporary rendering of the Bible from the original languages, crafted to present its tone, rhythm, events, and ideas in everyday language.*" So, contrary to commonly held opinion, this translation is not a paraphrase, rather one that follows the dynamic equivalency method of translation in more contemporary language than most. I have found this translation to express more insightfully the intention of this portion of the text than other versions. Passages of scripture included in this book for which versions are unspecified are quoted from the New Revised Standard Version (NRSV).

3. Maduro, *Mapas para la fiesta*, 10. My translation.

4. Ibid., 31.

5. Thomas Aquinas, *Summa theologica of Saint Thomas*, trans. Fathers of the English Dominican Province (New York: Benzinger Bros., 1948), Ia, IIae, Q. 4, A. 8.

6. Ibid., IIa, IIae, Q. 23, A. 1.

7. See Catherine Mowry LaCugna, *God for Us: The Trinity and Christian Life* (New York: HarperSanFrancisco, 1991).

8. Aristotle, *Nicomachean Ethics*, trans. Joe Sachs (Newburyport, MA: Focus Publishing/R. Pullins Co., 2008), Book IX, viii, 1169b.

9. See ibid., Book I, vii–x.

10. LaCugna, *God for Us*, 161, 243–317.

11. See the use of metaphysical concepts in specific and the elevation of metaphysics to wisdom in Thomas Aquinas, *Commentary on the Metaphysics of Aristotle*, trans. John P. Rowan (Chicago: Henry Regnery, 1961).

12. Kevin J. Vanhoozer, "Theology and the Condition of Postmodernity," in *Cambridge Companion to Postmodern Theology* (Cambridge: Cambridge University Press, 2003).

13. Ibid., 8.

14. See an analysis akin to feminism in John B. Cobb, Jr., and David Ray Griffin, *Process Theology: An Introductory Exposition* (Louisville, KY: Westminster John Knox Press, 1976), 9–10.

15. Joseph A. Bracken, *The One in the Many: A Contemporary Reconstruction of the God-World Relation* (Grand Rapids, MI: William B. Eerdmans, 2001), 24.

16. Barbara A. Babcock, "Ritual Undress and the Comedy of Self and Other: Bandelier's the Delight Makers," in *A Crack in the Mirror: Reflexive Perspectives in Anthropology* (Philadelphia: University of Pennsylvania Press, 1982), 192. Her thoughts may be compared with those of Marcella Althaus-Reid, *Indecent Theology: Theological Perversions in Sex, Gender and Politics* (New York: Routledge, 2000).

17. Indeed, this book was born out of a desire for deeper insight into the Christian view of the God of love. Through a study of the term *eros*, the figure of the *beloved divine lover* emerges as the cornerstone of this study, and divine enjoyment as the focal point of the intimate relationship God has with the cosmos. Eros inevitably takes us along the paths of passionate love. Hence passion becomes a point of contention between classical theism and more recent relational forms of theism. The metaphor of lovemaking links all these thematic pieces, providing this study with its distinctively poetic interest.

18. Alfred North Whitehead, *Modes of Thought: Six Lectures Delivered in Wellesley College, Massachusetts, and Two Lectures in the University of Chicago* (New York: Macmillan, 1938), 174. I became aware of this theological argument through a paper presented by Catherine Keller, titled "'Each Thing

Sings': A Process Theological Reading of Cardenal's *Cosmic Canticles*," at a conference in Managua, Nicaragua, "Primer Encuentro de Cosmologías: Cardenal, Chardin, y Whitehead," September 2010.

19. Whitehead, *Modes of Thought*, 174.

20. Catherine Keller, *Face of the Deep: A Theology of Becoming* (New York: Routledge, 2003), 171.

21. Ivone Gebara, "La mujer hace theología: Un ensayo para la reflexión," in *El rostro femenino de la teología*, ed. Elsa Tamez (San José, CR: Departamento Ecuménico de Investigaciones, 1988), 11–23. My translation.

22. See Amos Niven Wilder, *Theopoetic Theology and the Religious Imagination* (Lima, OH: Academic Renewal Press, 2001). Wilder, in his use of the term "theopoetics," feels indebted to Stanley Hopper and his students, and the consultations they organized on hermeneutics and language at Drew University and Syracuse University (p. iv).

23. Ivone Gebara, *Longing for Running Water: Ecofeminism and Liberation* (Minneapolis, MN: Fortress Press, 1999), 55.

24. Ibid., 55.

25. My research reignited a torrid love affair with the work of Thomas Aquinas, whom I admired during my Catholic school years. Finding myself seduced once again by his thought, I keep him as a central figure in this book from beginning to end, while recognizing that his work is limited by his historical context.

26. See Jon Sobrino, "Awakening from the Sleep of Inhumanity," *Christian Century* 108, no. 11 (1991).

27. Teresa of Avila, *Conceptions of the Love of God*, trans. and ed. E. Allison Peers, vol. 2 of *The Complete Works of St. Teresa of Avila* (New York: Continuum, 2002), 389. This book of St. Teresa of Avila is her commentary on the Song of Songs.

1. PAIN: GROANS AND BIRTH PANGS OF THE DIVINE ENJOYMENT

1. Jon Sobrino, *Christology at the Crossroads: A Latin American Approach*, trans. John Drury (Maryknoll, NY: Orbis Books, 1978), 201.

2. Abraham J. Heschel, *The Prophets II* (Peabody, MA: Hendrickson, 1962), 42.

3. See Aristotle, *Nicomachean Ethics*, trans. and with a glossary and introductory essay by Joe Sachs (Newburyport, MA: Focus Publishing/R. Pullins Co., 2008).

4. See Aristotle, *Politics*, trans. Benjamin Jowett (Mineola, NY: Dover, 2000), I and III, in addition to those portions of the *Nicomachean Ethics* already included here.

5. Aristotle, *Nicomachean Ethics*, IX, ix, 1169b.

6. Ibid., VIII, vii, 1159a.

7. Ibid., VIII, viii, 1159a. A communal ethic that provides the basis for good living is also at play, for a *phileopolis* or city of friends promotes the happiness of all.

8. Ibid., VIII, x, 1160b.

9. Ibid., VIII, x, 1160b.

10. Ibid., VIII, vii, 1159a.

11. Heschel, *Prophets II*, 32.

12. See Aristotle, *Nicomachean Ethics*, X, viii, 1179a.

13. Thomas Aquinas, *Of God and His Creatures: An Annotated Translation of the Summa contra gentiles of Saint Thomas*, trans. and ed. Joseph Rickaby (Westminster, MD: Carroll Press, 1950), III, xc, 5. In seeking to share the thoughts of early thinkers such as St. Thomas Aquinas and mystics like St. Teresa of Avila as they wrote, this book maintains the male pronouns being used in reference for God, and in some instances to humanity, but not exclusively so. Throughout the chapters, female and neutral forms are also employed.

14. Aristotle, *Nicomachean Ethics*, X, viii, 1178b. Since the gods are the happiest and most blessed of all, to be contemplative or at-work is to be most happy. The person who is at-work with her or his soul is the happiest in that he or she cares for the things that are dear to the gods, for being-at-work is in accordance with virtue, in "acting rightfully and beautifully" (1179a), and thus is blessed or favored by the gods. The divine favor is analogous to how happy the person can be: the more favor, the happier the person. The person most favored is the wise person. Here the argument of being-at-work as opposed to Endymion's sleep provides an antithesis to a type of contemplation that lacks behavioral transformation. The myth behind Endymion's sleep may help illustrate this point. In the Greek pantheon, Endymion was the human who achieved eternal youth when put to sleep by Zeus, his father, at the request of Selene, the Titan goddess of the moon. She so loved how Endymion looked when asleep that she petitioned Zeus to keep Endymion eternally asleep so that she could contemplate his beauty. In another tale, Hypnos, the god of sleep, who, being also enthralled by the beauty of Endymion's face when asleep, and in order to be eternally inspired by him, caused Endymion to remain eternally in a state of sleep with his eyes open. Contemplation, unlike a state of eternal sleep, therefore, contains an element of virtue, the betterment of human behavior toward other fellow humans.

15. Don Adams, "Aquinas on Aristotle's Happiness," in *Medieval Philosophy and Theology*, ed. Norman Kretzmann et al. (Notre Dame, IN: University of Notre Dame Press, 1991), 98–99.

16. Anders Nygren, *Agape & Eros*, trans. Philip S. Watson (Chicago: University of Chicago Press, 1982), 44–45, 212.

17. The quotations are according to Aristotle, *Metaphysics*, trans. W. D. Ross (Sioux Falls, IA: NuVision Publications, 2005), XII. For a classical numbering of Aristotle's *Metaphysics* (as cited in the notes), see the translation of Joe Sachs from Green Lion Press (1999, 2002).

18. Aristotle, *Metaphysics*, XII, xi, 1071b 10–1072a 10.

19. Ibid., XII, xii, 1072b 20.

20. Ibid., XII, xiii, 1073a 20.

21. Gregory of Nyssa, *From Glory to Glory: Texts from Gregory of Nyssa's Mystical Writings*, trans. and ed. Herbert Musurillo (Crestwood, NY: St. Vladimir's Seminary Press, 1979), 102, 196–97.

22. Joseph A. Bracken, *The Divine Matrix: Creativity as Link between East and West* (Eugene, OR: Wipf and Stock, 1995), 11.

23. Aristotle, *Metaphysics*, trans. W. D. Ross (Sioux Falls: IA: NuVision Publications, 2005), XII, ix, 1074b 30.

24. Aristotle, *Nicomachean Ethics*, X, vi, 1177a.

25. Ibid., I, xiii, 1102b.

26. Heschel, *Prophets II*, 30.

27. With the use of the term "anesthetization," Heschel seems to be offering a critique of some forms of Greek thought, such as Stoicism, which posited that a sage, or a person of moral and intellectual perfection, would not suffer destructive emotions. For the Stoics, virtue was sufficient for happiness, and the sage whose emotions were under control was immune to misfortune.

28. Heschel, *Prophets II*, 34. Words gain a higher meaning when used in speaking of God. The writers of the scriptures, as Heschel points out, knew of the difference between them and God, and so anthropomorphism was not one of their concerns. One example is found in Genesis 1:1, where the notion of a beginning of the world does not speak of cause, but rather posits the world as finite, and not ultimate. God pictured as human was not the same as God being human. Pathos was not merely a matter of resemblance but of relatedness. See also pp. 45 and 51.

29. See Aristotle, *Metaphysics*, XII, xi, 1072b 20.

30. Sobrino, *Christology at the Crossroads*, 197.

31. See Bracken, *The Divine Matrix*, 14.

32. Mark-Robin Hoogland, *God, Passion and Power: Thomas Aquinas on Christ Crucified and the Almightiness of God* (Leuven: Peeters Press, 2003), 89.

33. Thomas Aquinas, *Summa theologica of Saint Thomas*, trans. Fathers of the English Dominican Province (New York: Benzinger Bros., 1948), Ia, Q. 12.

34. Aristotle, *Aristotle's Physics*, trans. Richard Hope (Lincoln: University of Nebraska Press, 1961), VIII, v, 256b.

35. Heschel, *Prophets II*, 14.

36. Jürgen Moltmann, *The Crucified God: The Cross of Christ as the Foundation and Criticism of Christian Theology*, trans. R. A. Wilson and John Bowden (Minneapolis, MN: Fortress Press, 1993), 222.

37. Heschel, *Prophets II*, 4.

38. Ibid., 4.

39. Aristotle, *Nicomachean Ethics*, IX, xi.

40. See Jon Sobrino, "Awakening from the Sleep of Inhumanity" (*Christian Century* 108, no. 11 [1991]: 364–70), where he argues that God follows in the footsteps of those who have been crucified throughout history, thus becoming like humanity via the Crucifixion. Solidarity therefore precedes atonement.

41. Moltmann, *Crucified God*, 230.

42. Several arguments support the view that God cannot suffer. For one, suffering has been linked with evil as well as sin, and God, in whom evil and sin cannot be found, cannot endure suffering. Creatures suffer as a result of sin having entered the creaturely existence after the Fall. That the freedom of God is perfect also implies that God is not capable of experiencing suffering, since God's choices are altogether good. Moreover, God is absolute and unlimited, and suffering implies a limitation. While God may experience some form of empathy, God is incapable of suffering with the created order. Instead, what God experiences is unmixed enjoyment, as discussed above.

43. See Tertullian, *Against Praexas*, xxix, in *The Ante-Nicene Fathers*, ed. Alexander Roberts and James Donaldson (Edinburgh: T&T Clark; Grand Rapids, MN: William B. Eerdmans, 1989).

44. In Christian theology, *patripassianism* (from Latin *patri-*, "father," and *passio*, "suffering") is the belief that God suffers in the sense of the Father being incarnate and suffering on the cross. The Trinitarian party maintained, on the contrary, that Christ and the Father were different persons, and that Christ suffered on the cross, but not the Father, thereby maintaining the doctrine of divine apathy. The majority of early Christian teachers came to regard *patripassianism* as a non-Trinitarian heresy.

45. Athanasius, *Orations against the Arians*, III, xvi, 30–31, in *The Nicene and Post-Nicene Fathers*, ed. Philip Schaff and Henry Wace (Edinburgh: T&T Clark, 1987).

46. Ibid., III, xvi, 33.

47. Apollinaris of Laodicea, in *The Christological Controversy*, trans. and ed. Richard A. Norris (Philadelphia: Fortress Press, 1980), 108.

48. Ibid., 110.

49. Hippolytus, *Against the Heresy of One Noetus*, in Roberts and Donaldson, *The Ante-Nicene Fathers*, 18.

50. Tertullian, *Against Praexas*, xxvii.

51. Alexander of Alexandria, in *The Trinitarian Controversy*, ed. William G. Rusch (Philadelphia: Fortress Press, 1980), 40–41.

52. Athanasius, *Orations against the Arians*, I, x, 35–36.

53. Aquinas, *Summa theologica*, IIIa, Q. 16, A. 5.

54. For one, Jesus's soul was rational, untouched by the flesh, so there would be no possibility of sin (see Origen, *On First Principles*, II, vi, 5, in Roberts and Donaldson, *The Ante-Nicene Fathers*), and since suffering is related to sin and evil, in the end this is taken to mean that the soul of Jesus could not suffer.

55. Thomas Aquinas, *On Love and Charity: Readings from the "Commentary on the Sentences of Peter Lombard,"* trans. Peter A. Kwasniewski, Thomas Bolin, and Joseph Bolin, with an introduction and notes by Peter A. Kwasniewski (Washington, DC: Catholic University of America Press, 2008), S. III, D. 27, Q. 1, A. 1, response.

56. Thomas Aquinas, *Summa contra gentiles*, trans. Anton C. Pegis (Notre Dame, IN: University of Notre Dame Press, 1975), I, lxxxix, no. 3 and 5.

57. Eberhard Jüngel, *God as the Mystery of the World: On the Foundation of the Theology of the Crucified One in the Dispute between Theism and Atheism*, trans. Darrell L. Guder (Grand Rapids, MI: William B. Eerdmans, 1983), 13.

58. See, for example, Moltmann, *Crucified God*, 87.

59. Ibid., 269.

60. This understanding of self-limitation is first conceived as a Trinitarian affair. God pours or self-empties Godself out of God in the relationship with the two other persons of the Trinity (Moltmann, *Crucified God*, 206). In alignment with Heschel's principles, though not with Jewish theology, he has in sight a Trinitarian participation exemplified in the event of the cross. God is *sympatheticus* or *patheticus* as God opens Godself in freedom to the other, and is vulnerable to the pain and even the death of the other (pp. 270–74). The dynamic participation of love of one person of the Trinity in the other leads to a fuller Trinitarian view of the God who limits the divine self voluntarily. As found in the work of Geddes MacGregor, each person willingly self-limits in surrender before the other two (see MacGregor, *He Who Lets Us Be: A Theology of Love* [New York: Seabury Press, 1975], 120). This divine relationship is an act of divine limitation that brings pain into the self of God. Thus one can argue that the divine pain is ontological. Moreover, this Trinitarian affair of self-limitation also entails a communication of pain in the reciprocity of natures between all members of the Trinity. In particular, Martin Luther's understanding of the doctrine of the *communicatio idiomatum* or communication of Jesus's human and divine attributes, Kazoh Kitamori's Mahayana-Buddhism, and Lutheran theology underpin this aspect of Moltmann's theology. Luther took his concept in

the direction of the *theologia crucis* and *deus absconditus*, that is, the hidden-ness of God in his theology of the cross, regarding the doctrine of the communication of attributes (see Moltmann, *Crucified God*, 47), while Moltmann sought to emphasize God's suffering, a view more akin to Kitamori's. Another document that sheds some light on the matter is Luther's *Heidelberg Disputation*.

It's also important to keep in mind that the doctrine of the *communicatio idiomatum* is attributed first to Athanasius (see *Orations against the Arians*, I, vi, 21; x, 35–36) and second to John of Damascus (see John of Damascus, *An Exact Exposition of the Orthodox Faith*, I, viii, in *The Nicene and Post-Nicene Fathers*, ed. Philip Schaff and Henry Wace, vol. 9 [Edinburgh: T&T Clark; Grand Rapids, MI: William. B. Eerdmans, 1989]). Athanasius argued for the unity between the divine and the human in Christ while affirming that the two natures interact without mixing. The human nature of Jesus, for example, would be informed by his divine nature in matters concerning knowledge. John of Damascus sought to explain the communication of the properties in terms of penetration. Through penetration, each of the natures communicates to the other its own. Athanasius is also one who understands the *communicatio idiomatum* as akin to a dance—*perichoresis*. The notion of *perichoresis* is briefly explained in Chapter 2.

61. Kazoh Kitamori, *Theology of the Pain of God: The First Original Theology from Japan* (Eugene, OR: Wipf and Stock, 2005).

62. In Christianity, *docetism* (from the Greek δοκέω [dokeō], "to seem") held that Jesus was in reality incorporeal, and so on the cross, Jesus did not physically die. Statements that refer to Jesus as having lived in the "flesh" (i.e., John 1:14) were merely metaphorical.

63. Kitamori, *Theology of the Pain of God*, 41. Moltmann interprets Kitamori, and most others in agreement with him, in light of how the divine person assumed the human nature in the incarnation (which makes the existence of Jesus concrete). For him, the divine nature is able to experience what the human nature is experiencing. What one feels the other also feels (Moltmann, *Crucified God*, 232). By sharing or partaking of attributes (human and divine), God shares God's divinity with the Son, and the Son shares his human attributes with God. Through the mutual partaking or *koinonia* of attributes there is negation and communion between the divine and the human, without the erasure of distinctions. God suffered the death of the Son but not according to patripassionism, for God died the death of the godless on the cross and yet did not die (Moltmann, *Crucified God*, 244). In the forsakenness of Jesus, God also surrendered Godself. This idea preserves the identity of both God and Son, while granting both flesh by love emerging from the grief of God in light of the death of the Son.

64. Jung Young Lee, "The Yin-Yang Way of Thinking: A Possible Method for Ecumenical Theology," *International Review of Missions* 60, no.

239 (July 1971): 363. See also Jung Young Lee, *God Suffers for Us: A Systematic Inquiry into a Concept of Divine Impassibility* (The Hague: Martinus Nijhoff, 1974).

65. Sobrino, *Christology at the Crossroads*, 220–21.

66. Kitamori, *Theology of the Pain of God*, 108.

67. Heschel, *Prophets II*, 43–46.

68. Luz Beatriz Arellano, "Women's Experience of God in Emerging Spirituality," in *With Passion and Compassion: Third World Women Doing Theology: Reflections from the Women's Commission of the Ecumenical Association of Third World Theologians*, ed. Virginia Fabella and Mercy Amba Oduyoye (Maryknoll, NY: Orbis Books, 1988), 136. The severity of the tragedies emanating from the civil wars in Latin America has been well documented. For example, the auxiliary archbishop Juan José Gerardi Conedera and the Interdiocesan Historical Memory Recovery Project (REMHI in Spanish) that he directed have reported the following in Guatemala alone: more than 150,000 deaths, 50,000 people who disappeared, one million refugees, 200,000 orphans, and 40,000 widows, making a total of 1,440,000 victims. See Archdiocese of Guatemala, *Guatemala: Never Again!* (Maryknoll, NY: Orbis Books, 1999). Sadly, these numbers reflect only the atrocities committed there between 1960 and 1996.

69. Responding to Moltmann, Sobrino firmly argues that the Christian faith finds its roots in no other doctrine than that of the "crucified God." See Sobrino, *Christology at the Crossroads*, 28–33. As such, one must not rush to speak of the resurrection. Relativizing the cross in light of the resurrection reduces its potential for being the scandal that the cross was meant to be.

70. Sobrino, *Christology at the Crossroads*, 196.

71. Ibid., 196.

72. Ibid., 188.

73. Ibid., 221.

74. Aristotle, *Metaphysics*, XII, xi, 1074b 30.

75. Sobrino, *Christology at the Crossroads*, 190.

76. Ibid., 166.

77. Ibid., 182.

78. Moltmann, *Crucified God*, 227.

79. Ibid., 207.

80. Dorothee Soelle, *Suffering* (London: Darton, Longman & Todd, 1975), 148. A story commonly included in early arguments on the God who suffers was Elie Wiesel's boy hanging on the gallows (based on an event that occurred in Auschwitz). Its implications for a God who suffers are internal to it. See Elie Wiesel, *Night* (London: Fontana/Collins, 1972), 76–77. This vision of the God who is "hanging here on the gallows" understandably drove the initial

Christian theological inquiry into divine impassibility. With much respect for the distinctiveness of Jewish thought and practice, we might tepidly note that Jewish understandings such as these do and must shed light on Christian views. This has been the case particularly for authors like Moltmann, who have formed their views of the crucified God in lieu of descriptive images of the Holocaust such as this one. Yet, without much delay, we must also note that the image of God hanging on the gallows should in no way be taken to mean the crucified Jesus, which would be an insult to many of the Jewish faith; and, more important, the despair of the little boy speaks first of all to the Jew in Auschwitz. Along with Johann-Baptist Metz and Kenneth Surin, one can recognize that to those who experienced such terrors, and to them only, is given the primary right to speak of the God being hanged on the gallows (see Johann-Baptist Metz, "Facing the Jews: Christian Theology after Auschwitz," in *The Holocaust As Interruption*, ed. Elisabeth Schüssler Fiorenza, and David Tracy [London: T&T Clark (Continuum) 1984], 29–30; Kenneth Surin, *Theology and the Problem of Evil* [Eugene, OR: Wipf and Stock, 2004], 118, 124). Its application for Christian thought is presented as a challenge. As Grace Jantzen attests, "Only a God who can suffer could command respect after Auschwitz" (see Jantzen, *God's World, God's Body* [Philadelphia, PA: Westminister Press, 1984], 84). Undeniably, such a narrative forces us to take a second look at the view on the impassible God of love. While God moves all things via love, God cannot remain unmoved by living beings other than God. Otherwise we stumble on the contradictions being presented in this project.

81. Surin, *Theology and the Problem of Evil*, 154.

82. María Clara Bingemer, "Chairete: Alegrai-vos a muller no futuro da teologia da liberção," *Revista Eclesistica Brasileira* 48, no. 191 (1988): 572, cited in María Pilar Aquino, *Our Cry for Life: Feminist Theology from Latin America*, trans. Dinah Livingstone (Maryknoll, NY: Orbis Books, 1993), 110–11.

83. María Teresa Porcile, "El derecho a la belleza en América Latina," in *El rostro femenino de la teología*, ed. Elsa Tamez (San José, CR: Departamento Ecuménico de Investigaciones, 1988), 87. I translate this quotation as follows: "A word about the God of fiesta and of beauty; a prophetic wisdom of the life experience with the living God among and from the poor, inhabiting the shapes and colors, the cries, is necessary in order to make poetry of peace (cf. Mt. 5:9), because the one who makes peace is a poet of peace."

84. Aristotle, *Nicomachean Ethics*, VIII, i, 1155a.

85. Sobrino, *Christology at the Crossroads*, 180.

86. Ibid.

87. Charles Hartshorne, *The Divine Relativity: A Social Conception of God* (New Haven, CT: Yale University Press, 1984), 45.

88. Arellano, "Women's Experience of God," 146.

89. Aquinas, *On Love and Charity*, S. III, D. 27, Q. 1, A. 1, response.

90. The reasons may vary. The inability of humans to see the whole can be one reason why there will always be conflicts as harmony is attempted, mostly because a narrow view of how harmony can be manifested is expressed and put into action. Often the attempt becomes monarchic and segregationalist, which leads to the enjoyment of a few who act in similar manner to one another, thus establishing the norm imposed on harmonious living.

91. See Alfred North Whitehead, *Adventures of Ideas* (New York: Free Press, 1961), 284–88.

92. Porcile, "El derecho a la belleza en América Latina," 91–92.

93. Ibid., 107.

94. Miguel Unamuno, *Tragic Sense of Life*, trans. J. E. Crawford Flitch (Charleston, SC: BiblioBazaar, 2007), 100.

95. Ibid., 222–24 passim.

96. Moltmann, *Crucified God*, 274.

97. Sobrino, *Christology at the Crossroads*, 227.

98. Ibid., 228. This is not to say that Sobrino embraces a panentheistic model of the God-cosmos relationship, as Moltmann does. He admits to finding no use for it in his own understanding of the crucified God (Sobrino, *Christology at the Crossroads*, 28–33). To me, however, this is one of the ways in which Sobrino's theology falters, and the point at which feminists from Latin America take on a more vulnerable approach to a theology of divine love, and at that, one that parallels panentheism in their views.

99. Sobrino, *Christology at the Crossroads*, 231.

100. The "*u*" of the *topos* or place is not so much in its usual Greek form of negation, as in "no-place." Rather, it serves to point to the "not yet-but-possible" or potentiality of becoming place, when it takes part of the human imagination.

101. Ibid., 232.

102. Moltmann, *Crucified God*, 247.

103. See Emmanuel Levinas, *Totality and Infinity: An Essay on Exteriority*, trans. Alphonso Lingis (Pittsburg, PA: Duquesne University Press, 1969).

104. Sobrino, *Christology at the Crossroads*, 203.

105. Ibid., 214.

106. Ibid., 225.

107. Kitamori, *Theology of the Pain of God*, 26.

108. Ibid., 96.

109. James H. Cone, *God of the Oppressed* (Maryknoll, NY: Orbis Books, 1997), 174.

110. Surin, *Theology and the Problem of Evil*, 150. Human life is complex. One cannot paint a complete picture of God from these human experiences. Even if metaphorically speaking, conceptualizing such an image of God is also a complex task and difficult to delineate in terms of issues of justice. What one

can affirm here, therefore, is that confronting evil places a demand on each and every one of us.

111. Ibid., 161.

112. Sobrino, *Christology at the Crossroads*, 200.

113. Leonardo Boff, *Passion of Christ, Passion of the World: Their Facts, Their Interpretation and Their Meaning for Yesterday and Today*, trans. Robert E. Barr (Maryknoll, NY: Orbis Books, 1987), 132–33.

114. Ibid., 132.

115. Surin, *Theology and the Problem of Evil*, 142–53.

116. In its earliest Christian expressions, divine friendship rent asunder from affect as a means to pose an immutable God parallels the manner in which being moved by another represents a tarnished *imago Dei*. This notion of immutable beginnings, when placed in relation to the passibility of the created order, means for early thinkers such as Gregory of Nyssa that immutability is the archetype and passion is a symbol of the Fall (*From Glory to Glory*, 112). The delights of Paradise were turned into toil and sickness (sorrow), and particularly for women into labor pains, and the one "who was familiar with impassibility has been transformed into a life of passion and death" (ibid., 88–90). Mutability is merely instrumental, for it leads nature to grow in good, to transform the soul progressively into the divine, who is always the same (ibid., 84). One can contend that feminists, by linking labor pains to God, are making a bold statement, one that turns the notion of "the curse" upside down.

117. María Clara Bingemer, "Reflections on the Trinity," in *Through Her Eyes: Women's Theology from Latin America*, ed. Elsa Tamez (Maryknoll, NY: Orbis Books, 1989), 80. Bingemer borrows some of her concepts on "womb love" from Phyllis Trible (see Trible, *Texts of Terror: Literary-Feminist Readings of Biblical Narratives* [Philadelphia: Fortress Press 1984]). This is not to say that the image of the Father can no longer be applicable to God. For Bingemer, God is a maternal Father and a paternal Mother. There is an exchangeability between Father and Mother images that is appealing in her work. Her main point is that as God is both Father and Mother, so are all three persons of the Trinity. Jesus and the Spirit acquire motherly characteristics along with the fatherly ones. Thus the divine love is both maternal and paternal.

118. Bingemer, "Reflections on the Trinity," 67.

119. Ibid., 76, 77, 66.

120. Ana María Tepedino, "Feminist Theology as the Fruit of Passion and Compassion," in *With Passion and Compassion: Third World Women Doing Theology: Reflections from the Women's Commission of the Ecumenical Association of Third World Theologians*, ed. Virginia Fabella and Mercy Amba Oduyoye (Maryknoll, NY: Orbis Books, 1988), 167.

121. Ibid., 167.

122. Bingemer, "Chairete," 575, cited in Aquino, *Our Cry for Life*, 112.

123. Bingemer, "Reflections on the Trinity," 77–78.

124. Ibid., 79.

125. Jürgen Moltman, *God in Creation: A New Theology of Creation and the Spirit of God. The Gifford Lectures 1984–1985* (New York: Harper & Row, 1985), 87.

126. Bingemer, "Chairete," cited in Aquino, *Our Cry for Life*, 111.

127. Alida Verhoeven, "The Concept of God: A Feminine Perspective," in *Through Her Eyes: Women's Theology from Latin America*, ed. Elsa Tamez (Maryknoll, NY: Orbis Books, 1989), 54–55.

128. Porcile, "El derecho a la belleza en América Latina," 90–91.

129. Verhoeven, "The Concept of God: A Feminine Perspective," 55.

130. Aquino, *Our Cry for Life*, 10.

131. Tepedino, "Femnist Theology," 168.

132. Aquino, *Our Cry for Life*, 154.

133. Teresa Cavalcanti, "El ministerio prefético de las mujeres en el Antiguo Testamento: Perspectivas de actualización," in *El rostro femenino de la teología*, ed. Elsa Tamez (San José, CR: Departamento Ecuménico de Investigaciones, 1988), 35. See Sandro Gallazi, "Os Macabeus: una luta pela liberdale de povo," in *A violénica dos opresores e o direito dos pobres à vida, na Bíblica*, Estudios bíblicos 6 (Petrópolis: Vozes, 1985), 47.

134. Aquino, *Our Cry for Life*, 151.

135. Jay B. McDaniel, "The Passion of Christ: Grace Both Red and Green," in *Cross Examinations: Readings on the Meaning of the Cross Today*, ed. Marit Trelstad (Minneapolis, MN: Augsburg Fortress, 2006), 197.

136. Aquinas, *Summa theologica*, Ia, IIae, QQ. 22–25.

137. Marcella Althaus-Reid, *Indecent Theology: Theological Perversions in Sex, Gender and Politics* (New York: Routledge, 2000), 134.

138. See Porcile, "El derecho a la belleza en América Latina," 90–91. Interestingly, this concept of festivity accompanied by the expression of the arts appears to be a universal means to raise human consciousness towards the common good. For example, in Cairo, after the political revolution that overthrew the presidency of Hosni Mubarak (2011), there was an emergence of a music style termed *mahraganat*, which in Arabic stands for "festivals." With this style of music, people dance as they listen to lyrics that speak of what they have in their minds, address their issues, and protest against inequality. See Ben Hubbard, "Out of Egypt's Chaos, Musical Rebellion," *New York Times*, May 12, 2012, A6, A12.

139. Porcile, "El derecho a la belleza en América Latina," 90.

140. Ibid., 90.

141. For Aristotle, and many of the thinkers in antiquity, by settling on a nobility whose task was governance, the task of labor rested on the shoulders of the workers such as craftsmen, artisans, and slaves, leaving these workers with

no opportunities for much leisure. I see the concept of *fiesta* as way to further disrupt this Greek paradigm of enjoyment. See, for example, Aristotle's *Politics*.

142. For the Latin American bishops who met in Puebla, faith too is being expressed in the *fiestas* and celebrations (see no. 454 de Puebla). Ivone Gebara, "La mujer hace theología: Un ensayo para la reflexión," in *El rostro femenino de la teología*, ed. Elsa Tamez (San José, CR: Departamento Ecuménico de Investigaciones, 1988), 23. Interestingly, Pope Francis also speaks of the value of leisure in counteracting competitiveness and consumerism in the book *Pope Francis: Conversations with Jorge Bergoglio: His Life in His Own Words*, ed. Sergio Rubin and Francesca Ambrogetti (New York: Putnam Adult, 2013). See also Mark Oppenheimer, "Pope Francis Has a Few Words in Support of Leisure," *New York Times*, April 27, 2013, A13.

143. Arellano, "Women's Experience of God," 207, cited in Aquino, *Our Cry for Life*, 156.

144. Porcile, "El derecho a la belleza en América Latina," 87.

145. "Wombier" is a term I am borrowing from Catherine Keller, who describes the divine-creaturely reality as womblike: Catherine Keller, *Face of the Deep: A Theology of Becoming* (New York: Routledge, 2003), 223.

2. YEARNING: TRACES OF THE DIVINE EROTIC EXISTENCE IN THE COSMOS

1. Ernesto Cardenal, *Love: A Glimpse of Eternity*, trans. Dinah Livingstone (Brewster, MA: Paraclete Press, 2006), 61.

2. Pseudo-Dionysius, *The Divine Names*, in *Pseudo-Dionysius: The Complete Works*, ed. John Farina, trans. Colm Luibheid (Mahwah, NJ: Paulist Press, 1987), 82.

3. Thomas Aquinas, *Summa theologica of Saint Thomas*, trans. Fathers of the English Dominican Province (New York: Benzinger Bros., 1948), Ia, IIae, Q. 28, A. 3. Emphasis his.

4. Anders Nygren, *Agape & Eros*, trans. Philip S. Watson (New York: Harper & Row, 1982), 212.

5. See Jacques Lacan, *On Feminine Sexuality: The Limits of Love and Knowledge, Book XX, Encore 1972–1973* (New York: W. W. Norton, 1998), 142. Divine *jouissance* or enjoyment is discussed throughout the book, and particularly from a feminist perspective in the third chapter.

6. Thomas Aquinas, *Devoutly I Adore Thee: The Prayers & Hymns of Saint Thomas Aquinas*, ed. Robert Anderson and Johann Moser (Manchester, NH: Sophia Institute Press, 1993), 33.

7. Thomas Aquinas, *Of God and His Creatures: An Annotated Translation of the Summa contra gentiles of Saint Thomas*, ed. and trans. Joseph Rickaby (Westminster, MD: Carroll Press, 1950), I, c.

8. Thomas Aquinas, *Summa contra gentiles*, trans. Anton C. Pegis (Notre Dame, IN: University of Notre Dame Press, 1975), I, c, n. 1.

9. John S. Morreall, *Analogy and Talking about God: A Critique of the Thomistic Approach* (Washington, DC: University Press of America, 1978), 9.

10. Plato, *Symposium*, trans. Robin Waterfield (Oxford: Oxford University Press, 1994), 206a.

11. Morreall, *Analogy and Talking about God*, 9.

12. Plotinus, *The Enneads*, trans. Stephen McKenna and B. S. Page (Hong Kong: Forgotten Books, 2007), VI, viii, 15.

13. Ibid., III, v, 1.

14. Ibid., VI, v, 12.

15. Ibid., V, v, 12.

16. For a similar approach, see, for example, the works of Bernard McGinn, "God as Eros: Metaphysical Foundations of Christian Mysticism," in *New Perspectives on Historical Theology: Essays in Memory of John Meyendorff*, ed. Bradley Nassif (Grand Rapids, MI: William B. Eerdmans, 1996); "The Language of Love in Christian and Jewish Mysticism," in *Mysticism and Language*, ed. Steven T. Katz (New York: Oxford University Press, 1992); "Tropics of Desire: Mystical Interpretations of the Song of Songs," in *That Others May Know and Love: Essays in Honor of Zachary Hayes, OFM*, ed. Michael F. Cusato and F. Edward Coughlin (St. Bonaventure, NY: St. Bonaventure University Press, 1997); and his book series titled *The Presence of God: A History of Western Christian Mysticism* (Spring Valley, NY: Crossroad, 1991–2012). Another author whose work seeks to bridge classical thought with mysticism is Andrew Louth. In addition to the works cited here on Denys the Areopagite, see "Eros and Mysticism: Early Christian Interpretation of the Song of Songs," in *Jung and the Monotheisms: Judaism, Christianity and Islam*, ed. Joel Ryce-Menubin (London: Routledge, 1994).

17. I thank the Latino theologian Orlando Espín for persuading me to approach St. Thomas Aquinas in this manner. His advice evolved into one of the guiding principles of this book's theme.

18. Andrew Louth, *Denys the Areopagite* (London: Continuum, 1989), 18.

19. Don Adams, "Aquinas on Aristotle's Happiness," in *Medieval Philosophy and Theology*, ed. Norman Kretzmann et al. (Notre Dame, IN: University of Notre Dame Press, 1991), 98–99.

20. Mark Jordan, *Rewritten Theology: Aquinas after His Readers* (Malden, MA: Blackwell, 2006), 89. Jordan also explains how even the *Summa theologica* was written as "an ideal of curricular reform for Dominican theology, that is, for the teaching of his own religious order, and by extension for other Christian priests or religious" (p. 7). See *Rewritten Theology*'s chapter 6 for a brief narrative on the moral formation of the *Summa*. His teaching was performative, written as a dialogue, and sought to express the creeds under a new language. It was also through a process of rewriting entrusted to communities with dispositions

of institutional power that the *Summa* took its final form as a theological authority, argues Jordan (pp. 7–17). The combination of sources on which he draws and the diversity of languages attest to the fact that Aquinas felt free to explore new ways of teaching each particular doctrine.

21. Averroës, *Averroës' Three Short Commentaries on Aristotle's "Topics," "Rhetoric," and "Poetics,"* ed. and trans. Charles E. Butterworth (Albany: State University of New York Press, 1977), 83.

22. Ibid., 84.

23. Pseudo-Dionysius, *The Divine Names*, 53.

24. See the preface to St. Thomas Aquinas, *Commentary on the Posterior Analytics of Aristotle*, ed. Richard Berquist and Ralph McInerny (South Bend, IN: St. Augustine's Press, 2008); and *Summa theologica*, Ia, QQ. 1, 12–13.

25. Richard A. Norris, ed., *The Song of Songs: Interpreted by Early Christian and Medieval Commentators* (Grand Rapids, MI: William B. Eerdmans, 2003), 1. The series in which this work appears, *The Church's Bible*, contains lengthy excerpts of the original work of ancient commentaries. In the case of this volume, edited by Norris, the commentary and homiletic work under exploration is on the Song of Songs. In this book I make much use of the excerpts contained in this volume, not only because of the systematic manner in which Norris conveniently arranges the material but also because I find his translations fresh and insightful, containing terminology that comes closest to the meaning I intend to convey in this book. Also, some of the commentaries or materials on the Song of Songs included here are difficult to locate in English. Sadly, Norris's volume lacks the contributions of female authors. I also use other translations of sermons, commentary, and written material of classical thinkers in this book (if available in English) to complement Norris, as certain terms employed in other translations more closely communicate my desired meaning in the English language.

26. Gregory the Great, in Norris, *The Song of Songs*, 9. See also Gregory the Great, *On the Song of Songs*, trans. and with an introduction by Mark DelCogliano (Collegeville, MN: Liturgical Press, 2012), 5.

27. Origen, *The Song of Songs*, 24.

28. Ibid., 29–40 passim.

29. Origen, *On First Principles*, in *The Ante-Nicene Fathers*, ed. Alexander Roberts and James Donaldson (Edinburgh: T&T Clark; Grand Rapids, MN: William B. Eerdmans, 1989), III, vi, 1.

30. Origen, *Homilies on Numbers*, Homily 17: Numbers 23:25–30; 24:1–9, iv, 2. See *Ancient Christian Texts*, ed. Thomas P. Scheck, trans. Christopher A Hall (Downers Grove, IL: IVP Academic, 2009).

31. Origen, *The Song of Songs, Commentary and Homilies*, trans. and ann. R. P. Lawson (New York: Newman Press, 1956), 58.

32. Gregory of Nyssa, *From Glory to Glory: Texts from Gregory of Nyssa's Mystical Writings*, trans. and ed. Herbert Musurillo (Crestwood, NY: St. Vladimir's Seminary Press, 1979), 206.

33. Ibid., 145.

34. Ibid., 213.

35. Ibid., 146.

36. Ibid., 146.

37. Ibid., 149.

38. Ibid., 212, 213.

39. Ibid., 270.

40. See, for example, Origen's *The Song of Songs, Commentary and Homilies*, particularly the first part of the prologue, where he discusses the themes of the Song of Songs.

41. Mechtild of Magdeburg, *Flowing Light of the Godhead*, trans. Frank Tobin, ed. and with a preface by Margot Schmidt (Mahwah, NJ: Paulist Press, 1998), 58.

42. Ibid., 62.

43. Hadewijch, *Hadewijch: The Complete Works*, trans. Mother Columba Hart (New York: Paulist Press, 1980), 12.

44. Ibid., 66.

45. Ibid., 80.

46. Ibid., 224–25, 239.

47. Ibid., 112. Hadewijch uses the term "love" to refer to God, or love becomes a divine persona, and so in her work Love is capitalized. To preserve her thoughts, here in this quotation Love is also capitalized, whereas when referring to the divine act of loving or the quality of love, and elsewhere in the chapter, it isn't.

48. Ibid., 181.

49. Denys Turner, *Eros & Allegory: Medieval Exegesis of the Song of Songs* (Kalamazoo, MI: Cistercian Publications, 1995), 139.

50. Ibid., 139.

51. William of Saint-Thierry, in *The Song of Songs: Interpreted by Early Christian and Medieval Commentators*, ed. Richard A. Norris (Grand Rapids, MI: William B. Eerdmans, 2003), 17. See also William of Saint-Thierry, *Exposition on the Song of Songs*, trans. Mother Columba Hart, with an introduction by J.-M. Déchanet (Kalamazoo, MI: Cistercian Publications, 1968), 25.

52. Gregory the Great, *On the Song of Songs*, 3.

53. Gregory of Nyssa, *From Glory to Glory*, 154.

54. Ibid., 156, 183.

55. Pseudo-Dionysius, *The Divine Names*, 80–83.

56. Ibid., 95.

57. See Umberto Eco, *The Aesthetics of Thomas Aquinas*, trans. Hugh Bredin (Cambridge, MA: Harvard University Press, 1988), chap. 1.

58. Aquinas, *Of God and His Creatures*, I, c, n. 2.

59. Aristotle, *Metaphysics*, trans. W. D. Ross (Sioux Falls, IA: NuVision Publications, 2005), XII, xii, 1072b 20. The notion of contemplation here appears to refer to the manner in which philosophers withdraw from all daily activities to examine their ideas. Such mental activity is accompanied by leisure and

avoids being troubled with cares. See, for example, René Descartes' description of how he undertook the task of reflection: "I was then in Germany, where I had gone because of the desire to see the wars which are still not ended; and while I was returning to the army from the coronation of the Emperor, I was caught by the onset of winter. There was no conversation to occupy me, and being untroubled by any cares or passions, I remained all day alone in a warm room. There I had plenty of leisure to examine my ideas." René Descartes, *Discourse on Methods and Meditations*, trans. Laurence J. Lafleur (Indianapolis: Bobbs-Merrill, 1960), 10. The regulation of passions therefore can lead to happiness (see p. 21).

60. Aristotle, *Metaphysics*, XII, ix, 1074b 30.

61. See Nygren, *Agape & Eros*, 44–45.

62. .Ibid.

63. Aristotle, *Nicomachean Ethics*, trans. and with a glossary and introductory essay by Joe Sachs (Newburyport, MA: Focus Publishing/R. Pullins Co., 2008), I, viii–ix.

64. Aquinas, *Of God and His Creatures*, I, c, n. 2.

65. Ibid., I, c, n. 4.

66. Ibid., I, ci.

67. Ibid.

68. Fran O'Rourke, *Pseudo-Dionysius and the Metaphysics of Aquinas* (Notre Dame, IN: University of Notre Dame Press, 2005), 197.

69. Ibid., 152.

70. Ibid., 178. See also Majid Fakhry, *Averroes (Ibn Rushd): His Life, Works and Influence* (Oxford: Oneworld, 2001). According to Fakhry, one can observe here the influence of Averroës on Aquinas's writings (possibly via Boethius). As he argues, the concept *esse per se subsistens* becomes one of Aquinas's most pivotal metaphysical expressions pertaining to God. It denotes that in God alone "is the unity of essence and existence safeguarded" (p. 141). He explains that one argument that supports this statement is that "God possesses all the perfections 'in a more excellent way' than all other things, because in Him they are one; whereas in other things they are diversified" (p. 141). See also Aquinas, *On Being and Essence*, trans. Armand Maurer, rev ed. (Toronto: Pontifical Institute of Medieval Studies, 1968), 62, where, as Fakhry points out, Aquinas draws from principles laid out in Aristotle's *Metaphysics* V, xvi, 1021b 30, and Averroës's *In Metaphysicoprum* V, f.c. 21, fol. 62r., 10–13. Contra Avecina, it also means that God possesses being essentially and not accidentally (p. 142). His dialogue with Islamic philosophy is beyond the purview of this book.

71. O'Rourke, *Pseudo-Dionysius and the Metaphysics of Aquinas*, 197.

72. Aquinas, *Of God and His Creatures*, I, cii, n. 7.

73. See Emmanuel Levinas, *Totality and Infinity: An Essay on Exteriority*, trans. Alphonso Lingis (Pittsburgh, PA: Duquesne University Press, 1969), 210.

74. Ibid., 179–80.

75. Aquinas, *Summa contra gentiles*, I, c, n. 1.

76. Charles Hartshorne, *Aquinas to Whitehead: Seven Centuries of Metaphysics of Religion. The Aquinas Lecture, 1976*. Aquinas Lecture 40 (Milwaukee, WI: Marquette University Publications, 1976), 48.

77. Aquinas, *Summa contra gentiles*, I, c, n. 1.

78. Joseph A. Bracken, *The Divine Matrix: Creativity as Link between East and West* (Eugene, OR: Wipf and Stock, 1995).

79. Aristotle, *Metaphysics*, XII, ix, 1074b 30.

80. Aquinas, *Summa theologica*, Ia, Q 2, A 1.

81. Bracken, *The Divine Matrix*, 26.

82. Ibid., 35. See also, for example, Karl Rahner, *Spirit in the World*, trans. William Dych (New York: Continuum, 1994). For him, knowledge and love in the work of Aquinas go hand in hand.

83. Thomas Aquinas, *On Love and Charity: Readings from the "Commentary on the Sentences of Peter Lombard,"* trans. Peter A. Kwasniewski, Thomas Bolin, and Joseph Bolin, with an introduction and notes by Peter A. Kwasniewski (Washington, DC: Catholic University of America Press, 2008), S. III, D. 32, notes.

84. Aquinas, *Summa theologica*, Ia, Q. 27, A. 4.

85. Ibid., Ia, Q. 27, A. 4. In this chapter and elsewhere in the book, whenever the term Spirit is capitalized, it refers to the third person of the Trinity. In such instances where "spirit" denotes a divine quality or operation or is used as a universal term, it is written in lowercase. Similarly, terms like "word" and "love," when referring specifically to the Son and the Spirit, will be capitalized (Word, Love). These two terms will acquire breath in meaning when used in lowercase. For example, the Spirit is Love proceeding from God, but also the divine love is an impulse that stirs all things toward love. The term "advent" in lowercase implying its inclusive but not solely liturgical meaning is another example of my intended broad meaning.

86. Ibid., Ia IIae, Q. 28, A. 2.

87. Ibid., Ia, Q. 79, A. 1.

88. Ibid., Ia, Q. 27, A. 5.

89. This term first appeared in the fourth century A.D. in Epistle 101 of Gregory Nazianzen, and is later used in the work of John of Damascus in his *An Exact Exposition of the Orthodox Faith* to explain the Trinitarian aspect of three being one. The Damascene describes it the following way: "Wherefore we do not speak of three Gods, the Father, the Son, and the Holy Spirit, but rather of one God, the holy Trinity, the Son and Spirit being referred to one cause, and not compounded or coalesced according to the synaeresis of Sabellius. For, as we said, they are made one not so as to commingle, but so as to cleave to each other, and they have their being in each other without any coalescence or commingling." John of Damascus, *An Exact Exposition of the Orthodox Faith*, I, viii,

in *The Nicene and Post-Nicene Fathers*, ed. Philip Schaff and Henry Wace, vol. 9 (Edinburgh: T&T Clark; Grand Rapids: William B. Eerdmans, 1989).

90. See John Zizioulas, *Being as Communion: Studies in Personhood and the Church* (Crestwood, NY: St. Vladimir's Seminary Press, 1985). See also Patricia Wilson-Kastner, *Faith, Feminism, and the Christ* (Philadelphia, PA: Fortress Press, 1983).

91. Pseudo-Dionysius, *The Divine Names*, in *The Complete Works*, 61.

92. Catherine Mowry LaCugna, *God for Us: The Trinity and Christian Life* (New York: HarperSanFrancisco, 1991), 271.

93. Ibid., 270.

94. Joseph A. Bracken, *The One in the Many: A Contemporary Reconstruction of the God-World Relation* (Grand Rapids, MI: William B. Eerdmans, 2001), 40. This does not mean that the notion of God as relational is being replaced, or that matters concerning the subject and the body are being erased. Rather, I seek to open up the space for envisioning more permeable understandings of God. By highlighting the movement of divine love, even as I discuss the divine flesh, I create a space for greater and more diverse forms of divine enjoyment to surface throughout the book.

95. Ivone Gebara, *Longing for Running Water: Ecofeminism and Liberation*, trans. David Molineaux (Minneapolis, MN: Fortress Press, 1999), 116.

96. This aspect is revisited in Chapter 3, in a discussion of the postmodern view of Jean-Luc Marion, whose concerns address love as primary to the question of being.

97. Bracken, *The Divine Matrix*, 55.

98. Levinas, *Totality and Infinity*, 50.

99. See Aristotle, *Aristotle's Physics*, trans. Richard Hope (Lincoln: University of Nebraska Press, 1961), VIII. See also Matthew Fox, *Sheer Joy: Conversations with Thomas Aquinas on Creation Spirituality* (New York: HarperSanFrancisco, 1992), 62.

100. Aquinas, *Summa theologica*, Ia, Q. 8, AA. 1, 3.

101. Ibid., Ia IIae, Q. 26, A. 2

102. Ibid., Ia, Q. 20, A. 1.

103. Aquinas, *On Love and Charity*, S. III, D. 27, Q. 1, A. 1.

104. Akin to the thought prevalent in Ignatius of Loyola, yearning is love as both *eros* and *agape*, having one and the same meaning. Even defending the term eros, he claims that "real yearning" is appropriate of God. See Pseudo-Dionysius, *The Divine Names*, 81.

105. Aquinas, *Summa contra gentiles*, I, c, n. 1.

106. Aquinas, *On Love and Charity*, S. III, D. 32, A. 1.

107. Aquinas, *Summa theologica*, IIa, IIae, Q. 175, A. 2.

108. O'Rourke, *Pseudo-Dionysius and the Metaphysics of Aquinas*, 217.

109. Aquinas, *Summa theologica*, Ia, Q. 43, A. 5.

110. Ibid., Ia, Q. 43, A. 1.

111. Ibid., Ia, Q. 43, A. 2.

112. Aquinas, *Summa contra gentiles*, I, xci, n. 6.

113. Aquinas, *Summa theologica*, Ia, IIae, Q. 26, A. 2. Emphasis his.

114. Aquinas, *Summa contra gentiles*, I, xci, n. 4.

115. Aquinas, *Summa theologica*, Ia, IIae, Q. 28, A. 3.

116. Ibid., Ia, IIae, Q. 28, A. 2.

117. Ibid., Ia, Q. 14, A. 6. Literally speaking, it is in all things as cause.

118. Ibid., Ia, Q. 20, A. 2.

119. Ibid., Ia, Q. 20, A. 1. Emphasis his. For Aristotle, a circular motion can be both single and continuous, and therefore not only infinite but also perfect. In a circle there is a simple and continuous turning back to the starting point. That is, there are neither interruptions nor changes of direction but one single movement toward its source.

120. Aquinas, *Summa contra gentiles*, I, lxxxviii, n. 2. A similar thought is found in Denys the Areopagite, who argues that the "Cause of all . . . is not a material body . . . suffers neither disorder nor disturbance and is overwhelmed by no earthly passion" (see Pseudo-Dionysius, *Mystical Theology*, in *The Complete Works*, 141).

121. O'Rourke, *Pseudo-Dionysius and the Metaphysics of Aquinas*, 178, 190, 178. This book does not engage the already well-debated aspect of cause and effect in Aquinas but rather focuses on the notion of the activity of love in ways that imply something other than cause and effect, as in a more process view, in which impulse is rather purposeful but open-ended.

122. According to Aquinas, "Divine providence provides for all things according to their mode of existence lxxiii, n. 2). But is proper to man and to every rational creature to act voluntarily and to be a master of his own acts; and compulsion is contrary to voluntariness." God, who loves all creatures wishes their good, thus guards them, but in a manner that allows for their volitions and choices. See Aquinas, *Of God and His Creatures*, III, cli, n. 2; cxlix, n. 2.

123. Aquinas, *Summa theologica*, IIa, IIae, Q. 23, A. 2.

124. Ibid., IIa, IIae, Q. 23, A. 2. Emphasis his.

125. Aquinas, *On Love and Charity*, S. II, D. 38, A. 1, response.

126. Aquinas, *Of God and His Creatures*, III, cli, n. 2.

127. Ibid., III, cli, n. 5.

128. Ibid., III, clii, n. 1.

129. Pseudo-Dionysius, *The Divine Names*, 73

130. Ibid., 82.

131. Aquinas, *Summa theologica*, Ia, Q. 20, A. 2.

132. See ibid., Ia, IIae, Q. 4, A. 8. Aquinas also argues that to love with benevolence is "to wish good" to another (ibid., IIa IIae, Q. 23, A. 1.)

133. Ibid., Ia IIae, Q. 28, A. 5.

134. Ibid., Ia IIae, Q. 27, A. 1.

135. The term *visio beatifica* refers to the mystical act of seeing God face to face by means of being in union with God.

136. Aquinas, *On Love and Charity*, S. I, D. 1, Q. 1, A. 1, response.

137. Aquinas, *Summa theologica*, Ia, IIae, Q. 3, A. 8.

138. Ibid., Supp., Q. 92, A. 1. Happiness, which is a pleasure of the soul, he argues, "belongs principally to the sight. But natural pleasure belongs principally to the touch" (ibid., Ia, IIae, Q. 31, A. 6). Arguing on the basis of etymology, he states, "For *theos* [*theos* with a Greek spelling], which among Greeks signifies God, comes from *theaste* [*theastai* with a Greek spelling], which means to consider or to see" (*Summa Contra Gentiles*, I, xliv, n. 10). Feminists like Luce Irigaray have argued against the primacy of sight over touch, which favors the intellect in the end. A postmodern feminist understanding of tactile and embodied forms of enjoyment will be more fully developed in Chapter 3 of this book and onward.

139. Fox, *Sheer Joy*, 63.

140. O'Rourke, *Pseudo-Dionysius and the Metaphysics of Aquinas*, 217, 221, 216. As we shall see, something else would need to be added for there to be a real opening to the cosmos.

141. Aquinas, *Summa contra gentiles*, I, c, n. 4.

142. Pseudo-Dionysius, *The Divine Names*, 73.

143. Ibid., 75.

144. Ibid., 79.

145. Ibid., 82.

146. Aquinas, *Of God and His Creatures*, I, c, n. 3.

147. Peter Lombard, *The Sentences: Book 2. On Creation*, trans. Giulio Silano (Toronto: Pontifical Institute of Medieval Studies, University of Toronto, 2008), II, iv, n. 1.

148. Aquinas, *Of God and His Creatures*, III, lxiii, n. 1.

149. Aquinas, *Summa contra gentiles*, III, li.

150. Aquinas, *Devoutly I Adore Thee*, 84–85.

151. Pseudo-Dionysius, *The Divine Names*, 82.

152. Aquinas, *Summa theologica*, Ia IIae, Q. 28 A. 2.

153. Ibid., Ia, IIae, Q. 28.

154. Ibid., Ia, IIae, Q. 26, A. 2.

155. Aquinas, *Summa theologica*, Ia, IIae, Q. 26, A. 2 Implications for notions of Sabbath, recreation, and leisure in relation to the Trinity are discussed in Chapter 5 of this book.

156. Ibid., Ia, IIae, Q 2, A. 8.

157. Gregory of Nyssa, *From Glory to Glory*, 210. It also translates as freedom from passion, so this concept of the nuptial bed could also be problematic.

158. Ibid., 237.

159. Ibid., 286.

160. Aquinas, *Summa theologica*, Ia, IIae, Q. 1, A. 7.

161. Catherine Keller, *Face of the Deep: A Theology of Becoming* (New York: Routledge, 2003), 195.

162. Aquinas, *Summa contra gentiles*, I, xci, n. 17.

163. Keller, *Face of the Deep*, 198. Emphasis hers.

164. Bracken, *The Divine Matrix*, 27.

165. Bracken, *The Divine Matrix*, 27, 29.

166. While Bracken makes reference to this key aspect of love in dialogue with Jean-Luc Marion, as found in 1 John 4:8, he does not develop this concept of love as permeable and transfigurative as I do in his understanding of the divine essence (see Bracken, *The One in the Many*, 25). A discussion of Bracken's views on Marion's work on the divine essence of love follows in Chapter 3. What his arguments contain that I seek to appropriate is an insightful view of Aquinas and the dynamic aspect of the nature of God, which I interpret as complex desire. More on the development of his views in conversation with mine appears in the chapters that follow.

167. Aquinas, *Summa theologica*, Ia, IIae, Q. 20

168. Bracken, *The Divine Matrix*, 29.

169. Ibid., 30.

170. Aquinas, *Summa contra gentiles*, I, xiii, n. 21.

171. Bracken, *The Divine Matrix*, 30.

172. Marguerite Porete, *A Mirror of Simple Souls: The Mystical Work of Marguerite Porete*, ed. and trans. Anne L. Barstow (Spring Valley, NY: Crossroad, 1990), 52, 72.

173. Ibid., 73.

174. Ibid., 58.

175. Hartshorne, *Aquinas to Whitehead*, 44.

176. Aquinas, *Summa theologica*, Ia, Q. 28, A. 1.

177. Aristotle, *Metaphysics*, XII, vi, 1072a 10.

178. A case in point is the concept of divine repentance. Philo, an early Jewish thinker who influenced Christianity, argued the following: "Some believe that the repentance of the Deity is shown by these words, but not rightly do they so believe, for the Deity is without change" (see Philo, *Questions and Answers on Genesis*, I, xciii, in *The Loeb Classical Library*, Supplement I, trans. Ralph Marcus from the ancient Armenian version of the original Greek [Cambridge, MA: Harvard University Press; London: William Heinemann, 1953]). A similar mode of reasoning is found in Origen. In his *On First Principles*, he states the following: "And now, if, on account of those expressions which occur in the Old Testament, as when God is said to be angry or to repent, or when any other human affection or passion is described, . . . we do not take such expressions literally, but seek in them a spiritual meaning" (Origen, *On First Principles*, II, iv, 4).

The same concern comes in relation to the passage in Jeremiah 18 that hints at God repenting. On this point he argues that it has to do with God condescending to the human mode of speech (Origen, *Homilies on Jeremiah and 1 Kings 28*, in *The Fathers of the Church*, vol. 97, trans. John Clark Smith [Washington, DC: Catholic University of America Press, 1998], xviii).

179. Louth, *Denys the Areopagite*, 108.

180. Ibid., 95.

181. Aquinas, *On Love and Charity*, S. III, D. 32, A. 1.

182. Aquinas, *Summa theologica*, Ia, IIae, Q. 28, A. 3.

183. Aquinas, *Of God and His Creatures*, I, cii, n. 7.

184. Aquinas, *Summa theologica*, Ia, IIae, Q. 28, A. 1.

185. Ibid., Ia, Q. 29, A. 3.

186. Ibid., Ia, IIae, Q. 22, A. 3.

187. Abraham Heschel, *The Prophets II*, (Peabody, MA: Hendrickson, 1962), 11.

188. Aquinas, *Of God and His Creatures*, I, ci. See also Aquinas, *Summa theologiae*, Ia, IIae, Q. 30, A. 1. This is not to say that thinkers like Aquinas do not highly value the pleasures that the senses offer. For him, for example, it is good that they are readily known to us through the body's experience, since they tend to alter something in the body itself and can even be medicinal in that they can bring relief to an ailment such as grief. Neither can we say that for Aquinas, all pleasures are evil, for the scriptures invite us to delight in the Lord (Ps. 36:4). Some pleasures are good and some are evil, for pleasure as such "is a repose of the appetitive power in some loved good" (*Summa theologica*, Ia, IIae, Q. 34, A. 1). All pleasures that go beyond the intellect or that obstruct the intellect are not necessarily considered evil, either. Pleasure that comes through the conjugal union, for example, is said to go beyond the mind or to obstruct thinking, yet is not morally evil (*Summa theologica*, Ia, IIae, Q. 34, A. 1). Yet also for him, pleasures, particularly those of the body, ultimately do not lead to happiness. Rather, they are a hindrance to the path toward God, which is the end of every creature. According to Aquinas, "But bodily pleasures injure a man from any close approach to God: for God is approached by contemplation, and the aforesaid pleasures are a hindrance to contemplation." And so temperance and abstinence from bodily pleasures are praiseworthy. Particularly since "the desire of pleasurable enjoyments" pursued in the life of pleasure, as he argues, can become intemperate and incontinent (*Of God and His Creatures*, III, xxvii, n. 9). Aquinas's view hints at a particular monastic spirituality. His work contains traces of his spiritual life during his time in the monastery in Italy and of his calling as someone who was training Dominican friars. So he emphasizes a path toward God in which one is able to abstain not only from engaging in sexual activity but also from amassing fortune, or earning honor, or accumulating virtues. While abstaining from such pleasures, one finds the final happiness,

which consists "in the contemplation of truth." According to him, this will be a contemplation "guided by wisdom to the study of the things of God" (*Of God and His Creatures*, III, xxxvii; lxiii, n. 5).

189. This is one of the reasons for atheism that Jürgen Moltmann posits. See Jürgen Moltmann, *The Crucified God: The Cross of Christ as the Foundation and Criticism of Christian Theology*, trans. R. A. Wilson and John Bowden (Minneapolis, MN: Fortress Press, 1993), chap. 6.

190. Gregory the Great, *On the Song of Songs*, 4.

191. Gregory the Great, in Norris, *The Song of Songs*, 10. See also Gregory the Great, *On the Song of Songs*, 5.

192. Gregory of Nyssa, in Norris, *The Song of Songs*, 18.

193. William of Saint-Thierry, in Norris, *The Song of Songs*, 106. See William of Saint-Thierry, *Exposition on the Song of Songs*, 117.

194. Gregory of Nyssa, *From Glory to Glory*, 112.

195. Ibid., 116.

196. Ibid., 89.

197. Michelle González, *Created in God's Image: An Introduction to Feminist Theological Anthropology* (Maryknoll, NY: Orbis Books, 2007), 44.

198. Aquinas, *Summa theologica*, Ia, Q. 3, A. 1.

199. Gebara, *Longing for Running Water*, 79.

200. Aquinas, *Summa theologica*, Ia, Q. 29, A. 1.

201. Ibid., Ia, Q. 27, A. 1.

202. *Suppositum* means "the individual substance of a certain kind which is the subject of existence and all accidental modifications which constitute the individual, synonym of *hypostasis*, *subiectum*, and *substantia*" (Roy J. Deferrari, Sister M. Inviolata Barry, and Ignatius McGuiness, *A Lexicon of St. Thomas Aquinas* [Baltimore, MD: John D. Lucas Printing Co., 1948], 1079). The difference between modes of relationship is the way in which Aquinas brings in relative opposition, thus distinction between the triune persons. The focus is not on the interpenetration but rather on the plurality of relations and their distinction from each on the basis of relative opposition, paternity and *filiation* belonging to two distinct persons, Father and Son, respectively, and *spiration* of the Spirit from the Father and the Son (as per the *filioque*) belonging to the Spirit.

203. Aquinas, *Summa theologica*, Ia, Q. 28, A. 3.

204. LaCugna, *God for Us*, 153.

205. Ibid., 160. Though the term "absolute" is not included in this passage, she makes use of it in most passages in which she speaks of self-sufficiency (subsistence).

206. Aquinas, *Summa theologica*, Ia, Q. 28, A. 1.

207. Aquinas, *Of God and His Creatures*, I, c, n. 4.

208. Ibid., I, c.

209. Ibid., I, c. The statement that love and joy are "properly" in God means that these are found in God as such and not just metaphorically or analogically.

210. Aquinas, *Summa theologica*, II, IIae, Q. 23, A. 2.

211. Pseudo-Dionysius, *The Divine Names*, 84.

212. As already argued, for Aquinas, "man's last end may be said to be either God Who is the Supreme Good simply; or the enjoyment of God, which implies a certain pleasure in the last end. And in this sense a certain pleasure of man may be said to be the greatest among human goods." See *Summa theologica*, Ia, IIae, Q. 34, A. 3.

213. Aquinas, *Summa theologica*, Ia, IIae, Q. 3, A. 1.

214. Heschel, *The Prophets II*, 440.

215. O'Rourke, *Pseudo-Dionysius and the Metaphysics of Aquinas*, 221, 216. As we shall see, something else would need to be added in order for there to be a real opening to the cosmos.

216. Ibid., 230, 252, 230.

217. Pseudo-Dionysius, *The Divine Names*, 67.

218. O'Rourke, *Pseudo-Dionysius and the Metaphysics of Aquinas*, 153.

219. Aquinas, *Summa theologica*, Ia, Q. 20, A. 2.

220. Aquinas, *Summa contra gentiles*, I, xc, n. 6; xxxviii, n. 5.

221. Ibid., I, xxxviii, n. 5.

222. Aquinas, *On Love and Charity*, S. III, D. 32, A. 1.

223. Aquinas, *Summa contra gentiles*, I, xci, n. 4.

224. Aquinas, *Of God and His Creatures*, I, cii, n. 2.

225. Jean-Luc Marion, *On the Ego and on God: Further Cartesian Questions*, ed. John D. Caputo, trans. Christina M. Gschwandtner (New York: Fordham University Press, 2007), 89, 95, 98.

226. Ibid., 5.

227. Jean-Luc Marion, *Prolegomena to Charity*, trans. Stephen E. Lewis (New York: Fordham University Press, 2002), 76.

228. Ibid., 77.

229. Jean-Luc Marion, *The Erotic Phenomenon*, trans. Stephen E. Lewis (Chicago: University of Chicago Press, 2007), 59.

230. Ibid., 61. Note that Marion is careful not say "the glory of God." Here Marion is making a comparison to an older philosophical understanding of the gods of antiquity.

231. Marion, *On the Ego and on God*, xxviii.

232. Aquinas, *Summa theologica*, Ia, Q. 98, A. 2.

3. PERMEABILITY: THE OPEN WOUNDS OF THE LOVERS' FLESH

1. Teresa of Avila, *Conceptions of the Love of God*, vol. 2 of *The Complete Works of St. Teresa of Avila*, trans. and ed. E. Allison Peers (New York: Continuum, 2002), 389.

2. Jean-Luc Marion, *The Erotic Phenomenon*, trans. Stephen E. Lewis (Chicago: University of Chicago Press, 2007), 221–22.

3. Marcella Althaus-Reid, *Indecent Theology: Theological Perversions in Sex, Gender and Politics* (New York: Routledge, 2000), 120.

4. One can think of Jacques Derrida. Angelus Silesius, for example, influenced his thought on the God without a name. See Jacques Derrida, *On the Name*, trans. David Wood (Stanford, CA: Stanford University Press, 1995).

5. Thomas Aquinas, *Summa theologica of Saint Thomas*, trans. Fathers of the English Dominican Province (New York: Benzinger Bros., 1948), Ia, Q. 13, AA. 2, 3.

6. Jean-Luc Marion, *In Excess: Studies on Saturated Phenomena*, trans. Robyn Horner and Vincent Berraud (New York: Fordham University Press, 2002), 136.

7. Marion, *The Erotic Phenomenon*, 222.

8. As initially explored in the previous chapter, love has been dichotomized into two loves, agape and eros, each with its defined boundaries and characteristics, never to be mixed. One of the strongest statements of this dichotomy is found in Anders Nygren's *Agape & Eros*, translated by Philip S. Watson (New York: Harper & Row, 1982). Nygren pursued a method he called "motif research," which allowed him to isolate what he considered to be two sharply contrasting notions of love. For Nygren, agape and eros belong to two separate spiritual worlds that have no contact with each other. Agape is sublime and eros is vulgar. God's love is agape. Agape is the expression of God's sacrificial gift that humans receive that renders them worthy of love and enables them to love beyond eros, selflessly. This view is explicitly challenged in Marion's *Erotic Phenomenon*, p. 5. See also Virginia Burrus, "Introduction: Theology and Eros after Nygren," in *Toward a Theology of Eros: Transfiguring Passion at the Limits of Discipline*, ed. Virginia Burrus and Catherine Keller (New York: Fordham University Press, 2006).

9. Jacques Lacan, *Feminine Sexuality: Jacques Lacan and the école Freudienne*, ed. Juliet Mitchell and Jacqueline Rose (Basingstock: Macmillan; New York: Pantheon Press, 1982), 146.

10. Ibid., 142–43.

11. Ibid., 153. As Frederick Depoortere explains, the term *jouissance* means "to enjoy," which can both refer "to experience pleasure and to have something at one's disposal (to possess)." The verb *jouir*, however, also means "'to come' (in the sense of having an orgasm)." See Frederick Depoortere, "Jouissance féminine? Lacan on Bernini's 'The Ecstasy of Saint Teresa' versus Slavoj Žižek on Lars von Trier's 'Breaking the Waves,'" in *Encountering Transcendence: Contributions to a Theology of Christian Religious Experience*, ed. L. Boeve, H. Geybels, and S. Van den Bossche (Leuven: Peeters Press, 2005), 33.

12. Jacques Lacan, *On Feminine Sexuality: The Limits of Love and Knowledge, Book XX, Encore 1972–1973* (New York: W. W. Norton, 1998), 62.

13. Lacan, *Feminine Sexuality*, 147.

14. Teresa of Avila, *Conceptions of the Love of God*, 382.

15. Ibid., 388.

16. William of Saint-Thierry, in *The Song of Songs: Interpreted by Early Christian and Medieval Commentators*, ed. Richard A. Norris (Grand Rapids, MI: William B. Eerdmans, 2003), 106. See also William of Saint-Thierry, *Exposition on the Song of Songs*, trans. Mother Columba Hart, with an introduction by J.-M. Déchanet (Kalamazoo, MI: Cistercian Publications, 1968), 117.

17. William of Saint-Thierry, in Norris, *The Song of Songs*, 105. See also William of Saint-Thierry, *Exposition on the Song of Songs*, 115.

18. Origen, *The First Homily*, in *The Song of Songs, Commentary and Homilies*, trans. and ann. R. P. Lawson, vol. 26 of *Ancient Christian Writers* (New York: Newman Press, 1956), 269.

19. Ibid., 273.

20. Origen, in *The Song of Songs: Interpreted by Early Christian and Medieval Commentators*, ed. Richard A. Norris (Grand Rapids, MI: William B. Eerdmans, 2003), 35.

21. Gregory of Nyssa and Gregory the Great, in *The Song of Songs: Interpreted by Early Christian and Medieval Commentators*, ed. Richard A. Norris (Grand Rapids, MI: William B. Eerdmans, 2003), 36. See Gregory the Great, *On the Song of Songs*, trans. and with an introduction by Mark DelCogliano (Collegeville, MN: Liturgical Press, 2012), 26.

22. William of Saint-Thierry, in Norris, *The Song of Songs*, 106. See also William of Saint-Thierry, *Exposition on the Song of Songs*, 115.

23. Gregory the Great, in Norris, *The Song of Songs*, 28. See Gregory the Great, *On the Song of Songs*, 13.

24. Honorius of Autun, in Norris, *The Song of Songs*, 24.

25. The Shulamite is the ascription given to the female character (considered the heroine) and one of two main protagonists of the Song of Songs in the Hebrew Bible. She is thought to be from Shulem and a young maiden of dark skin. According to Irigaray, she belonged to and represents a culture in which goddess worship was practiced. See Luce Irigaray, "Questions to Emmanuel Levinas," in *The Irigaray Reader*, ed. Margaret Whitford (Oxford: Blackwell, 1991).

26. Richard Kearney, *The God Who May Be: A Hermeneutic of Religion* (Bloomington: Indiana University Press, 2001), 54

27. Ibid., 57.

28. Origen, *Commentary*, in Norris, *The Song of Songs*, 59.

29. Kearney, *The God Who May Be*, 54.

30. Bernard of Clairvaux, in *The Song of Songs: Interpreted by Early Christian and Medieval Commentators*, ed. Richard A. Norris (Grand Rapids, MI: William B. Eerdmans, 2003), 23.

31. Ibid., 23.

32. Teresa of Avila, *Conceptions of the Love of God*, 393.

33. Ibid., 393. As E. Allison Peers writes in her introduction to Teresa of Avila's *Conceptions of the Love of God*, "So fervent a lover of God as St. Teresa could not fail to be inspired by the sublimity of the mystical conceptions which underlie the most ardent and luxuriant of love-songs in the world's literature" (p. 352). It remains closely connected to the *The Interior Castle* and the latter stages of contemplation in which there is union with God (see *The Interior Castle*, in *The Complete Works of St. Teresa of Avila*, vol. 2). Even today it is presumed that this book was meant to be read aloud, just as she would have read her meditations to her spiritual daughters.

34. Denys Turner, *Eros & Allegory: Medieval Exegesis of the Song of Songs* (Kalamazoo, MI: Cistercian Publications, 1995), 25. According to Turner, when imagery like this is used in Western Christianity to describe the relationship with God, it is notably erotic.

35. Teresa of Avila, *Conceptions of the Love of God*, 359.

36. Turner, *Eros & Allegory*, 41.

37. See Phyllis Trible, "Love Lyrics Redeemed," in *The Song of Songs: A Feminist Companion to the Bible* (1st ser.), ed. Athalya Brenner (Sheffield, IA: Sheffield Academic Press, 1993).

38. Turner, *Eros & Allegory*, 26.

39. Marion, *The Erotic Phenomenon*, 8.

40. Jean-Luc Marion, *The Visible and the Revealed*, trans. Christina M. Gschwandtner, ed. John D. Caputo (New York: Fordham University Press, 2008), 87.

41. Marion, *The Erotic Phenomenon*, 28.

42. Charles Hartshorne, *The Divine Relativity: A Social Conception of God* (New Haven, CT: Yale University Press, 1984). 17.

43. Marion, *The Erotic Phenomenon*, 92.

44. Ibid., 34–35. At times Marion argues against Aquinas's categorization of God as *ipsum esse*. Marion insightfully notes that Aquinas's affirmations of the perfections of God, though defining God in a quasi-absolute manner, yield to a *via eminentiae* that points toward unknowing. The problem lies, as he points out, in that even this unknowing in the end results in causality (*In Excess*, 136). God is first mover, efficient cause, the cause of a necessity, cause of perfection, and the final end. Aquinas also grants *ens* primacy, Marion argues, "over very other divine name" (*God without Being: Hors-Texte*, trans. Thomas A. Carlson [Chicago: University of Chicago Press, 1991), 72). For Aquinas, he states, "the one who is," is the most proper name of God, for it denotes *ipsum esse* or being itself, the essence of God (*God without Being*, 76). Elsewhere Marion asserts that Aquinas's use of the term *esse* is analogical and is a path toward knowledge of God (*On the Ego and on God: Further Cartesian Questions*,

trans. Christina M. Gschwandtner, ed. John D. Caputo [New York: Fordham University Press, 2007], 162). The God of Aquinas, he argues, is not according to *causa sui*, or the cause of itself, but rather beyond cause (*On the Ego and on God*, 142). For a similar argument on Aquinas's concept of *ipsum esse subsistens*, see Denys Turner, "On Denying the Right God: Aquinas on Atheism and Idolatry," in *Aquinas in Dialog: Thomas Aquinas for the Twenty-First Century*, ed. Jim Fodor and Frederick Christian Bauerschmidt (Oxford: Blackwell, 2004). For Turner, Aquinas's intention in using the concept of *ipsum esse subsistens* was to preserve God's distinction from other creatures while being able to predicate something about God even by means of human language (involving the negative step of affirmation). This statement helps illustrate Aquinas's tendency to make use of the *via eminentiae* (path of excessive affirmation), which speaks of the plenitude and excessiveness of God's being: unlike any other thing, God is not and God is. He argues, "When we say therefore that God is *ipsum esse subsistens*—hence, that there is no kind of thing that God is—we could mean that God's existence is 'unspecific' in either sense" (p. 144). Herein lies a paradox. The indeterminacy of the divine *esse* means that God's being is what Turner deems "beyond similarity and otherness," that is, "totally *inclusive*" (p. 144). One must note also that for Marion, however, the circularity of love connoted in the concept of *ipsum esse* translates into amorous autism, as demonstrated in the second chapter. In partaking of the Eucharist one would need to affirm some mystical reality of union with God that does away with solipsism (*God without Being*, 178–82). Thus the focus of this chapter is on this explicit critique of the concept of *ipsum esse subsistens* of Marion as it deals specifically with the notion of divine self-enjoyment in relationship to God as "the best lover."

45. Marion, *The Erotic Phenomenon*, 74–103 passim. Marion seeks to challenge the axiom of René Descartes that confines the phrase "I am" to thought. Descartes states, "But what then am I? A thinking being. What is a thinking being? It is a being which doubts, which understands, which conceives, which affirms, which denies, which wills, which rejects, which imagines also, and which perceives." See René Descartes, *Discourse on Methods and Meditations*, trans. Laurence J. Lafleur (Indianapolis: Bobbs-Merrill, 1960), 85. But for Marion, the primary thing that defines being is love, and not thought, an other that interpellates the self, and not doubt and certainty. Rather than to be is to know thyself, which can lead to notions of ataraxia, for Marion, "we are, insofar as we come to know ourselves, always already caught within the tonality of an erotic disposition—love or hate, unhappiness or happiness, enjoyment or suffering, hope or despair, solitude or communion." Love is what defines the "I," and not the other way around, being defining love. See Marion, *The Erotic Phenomenon*, 7, 20.

46. Marion, *The Erotic Phenomenon*, 131.

47. Ibid., 135.

48. See Marion, *The Visible and the Revealed*, 116–18.

49. Marion, *The Erotic Phenomenon*, 209.

50. Teresa of Avila, *Conceptions of the Love of God*, 393.

51. Marion, *The Visible and the Revealed*, 62.

52. Teresa of Avila, *The Interior Castle*, in vol. 2 of *The Complete Works of St. Teresa of Avila*, trans. and ed. E. Allison Peers (New York: Continuum, 2002), 277.

53. Karmen MacKendrick, *Counterpleasures* (Albany: State University of New York, 1999), 76.

54. Ibid., 82.

55. Ibid., 121.

56. Teresa of Avila, *Conceptions of the Love of God*, 360–61.

57. Ibid., 363.

58. Ibid., 387.

59. Ibid., 389.

60. Ibid., 388. While in some early writers this cellar of wine was solely placed in relationship to knowledge, here in the words of St. Teresa one can appreciate the manner in which this storeroom of so many pleasures is not circumscribed to thought.

61. Ibid., 384.

62. Ibid., 378.

63. Teresa of Avila, *The Interior Castle*, 291.

64. Gregory of Nyssa, *From Glory to Glory: Texts from Gregory of Nyssa's Mystical Writings*, trans. and ed. Herbert Musurillo (Crestwood, NY: St. Vladimir's Seminary Press, 1979), 126, 201.

65. William of Saint-Thierry, in Norris, *The Song of Songs*, 16. See also William of Saint-Thierry, *Exposition on the Song of Songs*, 23.

66. See Emmanuel Levinas, *Totality and Infinity: An Essay on Exteriority*, trans. Alphonso Lingis (Pittsburgh, PA: Duquesne University Press, 1969), 256–66.

67. Lacan, *Feminine Sexuality*, 147.

68. Levinas, *Totality and Infinity*, 258.

69. Lacan, *Feminine Sexuality*, 140, 145.

70. Ibid., 145. In answering this question, a careful look at the term *ek-sistence* can be helpful for this study. As in the work of Martin Heidegger, here her existence refers to its equivalent in "the Greek *ekstasis* and the German *Ekstase*," which "means to 'stand outside something', or 'apart' from something," as Frederick Depoortere explains. Lacan makes use of the term "to designate that which does not exist, but only exists from outside the symbolic order and as a consequence does not possess any reality (because only that which belongs to the symbolic order has reality)" (see Depoortere, "Jouissance féminine?," 32). One can agree with Lacan to a point, the *jouissance* of the cosmos is beyond

rationality in the sense that it exceeds the symbolic mirrors of the "good old God" of Aristotle. But problems persist, as argued above, when the words of the one who, like St. Teresa of Avila, enjoys herself fall into silence.

71. St. Teresa's *jouissance* falls prey to the tendency to name her pleasure, in order to dissect it and catalogue it, as Irigaray argues (see Irigaray, "Così Fan Tuti," in *This Sex Which Is Not One* [Ithaca, NY: Cornell University Press, 1985], 90). And as Cristina Mazzoni asserts, Lacan did not move much beyond the prevalent view of female *jouissance*, particularly St. Teresa's. Her enjoyment in the shape realized by Bernini had become "the quintessential mystical (and thus, for some, erotically predisposed) woman, mentioned time and again by turn-of-the-century writers" (see Cristina Mazzoni, *Saint Hysteria: Neurosis, Mysticism, and Gender in European Culture* [Ithaca, NY: Cornell University Press, 1996], 37). Thinkers like Jean-Martin Charcot would contemplate visuals and photographs without listening to or reading St. Teresa's actual words. Under such scrutiny she would become "the model and the protectress of those women whose aching wombs prevent them from appropriating the language of their own sexuality. The *globus hystericus* rising and falling in their throat, that potent image of the displaced and wandering uterus, forbids them to speak of the painful eros," Mazzoni insightfully states (*Saint Hysteria*, 42). Mazzoni rightly concludes that "Lacan is clearly making a reductive and patronizing move" by relying on the graven image of St. Teresa rather than on her verbal account, as other many thinkers like Charcot had done in the past (*Saint Hysteria*, 46–47).

72. Irigaray, "Così Fan Tuti," 96.

73. Ibid., 96. These arguments are mostly directed at Lacanian views with regard to female *jouissance*.

74. Elizabeth Grosz, *Sexual Subversions: Three French Feminists* (Crows Nest, NSW: Allen & Unwin, 1989), 151.

75. Teresa of Avila, *The Interior Castle*, 277.

76. Ibid., 342.

77. Irigaray, "La Mystérique," in *Speculum of the Other Woman*, 201.

78. Teresa of Avila, *The Interior Castle*, 277. Interestingly enough, *jouir*, as Depoortere explains, "can also mean to 'suffer severe pain'" (see Depoortere, "Jouissance féminine?," 33). In the concept of *jouissance*, pleasure and pain come together. He avers, "This also seems to be the case in the fragment from saint Teresa quoted above, in which sweetness and intense pain are mentioned side-by-side" (p. 34).

79. Teresa of Avila, *The Interior Castle*, 325.

80. Ibid., 324.

81. Teresa of Avila, *Conceptions of the Love of God*, 392.

82. Gregory of Nyssa, *From Glory to Glory*, 272.

83. Thomas Aquinas, *On Love and Charity: Readings from the "Commentary on the Sentences of Peter Lombard,"* trans. Peter A. Kwasniewski, Thomas Bolin, and Joseph Bolin, with an introduction and notes by Peter A. Kwasnieski (Washing-

ton, DC: Catholic University of America Press, 2008), S. III, D. 27, Q. 1, A. 1, reply 4. To argue for *com*penetration is not too unlike classical thought, as already intimated in relation to the concept of perichoresis.

84. I thank Catherine Keller for prompting me to look into this theological concept of sadomasochism as a way to explain the interplay between suffering and joy. For other works on sadomasochism from a feminist perspective, see Anna Mercedes, *Power For: Feminism and Christ's Self-Giving* (Edinburgh: Bloomsbury T&T Clark, 2011); Ken Stone, "'You Seduced Me, You Overpowered Me, and You Prevailed': Religious Experience and Homoerotic Sadomasochism in Jeremiah," in *Patriarchs, Prophets and Other Villains* (London: Equinox, 2007); Jeremy Carrette, "Intense Exchange: Sadomasochism, Theology and the Politics of Late Capitalism," *Theology & Sexuality* 11, no. 2 (2005); Anselm Haverkamp, "Christ's Case: The Stigma of Representation, Christian Sadomasochism," in *Stigmata: Poetiken der Körperinschrift* (Munich: Wilhelm Fink, 2004); Graham Ward, "Theology and Cultural Sadomasochism," *Svensk Teologisk Kvartalskrift* 78, no. 1 (2002); Mark Edmundson, *Nightmare on Main Street: Angels, Sadomasochism and the Culture of Gothic* (Cambridge, MA: Harvard University Press, 1997); Lynn S. Chancer, *Sadomasochism in Everyday Life: The Dynamics of Power and Powerlessness* (New Brunswick, NJ: Rutgers University Press, 1992); and Marcella Althaus-Reid, *The Queer God* (London: Routledge, 2003).

85. Althaus-Reid, *The Queer God*, 17.

86. Althaus-Reid, *Indecent Theology*, 155.

87. For Levinas, *voluptuosity* is pure desire, thus "remains desire at each instant, which as shown later in this chapter also refers to "an incessant recommencement of virginity" (see *Totality and Infinity*, 258).

88. Levinas, *Totality and Infinity*, 260.

89. Ibid., 261.

90. Ibid., 258.

91. Irigaray, "Così Fan Tuti," 90.

92. Elizabeth Grosz, *Jacques Lacan* (New York: Taylor & Francis, 2002), 146.

93. Irigaray, "Così Fan Tuti," 88.

94. Ibid., 91.

95. Irigaray, "'Woman's Jouissance,'" in *Speculum of the Other Woman*, 355.

96. Irigaray, "La Mystérique," 192.

97. Irigaray, "Women's Jouissance," 356.

98. Ibid., 357.

99. Irigaray, "La Mystérique," 200.

100. Marion, *The Erotic Phenomenon*, 44.

101. Julia Kristeva, *Tales of Love*, trans. Leon S. Roudiez (New York: Columbia University Press, 1983), 94.

102. Irigaray, "Così Fan Tuti," 90. Here Irigaray is also posing a critique of Gilles Deleuze's trope of the "body without organs." See Gilles Deleuze, *The Logic of Sense* (New York: Columbia University Press, 1990).

103. Irigaray, "La Mystérique," 196–97. While many of these ideas have been a part of my work all along, I found an affinity also reflected here with the paper "The Sense of Passion," delivered by William Robert at a 2010 meeting of the American Academy of Religion.

104. The wound, referring to an open space in the flesh where both pain and pleasure meet, points to an exchange of abandonments akin to withdrawals on the part of the lovers. Each makes space for the other in their flesh. There is no beginning or end in sight to this mutual wounding, *spacing* for the lovers' pleasures.

105. Teresa of Avila, *The Interior Castle*, 277.

106. Virginia Burrus, *The Sex Lives of Saints: An Erotics of Ancient Hagiography* (Philadelphia: University of Pennsylvania Press, 2004), 69. Here Burrus is using MacKendrick's language on expenditure from *Counterpleasures*, an expenditure that ensues in an increase.

107. Teresa of Avila, *Conceptions of the Love of God*, 395.

108. Ibid., 385–92.

109. Irigaray, "La Mystérique," 200. Pointing to the woman's slit does not necessarily confine *jouissance* to the sexual organs; rather, it includes them. See Morny Joy, *Divine Love: Luce Irigaray, Women, Gender and Religion* (Manchester: Manchester University Press, 2002), 18. She explains how for Irigaray, women's *jouissance* is not confined to one sexual organ or a unified sexuality. Parts of her body, such as the uterus and the womb, are also erotic zones of pleasure. Her sexuality is multiple, exceeding the boundaries of the male gaze and theoretical framework (which are male parameters). Motherhood and the clitoris both can play a significant role in female pleasure. See Irigaray, *Speculum of the Other Woman*, 233; see also Claire Elise Katz, "From Eros to Maternity: Love, Death, and the 'Feminine' in the Philosophy of Emmanuel Levinas," in *Women and Gender in Jewish Philosophy*, ed. Hava Tirosh-Samuelson (Bloomington: Indiana University Press, 2004).

110. Irigaray, "La Mystérique," 200.

111. Teresa of Avila, *Conceptions of the Love of God*, 389.

112. Ibid., 386.

113. Ibid., 385.

114. Ibid., 384.

115. Ibid., 361.

116. Ibid., 389.

117. Irigaray, "La Mystérique," 202.

118. In divine ecstasy, God withdraws Godself, and receives the divine self via the abandonment of Godself. God becomes the lover, in a sense, through the act of loving, giving or abandoning Godself (ecstasy). Similar to the concepts of *kenosis* or *zimzum* discussed in previous chapters, ecstasy as abandonment opens up a space of vulnerability for another to bring forth her enjoyment.

Hence here also lies the erotic dimension of the divine love that I see evident in that divine yearning is akin to God abandoning the divine self to gain intimacy with, and thus the feeling of, something or someone distinct from God.

119. Irigaray, "La Mystérique," 200.

120. Irigaray, *Marine Lover of Friedrich Nietzsche*, trans. Gillian C. Gill (New York: Columbia University Press, 1991), 137.

121. Jean-Luc Marion, *Prolegomena to Charity*, trans. Stephen E. Lewis (New York: Fordham University Press, 2002), 158–59.

122. Marion, *The Erotic Phenomenon*, 14.

123. Ibid., 221.

124. Irigaray, *Marine Lover*, 15.

125. Ibid., 7.

126. Irigaray, "Così Fan Tuti," 89.

127. Joy, *Divine Love*, 15.

128. Ibid., 17.

129. Mazzoni, *Saint Hysteria*, 193.

130. Teresa of Avila, *Conceptions of the Love of God*, 383–86.

131. Ibid., 392.

132. Turner, *Eros & Allegory*, 30.

133. Ibid., 55.

134. Luce Irigaray, *The Forgetting of Air in Martin Heidegger*, trans. Mary Beth Mader (Austin: University of Texas Press, 1999), 143.

135. Luce Irigaray, *The Way of Love*, trans. Heidi Bostic and Anthony Pluhacek (London: Continuum, 2002), vii. When Irigaray speaks of difference she is mainly referring to sexual difference. In this book I use difference or *alterity* in the broader sense.

136. Luce Irigaray, *Le corps-à-corps avec la mere* (Montreal: Editiones de la pleine lune, 1981), 48–49, cited in Grosz, *Sexual Subversions: Three French Feminists*, 170.

137. Marion, *The Erotic Phenomenon*, 221–22.

138. A discourse based on the Song of Songs protects the notions of eros, yearning, and appetite from the very concerns that Aquinas addressed but failed to resolve in his discussions of divine concupiscence. With this poetic aid, the divine love bound by any autarkic circularity of some metaphysical worldviews can begin to break free.

139. In this book I make use of Marion's term "eroticization," yet I nuance it to speak of an embodied flesh rather than merely a glorified flesh, even though I agree with him that the flesh "must not appear in equal footing with objects"—a possible danger, as he warns, of embodiment. See, for example, Marion, *The Erotic Phenomenon*, 115–17.

140. Marion, *The Erotic Phenomenon*, 38.

141. Ibid., 127.

142. Marion, *In Excess*, 92.

143. Ibid., 96.

144. Ibid., 98.

145. Irigaray, *Marine Lover*, 116.

146. Descartes, *Discourse*, 101.

147. See ibid., 92.

148. Levinas, *Totality and Infinity*, 99.

149. Marion, *Prolegomena to Charity*, 99. Here Marion is also challenging Aristotle's metaphysics, in which God, as efficient cause, is in the end the recipient of God's own goods (this is the notion of a circular love against which I argued in the second chapter). This notion of distance may have been inspired also by a dialogue that takes place between Martin Heidegger and Emmanuel Levinas on the notion of the opening or clearing of Being. The clearing is a space that opens at the center but that also encircles all that is, mostly described as the Nothing. This space guarantees a passage from nonbeing to being, from absence to presence, in Heidegger's thought. See, for example, Martin Heidegger, "The Origin of the Work of Art," in *Poetry, Language, Thought* (New York: HarperCollins, 1971), 51–54, and compare Heidegger's views with those of Levinas in *Totality and Infinity*, 187–93. The clearing in Heidegger lets things appear, lets them be. Levinas, arguing against Heidegger, posits that the clearing cannot be about a return to self, nothing is grasped (see also Emmanuel Levinas, *Basic Philosophical Writings*, ed. Adriaan T. Peperzak, Simon Critchley, and Robert Bernasconi [Bloomington: Indiana University Press, 1996], 59–63). Unlike Heidegger's clearing, there is no presence but the infinite Ab-solute absence of the other. The radical separation between the self and the other prevents the self from usurping the space of the other. Marion clearly takes these two understandings and posits a removal of the divine that quasi-appears but as a silhouette in a removal that is ecstatic.

150. Joseph A. Bracken, *The One in the Many: A Contemporary Reconstruction of the God-World Relation* (Grand Rapids, MI: William B. Eerdmans, 2001), 32.

151. Jacques Derrida, "*Ousia* and *Gramme*: Note on a Note from *Being and Time*," in *Margins of Philosophy*, trans. Alan Bass (Chicago: University of Chicago Press, 1982), 52.

152. Ibid., 52.

153. Ibid., 52.

154. See Jean-Luc Marion, *The Idol and Distance: Five Studies*, trans. Thomas A. Carlson (New York: Fordham University Press, 2001), 153.

155. Marion, *Prolegomena to Charity*, 167. It should also be noted that the manner in which Marion describes distance is not akin to the notion of exteriority as found in the work of Levinas, which seems to maintain an ontological difference, or to Derrida's *différance*, which eliminates not only the idol but also any divine advent altogether, and thus the God as a result (see Marion, *The*

Idol and Distance, 215–33; and Jacques Derrida, "Différance," in *Margins of Philosophy*, trans. Alan Bass [Chicago: University of Chicago Press, 1982]). For Marion, distance is like a clearing away that, rather than being voidlike (nothingness), shows forth what I consider to be a silhouette, that of the lover, thus offering greater possibility to talk about the divine lover as taking on a bodily shape.

156. This interpretation of the cherubs of the Ark of the Covenant is very fitting. As Julia Kristeva has indicated, the two cherubs became the manifestation of God as female, which later in the Talmud became split between the two genders: the male cherub came to represent God, "the female the people of Israel." See Kristeva, *Tales of Love*, 86–87.

157. Luce Irigaray, "Belief Itself," in *Sexes and Genealogies*, trans. Gillian C. Gill (New York: Columbia University Press, 1993), 45.

158. One may argue that St. Teresa of Avila advocated for chastity in her *Way of Perfection*, the book that stipulates the rules of living for her Carmelite order. Also, visions of the Virgin of Mt. Carmel inspired and even parallel many of her visions of God as lover. So, like St. John of the Cross and Bernard of Clairvaux, she is seen as denying ecstasy its flesh, thus making it more contingent on celibacy (see, e.g., Alicia Ostriker, "A Holy of Holies: The Song of Songs as a Countertext," in *The Song of Songs: A Feminist Companion to the Bible*, 2nd ser., ed. Athalya Brenner and Carole R. Fontaine [Sheffield: Sheffield Academic Press, 2000], 38). While these two aspects alone might imply a glorification of virginity on her part, her words explicitly point to an intimate and possibly sexual union, more so than in the writings of her male counterparts. Also, while she most likely was not sexually active on the physical level (something that may never be known for certain), she sought to embody her pleasure spiritually in her union with God. That the spiritual crosses over the physical in a manner such that is difficult to pinpoint where one ends and the other begins at the level of the experiential cannot be denied either. Whatever mystics experienced in the spirit orgasmicly could reverberate through their entire bodies. Moreover, we cannot disregard the time and location of her life's works, and the role that restrictions imposed by those who threatened to censure St. Teresa's works may have played. Under their scrutiny, she would have sought to impose this symbol of sanctity on her sisters as a means to legitimize her efforts—a practice already imposed on the male priests of the Church. Even so, there is something subversive about women seeking physical chastity rather than "proper" marriage, for "delayed pleasure" places them beyond the established strictures of the time (see MacKendrick, *Counterpleasures*). Virginity in the lives of medieval female saints could have been used as a means to offset patriarchy (see, e.g., Stacey Schlau, "Following Saint Teresa: Early Modern Women and Religious Authority," *Modern Language Notes* 117, no. 2 [2002]: 286–309). This is a very complex topic in feminism that greatly expands what

is being said here. Delving into these literary and historical arguments, while a worthy exercise, is beyond the scope of this book on God as passionate lover.

159. Gregory of Nyssa, *From Glory to Glory*, 98.

160. Ibid., 111.

161. Ibid., 204.

162. Ibid., 137.

163. See Marion, *The Erotic Phenomenon*, 157.

164. Levinas, *Totality and Infinity*, 256. See also the critique that Irigaray posits regarding this Levinasian concept of voluptuosity in "Questions to Emmanuel Levinas." For her, Levinas (even if unwillingly) reifies the circle of sameness and patriarchy. She argues, "solitary love does not correspond to the shared outpouring, to the loss of boundaries which takes place for both lovers when they cross the boundary of the skin into the mucous membranes of the body, leaving the circle which encloses my solitude to meet in a shared space, a shared breath, abandoning the relatively dry and precise outlines of each body's solid exterior to enter a fluid universe where the perception of being two persons [*de la dualité*] becomes indistinct, and above all, acceding to another energy, neither that of the one nor of the other, but an energy produced together and as a result of the irreducible difference of sex" (p. 180).

165. Levinas, *Totality and Infinity*, 257.

166. Ibid., 258.

167. Ibid., 258.

168. Kristeva, *Tales of Love*, 98.

169. Ibid., *Tales of Love*, 98.

170. Virginia Burrus and Stephen D. Moore, "Unsafe Sex: Feminism, Pornography, and the Song of Songs," *Biblical Interpretation* 11, no. 1 (2003): 24–52.

171. Luz Beatriz Arellano, "Women's Experience of God in Emerging Spirituality," in *With Passion and Compassion: Third World Women Doing Theology: Reflections from the Women's Commission of the Ecumenical Association of Third World Theologians*, ed. Virginia Fabella and Mercy Amba Oduyoye (Maryknoll, NY: Orbis Books, 1988), 146.

172. See MacKendrick, *Counterpleaures*, 146. MacKendrick, for example, attempts to explain the complexity of the interplay of desire and pleasure, which she finds having its roots in the early Christian bodily practices and thought of the ascetics and recent theological conversations on sadomasochism. She finds a fluid boundary that flirts and postpones satisfaction, thus disrupting certainty. According to MacKendrick's analysis, there can be forms of pleasure that refuse teleology. The prolongation of pain intensifies pleasure, taking the contours of desire. Here also the concepts of resistance

and withdrawal come into play. Paradoxically, the resistance and withdrawal of the desired object increase desire itself, which in turn produces intensity (increased desire that escapes comprehension). For her, as the prolongation of desire as described in the language of sadomasochism, *jouissance* hence does not fall prisoner to Western views of orgasm. For it outlasts orgasm in its defiance of a specific telos, hence subverting productivity and commodification, and holding no socially approved status. See MacKendrick, *Counterpleasures*.

173. Turner, *Eros & Allegory*, 84. With this in mind, the concerns of Beverly Harrison and Carter Heyward are being addressed. They critically suggest that the mystics' "delayed gratification" may point to a feeling or psychological effect that prominently features eschatology: "This disembodied spirituality, in which pleasure is fundamentally a state of mind, is steeped in the eschatological promise that the realm of the divine—a spiritual area of unity, joy and ecstasy—is, for Christians, here but not quite here; but not quite yet" (see Beverly Wildung Harrison and Carter Heyward, "Pain and Pleasure: Avoiding the Confusions of Christian Tradition in Feminist Theory," in *Sexuality and the Sacred: Sources for Theological Reflection*, ed. James B. Nelson and Sandra P. Longfellow [Louisville, KY: Westminster John Knox Press, 1994], 136). Such eschatology would seek to rid itself of bodies with their carnal passions, where there would be no pain as a result of the war of flesh with the spirit.

174. Turner, *Eros & Allegory*, 84–85.

175. These are three statements that Marion puts in relation to each other, without advocating for interminglings of the flesh. See his *The Erotic Phenomenon*, 131, 135.

176. Turner, *Eros & Allegory*, 88.

177. Gregory of Nyssa, *From Glory to Glory*, 179.

178. Ibid., 190–91

179. Ibid., 201.

180. Ibid., 199.

181. William of Saint-Thierry, in Norris, *The Song of Songs*, 11. See also William of Saint-Thierry, *Exposition on the Song of Songs*, 6.

182. William of Saint-Thierry, in Norris, *The Song of Songs*, 11. See also William of Saint-Thierry, *Exposition on the Song of Songs*, 6.

183. Irigaray, *Marine Lover*, 117.

184. Teresa of Avila, *Conceptions of the Love of God*, 386.

185. Ibid., 384.

186. Kristeva, *Tales of Love*, 96.

187. Turner, *Eros & Allegory*, 59.

188. Ostriker, "A Holy of Holies," 43.

189. Ibid., 51.

190. J. Cheryl Exum, "Ten Things Every Feminist Should Know about the Song of Songs," in Brenner, *The Song of Songs*, 26.

191. Exum, "Ten Things," 30.

192. Daphna V. Arbel, "'My Vineyard, My Very Own, Is for Myself,'" in *The Song of Songs: A Feminist Companion to the Bible*, 2nd ser., ed. Athalya Brenner with Carole R. Fontaine (Sheffield, IA: Sheffield Academic Press, 2000), 91.

193. Nicholas of Lyra, in Norris, *The Song of Songs*, 26.

194. Origen, *The Song of Songs*, 65.

195. Nilus of Ancyra, in Norris, *The Song of Songs*, 29.

196. See also William of Saint-Thierry, *Exposition on the Song of Songs*, 39–43. Richard Norris in his book *The Song of Songs* explains how while males were not commonly described as having breasts, early and medieval thinkers would not have considered it odd, since the Bridegroom was associated with divine Wisdom, which was female and was considered to nourish the soul with milk and to illumine the mind, bringing it into conformity or according to the image of God (Norris, *The Song of Songs*, 20). What I consider significant are also the implications, in addition to the analogical and allegorical language, of this queering of the divine to present a view that embraces female bodily pleasures or *jouissance* in a model of the divine enjoyment.

197. Teresa of Avila, *Conceptions of the Love of God*, 382.

198. Except at the end of the Songs. See Trible, "Love Lyrics Redeemed," 117.

199. Exum, "Ten Things," 33.

200. Ostriker, "A Holy of Holies," 49.

201. Kearney, *The God Who May Be*, 57. Here Kearney is paraphrasing André La Cocque's descriptions of the Shulamite's passion in his description of free love. See André LaCocque, "The Shulamite," in *Thinking Biblically: Exegetical and Hermeneutical Studies*, trans. David Pellauer, ed. Paul Ricoeur and André LaCocque (Chicago: University of Chicago Press, 1998), 245.

202. Turner, *Eros & Allegory*, 58–59.

203. Marion, *The Erotic Phenomenon*, 195.

204. Irigaray, *The Forgetting of Air*, 72.

205. Ibid., 40.

206. As discussed in the first chapter, for Aquinas, "*God's love is the divine ousia*," which implies a movement through which God as the lover is placed outside the divine self (suffers ecstasy), thus "made to pass into the object" of the divine love. Love as such is a unitive force or a divine impulse. See Aquinas, *Summa theologica*, Ia, Q. 20, A. 2; Q. 28, A. 1. See also Aquinas, *On Love and Charity*, III, D. 32, notes.

207. Jacques Derrida, "Step of Hospitality/No Hospitality," in *Of Hospitality* (Stanford, CA: Stanford University Press, 2000), 123. This concept of entering "without delay" is a Derridean view more specifically of hospitality.

208. Another point to consider is that in Spanish, *disfrutar* (the verb) and *disfrute* (the noun) would mean what the two French terms mean in terms of

enjoyment, except that in Spanish both *disfrutar* and *disfrute* etymologically come from *des-frutar* ("to take away the fruit"). See Depoortere, "Jouissance féminine?"

209. Irigaray, "La Mystérique," 200.

210. Luce Irigaray, "The Fecundity of the Caress: A Rereading of Levinas, *Totality and Infinity*, 'Phenomenology of Eros,'" in *Feminist Interpretations of Emmanuel Levinas*, ed. Tina Chanter (University Park: Pennsylvania State University Press, 2001), 122.

211. Teresa of Avila, *The Interior Castle*, 335.

212. Irigaray, *Marine Lover*, 105.

213. Ibid., 37.

214. Irigaray, *The Way of Love*, 65.

215. Irigaray, *The Forgetting of Air*, 53.

216. Turner, *Eros & Allegory*, 58–59.

217. Irigaray, *The Way of Love*, 134.

218. Ibid., 152.

219. Ibid., 153.

220. Ibid., 153.

221. Ibid., 132.

222. Irigaray, *The Forgetting of Air*, 76.

223. Kearney, *The God Who May Be*, 54.

224. Ibid., 4.

225. Irigaray, *The Forgetting of Air*, 96.

226. Turner, *Eros & Allegory*, 26.

227. Teresa of Avila, *Conceptions of the God of Love*, 392.

228. Bracken, *The One in the Many*, 25.

229. Irigaray, *The Way of Love*, 9.

230. Michel Foucault, "A Preface to Transgression," in *Language, Counter-memory, Practice: Selected Essays and Interviews by Michel Foucault* (Ithaca, NY: Cornell University Press, 1977), 37.

4. INTENSITY: PASSIONATE BECOMINGS OF THE DIVINE COMPLEX

1. Ernesto Cardenal, *Cosmic Canticle*, trans. John Lyons (Willimantic, CT: Curbstone Press, 1993), Cantiga 40, p. 415.

2. See, for example, Jean-Luc Marion, *The Erotic Phenomenon*, trans. Stephen E. Lewis. (Chicago: University of Chicago Press, 2007), 221–22.

3. Cardenal, *Cosmic Canticle*, Cantiga 42, p. 449.

4. Nicolas of Cusa, *Nicolas of Cusa: Selected Spiritual Readings*, trans. Frank Tobin, ed. and with a preface by Margot Schmidt (Mahwah, NJ: Paulist Press, 1997), 135, cited in Catherine Keller, *Face of the Deep: A Theology of Becoming* (New York: Routledge, 2003), 231–32. Relationship as a way to define the self is

a key theme in the works of Keller. For a more in-depth exploration of this aspect of relationship, see also Catherine Keller, *From a Broken Web: Separation, Sexism, and Self* (Boston: Beacon Press, 1986).

5. The term "reality-in-process" is used mostly by Ivone Gebara. See, for example, Gebara, *Longing for Running Water: Ecofeminism and Liberation*, trans. David Molineaux (Minneapolis, MN: Fortress Press, 1999), 55. I use it here to legitimately align her with other like-minded thinkers, mostly panentheistic and process scholars, without asserting that she herself is to be counted among them.

6. Thomas Aquinas, *On Love and Charity: Readings from the "Commentary on the Sentences of Peter Lombard,"* trans. Peter A. Kwasniewski, Thomas Bolin, and Joseph Bolin, with an introduction and notes by Peter A. Kwasniewski (Washington, DC: Catholic University of America Press, 2008), S. III, D. 27, Q. 1, A. 1, response.

7. Alfred North Whitehead, *Process and Reality: An Essay in Cosmology*, ed. David Ray and Donald W. Sherburne Griffin (New York: Free Press, 1978), 32.

8. Ibid., 346.

9. Thomas Aquinas, *Summa theologica of Saint Thomas*, trans. Fathers of the English Dominican Province (New York: Benzinger Bros., 1948), Ia, IIae, Q. 22, A. 3.

10. Ibid., Ia, IIae, Q. 28, A. 5.

11. Ibid., Ia, Q. 20, A. 1. See also Thomas Aquinas, *Of God and His Creatures: An Annotated Translation of the Summa contra gentiles of Saint Thomas*, trans. and ed. Joseph Rickaby (Westminster, MD: Carroll Press, 1950), I, xc.

12. Thomas Aquinas, *Summa contra gentiles: Book One: God*, trans. Anton C. Pegis. (Notre Dame, IN: University of Notre Dame Press, 1975), I, xci, n. 6.

13. Alfred North Whitehead, *Adventures of Ideas* (New York: Free Press, 1967), 147. For Whitehead, God is dipolar, or has two poles, one mental and the other physical. Causal feelings refer to the physical pole and conceptual feelings refer to the mental one. In this construct he goes beyond classical thought, which ascribes to God only intellectual capabilities (without Whitehead's doing away with them). See Whitehead, *Process and Reality*, 239–40.

14. Whitehead, *Adventures of Ideas*, 275.

15. Ibid., 148.

16. Whitehead, *Process and Reality*, 32.

17. Ibid., 67.

18. Ibid., 32.

19. Ibid., 102, 351.

20. Ibid., 9.

21. Otto Maduro, *Mapas para la fiesta: Reflexiones sobre la crisis y el conocimiento*, Temas de formación sociopolítical 40 (Atlanta: Asociación para la Educación Teológica Hispana, 1998), 31. Translation mine.

22. Aquinas, *Summa theologica*, Ia, IIae, Q. 28, A. 5.

23. Aquinas, *Summa contra gentiles*, I, xci, n. 6.

24. Whitehead, *Adventures of Ideas*, 169. Emphasis mine.

25. See Alfred North Whitehead, *Modes of Thought: Six Lectures Delivered in Wellesley College, Massachusetts, and Two Lectures in the University of Chicago* (New York: Macmillan, 1938), 68. Emphasis mine.

26. Ibid., 68.

27. Whitehead, *Process and Reality*, 344.

28. Ibid., 345. See also Joseph A. Bracken, *Divine Matrix: Creativity as Link between East and West* (Eugene, OR: Wipf and Stock, 1995), 29.

29. Whitehead, *Process and Reality*, 351.

30. Ibid., 351.

31. Ibid., 351.

32. Roland Faber, *God as Poet of the World: Exploring Process Theologies*, trans. Douglas W. Stott (Louisville, KY: Westminster John Knox Press, 2004), 190.

33. Alfred North Whitehead, *Religion in the Making* (New York: Fordham University Press, 1966), 151.

34. Whitehead, *Process and Reality*, 351.

35. Whitehead, *Adventures of Ideas*, 159.

36. Faber, *God as Poet of the World*, 294.

37. Whitehead, *Process and Reality*, 346.

38. Whitehead, *Modes of Thought*, 54.

39. Whitehead, *Process and Reality*, 88.

40. Ibid., 84.

41. See Faber, *God as Poet of the World*, 201–14. See also Whitehead, *Process and Reality*, 346.

42. Faber, *God as Poet of the World*, 251.

43. Ibid., 15. See also Whitehead, *Process and Reality*, 31, 351.

44. Aquinas, *On Love and Charity*, S. II, D. 38, A. 1, response.

45. Whitehead, *Modes of Thought*, 152.

46. Whitehead, *Process and Reality*, 66.

47. Ibid., 164.

48. Ibid., 289.

49. Ibid., 348.

50. Ibid., 220. "Potentiality" is a term that for Whitehead corresponds to or is correlative of *givenness* (p. 44).

51. This is unlike the relationless and independent being expressed mostly in classical Cartesian thinking.

52. Faber, *God as Poet of the World*, 64.

53. Ibid., 110–11.

54. Whitehead, *Process and Reality*, 41.

55. Ibid., 51–52.

56. Aquinas, *On Love and Charity*, S. III, D. 27, Q. 1, A. 1, n. 4.

57. Ibid., S. III, D. 27, Q. 1, A. 1, response.

58. Ibid., S. III, D. 27, Q. 1, A. 1, response.

59. Cardenal, *Cosmic Canticle*, Cantiga 42, p. 449.

60. Joseph A. Bracken, *The One in the Many: A Contemporary Reconstruction of the God-World Relation* (Grand Rapids, MI: William B. Eerdmans, 2001), 26. For Whitehead, the meaning of objectification is when "actual particulars become original elements for a new creation." In this, of course, his meaning takes postmodern views on objectification further (see Chapter 3), that is, it does so in a manner that addresses the concerns of postmodern thinkers. See Whitehead, *Process and Reality*, 210.

61. Whitehead, *Process and Reality*, 34.

62. Aquinas, *Of God and His Creatures*, I, lxxxii, n. 2.

63. Ibid., I, lxxxix, n. 5.

64. Fran O'Rourke, *Pseudo-Dionysius and the Metaphysics of Aquinas* (Notre Dame, IN: Notre Dame University Press, 2005), 97.

65. Bracken, *The Divine Matrix*, 31–32.

66. Ibid., 33.

67. Whitehead, *Process and Reality*, 343.

68. Whitehead, *Adventures of Ideas*, 277.

69. Whitehead, *Process and Reality*, 47.

70. Whitehead, *Religion in the Making*, 108.

71. Whitehead, *Process and Reality*, 12. This means that there is an aspect of God that derives from the divine relationship with the world, is consequent to it.

72. Ibid., 345.

73. Aquinas, *Summa theologica*, IIa IIae, Q. 175, A. 2, rep. obj. 2.

74. Whitehead, *Process and Reality*, 345–46.

75. Luce Irigaray, *The Way of Love*, trans. Heidi Bostic and Anthony Pluhacek (London: Continuum, 2002), 153.

76. Novelty is by determinateness prehending or ingressing indeterminateness (see Whitehead, *Process and Reality*, 345). Also, the intensity of each satisfaction is dependent on order; the less disorder, the more intense the satisfaction. Each concrescence ends with "the attainment of a fully *determinate* 'satisfaction'" (*Process and Reality*, 85). I thank Georgias Romero, a Chilean friend and process thinker, who while visiting the Metropolitan Museum of Art in New York City and admiring with me the painting *The Yellow Cow*, by Franz Marc, helped me visualize this Whiteheadian concept of discordance in terms of enjoyment.

77. Whitehead, *Process and Reality*, 349. For another perspective on multiplicity (nonprocess), see Laurel C. Schneider, *Beyond Monotheism: A Theology of Multiplicity* (New York: Routledge, 2007).

78. Ivone Gebara, *Out of the Depths: Women's Experience of Evil and Salvation*, trans. Ann Patrick Ware (Minneapolis, MN: Fortress Press, 2002), 131.

79. Keller, *Face of the Deep*, 223.

80. Aquinas, *Summa theologica*, Ia IIae, Q. 28, A. 2.

81. Teresa of Avila, *Conceptions of the Love of God*, in vol. 2 of *The Complete Works of St. Teresa of Avila*, trans. and ed. E. Allison Peters (New York: Continuum, 2002), 389.

82. Ibid., 386.

83. Denys Turner, *Eros & Allegory: Medieval Exegesis of the Song of Songs* (Kalamazoo, MI: Cistercian Publications, 1995), 58.

84. Whitehead, *Process and Reality*, 67.

85. Faber, *God as Poet of the World*, 102. See also Helmut Maasen, *Gott, das Gute und das Böse in der Philosophie A.N. Whiteheads* (Frankfurt: Lang, 1988).

86. Whitehead, *Process and Reality*, 47.

87. Alfred North Whitehead, *Science and the Modern World* (New York: Free Press, 1925), 194.

88. Charles Hartshorne, *The Divine Relativity: A Social Conception of God* (New Haven, CT: Yale University Press, 1984), 32.

89. Whitehead, *Religion in the Making*, 108.

90. Whitehead, *Process and Reality*, 343.

91. For example, see Bracken, *The Divine Matrix*, 4. For Bracken, the divine nature of love that grounds or is the dynamic source of the being of God resembles in its operation Whitehead's understanding of creativity and the extensive continuum.

92. Whitehead, *Adventures of Ideas*, 177. I adopt the definitions of Joseph Bracken on the divine continuum and creativity, which he conceives as existing in God, the divine nature or ground of being (see Bracken, *The Divine Matrix*, introduction and chapter 4). For him, the divine continuum is like a perichoretic field, which he describes as the spatial context that "provides a 'relational complex' in which all entities, both actual and potential, have their standpoint or niche" (p. 3). The continuum relates to creativity, another Whiteheadian term that Bracken defines as "an underlying activity which serves as the ontological ground for everything that exists" (pp. 2–3). These two distinct yet interrelated principles refer to the ground of all beings, including God. Like Bracken, I am aware that not all process thinkers will agree with this view, but I find it helpful in describing what I seek to explain in this book regarding the concept of "intermingling."

93. Aquinas, *Summa theologica*, Ia, Q.1, A. 9; Q. 3, A. 4.

94. Bracken, *The Divine Matrix*, 29.

95. Whitehead, *Process and Reality*, 87–88.

96. Ibid., 21.

97. Bracken, *The Divine Matrix*, 55.

98. Jorge Luis Nobo, *Whitehead's Metaphysics of Extension and Solidarity* (Albany: State University of New York Press, 1986), 255, cited in Bracken, *The Divine Matrix*, 58.

99. Plato, *Plato's Timaeus*, trans. Peter Kalkavage (Newburyport, MA: Focus Publishing, 2001), 80. Emphasis mine.

100. Whitehead, *Adventures of Ideas*, 134. Emphasis mine.

101. Ibid., 208. Emphasis mine.

102. Ibid., 150, 275.

103. Faber, *God as Poet of the World*, 105.

104. Ibid., 203.

105. Roland Faber, "De-ontologizing God: Levinas, Deleuze, and Whitehead," in *Process and Difference: Between Cosmological and Poststructuralist Postmodernisms*, ed. Catherine Keller and Anne Daniell (Albany: State University of New York Press, 2001), 222–23.

106. Bracken, *The Divine Matrix*, 55.

107. Ibid., 58.

108. Ibid., 29.

109. Ibid., 67.

110. Ibid., 137.

111. Teresa of Avila, *Conceptions of the Love of God*, 389.

112. Whitehead, *Process and Reality*, 349.

113. See Faber, *God as Poet of the World*, 317, 325. See also Roland Faber, "The Sense of Peace: A Para-doxology of Divine Multiplicity," in *Polydoxy: Theology of Multiplicity and Relation*, ed. Catherine Keller and Laurel C. Schneider (London: Routledge, 2011).

114. Whitehead, *Process and Reality*, 349.

115. Ibid., 346.

116. Hartshorne, *The Divine Relativity*, xvii.

117. Ibid., xvii.

118. Ibid.

119. Gloria L. Schaab, *The Creative Suffering of the Triune God: An Evolutionary Theory* (New York: Oxford University Press, 2007), 36.

120. Ibid., 51.

121. Jay B. McDaniel, "The Passion of Christ: Grace Both Red and Green," in *Cross Examinations: Readings on the Meaning of the Cross Today*, ed. Marit Trelstad (Minneapolis, MN: Augsburg Fortress, 2006), 200.

122. Jay B. McDaniel, "Can Animal Suffering Be Reconciled with Belief in an All-Loving God?," in *Animals on the Agenda: Questions about Animals for Theology and Ethics*, ed. Andrew Linzey and Dorothy Yamamoto (Urbana: University of Illinois Press, 1998), 164.

123. Whitehead, *Process and Reality*, 279–80.

124. Faber, *God as Poet of the World*, 102. See also Maasen, *Gott, das Gute und das Böse in der Philosophie A.N. Whiteheads*.

125. Faber, *God as Poet of the World*, 129.

126. Whitehead, *Process and Reality*, 47.

127. Faber, *God as Poet of the World*, 189.

128. Hartshorne, *The Divine Relativity*, 19.

129. Whitehead, *Adventures of Ideas*, 256–57.

130. Whitehead, *Process and Reality*, 45.

131. Ibid., 349.

132. Ibid., 87–89.

133. Whitehead, *Adventures of Ideas*, 260. Emphasis mine. Only as negative could discordance be a cause of enfeeblement.

134. Abraham J. Heschel, *The Prophets II* (Peabody, MA: Hendrickson, 1962), 34.

135. Whitehead, *Adventures of Ideas*, 261.

136. Ibid., 261.

137. Ibid., 263.

138. Hartshorne, *The Divine Relativity*, x–xi. See also Morris Cohen, *Preface to Logic* (New York: Henry Holt, 1944), 74–75.

139. Hartshorne, *The Divine Relativity*, 46.

140. Ibid., 128.

141. Charles Hartshorne, *Aquinas to Whitehead: Seven Centuries of Metaphysics of Religion. The Aquinas Lecture, 1976*, Aquinas Lecture 40 (Milwaukee, WI: Marquette University Publications, 1976), 27.

142. Hartshorne, *The Divine Relativity*, 143.

143. Ibid., 76. Emphasis mine.

144. Hartshorne, *Aquinas to Whitehead*, 33.

145. Ibid., 43.

146. Hartshorne, *The Divine Relativity*, 90.

147. Marion, *The Erotic Phenomenon*, 221–22.

148. Keller, *Face of the Deep*, 164.

149. Ibid., 178. See Faber, *God as Poet of the World*, 258–59; Nicolas of Cusa, *Nicolas of Cusa*, 140.

150. Keller, *Face of the Deep*, 206. See also Roland Faber, *Leben in Fuelle: Skizzen zur christlichen Spiritualitaet. Festschrift fuer Prof. Weismayer zu seinem 65. Geburtstag* (Muenster: LT, 2001), 80.

151. Keller, *Face of the Deep*, 206. See also Roland Faber, *Leben in Fuelle*, 80.

152. Whitehead, *Process and Reality*, 270–80.

153. Keller, *Face of the Deep*, 232.

154. Ibid., 219. Emphasis mine.

155. Ibid., 226.

156. Ibid., 10.

157. Ibid., 178. Here also Keller is drawing from the divine name "Elohim."

158. Ibid., 135.

159. Ibid., 136.

160. Aquinas, *On Love and Charity*, S. III, D. 27, Q. 1, A. 1, response.

161. "Pluriverse" is a term that Ernesto Cardenal uses metaphorically to speak of the cosmos. See Ernesto Cardenal, *Pluriverse: New and Selected Poems*, trans. Jonathan Cohen (New York: New Directions, 2009).

162. Keller, *Face of the Deep*, 219. Catherine Keller, *God and Power: Counter-Apocalyptic Journeys* (Minneapolis, MN: Fortress Press, 2005), 144.

163. Gebara, *Longing for Running Water*, 124.

164. See Keller, *God and Power*, 144. See also Gebara, *Out of the Depths*, 172–73. One must note that for Ivone Gebara, the term relatedness, while personal, does not seek to refer to God as a person. As she argues, relatedness refers to something that is "far more than simply personal," for she seeks to come to terms with something that is concomitant with the cosmos, meaning something not autonomously apart from it (Gebara, *Longing for Running Water*, 105). Also, this term "relatedness," as Gebara argues, "is not taken from any particular philosophy, thought system, or school of spirituality" (p. 83); rather, she sees it as a common term used in ecofeminism. Here in this chapter it is used in relation to process thought owing to its resemblance to the terms "creativity," "extensive continuum," and "khora" used by process theologians in their descriptions of the God-cosmos relationship.

165. See Gebara's use of McFague's metaphor of the "Body of God" in Gebara's *Longing for Running Water* (p. 104) and place it in conversation with Sallie McFague, *The Body of God: An Ecological Theology* (Minneapolis, MN: Fortress Press, 1993), 250–51, n. 13. Also in *Longing for Running Water* Gebara expresses a sympathetic view toward McFague's panentheism (pp. 123–24). As McFague herself indicates, the metaphor correlates directly with Charles Hartshorne's interpretation of Whitehead's philosophy of organism, hence the indirect and implicit conversation Gebara is having with process thought. For a more direct analysis of the use of the metaphor of the Body of God, see Charles Hartshorne, "The Theological Analogies and the Cosmic Organism," in *Man's Vision of God and the Logic of Theism* (New York: Willett, Clark, 1941). For other references to the cosmos as the Body of God, see Grace Jantzen, *God's World, God's Body* (Philadelphia, PA: Westminster Press, 1984). See also Sallie McFague, *Models of God: Theology for an Ecological, Nuclear Age* (Philadelphia: Fortress Press, 1987).

166. Gebara makes explicit use of the mathematical cosmological concepts of Brian Swimme (director of the Center for the Story of the Universe at the California Institute of Integral Studies) and of the Catholic ecotheologian Thomas Berry, who speak of a cosmology similar to that of Whitehead. See Gebara, *Out of the Depths*, 133. See also Gebara, *Longing for Running Water*, 55, 92, 211.

167. Keller in *God and Power* (p. 144) fittingly links the concept of "*esse*-diversity" more explicitly with the expression of *relatedness*.

168. Gebara, *Longing for Running Water*, 103.

169. Ibid., 116.

170. This aspect was visited in Chapter 3, in the discussion of the postmodern view of Jean-Luc Marion, whose concerns address this issue of love as primary to the question of being.

171. Gebara, *Longing for Running Water*, 83, 103. Emphasis mine.

172. Ibid., 103.

173. Aquinas, *On Love and Charity*, S. III, D. 32, notes. See the reference of Aquinas to love as the *ousia* or essence of God.

174. Gebara, *Longing for Running Water*, 108.

175. Ivone Gebara, "The Trinity and Human Experience: An Ecofeminist Approach," in *Women Healing Earth: Third World Feminism on Ecology, Feminism, and Religion*, ed. Rosemary Radford Ruther (Maryknoll, NY: Orbis Books, 1996), 16–17; Nobo, *Whitehead's Metaphysics of Extension and Solidarity*, 16–17.

176. Marion, *The Erotic Phenomenon*, 221–22.

177. See the previous chapter's discussion of the critique that Irigaray brings to the discourse with the use of "Yes" to speak of the divine-cosmos relationship.

178. Aquinas, *Summa theologica*, Ia, Q. 16, A. 1.

179. Ibid., Ia, 20, A. 1.

180. Ibid., Ia, IIae, Q. 22, A. 3.

181. Hartshorne's analogy is based on the Platonic cosmology that describes God as the soul of the world. The imagery gives him the basis on which to argue that God is intimately interconnected with the cosmos. Cosmos and God immediately share in their suffering. The idea of God being the soul of the body is problematic in that it remains too consequently bound to temporality, as Faber indicates (Hartshorne, *The Divine Relativity*, 51–63; Faber, *God as Poet*, 147–48).

182. Charles Hartshorne, *Omnipotence and Other Theological Mistakes* (Albany: State University of New York Press, 1984), 61.

183. Faber, *God as Poet of the World*, 87.

184. Ibid., 87. Arguments in Hartshorne's panentheism could be said to arrive at similar conclusions. See, for example, chapter 3 of the *Divine Relativity*.

185. Faber, *God as Poet of the World*, 126.

186. Whitehead, *Process and Reality*, 12–13.

187. Ibid., 340.

188. Ibid., 350.

189. Ibid., 73. I am considering here the concept of objective immortality that stems from perpetual perishing that resembles the interplay between a future not independent from its past.

190. Gebara, *Longing for Running Water*, 124.

191. Hartshorne, *Aquinas to Whitehead*, 29.

192. Ibid., 41.

193. For Whitehead, an organism is a nexus or can be an event composed of "a definite fact with a date" (*Process and Reality*, 215, 230). An event has "the

specific character of a place through a period of time" (*The Concept of Nature* [New York: Cosimo, 2007], 53).

194. Gebara, *Longing for Running Water*, 160.

195. See Gebara, *Out of the Depths*, 136, and compare it with the statements that follow in the next paragraph here in this section.

196. Gebara, *Longing for Running Water*, 161–62.

197. Gebara, *Out of the Depths*, 172–73.

198. Virginia Burrus, *The Sex Lives of Saints: An Erotics of Ancient Hagiography* (Philadelphia: University of Pennsylvania Press, 2004), 69. Here Burrus is using MacKendrick's language on expenditure, an expenditure that ensues in an increase.

199. Keller, *Face of the Deep*, 231. Here Keller is making use of Deleuze's understanding of Nicolas of Cusa. See Gilles Deleuze, *Difference and Repetition* (New York: Columbia University Press, 1995), 123.

200. Whitehead, *Process and Reality*, 72.

201. See Richard Kearney, *The God Who May Be: A Hermeneutics of Religion* (Bloomington: Indiana University Press, 2001).

202. Whitehead, *Process and Reality*, 73.

203. Ibid., 95.

204. Ibid., 111–12.

205. Keller, *Face of the Deep*, 169.

206. Ibid., 23.

207. Gebara, *Longing for Running Water*, 124.

208. Whitehead, *Adventures of Ideas*, 257.

209. See Faber, *God as Poet of the World*, 295–98.

210. Gebara, *Longing for Running Water*, 123.

211. Gebara, "The Trinity and Human Experience," 17. Nobo, *Whitehead's Metaphysics of Extension and Solidarity*, 17.

212. Gebara, *Out of the Depths*, 109.

213. Gebara, *Longing for Running Water*, 134.

214. Ibid., 116.

215. Whitehead, *Process and Reality*, 350.

216. Whitehead, *Process and Reality*, 350.

217. Keller, *Face of the Deep*, 169.

218. Keller, *Face of the Deep*, 170.

219. Gebara, *Out of the Depths*, 150–74.

220. Gebara, *Longing for Running Water*, 169.

221. Whitehead, *Adventures of Ideas*, 266.

222. Gebara, *Longing for Running Water*, 106.

223. Ibid., 106–7.

224. Maasen, *Gott, das Gute und das Böse in der Philosophie A.N. Whiteheads*, 109.

225. Whitehead, *Religion in the Making*, 87.

226. Keller, *Face of the Deep*, 221.

227. Gebara, *Longing for Running Water*, 124.

228. Katherine Keller and Anne Daniell, *Process and Difference: Between Cosmological and Poststructural Modernism* (Albany: State University of New York Press, 2001), 65–66.

229. Ibid., 66.

230. Gebara, *Longing for Running Water*, 55.

231. Keller, *Face of the Deep*, 139.

232. Ibid., 63.

233. Ibid., 80.

234. Whitehead, *Process and Reality*, 339.

5. IMPROPRIETY: INCARNATIONS OF CARNIVALESQUE PASSION
AND OPEN-ENDED BOUNDARIES

1. Mikhail Bakhtin, *Rabelais and His World*, trans. Helene Iswolsky (Bloomington: Indiana University Press, 1984), 26–27. From his work on carnivalesque language one can extract theological principles that help to imagine a God of passion that incarnates the flesh of the cosmos in all its diversity and ambiguity. Also, while I am aware that some have argued that carnivals in antiquity, such as the Roman Saturnalias, allowed for the practice of some forms of human and animal sacrifice, and thus were not wholly benevolent, the questions about and critiques of sacrifice, and implicitly of good and evil, are beyond the purview of this study. For a discussion of this matter, see, for example, James George Frazer, *The Golden Bough* (Sioux Falls, IA: NuVision Publications, 2006), 317–22. The point I seek to make implicitly addresses these concerns, as has been demonstrated so far and will become evident in this chapter.

2. Marcella Althaus-Reid, *The Queer God* (London: Routledge, 2003), 57. While I recognize the difficulties that attend the use of the word "orgy," particularly as the dancing human can become a god and the animals can become humanlike, I use it as a metaphor of interexchange without the abrogation of boundaries and identities.

3. For a God outside God's wits, see Pseudo-Dionysius [Denys the Areopagite], *The Divine Names*, in *Pseudo-Dionysius: The Complete Works*, trans. Colm Luibheid, ed. John Farina (Mahwah, NJ: Paulist Press, 1987), 287.

4. Bakhtin, *Rabelais and His World*, 294.

5. Julia Kristeva, *Tales of Love*, trans. Leon S. Roudiez (New York: Columbia University Press, 1987), 97. To embrace more fully the flesh of enjoyment, here I make use of the language of the carnival to reinterpret how the cosmos and its multiple living forms find themselves in this excessive lover, much as God finds the divine self within the *manyness* of the cosmos. They displace

themselves by yearning for and loving one another. And as is implicitly found in the work of St. Thomas Aquinas, along with Joseph Bracken, one considers how the divine love (more fleshly so) can be a uniting activity through which they come to share their nature, the ground of their existence, and the source of their enjoyment. The divine enjoyment is about a surplus of movement of one self into the other, and then back to the self.

6. God is in love and seeks to intermingle with more than one person and living being—loves excessively. See, for example, Friedrich Nietzsche, *The Birth of Tragedy*, trans. Walter Kauffmann (New York: Modern Library, 2000), 39, and compare it with Althaus-Reid, *The Queer God*, 55.

7. Pseudo-Dionysius, *The Divine Names*, 287. Emphasis mine.

8. Thomas Aquinas, *Summa theologica of Saint Thomas*, trans. Fathers of the English Dominican Province (New York: Benzinger Bros., 1948), Ia, IIae, Q. 28, A. 3.

9. See the concept of theopoetics which has been in conversation with the biblical understanding of dance and music characteristic of the festivals. Amos Niven Wilder, *Theopoetic Theology and the Religious Imagination* (Lima, OH: Academic Renewal Press, 2001), 52.

10. Aquinas, *Summa theologica*, Ia, Q. 28, A. 5.

11. See Mark C. Taylor, *Critical Terms for Religious Studies* (Chicago: University of Chicago Press, 1998), 349–63. See also Julia Kristeva, *Desire in Language: A Semiotic Approach to Literature and Art*, trans. Thomas Gora, ed. Leon S. and Alice A. Jardine (New York: Columbia University Press, 1980), 65, 78, 144. Mark Taylor offers a brief treatment of Kristeva's concept of the carnival in relation to the definition of "woman" she presents in her work. Their views, while outside the purview of this study, can be quite fruitful in considering the theological implications of the concept of transmutation that I discuss in this chapter. See Mark C. Taylor, *Altarity* (Chicago: University of Chicago Press, 1987), 151–84. I would also like to take the opportunity to remember my doctoral class on ritual theory at Drew University with the distinguished anthropologist Karen Brown, who inspired me to take a look at the subversive meanings of carnivals and other rituals of urban cities from a religious standpoint.

12. Marcella Althaus-Reid, *Indecent Theology: Theological Perversions in Sex, Gender and Politics* (New York: Routledge, 2000), 54.

13. Aquinas, *Summa theologica*, Ia, IIae, Q. 28, A. 3.

14. John Caputo, "Hospitality and the Trouble with God," in *Phenomenologies of the Stranger: Between Hostility and Hospitality*, ed. Richard Kearney and Kascha Semonovitch (New York: Fordham University Press, 2011), 83.

15. Aquinas, *Summa theologica*, IIa, IIae, Q. 175, A. 2.

16. Ibid., Ia, Q. 28. A. 5.

17. Pseudo-Dionysius, *The Divine Names*, 107.

18. Ibid., 109.

19. Aquinas, *Summa theologica*, see Ia, QQ. 12–13, specifically Q. 12, A. 12, and Q. 13, A. 8.

20. Pseudo-Dionysius, *The Divine Names*, 287. Emphasis mine.

21. Jean-Luc Marion, *The Erotic Phenomenon*, trans. Stephen E. Lewis (Chicago: University of Chicago Press, 2007), 221–22.

22. Pseudo-Dionysius, *The Divine Names*, 82. Emphasis mine.

23. See Caputo's radical view of God as hospitality in "Hospitality and the Trouble with God."

24. Bernard of Clairvaux, in *The Song of Songs: Interpreted by Early Christian and Medieval Commentators*, ed. Richard A. Norris (Grand Rapids, MI: William B. Eerdmans, 2003), 23.

25. Gregory of Nyssa, *From Glory to Glory: Texts from Gregory of Nyssa's Mystical Writings*, trans. and ed. Herbert Musurillo (Crestwood, NY: St. Vladimir's Seminary Press, 1979), 239.

26. Ibid., 240.

27. Teresa of Avila, *Conceptions of the Love of God*, in vol. 2 of *The Complete Works of St. Teresa of Avila*, trans. and ed. E. Allison Peers (New York: Continuum, 2002), 384.

28. Pseudo-Dionysius, *The Divine Names*, 67. Emphasis mine.

29. Thomas Aquinas, *On Love and Charity, Readings from the "Commentary on the Sentences of Peter Lombard,"* trans. Peter A. Kwasniewski, Thomas Bolin, and Joseph Bolin, with an introduction and notes by Peter A. Kwasniewski (Washington, DC: Catholic University of America Press, 2008), S. III, D. 32, A. 1, Obj. 3. I must also remind the reader that for Aquinas, strictly speaking, transmutation in God would not include anger or sadness (imperfect passions) but only delight and enjoyment (perfect passions intellective). Also, as I have already emphasized, for him, reciprocal participation between the divine lover and others is basically null, occurring only in terms of God communicating the divine perfections to the creatures. See the response he gives to Peter Lombard in the same passage quoted above.

30. Luce Irigaray, *The Forgetting of Air in Martin Heidegger*, trans. Mary Beth Mader (Austin: University of Texas Press, 1999), 53.

31. Ibid., 60.

32. Luce Irigaray, *Marine Lover of Friedrich Nietzsche*, trans. Gillian C. Gill (New York: Columbia University Press, 1991), 133.

33. Caputo, "Hospitality and the Trouble with God," 93.

34. Ibid., 94.

35. Ibid., 95. In this Caputo is also explicitly acknowledging the contributions of Althaus-Reid and her indecent theology, and implicitly aligns his concept of hospitality with hers.

36. Aquinas, *Of God and His Creatures: An Annotated Translation of the Summa contra gentiles of Saint Thomas*, trans. and Joseph Rickaby (Westminster, MD: Carroll Press, 1950), III, li.

37. Teresa of Avila, *Conceptions of the Love of God*, 385.

38. Luis Maldonado, *Fiesta popular y el hieratismo sacramental* (Madrid: Imprenta S.M., 1986), 30.

39. Irigaray, *Marine Lover*, 58.

40. María Teresa Porcile, "El derecho a la belleza en América Latina," in *El rostro femenino de la teología*, ed. Elsa Tamez[o] (San José, CR: Departamento Ecuménico de Investigaciones, 1988), 86. The English translation of this statement from Porcile is mine. This chapter, in its use of the trope of *fiesta*, holds the same commitments as the introduction and the first chapter, even as it seeks to expand their meaning, make them more playfully revelatory. For the Latin American bishops who met in Puebla, faith too is being expressed in the fiestas and celebrations (see no. 454 de Puebla). See Ivone Gebara, "La mujer hace theología," 23.

41. Porcile, "El derecho a la belleza en América Latina," 104.

42. Maldonado, *Fiesta popular y el hieratismo sacramental*, 30.

43. Friedrich Nietzsche, "On Reading and Writing," in *Thus Spoke Zarathustra: A Book for None and All*, trans. Walter Kauffmann (London: Penguin Books, 1966), 41.

44. The name *teología festiva o dionisiaca* is one given by Luis Maldonado. I have chosen this term to include the works of Rubem Alves, José Vasconcelos, and Roberto Goizueta, even though they themselves do not refer to their theology as such. Also, both Alves and Vasconcelos make use of Nietzsche's understandings of Dionysius. And while Goizueta does not, he remains in conversation with Vasconcelos, and in some ways seems to have been influenced by the thoughts of Alves. What they all explicitly share is a use of aesthetics in their theology.

45. Maldonado, *Fiesta popular y el hieratismo sacramental*, 26.

46. Nietzsche, "On Reading and Writing," 41.

47. Maldonado, *Fiesta popular y el hieratismo sacramental*, 40. The other is the will to power, but it is beyond the purview of this study.

48. José Vasconcelos, *Obras completas*, 4 vol. (Mexico City: Libros Mexicanos Unidos, 1957–1961), 3:1394. I am aware that Vasconcelos is a controversial figure among certain Latino/a theological circles, and understandably so, since it can be argued that in his descriptions of *la raza cósmica*, for example, one can find evidence of an attempt to whiten and Europeanize the Mexican population. For a critical view of Vasconcelos's work on racial identities, see Ernesto Medina, *Mestizaje: (Re)mapping Race, Culture, and Faith in Latina/o Catholicism* (Maryknoll, NY: Orbis Books, 2009). While I am not minimizing the importance of this valuable critique, here Vasconcelos plays a critical role in providing a vinculum between the elements of Dionysian art and the notion of *fiesta* that Goizueta offers that to me is also worth engaging.

49. Maldonado, *Fiesta popular y el hieratismo sacramental*, 46.

50. Nietzsche, *The Birth of Tragedy*, 139.

51. Ibid., 132.

52. Ibid., 37. Here I am clearly extending the concept of "primordial unity" and the "primordially One" of Nietzsche toward a more multiple view as embraced by my agreement with Keller on her concept of the *Manyone* and her deconstructions of the name of Elohim (Catherine Keller, *Face of the Deep: A Theology of Becoming* [New York: Routledge, 2003], 178). Hence, this is not to argue for a fusion of selves as in pagan rites, as already stated. Rather, as Kearney argues in *The God Who May Be*, in drawing on Kristeva's texts on *jouissance* and taboo, one can say that "the *persona* paradox of the transfiguring God" maintains a certain beyond-our-grasp type of transcendentalism that can still be experienced as carnal lust, in that divine love involves "all the senses—sound, odor, touch, sight, taste—but unlike the old pagan rites of sexual fusion and sacrifice, it resists the phallic illusion of totality, finality of fullness" (see Richard Kearney, *The God Who May Be: A Hermeneutics of Religion* [Bloomington: Indiana University Press, 2001], 58–59).

53. Aquinas, *Summa theologica*, Ia, Q. 28, A. 1.

54. Ibid., Ia, Q. 28, A. 5, Obj. 2. See also IIa, IIae, Q. 175, A. 3.

55. Nietzsche, *The Birth of Tragedy*, 26.

56. Maldonado, *Fiesta popular y el hieratismo sacramental*, 46–49.

57. Porcile, "El derecho a la belleza en América Latina," 90. The term "maenads" or "enthusiasts," as she defines it, refers etymologically to "those filled with God," perhaps as with wine.

58. Nietzsche, *The Birth of Tragedy*, 38.

59. Ibid., 36.

60. Maldonado, *Fiesta popular y el hieratismo sacramental*, 49.

61. Vasconcelos, *Obras completas*, 3:1392–93. Emphasis mine.

62. Nietzsche, *The Birth of Tragedy*, 105.

63. Aristotle, *Nicomachean Ethics*, trans. and with a glossary and introductory essay by Joe Sachs (Newburyport, MA: Focus Publishing/R. Pullins Co., 2008), I, xiii, 1102b.

64. Nietzsche, *The Birth of Tragedy*, 35–36.

65. Abraham Heschel, *The Prophets II* (Peabody, MA: Hendrickson, 1962), 34.

66. Nietzsche, *The Birth of Tragedy*, 61.

67. Karmen MacKendrick, *Counterpleasures* (Albany: State University of New York Press, 1999), 78.

68. Ibid., 126.

69. Nietzsche, *The Birth of Tragedy*, 52.

70. Ibid., 64.

71. Jean-Luc Marion, *The Idol and Distance: Five Studies*, trans. Thomas A. Carlson (New York: Fordham University Press, 2001), 36–55. Marion is critical

of the Nietzschean Dionysius since this figure dominates that of the Christ, an aspect that is beyond the purview of this study.

72. Roberto S. Goizueta, "Fiesta: Life in the Subjunctive," in *From the Heart of Our People: Latino/a Explorations in Catholic Systematic Theology*, ed. Orlando O. Espín and Miguel H. Díaz (Maryknoll, NY: Orbis Books, 1999), 92.

73. Maldonado, *Fiesta popular y el hieratismo sacramental*, 21.

74. Ibid., 30.

75. Ibid., 31. In *la fiesta*, enjoyment becomes creatively expansive, spilling over zones and territories, and so interconnecting multiple life forms and forms of living through that which is shared in common. Consequently, excess is in the communal in the form of its multiple expressions of enjoyment, a dissonant symphony of many voices singing their songs of jubilee.

76. Ibid., 24. I'm thinking of the Day of the Dead, a Latin American celebration observed on November 1 all around the world, and of two dear friends in Brooklyn who open their home each year to the friends and family members of those who have died of AIDS.

77. Goizueta, "Fiesta: Life in the Subjunctive," 87.

78. Ibid., 92. According to Victor Turner, symbols, though stemming from familiar social and cultural contexts, can become factors of social action and change when they are appropriated and used in creative and innovative ways by means of comparison. In juxtaposing symbols, there is an in-between space, a threshold, an ingress, entered by leaving one meaning and taking another. This in-between space Turner calls *liminality*, which manifests as a space of antistructure or a disorder of structures. *Liminality* allows for "freed" time that can be used for the purpose of defamiliarizing the familiar and recombining in creative ways cultural elements. See Victor Turner, *The Ritual Process: Structure and Anti-Structure* (New York: Aldine De Gruyter, 1995).

79. Jon Sobrino, *Christology at the Crossroads: A Latin American Approach*, trans. John Drury (Maryknoll, NY: Orbis Books, 1978), 221.

80. Rubem A. Alves, *Tomorrow's Child: Imagination, Creativity, and the Rebirth of Culture* (New York: Harper & Row, 1972), 98.

81. Nietzsche, *The Birth of Tragedy*, 72.

82. Ibid., 46. For Nietzsche this is evident in the political drive to form states and to generate patriotism, the ultimate affirmation of individual personality.

83. Ibid., 46.

84. Ibid., 129.

85. Ibid., 36. For Nietzsche, "self-forgetfulness" is tightly connected to the act of embracing "nature's cruelty." Its form of pleasure mixed with pain is expressed through bewitching sounds of ecstasy and "piercing shrieks" (46, 113).

86. Irigaray, *Marine Lover*, 129.

87. Ivone Gebara, *Out of the Depths: Women's Experience of Evil and Salvation*, trans. Ann Patrick Ware (Minneapolis, MN: Fortress Press, 2002), 35.

88. Elizabeth Johnson, *Quest for the Living God: Mapping Frontiers in the Theology of God* (New York: Continuum, 2007), 149.

89. After all, was not this what Karl Marx was really after in his challenge to the alienation of labor but could not reach, since he remained bound to notions of labor himself? For him, the capacity to enjoy oneself is hindered by the process of alienation tightly knitted into the capitalist mode of production. Especially it refers to the way in which workers or proletariat hold no direct relation to or cannot enjoy the objects that they produce. Their talents are being used mostly to benefit others, the "bourgeoisie." Yet, as implied in Goizueta and explicitly criticized by Alves, play is another category that can be used to argue against the mastery of a value exchange system over aspects of human enjoyment. See Alves, *Tomorrow's Child*, 47–50, and the explanation below.

90. Vasconcelos, *Obras completas*, 3:1225.

91. Alves, *Tomorrow's Child*, 31. Several authors have pointed to the ambivalence of the festivals, particularly as they also participate in contemporary consumer capitalism. See, for example, Jon Gross, "Disquiet on the Waterfront: Reflections on Nostalgia and Utopia in the Urban Archetypes of Festival Marketplaces," *Urban Geography* 17, no. 3 (1996): 221–47. I hold to the view that while there are aspects of the festival that can fall within the market economy, many of its expressions of enjoyment go beyond it. The many ways in which the market economy serves the excess of the festival are beyond the purview of this study.

92. Alves, *Tomorrow's Child*, 31.

93. Ibid., 31.

94. For Aristotle, the purpose of the state is to ensure the happiness of its citizens, and when parsing the meaning of this, technically speaking, true happiness is allotted most to the "better men," who would be the most wise and free to contemplate what would be best for the city. By keeping each person within a class system, as well as maintaining that women are weaker, that the purpose of the slave is to assent to the requests of the master, and that the foreign could be enslaved by reason of being less rational, Aristotle can claim a greater happiness for some over others, though technically for him, the whole of the state moves together toward the common good, hence a collective happiness. For example, see Aristotle, *Politics*, trans. Benjamin Jowett (Mineola, NY: Dover, 2000), chap. I. In saying this, I am also mindful of antiquity's worldview, which may have prevented someone as contemplative as he to see beyond this class system.

95. Johnson, *Quest for the Living God*, 148.

96. Vasconcelos, *Obras completas*, 3:1049–50.

97. Ibid., 3:1050.

98. Rubem A. Alves, *The Poet, the Warrior, the Prophet* (London: SCM Press, 1990), 63.

99. Goizueta, "Fiesta: Life in the Subjunctive," 96.

100. Alves, *The Poet, the Warrior, the Prophet*, 99–101. See also Rubem A. Alves, "Theopoetics: Longing and Liberation," in *Struggles for Solidarity: Liberation Theologies in Tension*, ed. Lorine M. Getz, and Ruy O. Costa (Minneapolis, MN: Fortress Press, 1992).

101. Porcile, "El derecho a la belleza en América Latina," 87.

102. Maldonado, *Fiesta popular y el hieratismo sacramental*, 50.

103. Nietzsche, *The Birth of Tragedy*, 58, 49.

104. As already shown in Chapter 3, for feminists like Althaus-Reid, the interplay between pain and pleasure destabilizes "rigid dyads." Sadomasochism allows playful reversals that, for MacKendrick, extend desire via resistance and the withdrawal of the flesh, and that grant even the marks of death regenerative power, a surplus to the body of flesh, as Burrus sees it. See Althaus-Reid, *The Queer God*, 17; MacKendrick, *Counterpleasures*; Virginia Burrus, *The Sex Lives of Saints: An Erotics of Ancient Hagiography* (Philadelphia: University of Pennsylvania Press, 2004).

105. See Porcile, "El derecho a la belleza en América Latina," 90–91.

106. Ibid., 90.

107. Alves, *Tomorrow's Child*, 137.

108. Ibid., 93–94.

109. Goizueta, "Fiesta: Life in the Subjunctive," 94.

110. Johnson, *Quest for the Living God*, 148.

111. Goizueta, "Fiesta: Life in the Subjunctive," 96.

112. Johnson, *Quest for the Living God*, 148.

113. Nietzsche, *The Birth of Tragedy*, 125.

114. Ibid., 60.

115. Ibid., 42.

116. Irigaray, *Marine Lover*, 8.

117. Ibid., 7.

118. Alves, *The Poet, the Warrior, the Prophet*, 47.

119. See, for example, Ivone Gebara, "La mujer hace teología: Un ensayo para la reflexión," in *El rostro femenino de la teología*, ed. Elsa Tamez, 11–24 (San José, CR: Departamento Ecuménico de Investigaciones, 1988), 23.

120. Goizueta, "Fiesta: Life in the Subjunctive," 96.

121. Alfred North Whitehead, *Process and Reality: An Essay in Cosmology*, ed. David Ray and Donald W. Sherburne Griffin (New York: Free Press, 1978), 73.

122. Goizueta, "Fiesta: Life in the Subjunctive," 94.

123. Alves, *Tomorrow's Child*, 81. As Alves argues, with a condescending smile, pure realism says "Your utopias can be beautiful. But it is not for nothing that they are u-topias—according to the Greek, 'not a place.' Reality has no room for these hopes. Your utopias are unrealizable dreams, in no way different from the madness of magic or the foolishness of play" (*Tomorrow's Child*, 104).

124. Ibid., 201.

125. Ibid., 203.

126. Irigaray, *Marine Lover*, 103.

127. Althaus-Reid, *The Queer God*, 47.

128. Richard Kearney, *Strangers, Gods, and Monsters* (London: Routledge, 2003), 34.

129. Jean-Luc Marion, *God Without Being: Hors-Texte*, trans. Thomas A. Carlson (Chicago: University of Chicago Press, 1991), 20–21. We can see evidence of the concept of excess in Marion's work, for example in his discussion on the icon. The icon opens up to the invisible that gazes at us, and to a measureless depth that points to its excess. It points to "an origin without an original," to an abyss that the eyes cannot finish probing. In other words, it opens up to distance and thus distinction. For a more in-depth exposition of his notion of excess, see Jean-Luc Marion, *In Excess: Studies on Saturated Phenomena*, trans. Robyn Horner and Vincent Berraud (New York: Fordham University Press), 2002.

130. Althaus-Reid, *Indecent Theology*, 110.

131. Here the term "queer" carries a double meaning—same-gender loving person and stranger. I am aware that the term can be offensive to some from self-denominated lesbian, gay, bisexual, transsexual, intersexual, and queer (LGBTIQ) communities. But in this book I employ it in a subversive manner. I intend for it to defy heterosexual discourse seeking to suppress heteronormative expressions of enjoyment. In this I align myself with Althaus-Reid, for whom theological queering means "the deliberate questioning of heterosexual experience and thinking which has shaped our understanding of theology, the role of the theologian and hermeneutics" (*The Queer God*, 2). Like Althaus-Reid, I use this term, most applicable to LGBTIQ communities, to also refer to the stranger, and to argue for a radical form of hospitality. Thus, along with her, I seek to expand the meanings of this antigay epithet by turning it on its head. Other terms, like "gay" and "alien," acquire a similar multidimensionality.

132. The term *vejigantes* means gigantic bladder. These are clownlike characters who dance about in the streets in the carnivals of Puerto Rico, in the cities of Loíza and Ponce. These characters are spiritlike representations of African religious heritage that subvert normative Christian religion and the colonizing political systems. Another character would be the Saga man, who embodies a term used for men who seek sexual favors for money. In the carnivals of St. Thomas people make a mockery of him. See Gus Edwards, "Caribbean Narrative: Carnival Characters—In Life and in the Mind," in *Black Theatre: Ritual Performance in the African Diaspora*, ed. Paul Carter Harrison and Gus Edwards (Philadelphia: Temple University Press, 2002).

133. Althaus-Reid, *Indecent Theology*, 47–48.

134. Bakhtin, *Rabelais and His World*, 197–99.

135. Ibid., 208.

136. Althaus-Reid, *Indecent Theology*, 25.

137. Ibid., 91.

138. While for Nietzsche the world is the ground of all existence, in this study I adopt a panentheistic view: God also as the ground/lessness of all things. See Nietzsche, *The Birth of Tragedy*, 79.

139. Althaus-Reid, *The Queer God*, 9.

140. Ibid., 14.

141. Ibid., 25. For Althaus-Reid the term most related to excess is *libertinaje*, which translates as licentiousness, with a meaning inclusive of but not limited to sexuality. More specifically, it is a concept that for many Argentinians holds a political ideal initiated by General Juan Domingo and Evita Perón in their efforts to establish the social welfare of the poor and the overthrow of the oligarchy. For Althaus-Reid, one way to address liberation theology's concerns and commitments is to free concepts of sexuality, an interpretative project that is also embraced in this book.

142. See Aristotle, *Metaphysics*, XII, ix, 1074b 30.

143. Althaus-Reid, *The Queer God*, 100. I see Althaus-Reid drawing theological principles from indigenous religions of Latin America and recapturing in her theology depictions of female deities. As Irigaray also observes, at one time female goddesses were represented by women's sexual organs, a visual practice that Christianity has sought to erase. See Irigaray, "Questions to Emanuel Levinas," in *The Irigaray Reader*, ed. Margaret Whitford (Oxford: Blackwell, 1991, 1993), 178.

144. See, for example, Pseudo-Dionysius, *The Celestial Hierarchy*, in *Pseudo-Dionysius: The Complete Works*, 145–91; and Aquinas's understanding of the angels in his *Summa theologica*, Ia, QQ. 50–63.

145. Bakhtin, *Rabelais and His World*, 400–3.

146. See the reasons why Aquinas keeps the argument on God's love closely related to the "intellect" in Chapter 2.

147. Understandably, this is the case. Aquinas would not hint at sexuality, since Aquinas was a celibate friar training other men in pursuit of the priesthood. Now one must also note that Aquinas, by favoring Aristotle and not Plato, also sought to present a more incarnational theology than Plato's influential thought would have allowed (body, senses). In addition, that his work seeks to be more in agreement with Denys the Areopagite than with Augustine is of significance. On this point, Matthew Fox is helpful. For him, "A sacralization of all nature was as important for Dionysius as for Aquinas. Dionysius had a creation-centered approach to spirituality and a cosmic one that Augustine lacked" (Fox, *Sheer Joy: Conversations with Thomas Aquinas on Creation Spirituality* [New York: HarperSan Francisco, 1992], 23).

148. Bakhtin, *Rabelais and His World*, 240–41. Bakhtin makes this statement in comparing popular comic tradition with womanhood.

149. Ibid., 314.

150. Ibid., 175.

151. Ibid., 378, 383.

152. Ibid., 217.

153. Ibid., 50.

154. Ibid., 335. For Bakhtin, something like urine or defecation are key to understanding degeneration as well as rebirth—they speak of life coming from the body itself. In this I see a similarity to the work of the liberation theologian Ivone Gebara, for whom God can be found even "in the squalor of our lives" for the purposes of resurrection. See Gebara, *Longing for Running Water: Eco-feminism and Liberation*, trans. David Molineaux (Minneapolis, MN: Fortress Press, 1999), 106.

155. Bakhtin, *Rabelais and His World*, 317.

156. Ibid., 163.

157. Ibid., 339.

158. See especially Friedrich Nietzsche, "Ariadne's Complaint," in *Dithyrambs of Dionysius*, trans. and with an introduction and notes by R. J. Hollingdale (London: Anvil Press Poetry, 1984).

159. Marion, *The Idol and Distance*, 53.

160. Althaus-Reid, *Indecent Theology*, 47.

161. Ibid., 117–23. For example, Althaus-Reid tells us that among the Incas from the town called Moya there are three divine mountains that portray their sexual cosmology of male, female, and bisexual orders. Two mountain divinities are male. And the other, called Apu Yaya, with its back considered to be male and its front female, is usually represented as a male and female elderly couple walking together.

162. Irigaray, *Marine Lover*, 149.

163. Althaus-Reid, *The Queer God*, 8.

164. Ibid., 25.

165. Althaus-Reid, *Indecent Theology*, 92.

166. Ibid., 36.

167. Keller, *Face of the Deep*, 199.

168. Ibid., 23.

169. Althaus-Reid, *The Queer God*, 69.

170. Ibid., 120.

171. Ibid., 135.

172. Ibid., 57.

173. Ibid., 58.

174. Ibid., 44, 51.

175. Ibid., 36.

176. Ibid., 83.

177. Nietzsche, *The Birth of Tragedy*, 30.

178. Aquinas, *Of God and His Creatures*, I, cii, n. 7.

179. Althaus-Reid, *The Queer God*, 17.

180. Ibid., 25.

181. Another location comes to play that more explicitly refers to the external and lower portions of the body, to the openings as the sites of transit that offer passage to the multitude of living forms and their enjoyments. It offers passage also to God, who becomes excessively welcoming of mutations of the divine self even after the fashion of the animal and plantlike amorphisms.

182. Althaus-Reid, *The Queer God*, 47.

183. Keller, *Face of the Deep*, 136.

184. Here I'm keeping in mind the nongeometrical space (third space) of Plato who explored the concept of the khora in the *Timaeus*, 49A–53B; Derrida's view of a hospitable space, in *Khora*, in *On the Name* (Stanford, CA: Stanford University Press, 1995); and of Keller's sensuous and earthened view of the khora, more akin to feminism, in the *Face of the Deep*, 165–69.

185. John D. Caputo, "Hospitality and the Trouble with God," in *Phenomenologies of the Stranger: Between Hostility and Hospitality*, ed. Richard Kearney and Kascha Semonovitch (New York: Fordham University Press, 2011), 85.

186. Nietzsche, *The Birth of Tragedy*, 37.

187. Ibid., 37.

188. Ibid., 38, 61.

189. Ibid., 85.

190. Ibid., 61.

191. Bakhtin, *Rabelais and His World*, 29.

192. Ibid., 32. Emphasis mine.

193. Ibid., 318.

194. Keller, *Face of the Deep*, 169–70.

195. Bakhtin, *Rabelais and His World*, 229–30.

196. Nietzsche, *The Birth of Tragedy*, 106.

197. Ibid., 39–40, 107.

198. Gebara, *Out of the Depths*, 172.

199. Bakhtin, *Rabelais and His World*, 40.

200. Ibid., 341.

201. Ibid., 256.

202. Nietzsche, *The Birth of Tragedy*, 104.

203. Bakhtin, *Rabelais and His World*, 255.

204. Ibid., 43.

205. Althaus-Reid, *The Queer God*, 32.

206. John D. Caputo, *The Weakness of God: A Theology of the Event* (Bloomington: Indiana University Press, 2006), 134.

207. Ibid., 33.

208. Althaus-Reid, *The Queer God*, 54.

209. Gebara, *Longing for Running Water*, 57.

210. I have found inspiration for these concepts in John Sallis, *Chorology: Beginning in Plato's Timaeus* (Bloomington: Indiana University Press, 1999), 7–45.

211. Gebara, *Out of the Depths*, 172.

212. They would be simply for use and the instruments of human happiness. See Aristotle's *Politics*, I, i, 12–13 (in reference to the household).

213. Althaus-Reid, *Indecent Theology*, 147.

214. Ibid., 171.

215. See also Franz Fanon's criticism of the enlightenment's way of categorizing according to skin color and its effort to establish a system of good manners among the colonized in *Black Skin, White Masks*, trans. Richard Philcox (New York: Grove Press, 2008).

216. Althaus-Reid, *The Queer God*, 149.

217. Nietzsche, *The Birth of Tragedy*, 107.

218. Ibid., 39–40.

219. Ibid., 49.

220. Maduro, *Mapas para la fiesta*, 31.

221. Althaus-Reid, *The Queer God*, 66.

222. Ibid., 44.

223. Ibid., 57.

224. Keller, *Face of the Deep*, 123.

225. Althaus-Reid, *Indecent Theology*, 97.

226. Ibid., 99.

227. Maduro, *Mapas para la fiesta*, 31.

Adams, Don. "Aquinas on Aristotle's Happiness." In *Medieval Philosophy and Theology*, edited by Norman Kretzmann et al., 98–118. Notre Dame, IN: University of Notre Dame Press, 1991.

Althaus-Reid, Marcella. *Indecent Theology: Theological Perversions in Sex, Gender and Politics*. New York: Routledge, 2000.

———. *The Queer God*. London: Routledge, 2003.

Alves, Rubem A. *Tomorrow's Child: Imagination, Creativity, and the Rebirth of Culture*. New York: Harper & Row, 1972.

———. *The Poet, the Warrior, the Prophet*. The Edward Cadbury Lectures 1990. London: SCM Press; Philadelphia: Trinity Press International, 1990.

———. "Theopoetics: Longing and Liberation." In *Struggles for Solidarity: Liberation Theologies in Tension*, edited by Lorine M. Getz and Ruy O. Costa. Minneapolis, MN: Fortress Press, 1992.

Anderson, Gary A. *A Time to Dance: The Expression of Grief and Joy in Israelite Religion*. University Park: Pennsylvania State University Press, 1955.

Aquinas, Thomas. *Concerning Being and Essence*. Translated by George G. Leckie. New York: Appleton-Century-Crofts, 1937.

———. *Summa theologica of Saint Thomas*. Translated by the Fathers of the English Dominican Province. New York: Benzinger Bros., 1948.

———. *Of God and His Creatures: An Annotated Translation of the Summa contra gentiles of Saint Thomas*. Translated and edited by Joseph Rickaby. Westminster, MD: Carroll Press, 1950.

———. *Commentary on the Metaphysics of Aristotle*. Translated by John P. Rowan. Chicago: Henry Regnery, 1961.

———. *Summa contra gentiles: Book One: God*. Translated by Anton C. Pegis. Notre Dame, IN: University of Notre Dame Press, 1975.

———. *Devoutly I Adore Thee: The Prayers and Hymns of St. Thomas Aquinas*. Translated by Robert Anderson and Johann Moser. Manchester, NH: Sophia Institute Press, 1993.

———. *Commentary on the Posterior Analytics of Aristotle*. Edited by Richard Berquist and Ralph McInerny. South Bend, IN: St. Augustine's Press, 2008.

———. *On Love and Charity: Readings from the "Commentary on the Sentences of Peter Lombard."* Translated by Peter A. Kwasniewski, Thomas Bolin, and Joseph Bolin. Introduction and notes by Peter A. Kwasniewski. Washington, DC: Catholic University of America Press, 2008.

Aquino, María Pilar. *Our Cry for Life: Feminist Theology from Latin America*. Translated by Dinah Livingstone. Maryknoll, NY: Orbis Books, 1993.

Arellano, Luz Beatriz. "Women's Experience of God in Emerging Spirituality." In *With Passion and Compassion: Third World Women Doing Theology: Reflections from the Women's Commission of the Ecumenical Association of Third World Theologians*, edited by Virginia Fabella and Mercy Amba Oduyoye. Maryknoll, NY: Orbis Books, 1988.

Aristotle. *Aristotle's Physics*. Translated by Richard Hope. Lincoln: University of Nebraska Press, 1961.

———. *Politics*. Translated by Benjamin Jowett. Mineola, NY: Dover, 2000.

———. *Metaphysics*. Translated by W. D. Ross. Sioux Falls, IA: NuVision Publications, 2005.

———. *Nicomachean Ethics*. Translated and with a glossary and introductory essay by Joe Sachs. Newburyport, MA: Focus Publishing/R. Pullins Co., 2008.

Averroës, *Averroës' Three Short Commentaries on Aristotle's "Topics," "Rhetoric," and "Poetics."* Translated and edited by Charles E. Butterworth. Albany: State University of New York Press, 1977.

Bakhtin, Mikhail. *Rabelais and His World*. Translated by Helene Iswolsky. Bloomington: Indiana University Press, 1984.

Bingemer, María Clara. "Chairete: Alegrai-vos a muller no futuro da teologia da liberção." *Revista Eclesistica Brasileira* 48, no. 191 (1988): 565–87.

———. "Reflections on the Trinity." In *Through Her Eyes: Women's Theology from Latin America*, edited by Elsa Tamez, 56–80. Maryknoll, NY: Orbis Books, 1989.

Boff, Leonardo. *Passion of Christ, Passion of the World: Their Facts, Their Interpretation and Their Meaning for Yesterday and Today*. Translated by Robert R. Barr. Maryknoll, NY: Orbis Books, 1987.

Bracken, Joseph A. *The Divine Matrix: Creativity as Link between East and West*. Eugene, OR: Wipf and Stock, 1995.

———. *The One in the Many: A Contemporary Reconstruction of the God-World Relation*. Grand Rapids, MI: William B. Eerdmans, 2001.

Brenner, Athalya, ed. *The Song of Songs. A Feminist Companion to the Bible*, 1st ser. Sheffield, IA: Sheffield Academic Press, 1993.

Brenner, Athalya, with Carole R. Fontaine, eds. *The Song of Songs. A Feminist Companion to the Bible*, 2nd ser. Sheffield, IA: Sheffield Academic Press, 2000.

Burrus, Virginia. *The Sex Lives of Saints: An Erotics of Ancient Hagiography*. Philadelphia: University of Pennsylvania Press, 2004.

———. "Introduction: Theology and Eros after Nygren." In *Toward a Theology of Eros: Transfiguring Passion at the Limits of Discipline*, edited by Virginia Burrus and Catherine Keller, xiii–xxi. New York: Fordham University Press, 2006.

Burrus, Virginia, and Catherine Keller, eds. *Toward a Theology of Eros: Transfiguring Passion at the Limits of Discipline*. New York: Fordham University Press, 2006.

Burrus, Virginia, and Stephen D. Moore. "Unsafe Sex: Feminism, Pornography, and the Song of Songs." *Biblical Interpretation* 11, no. 1 (2003): 24–52.

Caputo, John D. *The Weakness of God: A Theology of the Event*. Bloomington: Indiana University Press, 2006.

———. "Hospitality and the Trouble with God." In *Phenomenologies of the Stranger: Between Hostility and Hospitality*, edited by Richard Kearney and Kascha Semonovitch, 83–97. New York: Fordham University Press, 2011.

Cardenal, Ernesto. *Cosmic Canticle*. Translated by John Lyons. Willimantic, CT: Curbstone Press, 1993.

———. *Love: A Glimpse of Eternity*. Translated by Dinah Livingstone. Brewster, MA: Paraclete Press, 2006.

———. *Pluriverse: New and Selected Poems*. Translated by Jonathan Cohen. New York: New Directions, 2009.

Cobb, John B., Jr., and David Ray Griffin. *Process Theology: An Introductory Exposition*. Louisville, KY Westminster John Knox Press, 1976.

Cone, James H. *God of the Oppressed*. Maryknoll, NY: Orbis Books, 1997.

Depoortere, Frederick. "Jouissance féminine? Lacan on Bernini's 'The Ecstasy of Saint Teresa' versus Slavoj Žižek on Lars von Trier's 'Breaking the Waves.'" In *Encountering Transcendence: Contributions to a Theology of Christian Religious Experience*, edited by L. Boeve, H. Geybels, and S. Van den Bossche, 21–37. Leuven: Peeters Press, 2005.

Derrida, Jacques. "Différance." In *Margins of Philosophy*. Translated by Alan Bass. Chicago: University of Chicago Press, 1982.

———. *On the Name*. Translated by David Wood. Stanford, CA: Stanford University Press, 1995.

———. *Of Hospitality*. Stanford, CA: Stanford University Press, 2000.

Descartes, René. *Discourse on Methods and Meditations*. Translated by Laurence J. Lafleur. Indianapolis: Bobbs-Merrill, 1960).

Eco, Umberto. *The Aesthetics of Thomas Aquinas*. Translated by Hugh Bredin. Cambridge, MA: Harvard University Press, 1988.

Edwards, Gus. "Caribbean Narrative: Carnival Characters—In Life and in the Mind." In *Black Theatre: Ritual Performance in the African Diaspora*, edited by

Paul Carter Harrison and Gus Edwards, 108–14. Philadelphia: Temple University Press, 2002.

Faber, Roland. "De-ontologizing God: Levinas, Deleuze, and Whitehead." In *Process and Difference: Between Cosmological and Poststructuralist Postmodernisms*, edited by Catherine Keller and Anne Daniell, 209–34. Albany: State University of New York Press, 2001.

———. *God as Poet of the World: Exploring Process Theologies*. Translated by Douglas W. Stott. Louisville, KY: Westminster John Knox Press, 2004.

———. "The Sense of Peace: A Para-doxology of Divine Multiplicity." In *Polydoxy: Theology of Multiplicity and Relation*, edited by Catherine Keller, and Laurel C. Schneider, 36–56. London: Routledge, 2011.

Foucault, Michel. "A Preface to Transgression." In *Language, Counter-memory, Practice: Selected Essays and Interviews by Michel Foucault*. Edited by Donald F. Bouchard. Ithaca, NY: Cornell University Press, 1977.

Fox, Matthew. *Sheer Joy: Conversations with Thomas Aquinas on Creation Spirituality*. New York: HarperSan Francisco, 1992.

Gebara, Ivone. "La mujer hace teología: Un ensayo para la reflexión." In *El rostro femenino de la teología*, edited by Elsa Tamez, 11–24. San José, CR: Departamento Ecuménico de Investigaciones, 1988.

———. "The Trinity and Human Experience: An Ecofeminist Approach." In *Women Healing Earth: Third World Feminism on Ecology, Feminism, and Religion*, edited by Rosemary Radford Ruther, 13–23. Maryknoll, NY: Orbis Books, 1996.

———. *Longing for Running Water: Ecofeminism and Liberation*. Translated by David Molineaux. Minneapolis, MN: Fortress Press, 1999.

———. *Out of the Depths: Women's Experience of Evil and Salvation*. Translated by Ann Patrick Ware. Minneapolis, MN: Fortress Press, 2002.

Goizueta, Roberto S. "Fiesta: Life in the Subjunctive." In *From the Heart of Our People: Latino/a Explorations in catholic Systematic Theology*, edited by Orlando O. Espín and Miguel H. Díaz, 84–99. Maryknoll, NY: Orbis Books, 1999.

González, Michelle. *Created in God's Image: An Introduction to Feminist Theological Anthropology*. Maryknoll, NY: Orbis Books, 2007.

Gregory of Nyssa. *From Glory to Glory: Texts from Gregory of Nyssa's Mystical Writings*. Translated and edited by Herbert Musurillo. Crestwood, NY: St. Vladimir's Seminary Press, 1979.

Gregory the Great. *On the Song of Songs*. Translated and introduction by Mark DelCogliano. Collegeville, MN: Liturgical Press, 2012.

Gross, Jon. "Disquiet on the Waterfront: Reflections on Nostalgia and Utopia in the Urban Archetypes of Festival Marketplaces." *Urban Geography* 17, no. 3 (1996): 221–47.

Grosz, Elizabeth. *Sexual Subversions: Three French Feminists*. Crows Nest, NSW: Allen & Unwin, 1989.

———. *Jacques Lacan*. New York: Taylor & Francis, 2002.

Hadewijch. *Hadewijch: The Complete Works*. Translated by Mother Columba Hart. New York: Paulist Press, 1980.

Hartshorne, Charles. *Man's Vision of God and the Logic of Theism*. New York: Willett, Clark, 1941.

———. *Aquinas to Whitehead: Seven Centuries of Metaphysics of Religion. The Aquinas Lecture, 1976*. Aquinas Lecture 40. Milwaukee, WI: Marquette University Publications, 1976.

———. *Omnipotence and Other Theological Mistakes*. Albany: State University of New York Press, 1984.

———. *The Divine Relativity: A Social Conception of God*. New Haven, CT: Yale University Press, 1984.

Heschel, Abraham J.. *The Prophets II*. Peabody, MA: Hendrickson, 1962.

Hoogland, Mark-Robin. *God, Passion and Power: Thomas Aquinas on Christ Crucified and the Almightiness of God*. Leuven: Peeters Press, 2003.

Irigaray, Luce. "La Mysterique." In *Speculum of the Other Woman*. Translated by Gillian C. Gill. Ithaca, NY: Cornell University Press, 1985.

———. *Speculum of the Other Woman*. Translated by Gillian C. Gill. Ithaca, NY: Cornell University Press, 1985.

———. "Così Fan Tuti." In *This Sex Which Is Not One*. Translated by Catherine Porter and Carolyn Burke. Ithaca, NY: Cornell University Press, 1985.

———. *This Sex Which Is Not One*. Translated by Catherine Porter and Carolyn Burke. Ithaca, NY: Cornell University Press, 1985.

———. *Marine Lover of Friedrich Nietzsche*. Translated by Gillian C. Gill. New York: Columbia University Press, 1991.

———. "Questions to Emmanuel Levinas." In *The Irigaray Reader*, edited by Margaret Whitford, 178–89. Oxford: Blackwell, 1991, 1993.

———. *Sexes and Genealogies*. Translated by Gillian C. Hill. New York: Columbia University Press, 1993.

———. *The Forgetting of Air in Martin Heidegger*. Translated by Mary Beth Mader. Austin: University of Texas Press, 1999.

———. "The Fecundity of the Caress: A Reading of Levinas, *Totality and Infinity*, 'Phenomenology of Eros.'" In *Feminist Interpretations of Emmanuel Levinas*, edited by Tina Chanter, 119–44. University Park: Penn State University Press, 2001.

———. *The Way of Love*. Translated by Heidi Bostic and Anthony Pluhacek. London: Continuum, 2002.

Jantzen, Grace. *God's World, God's Body*. Philadelphia, PA: Westminster Press, 1984.

Johnson, Elizabeth. *Quest for the Living God: Mapping Frontiers in the Theology of God*. New York: Continuum, 2007.

Jordan, Mark. *Rewritten Theology: Aquinas After His Readers*. Malden, MA: Blackwell, 2006.

Joy, Morny. *Divine Love: Luce Irigaray, Women, Gender and Religion*. Manchester: Manchester University Press, 2002.

Jüngel, Eberhard. *God as the Mystery of the World: One the Foundation of the Theology of the Crucified One in the Dispute between Theism and Atheism*. Translated by Darrell L. Guder. Grand Rapids, MI: William B. Eerdmans, 1983.

Katz, Claire Elise. "From Eros to Maternity: Love, Death, and the 'Feminine' in the Philosophy of Emmanuel Levinas." In *Women and Gender in Jewish Philosophy*, edited by Hava Tirosh-Samuelson, 153–78. Bloomington: Indiana University Press, 2004.

Kearney, Richard. *The God Who May Be: A Hermeneutics of Religion*. Bloomington: Indiana University Press, 2001.

———. *Strangers, Gods, and Monsters*. London: Routledge, 2003.

Kearney, Richard, and Kascha Semonovitch, eds. *Phenomenologies of the Stranger: Between Hostility and Hospitality*. New York: Fordham University Press, 2011.

Keller, Catherine. *From a Broken Web: Separation, Sexism, and Self*. Boston: Beacon Press, 1986.

———. "Process and Chaosmos: The Whiteheadian Fold in the Discourse of Difference." In *Process and Difference: Between Cosmological and Postructuralist Postmodernisms*, edited by Catherine Keller and Anne Daniell. Albany: State University of New York Press, 2001.

———. *Face of the Deep: A Theology of Becoming*. New York: Routledge, 2003.

———. *God and Power: Counter-Apocalyptic Journeys*. Minneapolis, MN: Fortress Press, 2005.

Keller, Catherine, and Anne Daniell, eds. *Process and Difference: Between Cosmological and Postructuralist Postmodernisms*. Albany: State University of New York Press, 2001.

Kitamori, Kazoh. *Theology of the Pain of God: The First Original Theology from Japan*. Eugene, OR: Wipf and Stock, 2005.

Kristeva, Julia. *Desire in Language: A Semiotic Approach to Literature and Art*. Translated by Thomas Gora. Edited by Leon S. Roudiez and Alice A. Jardine. New York: Columbia University Press, 1980.

———. *Tales of Love*. Translated by Leon S. Roudiez. New York: Columbia University Press, 1987.

Lacan, Jacques. *Feminine Sexuality: Jacques Lacan and the école freudienne*. Edited by Juliet Mitchell and Jacqueline Rose. Basingstock: Macmillan; New York: Pantheon Press, 1982.

———. *On Feminine Sexuality: The Limits of Love and Knowledge, Book XX, Encore 1972–1973*. Edited by Juliet Mitchell and Jacqueline Rose. New York: W. W. Norton, 1998.

LaCugna, Catherine Mowry. *God for Us: The Trinity and Christian Life*. New York: HarperSanFrancisco, 1991.

Lee, Jung Young. *God Suffers for Us: A Systematic Inquiry into a Concept of Divine Impassibility*. The Hague: Martinus Nijhoff, 1974.

———. "The Yin-Yang Way of Thinking: A Possible Method for Ecumenical Theology." *International Review of Missions* 60, no. 239 (July 1971): 363–70.

Levinas, Emmanuel. *Totality and Infinity: An Essay on Exteriority*. Translated by Alphonso Lingis. Pittsburgh, PA: Duquesne University Press, 1969.

———. *Basic Philosophical Writings*. Edited by Adriaan T. Peperzak, Simon Critchley, and Robert Bernasconi. Bloomington: Indiana University Press, 1996.

Lombard, Peter. *The Sentences: Book 2. On Creation*. Translated by Giulio Silano. Toronto: Pontifical Institute of Medieval Studies, University of Toronto, 2008.

Louth, Andrew. *Denys the Areopagite*. London: New York: Continuum, 1989.

———. "Eros and Mysticism: Early Christian Interpretation of the Song of Songs." In *Jung and the Monotheisms: Judaism, Christianity and Islam*, edited by Joel Ryce-Menubin, 241–69. London: Routledge, 1994.

Maasen, Helmut. *Gott, das Gute und das Böse in der Philosophie A.N. Whiteheads*. Frankfurt: Lang, 1988.

MacGregor, Geddes. *He Who Lets Us Be: A Theology of Love*. New York: Seabury Press, 1975.

MacKendrick, Karmen. *Counterpleasures*. Albany: State University of New York Press, 1999.

Maduro, Otto. *Mapas para la fiesta: Reflexiones sobre la crisis y el conocimiento*. Temas de formación sociopolitica 40. Atlanta: Asociación para la Educación Teológica Hispana, 1998.

Maldonado, Luis. *Fiesta popular y el hieratismo sacramental*. Madrid: Imprenta S.M., 1986.

Marion, Jean-Luc. *God without Being: Hors-Texte*. Translated by Thomas A. Carlson. Chicago: University of Chicago Press, 1991.

———. *The Idol and Distance: Five Studies*. Translated by Thomas A. Carlson. New York: Fordham University Press, 2001.

———. *In Excess: Studies on Saturated Phenomena*. Translated by Robyn Horner and Vincent Berraud. New York: Fordham University Press, 2002.

———. *Prolegomena to Charity*. Translated by Stephen E. Lewis. New York: Fordham University Press, 2002.

———. *The Erotic Phenomenon*. Translated by Stephen E. Lewis. Chicago: University of Chicago Press, 2007.

———. *On the Ego and on God: Further Cartesian Questions*. Translated by Christina M. Gschwandtner. Edited by John D. Caputo. New York: Fordham University Press, 2007.

———. *The Visible and the Revealed.* Translated by Christina M. Gschwandtner. Edited by John D. Caputo. New York: Fordham University Press, 2008.

Mazzoni, Cristina. *Saint Hysteria: Neurosis, Mysticism, and Gender in European Culture.* Ithaca, NY: Cornell University Press, 1996.

McDaniel, Jay B. "Can Animal Suffering Be Reconciled with Belief in an All-Loving God?" In *Animals on the Agenda: Questions about Animals for Theology and Ethics,* edited by Andrew Linzey and Dorothy Yamamoto. 161–72. Urbana: University of Illinois Press, 1998.

———. "The Passion of Christ: Grace both Red and Green." In *Cross Examinations: Readings on the Meaning of the Cross Today,* edited by Marit Trelstad, 196–207. Minneapolis, MN: Augsburg Fortress, 2006.

McFague, Sallie. *Models of God: Theology for an Ecological, Nuclear Age.* Philadelphia: Fortress Press, 1987.

———. *The Body of God: An Ecological Theology.* Minneapolis, MN: Fortress Press, 1993.

Mechtild of Magdeburg. *Flowing Light of the Godhead.* Translated by Frank Tobin. Edited and with a preface by Margot Schmidt. Mahwah, NJ: Paulist Press, 1998.

Metz, Johann-Baptist. "Facing the Jews: Christian Theology after Auschwitz." In *The Holocaust As Interruption,* edited by Elisabeth Schüssler Fiorenza and David Tracy, 38–48. London: T&T Clark (Continuum), 1984.

Moltmann, Jürgen. *God in Creation: A New Theology of Creation and the Spirit of God. The Gifford Lectures 1984–1985.* New York: Harper & Row, 1985.

———. *The Crucified God: The Cross of Christ as the Foundation and Criticism of Christian Theology.* Translated by R. A. Wilson and John Bowden. Minneapolis, MN: Fortress Press, 1993.

Morreall, John S. *Analogy and Talking about God: A Critique of the Thomistic Approach.* Washington, DC: University Press of America, 1978.

Nicolas of Cusa. *Nicolas of Cusa: Selected Spiritual Readings.* Translated by Frank Tobin. Edited and with a preface by Margot Schmidt. Mahwah, NJ: Paulist Press, 1997.

Nietzsche, Friedrich. *Dithyrambs of Dionysius.* Translated with introduction and notes by R. J. Hollingdale. London: Anvil Press Poetry, 1984.

———. *Thus Spoke Zarathustra: A Book for None and All.* Translated by Walter Kauffmann. London: Penguin Books, 1966.

———. *The Birth of Tragedy.* Translated by Walter Kauffmann. New York: Modern Library, 2000.

Nobo, Jorge Luis. *Whitehead's Metaphysics of Extension and Solidarity.* Albany: State University of New York Press, 1986.

Norris, Richard A., trans. and ed. *The Christological Controversy.* Minneapolis, MN: Fortress Press, 1980.

Norris, Richard A., ed. *The Song of Songs: Interpreted by Early Christian and Medieval Commentators.* Grand Rapids, MI: William B. Eerdmans, 2003.

Nygren, Anders. *Agape & Eros*. Translated by Philip S. Watson. New York: Harper & Row, 1982.

O'Rourke, Fran. *Pseudo-Dionysius and the Metaphysics of Aquinas*. Notre Dame, IN: University of Notre Dame Press, 2005.

Origen. *The Song of Songs: Commentary and Homilies*. Translated and annotated by R. P. Lawson. Ancient Christian Writers 26. New York: Newman Press, 1956.

Ostriker, Alice. "A Holy of Holies: The Song of Songs as a Countertext." In *The Song of Songs: A Feminist Companion to the Bible*, 2nd ser., edited by Athalya Brenner and Carole R. Fontaine. Sheffield, IA: Sheffield Academic Press, 2000.

Plato. *Symposium*. Translated by Robin Waterfield. Oxford: Oxford University Press, 1994.

———. *Plato's Timaeus*. Translated by Peter Kalkavage. Newburyport, MA: Focus Publishing, 2001.

Plotinus. *The Enneads*. Translated by Stephen McKenna and B. S. Page. Hong Kong: Forgotten Books, 2007.

Porcile, María Teresa. "El derecho a la belleza en América Latina." In *El rostro femenino de la teología*, edited by Elsa Tamez, 85–107. San José, CR: Departamento Ecuménico de Investigaciones, 1988.

Porete, Marguerite. *A Mirror of Simple Souls: The Mystical Work of Marguerite Porete*. Translated and edited by Anne L. Barstow. Spring Valley, NY: Crossroad, 1990,

Pseudo-Dionysius [Denys the Areopagite]. *Pseudo-Dionysius: The Complete Works*. Translated by Colm Luibheid. Edited by John Farina. Mahwah, NJ: Paulist Press, 1987.

Roberts, Alexander, and James Donaldson, eds. *The Ante-Nicene Fathers*. Edinburgh: T&T Clark; Grand Rapids, MN: William B. Eerdmans, 1989.

Rusch, William G., ed. *The Trinitarian Controversy*. Philadelphia: Fortress Press, 1980.

Schaab, Gloria L. *The Creative Suffering of the Triune God: An Evolutionary Theory*. New York: Oxford University Press, 2007.

Schaff, Philip, and Henry Wace, eds. *The Nicene and Post-Nicene Fathers*. Edinburgh: T&T Clark, 1987.

Sobrino, Jon. *Christology at the Crossroads: A Latin American Approach*. Translated by John Drury. Maryknoll, NY: Orbis Books, 1978.

———. "Awakening from the Sleep of Inhumanity." *Christian Century* 108, no. 11 (1991): 364–70.

Soelle, Dorothee. *Suffering*. London: Darton, Longman & Todd, 1975.

Surin, Kenneth. *Theology and the Problem of Evil*. Eugene, OR: Wipf and Stock, 2004.

Tamez, Elsa, ed. *El rostro femenino de la teología*. San José, CR: Departamento de Investigaciones, 1988.

Taylor, Mark C. *Altarity*. Chicago: University of Chicago Press, 1987.

———. *Critical Terms for Religious Studies*. Chicago: University of Chicago Press, 1998.

Teresa of Avila. *The Complete Works of St. Teresa of Avila: Vol. 2: The Interior Castle*. Translated and edited by E. Allison Peers, 187–351. New York: Continuum, 2002.

———. *The Complete Works of St. Teresa of Avila: Vol. 2: Conceptions of the Love of God*. Translated and edited by E. Allison Peers, 352–399. New York: Continuum, 2002.

Tepedino, Ana María. "Feminist Theology as the Fruit of Passion and Compassion." In *With Passion and Compassion: Third World Women Doing Theology: Reflections from the Women's Commission of the Ecumenical Association of Third World Theologians*. Edited by Virginia Fabella and Mercy Amba Oduyoye. Maryknoll, NY: Orbis Books, 1988.

Trible, Phylis. *God and the Rhetoric of Sexuality*. Philadelphia: Fortress Press, 1978.

———. *Texts of Terror: Literary-Feminist Readings of Biblical Narratives*. Philadelphia: Fortress Press 1984.

Turner, Denys. *Eros & Allegory: Medieval Exegesis of the Song of Songs*. Kalamazoo, MI: Cistercian Publications, 1995.

———. "On Denying the Right God: Aquinas on Atheism and Idolatry." In *Aquinas in Dialog: Thomas Aquinas for the Twenty-First Century*. Edited by Jim Fodor and Frederick Christian Bauerschmidt, 137–58. Oxford: Blackwell, 2004.

Turner, Victor. *From Ritual to Theatre: The Human Seriousness of Play*. New York City: Performing Arts Journal of Publications, 1982.

———. *The Ritual Process: Structure and Anti-Structure*. New York: Aldine De Gruyter, 1995.

Unamuno, Miguel. *Tragic Sense of Life*. Translated by J. E. Crawford Flitch. Charleston, SC: BiblioBazaar, 2007.

Vasconcelos, José. *Obras completas*. 4 volumes. Mexico City: Libros Mexicanos Unidos.1957–1961.

Verhoeven, Alida. "The Concept of God: A Feminine Perspective," in *Through Her Eyes: Women's Theology from Latin America*, edited by Elsa Tamez. Maryknoll, NY: Orbis Books, 1989,

Whitehead, Alfred North. *Science and the Modern World*. New York: Free Press, 1925.

———. *Modes of Thought: Six Lectures Delivered in Wellesley College, Massachusetts, and Two Lectures in the University of Chicago*. New York: Macmillan, 1938.

———. *Adventures of Ideas*. New York: Free Press, 1961.

———. *Process and Reality: An Essay in Cosmology*. Edited by David Ray and Donald W. Sherburne Griffin. New York: Free Press, 1978.

———. *Religion in the Making*. New York: Fordham University Press, 1996.

———. *The Concept of Nature.* New York: Cosimo, 2007.

Wilder, Amos Niven. *Theopoetic Theology and the Religious Imagination.* Lima, OH: Academic Renewal Press, 2001.

William of Saint-Thierry. *Exposition on the Song of Songs.* Translated by Mother Columba Hart. Introduction by J.-M. Déchanet. Kalamazoo, MI: Cistercian Publications, 1968.

Wilson-Kastner, Patricia. *Faith, Feminism, and the Christ.* Philadelphia: Fortress Press, 1983.

Zizioulas, John. *Being as Communion: Studies in Personhood and the Church.* Crestwood, NY: St. Vladimir's Seminary Press, 1985.

banquet, 11, 70–71, 158–60, 163, 166–67,
169, 177–78, 180, 199
beauty, 19–20, 30, 40–43, 48, 51, 53,
66–67, 69–70, 78, 88, 93, 109, 143,
154–55, 161, 167, 172–73, 178, 198,
204n14, 210n83
becomings, 116, 127, 146, 148, 151, 153,
170, 181, 186, 194, 196
being-at-work, 20, 204n14; being-in-
one, 128; beingness, 164, 190
Bernard of Clairvaux, 92, 165
Bernini, Giovanni Lorenzo, 97–98,
232n71; *The Ecstasy of St. Teresa*, 97
bestial, 145, 191–93, 196
Bingemer, María Clara, 29, 37–40,
212n112
birth canal, 23; birthing, 10, 13, 23,
37–38, 41, 43–44, 100, 129, 145, 154,
185, 191, 192, 194–95
body, 5, 48, 54, 77–78, 90–91, 93, 100–1,
104, 107, 109, 112–14, 133, 149, 151,
153, 155–57, 159, 172, 175, 178, 181,
183–85, 187–91, 193, 197, 199,
224n188, 237n155, 238n172, 239n173,
240n196
Boethius, 49, 69, 76, 218n70
Boff, Leonardo, 36
border, 4, 156, 172, 187–89, 191, 195,
197–98
boundaries, 4, 16, 18, 24, 46, 87, 139,
159, 162, 171, 173–75, 177–79, 181,
194, 196–97, 227n8, 234n109,
238n164, 238n172, 251n2
bowels, 37, 39, 44, 60, 65, 70, 74, 95, 115,
118, 121, 133–34, 145, 148, 159, 184–85
Bracken, Joseph, 5, 18, 20, 58, 59, 61,
62, 71, 73, 76, 108, 118, 130, 134–37,
146–48, 150, 223n166, 245n91, 245n92,
252n5
bride, 51, 90, 92–93, 111
bridegroom, 51, 90, 91, 113, 240n196
Burrus, Virginia, 102, 153, 234n106,
250n198, 258n104

capitalism, 28, 257n89, 257n91
Caputo, John, 163, 166, 192, 194
Cardenal, Ernesto, 45, 63, 121–22, 130,
248n161
carnival, 5, 8, 10, 157, 161–62, 164, 167,
178, 182, 186–94, 197, 251n1, 251n5,

252n11, 259n132; carnivalesque
passion, 10, 157, 160, 166, 182–84,
187–89, 192–95, 197–98, 251n1
Cartesian, 82, 108, 128, 243n51;
non-Cartesian, 128
cartography of enjoyment, 2
celebration, 2, 33, 38, 42, 48, 155,
158–60, 166–67, 175–78, 180–81, 186,
192, 194, 197, 199–200, 201n1,
214n142, 254n40, 256n76
chaos, 124, 132, 153, 156–57, 161, 172,
174, 180, 191–92
chaosmos, 166
chaotic carnality, 188; chaotic disruption,
156; chaotic divine body, 154; chaotic
edges, 195; chaotic intensity, 155;
chaotic multiplicity, 155; chaotic nexus,
152–53, 168; chaotic potentiality, 153
chesed, 37
childbearing, 37, 114
choral motion, 7–8
circle, 9, 28, 58, 63, 76, 80, 221n119,
238n164; eternal, 68; of love, 61, 74,
194, 230n44; of perfection, 85
circularity, 75, 82, 93, 98, 100, 108, 109
cloud of unknowing, 109
coconstituted, 10
cocreators, 147
coincidentia oppositorum, 144
coinherence, 61
coitus, 107, 114
communal enjoyment, 4
communitarian, 2
compassion, 24, 37–38, 54, 156, 197
Cone, James, 35
Confucian, 26
consummation, 51, 53, 110–12, 115
contemplation, 18–19, 21, 28, 36, 48–51,
55, 58–59, 68, 70, 77, 97, 204n14,
217n59, 224n188
continuity, 25–26, 39, 154, 154, 190
cosmic copulation, 121–22, 130, 162, 187
cosmos, 2, 4–13, 15–16, 18–22, 24, 26–31,
33–40, 43, 46, 48, 55, 57–59, 61–62,
64–69, 71–81, 83–85, 87, 96, 98, 105–6,
118–24, 126–28, 130–33, 137–42,
144–46, 148–50, 152–55, 157–60,
162–63, 166, 168, 171, 175, 177, 180,
184, 190, 193, 199, 211n98, 222n140,
248n161, 248n164, 251n1, 251n5